SAFEGUARDING
FINANCIAL STABILITY
Theory and Practice

Garry J. Schinasi

INTERNATIONAL MONETARY FUND

Production: IMF Multimedia Services Division
Cover design: Lai Oy Louie
Cover photo: Bruno Budrovic, © Images.com/CORBIS

Cataloging-in-Publication Data

Schinasi, Garry J.
    Safeguarding financial stability : theory and practice / Garry J.
Schinasi — Washington, D.C. : International Monetary Fund, 2005.
    p.   cm.

    Includes bibliographical references and index.
    ISBN 1-58906-440-2

    1. Finance. 2. Banks and banking, Central. 3. Risk. I. International
Monetary Fund.
    HG101.S35 2005

Disclaimer: The views expressed in this work are those of the author and do not necessarily represent those of the IMF or IMF policy.

Price: $28.00

Please send orders to:
International Monetary Fund, Publication Services
700 19th Street, NW
Washington, DC 20431 USA
Telephone: (202) 623-9730   Telefax: (202) 623-7201
Internet: http://www.imf.org

I dedicate this book to my parents,
Jack (deceased) and Josephine Schinasi.

Here's what the experts are saying about

Safeguarding Financial Stability
Theory and Practice

By Garry J. Schinasi

"*Safeguarding Financial Stability* explicates why financial stability matters, what it means, and the challenges in securing it. . . . [It is] a thoughtful and thought-provoking volume that is a must read not just for central bankers but for all concerned with financial stability—and if you are not concerned about the latter, you soon will be!"

—Gerard Caprio, Jr., *World Bank*

"Garry Schinasi provides a unique and comprehensive framework for understanding financial stability and for assessing the risks posed by new financial instruments in increasingly unregulated markets in an increasingly globalized world. The channels of monetary policy management have changed tremendously, as anyone who follows the striking stability of long-term bond yields in the face of rising short-term interest rates will attest. The global business cycle is maturing, entering into a period of high financial risk, as discussed by Dr. Schinasi. Anyone who does not read this book today will regret not doing so, as the next financial shock and test of the stability of the global financial system is not long in coming."

—Gail D. Fosler, *The Conference Board*

"The economic and institutional transformation of central banking that has taken place over the past four decades has been driven mainly by monetary policy issues. However, it has profoundly affected another historical mission of central banks—the preservation of financial stability. Financial stability is gradually emerging as a distinct policy function, requiring its own body of scholarship, not to be confused with monetary policy on the one side, and supervision on the other side, although it is related to both.

"Building an analytical approach and a policy paradigm consistent with this new setting as well as with the changing landscape of financial markets and institutions is one of the tasks of today's research and policy agenda.

"Garry Schinasi takes us a big step forward in the fulfilment of this task. His book *Safeguarding Financial Stability* represents a brilliant attempt to provide solid and updated foundations to policies aiming at financial stability. The book is based on a thorough acquaintance with the literature, understanding of the real world, analytical skill, sense of the policy issues, familiarity with the diversity of country situations, and good judgement.

"The book can already be considered required reading for anyone interested in the subject of financial stability. Its clarity makes it accessible to practitioners as well as policymakers. At the same time, the book will stir debate and further research in academic circles."

—Tommaso Padoa-Schioppa, *European Central Bank*

". . . this is a great book. It synthesizes a large literature on financial stability, . . . and it fills in a number of crucial holes. . . . I think it will be remembered as the first concrete attempt to analyze, define, and move toward operationalizing assessment of financial stability."

—R. Todd Smith, *University of Alberta*

Contents

List of Tables

List of Figures

List of Boxes

Preface

This book was written because I could not find one like it in bookstores or in central bank libraries. In effect, it fills a gap—albeit imperfectly—in the existing policy, academic, and commercial literatures on financial stability issues.

The motivation for undertaking this project came to me in early 2003, after having spent nearly 10 years engaging in international capital market surveillance—first in the IMF's Research Department (both as Deputy Chief and Chief of the Capital Market and Financial Studies Division) and then in the newly created International Capital Markets Department (as Chief of the Financial Markets Stability Division). Part of the challenge of the job was to understand the implications of structural changes in finance (including financial institutions, markets, and infrastructures), which required talking to market participants and the relevant authorities (including central banks and supervisory authorities). The job always entailed keeping management and colleagues well informed about capital market developments, prospects, issues, and most important, sources of risks and vulnerabilities.

The time spent searching for potential risks and vulnerabilities (or "potholes" as we called them) in the international monetary and financial system, especially in the more mature markets, challenged my colleagues and me to search continuously for new ways of understanding how calm market conditions can lead to turbulence, why changes in market sentiment often occur without much warning, and how the private and official sectors can adapt and learn to prevent and better cope with financial difficulties and crises. By mid-2003 I felt it was time to step back from the events as they were occurring and to reflect more systematically—and with less pressure—on what kind of framework would advance the understanding of financial stability issues, how to communicate the importance of these issues, and how to encourage and energize a greater focus on optimizing the benefits of finance for societies at large.

Before actually reaching the decision to take a one year sabbatical from the IMF, I challenged myself to produce an outline of a study on financial stability issues that I was fairly certain I could write, if given sufficient free time. Instead, I produced an outline of a book that I wanted to read, but which I was uncertain I was capable of writing. I will leave it to the reader to decide whether the outcome was worth the effort. My only hope in publishing this study is that practitioners—that is, those who safeguard financial stability—will be motivated to think about these issues in a new and more productive way and that the relevant professions will be encouraged to develop useful, policy-oriented frameworks for achieving and maintaining national and international financial stability.

Acknowledgements

This study was researched and partly written during a one-year sabbatical from the International Monetary Fund (IMF). I gratefully acknowledge the IMF's generous financial support under its Independent Study Leave Program.

I also gratefully acknowledge the support and encouragement of the European Central Bank (ECB) and De Nederlandsche Bank (DNB) while visiting them in 2003 and 2004, and would like to thank especially Tommaso Padoa-Schioppa, Mauro Grande, and John Fell at ECB and Henk Brouwer, Jan Brockmeijer, Aerdt Houben, and Jan Kakes at DNB.

Chapters 2, 3, 5, and 6 are based, in part, on material researched and presented in various drafts of several papers (which were later revised and repackaged and issued as IMF Working Papers WP/04/101, WP/04/120, and WP/04/187). These and other related papers benefited from discussions with, and comments from, many colleagues both within and outside the IMF. These include Bill Alexander, Ivan Alves, Michael Bordo, Burkhard Drees, Christine Cumming, Udaibir Das, Phil Davis, Charlie Kramer, Myron Kwast, John Fell, Bob Flood, Andy Haldane, Aerdt Houben, Jan Kakes, Russell Kincaid, Donald Mathieson, Leena Mörttinen, Tommaso Padoa-Schioppa, Lars Pedersen, Eric Peree, and James R. White. I also received useful comments during seminars at ECB, DNB, the European Investment Bank, the University of Hong Kong, and from other IMF colleagues during the review process for IMF working papers.

The chapters presented in Part III of this study are based, at least in part, on material that was originally cowritten with IMF colleagues and published in various editions of the IMF's *International Capital Markets—Developments, Prospects and Key Policy Issues* during 1995–2001, and *Global Financial Stability Report* during 2002–2003. I would like to acknowledge the following coauthors for their contributions to this earlier work and the more recent manifestations of it presented in this study: Charlie Kramer (Chapters 9, 10, and 11); Burkhard Drees (Chapter 9); Todd Smith (Chapter 10); Peter Breuer (Chapter 11); and Oksana Khadarina provided essential assistance in preparing the quantitative part of Chapter 8. I am also grateful to my coauthors Aerdt Houben and Jan Kakes (of DNB) for allowing me to use material from our joint IMF Working Paper WP04/101 and DNB Occasional Paper, "Toward a Framework for Safeguarding Financial Stability," which we jointly researched, brainstormed, and drafted during a four-month period ending in mid-February 2004, and which makes up part of Chapter 6. I am grateful to my coauthor John Fell for allowing me to use material from our joint paper, "Assessing Financial Stability: Exploring the Boundaries of Analysis," published in a special financial-stability edition of *National Institute Economic Review* (April 2005). I am especially grateful to John Fell for providing a fertile environment at ECB for the early stages of my work and for his persistent encouragement to complete this project. In all other instances in which I use material drawn from the work of colleagues both within and outside the IMF it is acknowledged in footnotes. I am grateful to Oksana Khadarina for untiring efforts in producing and updating the tables and charts and also to Yoon Kim for assisting in a part of this effort. Special thanks to Margo and Tom Vuicich for providing a sunny environment for thinking and writing part of this study.

Thanks are due also to Jeanette Morrison, Anne Logue, and Sherrie Brown for their editorial and publishing expertise. I am particularly grateful to Sean M. Culhane for providing expert professional advice and encouragement during each phase of the editorial and production process.

I owe thanks to Michael Mussa (IMF Economic Counsellor and Director of Research, 1993–2001) and David Folkerts-Landau (Assistant Director of Research until 1998) for providing me with the opportunity to be a part of the IMF's international capital markets surveillance team in 1994–95.

Finally, I thank Katherine, Jack, and Sarah for their loving support throughout these and many other efforts.

Abbreviations

ART	alternative risk transfer
CDO	collateralized debt obligation
CDS	credit default swaps
CFTC	Commodity Futures Trading Commission
CLS	Continuous Linked Settlement
ERISA	Employee Retirement Income Security Act
FA	funding arrangements
FSAP	Financial Sector Assessment Program
GDP	gross domestic product
GIC	guaranteed investment contracts
GKO	ruble-denominated discount instrument
HKMA	Hong Kong Monetary Authority
IAIS	International Association of Insurance Supervision
ISDA	International Swaps and Derivatives Association
LIBOR	London Inter-Bank Offer Rate
LTCM	Long-Term Capital Management
NDF	nondeliverable forward (market)
OCC	Office of the Comptroller of the Currency
OFZ	ruble-denominated coupon bonds
OTC	over the counter
SAR	Special Administrative Region (Hong Kong)
SEC	Securities and Exchange Commission
SPV	special purpose vehicle
TARGET	Trans-European Automated Real-Time Gross Settlement Express Transfer System

1

Introduction and Summary

The objective of this book is to develop and present a framework for safe-guarding financial stability. Part I reviews important logical founda-tions that show how the process of finance is related to real economic processes and why finance can and should be viewed as providing public goods and requiring forms of private-collective and public policy action. Part II proposes and develops a comprehensive and practical framework for safe-guarding financial stability encompassing both the prevention and the reso-lution of financial imbalances, problems, and crises. Part III examines ongoing real world challenges to financial stability posed by recent structural financial changes such as the globalization of finance, the growing reliance on over-the-counter derivative instruments and markets, the growth of credit derivatives markets, and the capital market activities of insurance and rein-surance companies.

This Book and the Financial Stability Questions

Does financial stability require the soundness of institutions, the stability of markets, the absence of turbulence, and low volatility—or something even more fundamental? Can stability be achieved and maintained through individual private actions and unfettered market forces alone? If not, what is the role of the public sector, as opposed to private-collective action, in fos-tering financial stability? Should the public sector just make way for the pri-vate sector to achieve an optimum on its own, or is a more proactive role necessary for achieving the full private and social benefits of finance? Is there a consensus on how to achieve and maintain financial stability?

The role of the public sector is not likely to be clear and appropriately focused without an understanding of the requirements for financial stabil-ity in the first place. Likewise, the requirements for financial stability are not likely to be well understood without an analytical framework that can rigorously consider the questions above, individually and collectively. Unfortunately, there is no single, widely accepted framework for monitoring, assessing, and safeguarding financial stability; in fact, there is not even a widely accepted definition of financial stability. Perhaps this is the root of the problem, because without a good working definition of financial stability, the quickly growing financial-stability profession will continue to have difficulties developing useful analytical frameworks for examining policy issues, for monitoring and assessing the financial-stability performance of financial systems, and for dealing with financial systemic problems should they arise.

The core objective of this study is to develop a practical framework for safeguarding financial stability. As anyone who has tried to engage in financial-stability analysis knows, there are few if any widely accepted models or analytical frameworks for monitoring and assessing financial-system stability and for examining policy issues, as there are for economic systems and in other disciplines. The practice of financial-stability analysis is still in its infancy when compared with, for example, the analysis of monetary stability or macroeconomic stability. In the rare cases in which financial systems are expressed rigorously, they constitute one or two equations in much larger macroeconomic models possessing most of the usual macro-equilibrium and macro-stability conditions. In addition, there are reasons to doubt strongly that a single measurable target variable can be found for defining and achieving financial stability, as there is believed to be for defining and achieving monetary stability (such as an inflation target), although many doubt that a single target variable approach accurately represents actual practice in monetary policymaking.

Lacking a framework for financial stability, a set of models for analyzing and understanding it, or even a concept of financial-system equilibrium and stability, it is difficult to envision a framework for safeguarding financial stability (including a practical definition) akin to what economists normally demand and use. Nevertheless, it would be useful to have a framework that not only encompasses, but also requires, the continuous development and use of both analytical tools and policy analyses.

This study develops and proposes such a framework. The approach developed here is not a final blueprint, however, and it should be seen as one further step in the evolution of the practice of safeguarding financial stability. In researching and writing about many of the issues the book addresses, the choice often had to be made to be practical and policy relevant rather than scientific and rigorous, in part because assessing financial stability is still more of an art form than a rigorous discipline or science.

Accordingly, there is great scope for more scientific and rigorous efforts, as will be discussed later in the study.

The Increasing Importance of Financial Stability Issues

Since the early 1990s, safeguarding financial stability has become an increasingly dominant objective in economic policymaking. This is illustrated by the periodic financial stability reports launched by more than a dozen central banks and several international financial institutions (including the IMF, the Bank for International Settlements [BIS], and the World Bank), as well as by the more prominent place given to financial stability in the organizational structures and mandates of many of these institutions. The greater emphasis on financial stability is related to several major trends in financial systems during the past few decades. These trends reflect the expansion, liberalization, and subsequent globalization of financial systems—all of which have increased the possibility of larger adverse consequences of financial instability on economic performance (see Chapter 8 of this volume on the potential effects of globalization).

First, financial systems expanded at a significantly higher pace than the real economy. In advanced economies, total financial assets now represent a multiple of annual economic production. Table 1.1 illustrates this expansion over the period 1970–2004 for a heterogeneous group of advanced economies with relatively mature financial systems. For example, while currency remained relatively steady as a percentage of GDP over the period, total assets in financial institutions grew from 110 percent of GDP in 1980 to 377 percent in 2000 in the United Kingdom, from 182 percent in 1980 to 353 percent in 2000 in Germany, and from 111 percent in 1980 to 257 percent in 2000 in the United States. The growth of assets in the equity and bond markets is just as phenomenal. While differences between countries reflect their more market- or bank-oriented financial systems, most aggregates have increased. The broad measures of an economy's total financial assets invariably involve some double counting due to claims between financial institutions, but even these mutual holdings are relevant for financial stability because they represent the links, interactions, and complexities in the financial system.

Second, this process of financial deepening has been accompanied by changes in the composition of the financial system, with a declining share of monetary assets (aggregates), an increasing share of nonmonetary assets, and, by implication, greater leverage of the monetary base. The amount of currency relative to GDP has been broadly stable or decreased in all countries except Japan. In the United States, even the sizes of both M1 and M2 have fallen as financial innovation has progressed. For outlier Japan, the

Table 1.1. Changes in Key Financial Aggregates
(In percent of GDP)

United States

	1970	1980	1990	2000	2004
1 Currency	6	5	5	6	6
2 M1	21	15	14	11	11
3 M2	60	57	56	50	53
4 M3	65	72	72	73	79
5 Total bank assets[1]	54	54	53	58	53
6 Total financial institution assets	...	111	171	257	...
7 Equity	34	25	35	132	114
8 Bonds	47	53	108	157	159
6+7+8	...	189	314	546	...

United Kingdom

	1970	1980	1990	2000	2004
1 Currency	8	5	3	4	3
2 M4	52	50	86	93	110
3 Total bank assets[1]	51	47	108	156	262
4 Total financial institution assets	...	110	242	377	...
5 Equity	41	23	57	167	133
6 Bonds	52	31	33	74	70
4+5+6	...	164	332	618	...

Germany

	1970	1980	1990	2000	2004
1 Currency	5	6	7	6	7
2 M1	15	17	22	28	30
3 M2	25	29	39	...	65
4 M3	42	48	59	68	70
5 Total bank assets[1]	121	160	216	303	146
6 Total financial institution assets	...	182	259	353	...
7 Equity	11	7	17	48	38
8 Bonds	26	37	67	112	70
6+7+8	...	226	343	513	...

Japan

	1970	1980	1990	2000	2004
1 Currency	8	9	10	13	15
2 M1	29	29	27	48	71
3 M2	74	86	114	127	137
4 M3	127	136	180	219	227
5 Total bank assets[1]	66	77	134	127	168
6 Total financial institution assets	122	157	269	260	...
7 Equity	41	25	76	70	71
8 Bonds	23	60	78	124	141
6+7+8	186	242	423	454	...

France

1 Currency	10	5	4	3	6
2 M1	29	24	25	23	30
3 M2	44	51	44	44	58
4 M3	62	69	74	65	78
5 Total bank assets[1]	...	...	...	...	255
6 Total financial institution assets	...	...	...	...	...
7 Equity	6	4	14	84	65
8 Bonds	14	19	42	55	86
6 + 7 + 8	...	...	...	...	...

Canada

1 Currency	4	3	3	3	3
2 M1	11	9	7	11	13
3 M2	38	47	56	48	49
4 M3	46	63	64	65	69
5 Total bank assets[1]	...	...	...	...	152
6 Total financial institution assets	...	...	...	...	...
7 Equity	9	18	26	87	89
8 Bonds	33	52	68	76	67
6+7+8	...	...	...	...	...

Italy

1 Currency	10	7	6	7	6
2 M1	44	42	35	18	43
3 M2	76	79	67	...	60
4 M3	76	89	88	...	73
5 Total bank assets[1]	...	...	...	...	149
6 Total financial institution assets	...	...	...	...	...
7 Equity	7	3	10	57	42
8 Bonds	...	39	65	108	120
6+7+8	...	...	...	...	...

Netherlands

1 Currency	8	6	7	5	6
2 M1	23	21	25	35	40
3 M2	...	...	...	...	100
4 M3	53	60	77	92	105
5 Total bank assets[1]	71	129	184	254	362
6 Total financial institution assets	116	191	285	431	...
7 Equity	41	16	38	185	97
8 Bonds	11	25	73	85	98
6+7+8	168	232	396	701	...

Sources: Thomson Financial, IMF, Bank for International Settlements, Merrill Lynch, Salomon Smith Barney, and various national sources.

Note: Currency is coins and bank notes in circulation; M1, M2, M3, and M4 are national definitions. Total assets of financial institutions consist of total bank assets and (depending on data availability) assets of insurers, pension funds, and mutual funds.

[1] Figure in 2004 column is from 2003.

Figure 1.1 Composition of Key Financial Aggregates in 1970 and 2000
(In percent of GDP, average of the United States, Germany, the United Kingdom, Japan, France, Italy, Canada, and the Netherlands)

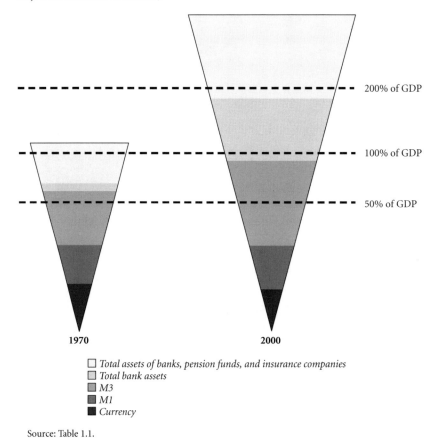

Source: Table 1.1.

increasing importance of narrow money in the 1990s may be attributable to greater incentives to hold money due to the Japanese financial sector's fragile state and enduring deflationary pressures.

The simple average expansion of the financial systems shown in Table 1.1 is illustrated in Figure 1.1, in which total assets of financial institutions are reflected by the triangle's surface. Figure 1.1 shows rather dramatically that between 1970 and 2000 the size of these assets almost tripled relative to GDP. Note also how the average of the financial systems has become more highly leveraged, in the sense that the broader monetary and financial assets represent a much greater share of the triangle in 2000 than in 1970 relative to central bank money (or currency).

Figure 1.2. Growth of Key Financial Assets, 1970–2004
(Average for the United States, Germany, the United Kingdom, Japan, France, Italy, Canada, and the Netherlands)

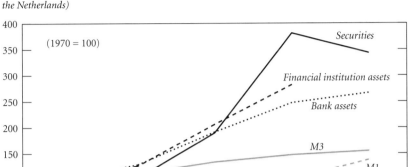

Source: Table 1.1.

Figure 1.2 shows the change in composition of the financial system over the past decades by expressing key financial aggregates as a percentage of their value in 1970 (all deflated by GDP). Clearly, the relative importance of monetary aggregates has decreased, while nonmonetary components have increased rapidly.

Third, as a result of increasing cross-industry and cross-border integration, financial systems are more integrated, both nationally and internationally. Financial institutions now encompass a broader range of activities than that of a traditional bank, which takes deposits and extends loans. This is reflected in the rise in financial conglomerates, which provide a vast array of banking, underwriting, brokering, asset-management, and insurance products and services.[1] In the 1990s, the number of mergers and acquisitions within the financial sector soared (Figure 1.3). Some of these transactions involved different industries or countries, especially in Europe where roughly half the deals in this period were either cross-border, cross-industry, or both (Table 1.2). In addition, cooperation between financial institutions intensified through joint ventures and strategic alliances. The greater international orientation of financial systems is also reflected in the

---

[1]See the various issues of the IMF's *International Capital Markets* report and Group of Ten (2001).

Figure 1.3. Financial Sector Mergers and Acquisitions, 1990–1999
(Number of mergers and acquisitions in Group of Ten countries)

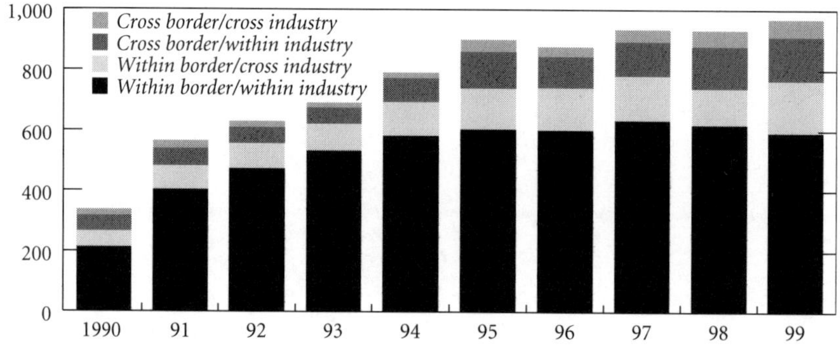

Source: Group of Ten, 2001.

increasing size of cross-border transactions in bonds and equity relative to GDP (see Table 1.3). On this score, the amount of outstanding international debt securities surged over the past decades (Table 1.4).

Fourth, the financial system has become more complex in terms of the intricacy of financial instruments, the diversity of activities, and the concomitant mobility of risks. Deregulation and liberalization created scope for financial innovation and enhanced the mobility of risks. In general, this greater complexity, especially the increase in risk transfers (see Chapter 10), has made it more difficult for market participants, supervisors, and policymakers alike to track the development of risks within the system and over time. To illustrate the higher mobility of risks, Table 1.5 presents the worldwide development of several types of derivatives since the mid-1980s. In nominal terms, total notional amounts outstanding have increased more than 40 times, while the number of derivative contracts has increased fivefold. (Chapter 9 provides a description of the potential risks to financial stability introduced by the widespread and more active use of over-the-counter derivatives.)

These trends and developments reflect important advances in finance that have contributed substantially to economic efficiency, both nationally and internationally. They evidently also have had implications for the nature of financial risks and vulnerabilities and the potential impact of risks and vulnerabilities on real economies, as well as implications for the role of policymakers in promoting financial stability. Consider financial system and market developments in the 1990s and early 2000s—a period during which global inflation pressures subsided and in many countries were eliminated. During this period, reflecting in part the above-mentioned trends, national financial systems around the world either experienced, or were

Table 1.2. **Distribution of Financial Sector Mergers and Acquisitions, 1991–1999**
(In percent)

	North America	Europe	Japan and Australia
Within border/within industry	80	53	64
Within border/cross industry	12	19	16
Cross border/within industry	6	21	14
Cross border/cross industry	2	8	5
Total	100	100	100

Source: Group of Ten, 2001.

exposed to, repeated episodes of unpleasant financial-market dynamics including asset-price volatility and misalignments; volatile if not unsustainable financial and capital flows; extreme market turbulence, at times leading to concerns about potential systemic consequences; and a succession of costly country crises in 1994–95, 1997, 1998, 1999, and in the early 2000s (Table 1.6). The experiences of, and fallout from, these financial stresses and strains occurred within both advanced countries with highly sophisticated financial markets and developing countries with financial systems of varying degrees of immaturity and dysfunction.

As these developments were occurring, economic and financial policymakers became increasingly concerned that global financial stability was becoming more difficult to safeguard.

The Need for an Analytical Framework

While dealing with the urgencies of financial-market and country crises in the 1990s, those situated at the front lines of financial-system policy-making—including at the major central banks and supervisory authorities, and at the IMF—searched widely and intensively for ways to advance their understanding of the ongoing problems and to reform national and international "financial architectures" to prevent and better cope with the potential for financial distress and crises. Some lessons were learned and efforts made to reform the rules of the game of international finance, many of which are documented in case studies and review articles.[2] Monitoring efforts were stepped up considerably, both nationally and internationally. Most notable are the IMF's efforts to strengthen its ongoing surveillance

---

[2]Much of this material can be found on the Web sites of the Bank for International Settlements, the Financial Stability Forum, the IMF, and the World Bank. Also see the Web site of the RGEMonitor at http://www.stern.nyu.edu/globalmacro/.

Table 1.3. Cross-Border Transactions in Bonds and Equities
(In percent of GDP)

	1975–79	1980–84	1985–89	1990–94	1995–99	2000–2003	2001	2002	2003
United States									
Bonds	4.0	9.4	63.6	93.9	139.0	188.0	161.4	208.4	262.1
Equities	1.9	3.6	9.9	14.7	45.0	90.8	87.4	85.0	82.1
Japan									
Bonds	2.2	9.8	115.3	72.9	63.7	70.2	73.7	73.8	77.8
Equities	1.1	4.4	14.9	9.6	17.2	36.5	36.7	33.1	35.3
Germany									
Bonds	5.3	9.7	37.8	86.5	208.7	350.5	378.7	351.1	394.0
Equities	1.9	3.4	11.7	14.9	48.6	132.6	133.6	115.6	112.2
France									
Bonds	…	6.8	21.9	108.6	233.5	293.9	288.1	299.3	362.0
Equities	…	2.4	12.1	16.9	56.1	150.7	140.2	138.1	154.0
Canada									
Bonds	1.2	3.9	29.3	104.5	216.6	149.5	135.6	157.0	175.8
Equities	3.3	6.5	14.8	19.2	52.3	122.8	101.9	151.5	132.1
Italy[1]	0.9	1.4	9.4	114.7	518.8	1,126.5	821.9	1,197.0	1,705.2

Sources: Bank for International Settlements; and national balance of payments data.
Note: Gross purchases and sales of securities between residents and nonresidents.
[1]No breakdown between bonds and equities is available.

Table 1.4. Outstanding International Debt Securities by Nationality of Issuer
(In percent of GDP)

	1970	1980	1990	2000	2003	2004
United States	0.1	0.7	3.1	17.8	27.9	28.6
Japan[1]	0.0	1.5	10.5	6.0	6.3	6.4
Germany[2]	0.1	0.4	4.5	47.9	80.5	86.4
France[1]	0.1	2.1	7.8	24.0	42.2	45.9
Italy	0.1	0.5	4.6	19.4	35.8	40.6
United Kingdom[1]	0.2	2.3	14.9	40.8	63.0	68.0
Canada	0.2	13.4	18.6	27.9	31.0	29.9
Netherlands	0.6	2.4	13.0	79.4	112.6	118.6
Sweden[1]	0.3	7.5	20.1	44.5	52.4	52.4
Switzerland[2]	0.5	1.7	4.5	41.2	49.0	72.9
Belgium	0.4	2.1	15.0	57.3	82.5	85.9

Sources: Bank for International Settlements; and IMF, *World Economic Outlook* database.
[1]Figure in 1970 column is from 1971.
[2]Figure in 1970 column is from 1972.

over member countries' macroeconomic policies, to assess national financial systems' compliance with international financial standards and codes (under the new and voluntary Financial Sector Assessment Program implemented jointly with the World Bank), and to enhance its multilateral surveillance of the global economy and financial system. Moreover, there is also now a general sense that policy responses in the future are likely to require coordination between a greater number of authorities from a greater number of countries.

As a result of these experiences and lessons, safeguarding financial stability is widely recognized as important to maintaining macroeconomic and monetary stability, and to achieving sustainable growth. Many advanced-country central banks (including under the auspices of the Bank for International Settlements), as well as the IMF, devote considerable resources to monitoring and assessing financial stability and to publishing financial-stability reports. A casual reading of these publications would suggest that financial-stability practitioners share some common understandings:

- Finance is fundamentally different from other economic functions such as exchange, production, and resource allocation.
- Finance contributes importantly to other economic functions and facilitates economic development, growth, efficiency, and ultimately social prosperity.
- Financial stability is an important social objective—a public good—even if it is not widely seen as being on par with monetary stability.
- Monetary and financial stability are closely related, if not inextricably intertwined, even though there is no consensus on why this is so.

Table 1.5. Exchange-Traded Derivative Financial Instruments: Notional Principal Amounts Outstanding and Annual Turnover

	1986	1990	1995	2000	2001	2002	2003	2004
Notional principal amounts outstanding				*(In billions of U.S. dollars)*				
Interest rate futures	370.0	1,454.8	5,876.2	7,907.8	9,269.5	9,955.6	13,123.8	18,191.5
Interest rate options	144.0	595.4	2,741.8	4,734.2	12,492.8	11,759.5	20,793.8	24,605.0
Currency futures	10.2	17.0	33.8	74.4	65.6	47.0	80.1	104.5
Currency options	39.2	56.5	120.4	21.4	27.4	27.4	37.9	60.8
Stock market index futures	13.5	69.1	172.2	371.5	333.9	325.5	501.9	634.9
Stock market index options	37.8	93.6	337.7	1,148.3	1,574.9	1,700.8	2,202.3	3,024.8
Total	614.8	2,286.4	9,282.1	14,257.7	23,764.1	23,815.7	36,739.8	46,621.5
North America	514.6	1,264.4	4,852.3	8,167.9	16,203.2	13,693.8	19,504.0	27,612.3
Europe	13.1	461.4	2,241.3	4,197.4	6,141.3	8,800.4	15,406.1	16,307.9
Asia and Pacific	87.0	560.5	1,990.2	1,606.2	1,308.5	1,192.4	1,613.2	2,452.4
Other	0.1	0.1	198.3	286.2	111.1	129.1	216.5	248.9
Annual turnover				*(In millions of contracts traded)*				
Interest rate futures	91.0	219.1	561.0	781.2	1,057.5	1,152.0	1,576.8	1,902.6
Interest rate options	22.2	52.0	225.5	107.6	199.6	240.3	302.2	361.0
Currency futures	19.9	29.7	99.6	43.6	49.1	42.7	58.7	83.8
Currency options	13.0	18.9	23.3	7.1	10.5	16.1	14.3	13.1
Stock market index futures	28.4	39.4	114.8	225.2	337.1	530.2	725.7	804.3
Stock market index options	140.4	119.1	187.3	481.4	1,148.2	2,235.4	3,233.9	2,980.1
Total	314.9	478.2	1,211.6	1,646.1	2,802.0	4,216.8	5,911.7	6,144.6
North America	288.7	312.3	455.0	461.3	675.7	912.2	1,279.7	1,633.6
Europe	10.3	83.0	354.7	718.5	957.8	1,074.8	1,346.4	1,412.6
Asia and Pacific	14.3	79.1	126.4	331.3	985.1	2,073.1	3,111.5	2,847.5
Other	1.6	3.8	275.5	135.0	183.4	156.7	174.1	250.9

Source: Bank for International Settlements.

Table 1.6. Market Turbulence and Crises in the 1990s and Early 2000s

1992	Exchange rate crises involving Italy and the United Kingdom
1994	Bond market turbulence in Group of Ten countries
1994–95	Mexican (*tesobono*) crisis Failure of Barings
1996	Bond market turbulence in United States
1997	U.S. equity market correction
1997–98	Asian crises (Thailand, Indonesia, Republic of Korea)
1998	Russian default Long-Term Capital Management crisis and market turbulence
1999	Argentina and Turkey crises
2000	Global bursting of equity price bubble
2001	Corporate governance problems—Enron, WorldCom, Marchoni, Global Crossing, and so forth September 11 terrorist attacks
2001–2002	Argentina crisis and default Parmalat

The academic literature also continues to grow, much of it covering specific financial-stability topics in considerable depth and some of it providing rigorous anchors for debating substantive and policy issues. For example, the extensive literature on banking covers the special role and fragility of banks in finance; the costs and benefits of deposit insurance; and the causes, consequences, and remedies for bank failures. Moreover, recent empirical studies have highlighted the rising incidence of banking crises,[3] as well as their considerable costs.[4] At the same time, central bank concerns with financial stability are as old as central banks themselves, given their ultimate responsibility for confidence in the national currency.[5] For example, the principal reason for the founding of the U.S. Federal Reserve System in 1913 was to assure stable and smoothly functioning financial and payments systems.[6] The literature on market sources of financial fragility and systemic risk more generally also continues to grow.[7]

---

[3]Bordo and others, 2001.

[4]Lindgren, Garcia, and Saal, 1996; Caprio and others, 1997, 2000, and 2003; Hoggarth and Saporta, 2001.

[5]Padoa-Schioppa, 2003; Schinasi, 2003.

[6]Volcker, 1984.

[7]For examples see Acharya, 2001; Allen and Gale, 2004; Allen, 2005; and Bernardo and Welch, 2004.

Despite this practical and intellectual progress in financial-stability analysis in recent years, it is still in a formative stage when compared with macroeconomic and monetary analysis. The various literatures taken together do not yet provide cohesive and practical toolkits useful for thinking about and *analyzing systemic financial-stability issues* and controversies, for *monitoring* and *assessing* financial stability in real time, for *preventing* problems from becoming potentially systemic, for *resolving* them when they do occur, and for *designing policies* more broadly to optimize the net social benefits of finance. Even the now ubiquitous phrase "financial stability" has no widely understood and accepted definition.

In short, the discipline lacks a generally accepted and useful "framework." To use a nautical metaphor—and to exaggerate somewhat—the profession is sailing on the high and at times turbulent seas with neither a well-conceived and time-tested map nor a reliable compass. The fact that many advanced-country financial markets and the international financial system remained resilient and that financial resilience (if not stability) has been reasonably well maintained in the early 2000s—especially in the mature markets—may have as much to do with good luck as with successful preventive policy design and market surveillance.[8]

That this is so is no fault of the relevant professions. It is an occupational hazard that financial crises are difficult to foresee, even when they are closely upon us. The financial world has changed rapidly, the problems requiring solutions are complicated, and stresses and strains arise within a poorly understood set of dynamic financial markets and institutions. In short, the challenges have been and still are daunting, even with important progress in understanding specific financial-stability issues.

Although the movement toward greater attention for financial-stability issues is clear, the point of focus of this attention is not. Consensus has yet to be reached on how to define the concept of financial stability, how to assess developments under this objective, and what role public policy should play.

Nevertheless, the practice of assessing and safeguarding financial stability is ongoing.

Specific Objectives of This Study

In this light, this study proposes a basic framework for financial-stability analysis and policy. At its core, the study develops both a working defini-

---

[8]Stock and Watson (2003) provide arguments and evidence for this view for macroeconomic policymaking during the fight in the 1990s against inflation. It seems to apply equally to financial-system policymaking.

tion of financial stability and a broad practical framework for monitoring, assessing, and maintaining it. Although most financial systems are still analyzed at the national level, the scope of this framework can be easily extended to international financial-stability issues.

One possible reason for the lack of a widely accepted definition of financial stability and a framework is that there is no widely accepted or articulated logical foundation for why private finance should be the purview of collective action, including public policy action and involvement. Modern finance is often portrayed to nonspecialists as a purely private activity having little to do with, or need for, private-collective or government involvement. Likewise, the benefits of finance are seen primarily, if not exclusively, as conveying to private counterparts engaged in specific financial activities and markets.

While there is some truth in the characterization of finance as primarily a private affair, it would be an illusion to evaluate the effectiveness of private finance and its enormous real economic benefits either entirely as private or exclusively as the result of individual private actions and unrestrained market forces. Regardless of what is thought about the necessity and efficacy of collective action and public policies, obtaining the full extent of the private net benefits of modern finance requires, at a minimum, the existence and effectiveness of many private-collective, publicly sanctioned, publicly mandated, and taxpayer-financed conventions, arrangements, and institutions.

Although finance would no doubt exist and bestow private and collective benefits without the particular social arrangements that have actually emerged and evolved, there would most likely be significantly fewer such benefits. Moreover, finance would most likely be significantly less efficient and supportive of economic activity, wealth accumulation, growth, and ultimately social prosperity. Is this not the case in many (if not most) developing countries in which financial systems have yet to reach a critical point of effectiveness and efficiency?

In short, the enormous and pervasive private benefits of modern finance and financial systems result from the existence of an effective financial system that has long been understood and supported as a public good. This is not meant to imply that all public policy involvement in private finance is appropriate, beneficial, or acceptable. Nor should this be taken to mean that all citizens benefit equally or have equal access to these private and social benefits. But the social benefits are there for the taking, especially in the more democratic societies with liberalized economies.

Although there now seems to be a consensus that many of the social conventions and arrangements that have developed over time are essential prerequisites for effective finance, this reflects a relatively new and modern understanding of the role of finance. Less than 75 years ago, society's mis-management of both money and finance played an important and devastating role in the Great Depression. More recently, some of these lessons are being learned again, in both mature markets and in an increasing number of emerging- and less-developed-market countries. For example, in the aftermath of recent corporate scandals in some mature markets in the early 2000s, improvements are being advocated and implemented—with accounting standards and their enforcement and the efficacy of existing corporate governance procedures and accountability, for instance. Likewise, as the result of recent financial crises in emerging-market countries, many of these social arrangements are being aggressively advocated for adoption in both less advanced and least developed economies and financial systems.

The obvious private and social benefits of finance as well as the sometimes disturbing events of the current era and their relationship to financial stability can be understood either to be the result of, or as at least reflecting, important strengths and weaknesses of finance. As discussed in Chapter 3, finance inherently embodies uncertainty and is associated with several other market imperfections:

- Some financial services provide positive externalities while others provide negative externalities.
- Some financial services are public goods.
- There are information failures in the provision of financial services.
- Financial contracts and markets are incomplete.
- Competition is not always perfectly balanced.

The practical import is that some market imperfections in finance can lead to the underconsumption and underproduction of some socially desirable financial activities, and the overconsumption and overproduction of some socially undesirable ones. In addition, these market imperfections can, at times, lead to the creation and accumulation of both economic and financial imbalances, which if not corrected could threaten financial stability.

As in other economic policy areas, it would seem reasonable to think that private-collective and public actions could be designed and implemented to address each source of market imperfection in finance, depending on how significant the efficiency losses associated with each might be. For example, for cases in which the presence of a market imperfection inhibits consumption and production of desirable financial activities, the challenge would be to provide incentives to supply and consume more of the activities that provide public benefits and positive externalities, that tend to open up new markets, and that increase competition unless there are natural monopolies. For cases in which a market imperfection encourages consumption and production of undesirable goods, the challenge would be to minimize the production and consumption of financial activities that result from these market failures. In considering this approach, the effectiveness of policies could be improved if they were designed and implemented in a cohesive fashion so that a policy designed to eliminate the negative impact of one kind of market imperfection does not offset the benefits of a policy designed to deal with another.

Because tendencies to underproduce and overproduce financial activities exist simultaneously, financial-system policies would be more effective if they strove to strike a socially optimal balance between *maximizing* the net social benefits of the positive externalities and public goods and *minimizing* the net social costs of the other market imperfections in finance. To what extent such policy cohesiveness and coordination is actually achieved in practice by countries or across borders is not clear. Striving to achieve the social optimum will undoubtedly entail difficult choices, including trading off some of the individual private benefits for the greater good, if and when this can be justified.

The public policy discussion in Part I deals first with the efficiency loss associated with market imperfections. However, each and every loss of efficiency does not require intervention. The desirability or necessity of some form of collective intervention is much clearer when a market imperfection in finance leads to an inefficiency that poses a significant threat to financial stability, because of the impact on either financial institutions or markets or both. Unfortunately, the financial-system policy literature rarely makes a clear distinction between sources of market imperfections that threaten stability and those that do not. Likewise, no framework exists now either for measuring the efficiency losses associated with market imperfections in finance or for assessing the risks to financial stability associated with market imperfections. These are some of the challenges in the period ahead, for which an analytical framework for financial stability would be useful for policy purposes. But this, too, is an enormous challenge.

In sum, while finance provides tremendous private and social benefits, important aspects of finance are associated with market imperfections and inherently hold the potential (although not necessarily a high likelihood) for fragility, instability, systemic risk, and adverse economic consequences. When private incentives and actions alone do not lead to an efficient pricing and allocation of capital and financial risks, it is possible that some combination of private-collective action and public policy could provide incentives to encourage the private sector to obtain a more efficient and desirable outcome.

Whether something can or should be done about this is the subject of active debate, but practically depends on the social net benefits of taking action. If the private and social benefits of taking action and providing incentives outweigh the private and social costs, they are worthy of consideration. A rule to consider, although difficult to implement, is that only policies that provide clear and measurable net benefits should be implemented.

This calculus most often involved both spatial and intertemporal trade-offs. While immediate benefits might be associated with specific private-collective or public sector policies, there may be greater future costs associated with private market reactions and adjustments to the policies. Examples include the costs of moral hazard and regulatory arbitrage.

Ultimately, it is a social and political decision whether private-collective and public sector involvement and intervention are appropriate. These cost-benefit, intertemporal, and social and political considerations are key reasons that financial-system policies are so difficult to devise and implement successfully.

In sum, this book addresses these and other closely related issues of immediate relevance to global finance. The study is divided into three somewhat separable parts:

- Part I presents foundations for thinking about financial-stability issues.
- Part II develops a working definition of financial stability and a broad framework for monitoring, assessing, and ensuring it.
- Part III examines ongoing challenges to financial stability posed by relatively recent structural financial changes, drawing on parts of the framework presented.

Organization of the Book

The remainder of this chapter lays out the organization of the study in somewhat more detail and summarizes some of its main findings.

The chapters in Part I provide a logical foundation for thinking about financial-stability issues. Chapter 2 lays out the essence of modern finance—the temporary transfer of the liquidity and payment services of money (legal tender and its very close substitutes) in return for a promise to return a greater amount of money to its original owner. The element of human trust in financial relationships and contracts is the source of both finance's strengths (efficiency gains) and weaknesses (fragility). In principle, both these strengths and weaknesses can be defined and measured in terms of the manner in which finance does or does not enhance the efficiency and effectiveness of other real economic processes, particularly intertemporal economic processes such as production, wealth accumulation, economic development and growth, and ultimately social prosperity. In reality, precise measurement is extremely difficult if not impossible.

After developing and examining this simple logic—drawn from disparate literatures—Chapter 3 applies some of the concepts from the economics of the public sector to finance. The chapter identifies sources of market imperfections in finance, justifies a role for both private-collective and public policy involvement, and argues that both fiat money and finance have the potential to convey significant positive externalities and the characteristics of a public good.

Chapter 4 briefly clarifies what is meant by efficiency and stability from an economic perspective. The implicit and practical import of this distinction is that not all market imperfections in finance may necessitate a private-collective or public policy response; whether intervention is desirable or necessary depends on the size and importance of the imperfection with regard to its impact on efficiency. While difficult to measure in practice, in principle the deviation from the efficient outcome should be part of the decision to intervene. The chapter distinguishes between volatility, fragility, and instability by drawing on the experience in the 1990s and early 2000s with market turbulence and country crises.

Part II then develops a broad policy-oriented framework for assessing and safeguarding financial stability and for resolving problems when they arise. The framework can be applied in a wide variety of existing ways of managing financial system policies in various countries. Chapter 5 develops a working definition of financial stability in terms of economic processes—in principle, measurable ones—and identifies several practical implications of the definition for financial-stability work. Based on this definition, Chapter 6 proposes a generic framework for financial-stability monitoring, assessment, and policy. The framework proposed is generic in three senses: it encompasses all the important aspects of financial systems (institutions, markets, and infrastructure); its implementation entails monitoring, analytical assessments, and policy adjustments when necessary; and it remains at a general level that allows it to be an umbrella framework for most existing frameworks. This chapter also identifies remaining analytical and measurement challenges. Chapter 7 discusses the role of central banks in ensuring financial stability, which in many countries might be a natural or special role.

Part III identifies and analyzes ongoing challenges to financial efficiency and stability posed by relatively recent structural changes in national and global finance. Each of these structural changes is no doubt improving financial and, it is hoped, economic efficiency, but may also be posing new risks or redistributing existing risks in ways that are poorly understood. The chapters in this part of the study are sequenced so that they progress from the general and broad in scope, to the more specific. Chapter 8 examines the stability implications of the globalization of finance and financial risk for both national financial systems and the international financial system. Chapter 9 examines the potential for instability in national and global financial markets related to the growing reliance on over-the-counter derivatives instruments and markets. Chapter 10 examines the implications for financial stability of the increased reliance on efficiency-enhancing risk transfer mechanisms, and focuses in particular on credit derivatives. Chapter 11 examines the supervisory, regulatory, and perhaps systemic challenges raised by the now greater role of insurance companies (and implicitly of other institutional investors) in financial and capital market activities.

Chapter 12 collects the main challenges to financial stability that are discussed in the book and that are likely to be faced in the future. Each of the areas identified in Part III taken separately, and certainly all of them taken together, lead to the strong conclusion that further and continuous reforms are desirable and should be aimed at striking a better balance between relying on market discipline and relying on official or private-collective action. In some countries—most of them advanced countries with mature markets—a rebalancing toward relying more on market discipline is desirable. In other countries—many of them with poorly developed markets—strong efforts need to be made to improve the financial infrastructure through private-collective and government expenditures and commitments and to target the role of government to enhance the effectiveness and efficiency of market mechanisms for finance. Specific areas where reforms are most needed include

- a realignment of private market incentives, including within firms—to improve internal governance at the board level, to improve management and risk controls, and to improve the alignment of incentives at the board, management, and staff levels;
- a reevaluation of regulatory incentives and their consistency with private market incentives—to reduce moral hazard;
- enhancements to disclosure by a wide range of financial and even nonfinancial entities—to improve the potential for effective market discipline and to improve private-collective and official monitoring and supervision;

- improvements to market transparency—to reduce asymmetries in markets and the tendency toward adverse selection;
- an enhancement to legal certainty where it is still ambiguous, such as with close-out procedures for swaps, credit derivatives, and other complex structured financial instruments;
- the development and implementation of comprehensive and appropriately targeted frameworks for monitoring, assessing, and safeguarding financial stability to better ensure financial stability and restore it when this fails;
- an increase in international cooperation and coordination in financial-system regulation, surveillance, and supervision—to eliminate international gaps in information and analysis and to reduce, if not eliminate, opportunities for regulatory arbitrage.

PART I

FOUNDATIONS

A s noted in Chapter 1, despite some professional consensus about why financial stability is an important policy objective and intellectual progress in analyzing certain financial-stability issues, the existing literature does not provide a cohesive framework. Moreover, within the financial-stability policy community, no fully articulated and widely accepted logical foundation yet exists that joins the elements of the consensus into a cohesive, consistent, and comprehensive whole. The articulation of such a logic could help identify where intellectual differences lie, and help establish a foundation on which to build a financial-stability framework.

The chapters in Part I develop such a logic—drawing ideas from and synthesizing important elements of disparate economic and finance literatures. One important conclusion of the analysis, and a lesson for the many less developed financial systems around the world, is that an effective (if not efficient) process of finance requires extensive private-collective and public policy involvement, to internalize and capture social economic benefits and public goods associated with finance. While much of this may be well understood and taken for granted in financial-system policymaking in mature, advanced-country financial systems, it is neither widely understood nor accepted more broadly.

Logic of the Arguments

Because the arguments of Part I are drawn from several literatures, a preview of the logic of the arguments is useful.

In modern economies, fiat money (legal tender) provides ultimate liquidity in the form of finality of payment; it also has the important quality of anonymity. A dollar bill is accepted in the United States irrespective of who is exchanging it, just as a euro coin is accepted in much of Europe and a yen coin in Japan. Together, liquidity and anonymity make fiat money society's surrogate for trust in trade and exchange. Used as a store of value, fiat money is imperfect and less unique, because its effectiveness depends on the ability of a small group of public servants (working in a monetary authority or central bank) to design and execute policies to maintain its value. Thus, an element of uncertainty surrounds the durability of the value of money.

Throughout recorded history—and even before the introduction of monies of various forms—societies have created and used alternative stores of value. Broadly construed, this is finance: a process, comprising private contracts and social arrangements (laws, institutions, codes of conduct, governance), that produces and exchanges stores of value. More specifically, finance creates instruments of no intrinsic value that enable private counterparts to temporarily transfer the finality-of-payment services of some form of money to others in exchange for a promise to reverse the transfer later, either for equal or greater value or to share in some reward (profit) in the future. Accordingly, finance embodies uncertainty about human trust and is closely tied to the characteristics, value, and dynamics of money.

Even though finance can be seen primarily as a dynamic network of private contracts, arrangements, and transactions, it provides both private and social benefits. It does so by enhancing and redistributing the characteristics and services of money, including as a public good. In so doing, finance facilitates and enhances opportunities for intertemporal economic processes and ultimately social prosperity. More specifically, it facilitates several economic processes: a greater amount of trade and exchange, production, savings, and investment; a more efficient allocation of resources; greater and more effective opportunities for wealth accumulation and economic development and growth; and greater opportunities and effectiveness in unbundling, repackaging, pricing, and trading financial and economic risks.

However, there are both private and social downside risks associated with certain aspects of finance. When the veracity of promises to pay comes to be doubted, uncertainty and risk tend to rise: financial counterparts reassess, reallocate, and reprice uncertainty about trust. This process usually occurs in an orderly fashion; but often enough it does not. In a worse-case scenario, widespread uncertainty about trust in finance leads to panic and a dramatic rise in the demand for society's surrogate for trust— some form of money as legal tender—until trust and confidence are restored. Because of the links between finance, money, intertemporal economic processes, and uncertainty about trust, when financial stability is called into question, monetary stability—and economic stability more generally—will also be at risk.

Organization

The topics of Part I are organized as follows:

Chapter 2 reviews important aspects of finance as a process of allocating and pricing resources and risks and how this process relates to real economic processes. The first section examines the relationship between finance and fiat money, organized around the conventional services of money, and identifies several important and unique aspects of finance. It asserts that finance intrinsically involves uncertainty about human trust—the source of both its strengths (facilitates economic processes and efficiency) and weaknesses (inherently includes the potential for market imperfections and fragility).

Building on these important characteristics, the second section of Chapter 2 discusses the enormous economic benefits provided by an effective process of finance. These benefits originate in the ways finance improves economic efficiency and, more specifically, facilitates important economic processes such as resource and risk allocation, wealth accumulation, growth, and social prosperity.

The third section of Chapter 2 examines characteristics of finance that can temporarily reduce private and social benefits, or worse, create the potential for financial and economic instability. It also briefly discusses some of the social arrangements that have evolved to deal with this potential fragility.

Chapter 3 frames the public policy aspects of finance described in Chapter 2. The first section applies the economics of the public sector to finance. In addition to the usual sources of inefficiency in finance—such as asymmetric information and incomplete markets—this section argues that widespread access to an effective process of finance is associated with significant positive externalities and that finance has the characteristics of a public good.

The second section of Chapter 3 discusses some of the main public policy implications of the fact that finance is a public good. One of these implications is that achieving the full private and net social benefits of finance requires maintaining a delicate balance of private-collective and public policy involvement in the main constituent parts of finance (infrastructure, institutions, and markets). In some countries, greater reliance on market discipline may be required, while in others a greater reliance on government involvement might be needed. A second implication is that achieving these objectives also requires a balance between maximizing the social benefits (associated with positive externalities and public goods) and minimizing the social costs (of the other sources of market imperfections). In countries with undeveloped markets this balance might be achieved through a greater emphasis on building the constituent parts of finance that create the positive externalities and public goods, while in the more advanced markets attaining this balance may require greater emphasis on warding off the adverse consequences of other sources of market imperfections.

Chapter 4 briefly illustrates, with some simple supply and demand graphs, the distinction between inefficiency and instability, drawing on the sources of market imperfections.

2

Money, Finance, and the Economic System

The examination of financial-stability issues requires considering the characteristics of finance that distinguish it from other important economic processes such as production, exchange, and savings and investment.[9] For example, in monetary economies, although economic processes make use of some or all of the characteristics of money, finance is uniquely related to money. Similarly, while production and exchange involve elements of human trust, finance uniquely embodies uncertainty about trust. This is so because finance intrinsically embodies promises that can be broken, as between borrowers and lenders. In these and other ways, finance plays important and unique roles in facilitating other economic processes. Recognizing these unique aspects of finance helps to explain why it is useful to think of finance and financial stability as conveying externalities and, in some ways, public goods.

Finance and Its Relation to Money

The unique aspects of finance, particularly its elemental relationship with human trust, are examined in this section.

What Is Finance?

According to Webster's Dictionary, finance is

(1) money or other liquid resources of a government, business, group, or individual; (2) the system that includes the circulation of money, the granting of

---

[9]Chapter 5 develops a working definition of financial stability.

credit, the making of investments, and the provision of banking facilities; (3) the science or study of the management of funds; (4) the obtaining of funds or capital. (*Merriam Webster's Collegiate Dictionary,* 10th edition)

The following analysis will make extensive use of the first two definitions, and more use of the second than the first. These definitions are not entirely useful or complete, however. First, there is no sense of what the "system" accomplishes or how it fits into the broader economic system. Second, these definitions do not provide a sense of whether finance is an end unto itself or just a means to an end. As an industry, finance produces measurable value-added and creates jobs. But there are other, less direct and less measurable benefits that may, in fact, add up to significantly more of a contribution than the measurable value-added.

The benefits of finance—both as a process and as an activity—originate primarily from the ways in which finance enhances the overall efficiency of resource and risk allocation, both spatially and intertemporally. By helping the economy allocate resources to their best uses through time, and allocating risks to those most capable of managing them, finance facilitates and supports the processes of production, wealth accumulation, economic growth, and the prosperity of societies more generally.

Accordingly, and for the purposes of designing and managing financial-system policies, finance is primarily a means by which important functions of the economic system are facilitated or achieved. This does not mean that finance does not directly contribute to production or that it plays a subordinate role. Throughout history, the need and search for more, and more effective, finance often led to discoveries and innovations in finance that themselves had a lasting, even a great, impact on economic systems and their evolution, at times for good—at times for evil.[10] Consider the positive, perhaps revolutionary, impact of the emergence of banking in Europe in the fifteenth century and of the invention of fiat money (and other forms of legal tender) in the seventeenth century.[11] These core elements of finance did not exist during most of recorded human history.

Economies still endure that have not developed finance to a sufficient extent to reap these broader benefits. Moreover, even in mature financial systems, the benefits of finance cannot be taken for granted. When finance is not performing properly—even in highly developed financial systems—it is likely to be reflected adversely in the economy's performance. The efficiency and effectiveness of finance in facilitating resource allocation may be

---

[10]This is a recurring theme in Kindleberger (1993); see page 5, for example.
[11]Michael Bordo suggested that the characteristics of fiat money discussed here also pertain to convertible monies (what most countries used as legal tender until the 1930s) and to fiduciary monies (such as bank money).

reduced, such as during a "credit crunch;" or worse, the potential for market imperfections and systemic problems (or systemic risk) may be introduced, such as occurs during the onset of financial crises. (Briefly, systemic risk is the risk that an event will trigger a loss of economic value or confidence in the financial system serious enough to have adverse effects on the real economy. Chapter 5 discusses this concept in more detail.)

How Is Finance Linked to Money?

In monetary economies, finance is intimately bound to the unique services of money. While this may be obvious, it is not trivial, as examined in the following discussion of the roles of money and money's relation to finance.

Services of fiat money

Although fiat money has no intrinsic value, it provides essential services that are part of every economic transaction in a monetary economy. Two of these services are as a unit of account and as a medium of exchange. The second role is more unique and defining than the first, in that fiat money—and more generally, legal tender—alone embodies the *finality of payment* in transactions.[12] Until legal tender is actually received by a party to a transaction (including in the form of an electronic transfer to a bank account), there will be uncertainty about whether an economic exchange of full contracted value has actually occurred. For example, and as is obvious, the certainty of receiving full value is immediate in a simple *exchange* of a commodity for legal tender.[13]

---

[12]Fiat money is a government-supplied means of payment—legal tender—of no intrinsic value. Throughout the discussion, the terms "fiat money," "money as legal tender," and "legal tender" are used interchangeably to represent media of exchange that embody the "finality of payment."

[13]Shubik (2001) notes on page 97: "Historically, weights of some commodity preceded coinage and were used for exchange around five thousand years ago in Babylon and Egypt. Coinage in precious metals entered trade around 630 BC and within a few years of its introduction in Asia Minor spread over the civilized world. Paper money became a serious economic force around the end of the seventeenth century with the founding of the Bank of England and the late twentieth century brought with it money as a pure abstraction." According to Kindleberger (1993), "The bill of exchange was a powerful innovation of the Italians in the thirteenth century that economized on the need to barter, clear books face to face, or to make payments in bulky coin, plate, or bullion. . . . by clearing or canceling a debt owed in one direction by one owed in the other or, more accurately, by one owed in another." He goes on to observe that, "Credit was involved in dealing in bills even when the request for payments was ostensibly at sight. Mails of the day took time. Bills were payable at sight, at 'usance,' or sometimes half-usance or double usance. Usance was the standard credit period for a given trade" (pp. 41–42).

More generally, any money that is universally accepted as a medium of exchange (or means of payment) facilitates trade and exchange. It could be a legally issued fiat currency, a commodity money such as rice or gold, or a *derivative* money—a bank deposit—that promises to pay a fixed amount of legal tender on demand (Tobin, 1992). Money facilitates trade and exchange by eliminating the timing of the receipt of income as a requirement for making expenditures. In this way, money removes an important individual constraint on economic activity.

Equally important, money facilitates efficient trade and exchange by eliminating the "double coincidence of wants" that is characteristic of, and intrinsic to, trade and exchange in barter economies.[14] A barter economy hinges on the costly requirement of finding someone who possesses the commodity you want to purchase, and who wants to purchase the commodity that you possess. If you have apples and want oranges, you would need to search and find a person who has oranges and wants apples, meet at a specific time and place, and decide how much to trade at what price. You may have to find several individuals and meet in several places and times to fully satisfy your demand for oranges. The search and transactions costs in barter economies are very high.

In a monetary economy, no such search and transactions costs are necessary: all you need to do is find someone who wants to sell the good for money. Because of its universal acceptance as supplying a medium-of-exchange service, money makes the processes of trade and exchange more efficient by driving search and transactions costs to a minimum. Thus, money enhances the efficiency of trade and exchange.

It is reasonable to ask, if money has no intrinsic value, why is it universally accepted? The answer is both complicated and unsatisfying but it also introduces an important human element of exchange. In effect, money is used as the universally accepted means of payment because of the expectation and *trust* that it will also be accepted by others. Because of this trust, it is self-fulfilling that money becomes the universally accepted medium of exchange. Fundamentally, in providing a vehicle for the finality of payment, money as legal tender is an *economy's surrogate for trust* in trade and exchange.[15]

A third service that can be provided by money is as a store of value. That legal tender can play this role is most obvious when the medium of

---

[14]Jevons (1871) coined this phrase.

[15]Shubik (1999) notes on page 33: "The unfortunate custom of talking about bank debt, whether in the form of private bank notes or deposits, as money has added considerably to the confusion and has made it more difficult to appreciate the critical role of fiat or outside money as the surrogate for trust in a modern economy."

exchange (the currency) is a commodity such as gold or silver coins. How-ever, even for these commodity monies, it cannot be taken for granted that their values—their purchasing power—will be maintained through time. Unlike unit-of-account and medium-of-exchange services, the effective-ness of money in providing a store-of-value service cannot be decreed by the government that issues it, unless the government can ensure it will maintain the value of the currency issued.[16]

There are incentives to create substitute stores of value. It would be sur-prising in any economy if the distribution of money perfectly matched the trade and exchange needs among individuals. Instead, it is reasonable to expect that at any given time some individuals would have more, and others less, than the amount of money required. Some individuals might be will-ing to pay something for the use of the medium-of-exchange services of money to obtain purchasing power that they do not presently have, but which they expect to earn in the future. At such times, it would seem that conditions would be favorable for a temporary exchange of money in return for a promise (an IOU) to return it, if only the promise of return could be properly valued and priced, if not guaranteed.

What is unique about finance?

Because economic agents typically prefer not to store value for long periods in the form of money, private contracts between third parties—financial instruments—have been created that provide both the store-of-value service (ownership claims on future income in the form of financial assets) and the medium-of-exchange service (for example, one can pay for a meal with a check drawn on a bank) of legal tender. These intertemporal contracts voluntarily reintroduce *uncertainty and risk about human trust,* a defining feature of finance. On the one hand, the re-introduction of uncer-tainty distinguishes finance from the means-of-payment services of fiat money. On the other hand, it allows finance to create potentially superior near-fiat-money substitutes as stores of value (the most obvious of which is bank credit). Finance can do this successfully only to the extent that uncertainty about trust can be priced and risk-managed. As examined

---

[16]This comes close to raising the issue of monetary stability and its relation to finance and financial stability, as in Padoa-Schioppa (2003), page 274: "... the role of central banks in financial stability is part of their genetic code. It was—and, I would say, still is—an insepa-rable component of their role as the bankers' banks and of their monopoly on ultimate liq-uidity." Using somewhat different arguments, Schinasi (2003) argues that central banks have a natural role to play, and interest, in ensuring financial stability.

below, the creation of fiat money substitutes for intertemporal exchange is the *essence of finance* and financial activities.

How does finance differ from exchange? To see the distinction more concretely, consider the elementary example of an exchange of money for a perishable good, say an apple. In such an exchange, both the unit-of-account and medium-of-exchange services are obviously relevant. Ownership and possession of the two items are exchanged with no intention of reversing or undoing the exchange at some later time. *The exchange of equal value, ownership, and possession is final.* Legal tender is accepted because it embodies the value of the commodity at that time, and it is trusted by the recipient of legal tender that the money can be used in other transactions immediately.

In this common exchange, the store-of-value service of money is not playing a major role if it is playing one at all. However, suppose the recipient of the money does not expect to use it soon or is uncertain about whether the value of money will be sustained until such time as the money is needed. Then the recipient might seek alternative and superior ways of storing future purchasing power (wealth) in some other value-safe form, or even in an alternative that might enhance the stored value. This would require finding other individuals that want (or need) to increase the amount of money they possess, either because they need more of the medium of exchange or want to use money as a store of value.

Essence of finance. What would the provider of legal tender accept in return? The answer is, a promise to pay back and enhance the same value at some future date. This is finance: a temporary exchange of the means-of-payment services of legal tender—society's surrogate for trust in exchange—in return for the promise of a superior store of value (See Table 2.1). Finance means giving up liquidity now for the promise of a future higher return.

Unlike in instantaneous and final exchanges of fiat money for a commodity or physical asset,[17] finance involves uncertainty and risk about human trust, the same element of trust that fiat money is designed to eliminate in instantaneous trade and exchange. However, in reintroducing this uncertainty, finance potentially creates superior stores of value that facilitate *intertemporal* exchange and other economic processes.

---

[17]Note that while financial transactions are exchanges of fiat money for an asset (the promise of a superior store of value), the transfer is temporary. This is fundamentally different from an outright purchase of physical assets, such as real estate, which is a final exchange of fiat money for physical assets. This difference remains even when the outright purchase is financed with a loan, except when the physical asset is used as collateral for the loan.

Table 2.1. **Finance As a Temporary Exchange of Services**

	Fiat money	Finance
Supplier of finance	**Sells** finality-of-payment service	**Buys** promise of superior store-of-value service
Demander of finance	**Buys** finality-of-payment service	**Sells** promise of superior store-of-value service

In finance, the initial exchange is followed by at least one other exchange between these two parties to *reverse* the initial exchange. This relationship in time between the supplier and demander of fiat money is based on the promise that the transfer will be reversed in the future: the initial exchange is not a completed transaction. *In essence, finance is a temporary exchange of the finality-of-payment services of fiat money for a promise, and this promise involves uncertainty about human trust.*[18]

More tangibly, debt contracts promise to pay back a fixed amount and, in most cases, a stream of interest payments. Equity contracts promise to pay back a share of the firm's profits, either in the form of dividends, or through a rise in the value of the shares, or both. If there is a lack of trust or few ways of eliminating trust as a consideration in financial transactions (such as collateral or hedging opportunities, for example), financial activity will be quite limited between the parties involved.

While other economic activities and relationships involve elements of human trust, in finance human trust is an essential part of the activity. For example, trust is involved in a relationship between workers and business owners: the owner of the firm promises to pay the worker for production, and the worker promises to produce a high-quality product. However, this trust relationship differs from that in finance in several important ways.

---

[18]Finance was probably born with the first loan, which may or may not have involved money as the unit of account or as the medium through which the loan temporarily transferred purchasing power from lender to borrower. According to Kindleberger (1993, page 21), while some historians have seen the natural progression of economic intercourse as evolving from barter, to monetary economies, and then to credit economies, the evidence contradicts this view. Credit was widely used in medieval times, and all three coexisted until modern times. "As late as the nineteenth century, the rural economy used a great deal of barter in such a country as France, the national economy organized along the roads used silver, and the international economy operating in ports and major financial centers used bills of exchange—a credit instrument—and settled balances that could not be cleared by bills in gold and silver payments (Braudel, 1977)." Shubik (2001) notes on page 97: "Credit has existed at least five thousand years as is evinced by the records of debt instruments in Sumer and the other ancient kingdoms in the fertile crescent. The granting of credit predated the invention of coinage by at least two thousand years."

Table 2.2. Relative Values of Services

Service	Fiat money	Finance
Unit of account	Absolute	Imperfect
Finality of payment	Absolute	No
Liquidity	Highest	Imperfect
Store of value	Useful	Potentially superior
Anonymity	Absolute	Imperfect

First, the promise in finance includes the possibility of the loss of principal (the amount of the loan); no such risk is typically taken on either side of the worker-owner promise. Second, the worker-owner promise involves an exchange of tangible items (goods produced for fiat money), whereas finance involves an exchange of a promise for fiat money. Third, the uncertainty associated with the worker-owner promise can be reduced significantly, in part by shortening the time between production and income payments to a week or two; in principle, workers could be paid every day, which would significantly reduce the promise element of the relationship.

More broadly, fiat money and finance provide different degrees of value-added as they supply specific services to members of society (see Table 2.2). In normal times, fiat money is a superior means of payment than are most forms of finance: both fiat money and finance can supply the service, but the reliability of vehicles that embody uncertainty about human trust clearly are inferior purely as means of payment, perhaps with the exception of bank money, a close substitute for fiat money as a means of payment. However, in normal times, finance has the potential to offer superior store-of-value services over those of fiat money, and in so doing offers superior services in facilitating intertemporal exchange. Both vehicles require the user to take some risk, but at least finance offers a higher reward.

✳ ✳ ✳ ✳ ✳

The analysis in this section, although elementary, aimed to (1) usefully examine the difference between money and finance, (2) elucidate the inextricable links between finance and money, (3) pinpoint the essence of finance, and (4) clarify the distinction between financial transactions and final exchanges of legal tender for physical goods and assets.

Finance uniquely complements the characteristics and qualities of money, for example, in the ways in which it facilitates (through lending) the preservation and potential growth of purchasing power through time, or in the ways in which it facilitates (through borrowing) the transfer of future earnings into present purchasing power. While these financial transfers through time could be performed, in principle, without the existence of universally accepted money, they would be performed with significantly less effectiveness and efficiency, and in significantly smaller amounts. Indeed, prior to the introduction of convertible monies in the eighteenth century, trade, exchange, and finance flourished in some parts of the world, but with significantly less breadth, scope, acceptance, and efficiency.

The discussion in this section also highlighted several unique and related characteristics of finance and financial activities in modern monetary economies:

- the temporary, intertemporal exchange of the finality-of-payment services of fiat money in return for the promise of a superior store of value;
- a trust agreement between counterparts;
- an intrinsic link to uncertainty.

Private and Social Economic Benefits of Finance

Because of its unique qualities, finance bestows enormous benefits privately and socially, and plays a fundamental role in facilitating the overall performance of economic systems. These private and social benefits and the role of finance have grown in importance in the latter half of the twentieth century. Throughout the course of the post–Second World War period, and beginning in earnest with the efforts toward financial liberalization in the late 1970s, the contribution of finance to the performance of economic systems has increased significantly in various dimensions, and in some cases immeasurably.[19] Moreover, financial activities also have grown in importance and in some economies constitute a relatively large direct share of employment and production of final goods and services.

Employment and production in the financial industry is perhaps the most visible and measurable contribution of finance to the performance of real economies, but it may not be the most fundamental or important. Finance contributes in several other, perhaps even more important ways.

---

[19]See the last several years of the IMF's *International Capital Markets: Developments, Prospects and Key Policy Issues*.

Facilitation of Intertemporal Economic Processes

Finance can be thought of as one important element of an economic system, one that facilitates the system's ability to perform intertemporal economic functions. In this respect, finance can be likened to other parts of an economic system's underlying infrastructure that together support (or in their absence, limit or inhibit) the performance of the economic system, such as the rule of law and enforcement of it. Similarly, finance provides fundamental services to the entire economy in much the same way that utility industries supply basic needs, such as water, power, and communications services. It is difficult to envision the benefits of modern economic life without these essential services; so too with the essential services of finance.[20]

Three important roles of finance in modern economies can be discerned.

First, finance enables the efficient allocation of real economic resources (now including human capital) at any given time and especially across time. It does so in many ways but one of the most important is by facilitating the matching of savers interested in postponing their consumption with end-user investors (most often through intermediaries) desiring to expand the capital base from which they can engage in productive activities.

Second, finance contributes to the performance of the real economy by facilitating the more effective management of the process of wealth accumulation for individuals, businesses, governments, and nations. Wealth or capital accumulation is one of the more fundamental requirements for a society to develop and grow. The more effective a society's financial mechanisms for wealth accumulation and management, the greater the opportunities for this society to enhance and sustain development and growth over time, and to weather the negative impact of unanticipated and unavoidable adverse events.

In the more highly developed and modern economies, the process of capital accumulation extends to the accumulation of human capital. In

---

[20]Levine (2003) and World Bank (1999) provide overviews of empirical work on the positive correlations between finance and economic development and growth. An important caveat is that the causality between the extent of financial intermediation and economic growth is difficult to determine empirically because these variables are inextricably linked and may both be endogenously determined. Theoretical approaches to this issue are developed in Acemoglu and Zilibotti (1997) and Greenwood and Jovanovic (1990). Recent emerging-market financial crises have highlighted the important adverse consequences that a dysfunctional financial system can have by either creating or exacerbating economic recessions, depressions, and crises. See various editions of the IMF's *International Capital Markets: Developments, Prospects, and Key Policy Issues,* for example, IMF (1995 and 1998a).

many economies individuals are now able to borrow against future earnings to enhance the prospects of their future levels of productivity, either through secondary and tertiary levels of education or vocational and job training.

A third role played by modern finance—one that has become increasingly important in the global economy and financial system—is its ability to aid in the management (including the diversification) of both economic and financial risks. Modern finance plays this role by providing greater opportunities for the unbundling, repackaging, pricing, transferring, and ownership of financial and economic risks, once the original economic or financial transaction has occurred. In fact, the essence of finance is that it is a process of transforming the risks and uncertainties associated with human trust (counterparty risk) into other not necessarily easily measurable, marketable, and manageable components (such as market risk and liquidity risk). Likewise, one could conceive of a useful alternative definition along these same lines. That is, finance and the financial system can be seen primarily as a large and dynamic network of financial contracts facilitating a vast diversity of economic functions. It is worthwhile examining this function of finance in greater detail, because it encompasses an increasingly important and fundamental role of finance in advanced countries and mature markets.

Modern Essence of Finance: Pricing and Allocating Risk

The development of derivatives markets in the past several decades and their maturation in the late 1990s is perhaps the best example of the more fundamental risk-allocation function of finance, particularly in modern economic systems.[21] For example, through the use of simple derivatives, such as interest-rate swaps, the financial risks inherent in a fixed-interest-rate loan can be easily transferred to another investor and swapped into a floating-interest-rate loan. Likewise, through the use of credit derivatives, the credit risk associated with a traditional loan can readily be swapped for another credit or insured; the loan could also be sold outright, perhaps through the securitization of the loan or a package of loans (known as asset-backed securities).

By allowing the unbundling and repackaging of risks, derivatives markets have helped transfer economic and financial risks to those most willing and capable of managing these risks. In so doing, finance in general,

---

[21]For the role of derivatives in modern banking, see Schinasi and others (2000).

and derivatives in particular, can help individual economic agents diversify their portfolios of economic and financial risks. At the same time, finance—derivatives in particular—benefits the economy as a whole, in part by providing mechanisms and opportunities for spreading economic and financial risk-taking throughout the economy. It also provides alternative channels for financing the same economic activity. As risk-transfer processes become more highly developed and mature, they can help to protect economic agents and the economy and its financial mechanisms by providing diverse opportunities for risk sharing, and burden sharing, too, when adverse consequences actually occur in particular markets or in the economy as a whole.

The spreading of modern finance techniques within economies has been associated with a tendency to make financial markets more complete. As a set of markets becomes more complete, those markets provide greater opportunities for creating private insurance contracts against a greater number of economic and financial risks. For example, the development of asset-backed security markets has enabled individuals in many countries to obtain consumer loans and home mortgages, and students to obtain loans for education and job training. Before asset-backed markets were developed and reached a level of maturity, many economies could not provide these financial services and transfer these risks, either among economic agents or through time.

In developing, refining, and providing these new and modern techniques, the mature financial systems are finding new ways for economic systems to capture the full benefits of finance. They are doing so by finding more (and more precise) ways of pricing and managing the risks inherent in temporarily transferring to other agents the purchasing power of money, including the risk and uncertainty about the human trust element in every financial instrument and transaction. Modern finance has also made this human trust element in transactions more transparent, and in so doing has identified ways to minimize the uncertainty of human trust, for example, by being better able to price in the market risks associated with collateral that acts as a surrogate for trust in many financial transactions.

Finance, Fragility, and Evolving Social Arrangements

As has been suggested but not yet explicitly stated, fiat money provides the ultimate *liquidity* service. However, finance also introduces the possibility of leverage. In combination, the liquidity- and leverage-enhancing features of finance provide potential benefits and costs, the latter as a result of the potential creation of financial fragility. Throughout recorded history, societies have created social and institutional arrangements that have attempted to capture the benefits of finance and minimize the potential for fragility and other potential costs.

Liquidity, Leverage, and Fragility

In providing universally accepted means-of-payment services, fiat money embodies instantaneous purchasing power with the lowest risk possible.

Finance enhances the liquidity services of fiat money by creating instruments that simultaneously provide superior store-of-value services to one counterpart and access to liquidity to the other counterpart, both spatially and intertemporally. These instruments are primarily in the form of promissory notes whereby one person's promise becomes another person's potential liquidity, provided the promise is transferable (marketable) with relative ease. By so enhancing the liquidity services of fiat money, finance can facilitate and fuel a pace of economic activity far beyond what fiat money alone can support.

Although finance provides superior store-of-value services, its incremental additions to the pool of liquidity are less perfectly liquid than fiat money, because finance embodies counterparty uncertainty and risk.[22] Taking a well understood example, traditional bank demand deposits are special forms of promissory notes that, by being widely accepted, are very close substitutes for fiat money. However, they are not universally accepted unconditionally in the way fiat money is. A bank's promissory note provides liquidity to the economic and financial system, but it is less liquid than fiat money because it encompasses counterparty risk—this is, in part, why banking is a fragile business. Promissory notes issued by individuals are even more imperfect.

Consequently, there are both potential benefits and costs associated with finance. On the one hand, finance enhances the private and social benefits of fiat money, in part by enlarging the pool of liquidity available for production, consumption, and exchange, and in part by facilitating and enhancing the efficiency of economic processes. On the other hand, finance inherently embodies uncertainty—about fulfilling promises—and thereby changes the nature of the original pool of pure liquidity by bringing in instruments of less perfect liquidity and acceptability than fiat money. This

---

[22]In his *Treatise on Money* (Vol. II), Keynes noted that one asset (or store of value) is more liquid than another if it is "more certainly realizable at short notice without loss" (1930b, p. 67).

introduces an element of uncertainty in individual private transactions, which has the potential for imposing costs (in terms of lost efficiency) for uninvolved third parties because of its potential adverse effects on liquidity. Thus, the inherent uncertainty in finance introduces a source of potential fragility and instability in financial markets that does not exist in most other markets in which tangible goods and services are traded. In this important respect finance is distinguishable from most other economic activities. Overall, the more positive features of finance provide efficiency enhancements and social benefits, while the more negative features entail the potential for instability and negative externalities (or contagion).

As a result, it is reasonable to see finance as encompassing both private and social trade-offs (and tensions). By embodying (and internalizing) uncertainty and risk about human trust tangible in intrinsically valueless instruments, finance enhances both private and social welfare. But by embodying a fragile human emotion like trust, finance is intrinsically fragile and, therefore, subject to instability under certain conditions. There are limits (albeit difficult to know and measure) to how far financial activity, liquidity, and leverage can be extended before too much finance is created on too little trust. When this situation is reached, imbalances tend to emerge and accumulate if left unchecked or if not self corrected.

Financial Institutions and Markets As Evolving Social Arrangements

As already suggested, the fundamental core of finance is the human promise to pay back fiat money to those willing to part with its services temporarily. The willingness of savers to do so involves a degree of trust that the promise will be honored.

In primitive or undeveloped economies, there tends to be significant uncertainty about whether promises will be kept, and limited enforceability of promises should they be broken (see Figure 2.1). Developed and modern societies have created social arrangements—such as social and business conventions and financial institutions and markets—in part to provide liquidity and pool risk and thereby to facilitate these intertemporal exchanges involving human promises and trust. These social innovations range from fundamental concepts of law and property rights, to institutional forums and structures that organize, process, and monitor information and pool risk taking. These forums run along a continuum roughly from individuals, to firms that provide intermediary services—or indirect finance, and extend to markets (both formal and informal) that allow individual lenders and borrowers to directly find matches of financial interests and comfort levels with uncertainty about human trust.

Figure 2.1. Evolution of Modern Finance

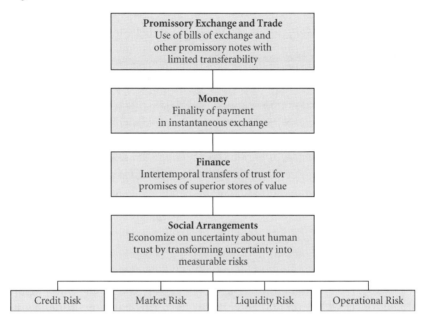

To consider this further, these social arrangements—in particular, financial institutions and markets—can be seen as society's way of minimizing, or economizing on, the need for individuals to rely on human trust in finance (Shubik, 1999). That financial institutions accomplish this is now conventional wisdom, and can be understood most clearly by considering the franchise of a traditional bank. On the asset side of their balance sheets, banks specialize, and are perceived as having a comparative advantage, in gathering, processing, and monitoring information on those members of society that want to issue promissory notes in return for temporary access to and use of fiat money. Accordingly, banks own assets in the form of promissory notes issued by such individuals (and firms). In return, banks provide liquidity in the form of access to fiat money, usually in the form of a deposit. On the liability side of their balance sheets, banks issue their own special kind of promissory note—demand deposits or checking accounts— to those members of society who would temporarily lend their excess fiat money to others, but who have neither the time nor the expertise to enter into bilateral relationships with potential borrowers to assess human trustworthiness. By issuing demand deposits, banks offer individuals the opportunity to store purchasing power and wealth in the form of a relatively safe asset with some commensurate return for the risks they are taking, namely of trusting the bank to pool and invest funds wisely. In this way, banks pool the liquidity of depositors and make it available to others. This franchise allows banks to profit from matching savers and borrowers.[23]

The bank franchise is one of society's arrangements for internalizing and pooling risk and uncertainty about human trust. In the absence of this pooling arrangement, uncertainty about trust would necessarily be embodied in bilateral promissory notes between individual savers and borrowers. By eliminating this need for finding a "double coincidence of wants" in exchanging promises for trust, financial intermediaries allow individuals the opportunity to avoid the costs of gathering information on the trustworthiness of those offering promises as stores of value. Banks likewise minimize the need for firms seeking finance to find that small subset of individuals possibly willing to enter into trust agreements.

Financial markets are another one of society's arrangements for internalizing and pooling uncertainties about trust and they accomplish similar objectives in very different ways. Markets facilitate the direct matching of savers and borrowers in both formal, organized ways (exchanges, clearinghouses, and so on) and informal ways (or over-the-counter, bilateral transactions). These forums provide information to participants for judging individual creditworthiness, although the information may be different from that gathered by a bank.

---

[23]Diamond and Rajan (2001, 2002) present models that formalize a bank's franchise value and its liquidity and fragility implications.

3

Public Policy Aspects of Finance

As examined in previous sections—based solely on the observation that finance intrinsically embodies uncertainty about human trust—finance can have both positive (or efficiency-enhancing) and negative effects on economic processes and systems. Both originate in the element of trust embodied in finance, and the balance between the two depends on the ways in which finance, as a process, facilitates the assessment, transformation, pricing, and allocation of the uncertainty and risks associated with this trust. The leaps of faith by members of society to engage in trust relationships so as to obtain private benefits have produced both private and social efficiency (and welfare) gains throughout history. However, history has also revealed that confidence in trust is a fragile feature of human interaction in all social endeavors, including economic and financial activities. When confidence in the trust underlying economic and financial transactions breaks down, so too can the ability of markets and financial institutions to perform their basic pricing, allocative, and intermediary functions. This breakdown can threaten financial stability. In effect, the element of human trust, and whether that trust is strong or weak, helps to determine the strength and stability of the economic and financial mechanisms that provide order to everyday economic life.

Can and will unfettered market forces lead to the right balance of these positive and negative aspects of finance? Is individual rationality (utility- and profit-maximizing behavior) sufficient to achieve collective rationality (or socially optimal outcomes) in finance?[24] If not, what steps can be taken to move society closer to the right balance?[25]

---

[24]This way of characterizing the issue echoes the seminal work of Olson (1965) and Sandler (1992).

[25]The Prisoner's Dilemma illustrates how the pursuit of self-interest can lead to an aggregate outcome that is inferior to other feasible outcomes; see Box 3.1.

Box 3.1. Prisoner's Dilemma

The prisoner's dilemma is a gaming situation often experienced in life and in financial markets. It illustrates how the pursuit of self-interest rather than cooperation can lead to an outcome for the collective that is inferior to other feasible outcomes.[1]

The original "game" was created by Albert Tucker, a Princeton mathematician. Tucker's dilemma was a more intuitive representation of a game discussed in a paper by a Rand mathematician, Merrill M. Flood; Flood's paper was followed by additional experiments at Rand with his colleague Melvin Dresher.[2] The original dilemma was posed as follows: Two men, charged with a joint violation of law, are held separately by the police. Each is told that

- if one confesses and the other does not, the former will be given a reward and the latter will be fined;
- if both confess, each will be fined.

At the same time, each has good reason to believe that if neither confesses, both will go free.

The incentives implicit in this situation are for each individual to follow the dominant strategy of confessing, which gives a smaller sentence to each prisoner for each of the choices the other prisoner might make. However, when each prisoner follows his dominant strategy, each receives a sentence greater than if neither confessed. In this situation, when both parties pursue their own interests exclusively and do not cooperate with each other, the outcome is worse for both of them, even though in any given situation, either party is better off not cooperating.[3]

In finance, it is not difficult to imagine situations like this classic dilemma. For example, in the midst of market turbulence in, say, the bond market, the five market makers accounting for most of the trading might encounter a situation in which each of them would strongly prefer to withdraw from market-making services so as to use inventory and liquidity to protect their own portfolios, including in other markets that might later be affected if the tur-

---

[1]For a readable and entertaining explanation, see *Prisoner's Dilemma* (Poundstone, 1992).
[2]See "Some Experimental Games" (Flood, 1952).
[3]See *A Mathematician Plays the Stock Market* (Paulos, 2003).

These are difficult, and in some ways philosophical questions. By applying certain features of the economics of the public sector, this chapter frames the public policy aspects of finance and financial stability considerations, and suggests that

- finance entails both positive and negative externalities;
- finance intrinsically embodies imperfect information (at the very least, uncertainty about human trust);

bulence turns to a widespread crisis. Thus, each has the incentive to withdraw, and if they all do so, the worst case scenario—a dysfunctional market—has a high probability of occurring. However, if they cooperate and all jointly decide to continue to supply market-making services, the turbulence would probably be limited and subside, leaving all of them better off.

An elaboration on the classic but simple and concrete prisoner's dilemma will make the problem clearer. A more modern adaptation might unfold as follows: Consider a situation involving two prisoners (although it can be generalized to any number participants). Two prisoners arrested on a minor charge are suspected of committing a major crime as well. Conviction carries a jail sentence of one year for the minor crime for each prisoner and a total of 10 years for the major crime. The police are having difficulty investigating the major crime and are under some pressure to resolve it. Each prisoner is questioned separately and is presented with the following choice: testify that the co-suspect committed the major crime (noncooperation) and go free, provided the co-suspect does not also testify, or remain silent and receive either a one-year sentence if the co-suspect remains silent or serve the full 10-year sentence if the co-suspect testifies. In the event both testify to the other's guilt, they split the prison sentence for the major crime (five years each).

The possible outcomes to these separate decisions follow:

- Both suspects remain silent. This is the cooperative solution, and they each receive a year in jail for the minor offense ($R = -1$, $R = -1$; R is the reward for cooperation). This is in fact the best outcome for each prisoner, as they would share the highest total payoff (-2).
- One suspect testifies against the other, while the other remains silent. Each is tempted to testify and go free (and receive $T = 0$; T is the temptation to confess). If one prisoner testifies against the other, and the other does not, the former goes free, while the latter receives the full 10-year sentence ($T = 0$, $S = -10$; S is the sucker payoff for remaining silent).
- Both testify against each other. If they both testify against each other, they will each receive a five-year sentence ($P = -5$, $P = -5$; P is the penalty payoff for confessing guilt).

- access to finance—the process that provides effective store-of-value services—is a public good, as is access to a universally accepted means of payment (fiat money);
- overall, some market imperfections produce "too little of a good thing" while others produce "too much of a good thing";
- because of market imperfections, maintaining effective finance and financial stability requires a balance between private market forces

Box 3.1. (*concluded*)

While the best outcome is for both prisoners to remain silent, each of them has little incentive to choose this option, knowing that the other prisoner understands the risks, and also understands that his choices do not affect his co-suspect's choices: each must choose independently, and without prior consultation. They also both have the strong temptation to squeal on the other prisoner and go free. Given these conditions, each prisoner has the strong incentive to make the choice that minimizes his prison term regardless of what the other prisoner chooses. Thus, it is rational for each prisoner to testify against the other and obtain a five-year sentence for the major crime, because remaining silent poses the risk of the worst outcome, a 10-year sentence. In this case, they take an equal share of the worst outcome of the game, rather than taking an equal share of the best outcome of the game.

These options can be represented in a payoff matrix as follows:

	B Silent	B Testifies
A Silent	$(-1, -1)$	$(-10, 0)$
A Testifies	$(0, -10)$	$(-5, -5)$

In general, for a two-person game to pose the Prisoner's Dilemma, the payoff matrix, and the structure of the various payoffs must be as follows: $T > R > P > S$, and $2R > T + S$.

	B Testifies	B Testifies
A Silent	(R, R)	(S, T)
A Testifies	(T, S)	(P, P)

and both private-collective and public sector action on behalf of members of society.

This chapter examines why fiat money and finance can and should be regarded as public goods and other public policy aspects of finance and financial stability. In order to do so, it first applies the economics of the public sector—particularly the concept of market imperfections or failures—to finance.

Sources of Market Imperfections in Finance

A *market imperfection* occurs when a market outcome (or market force) deviates from a standard used by economists to define the economically efficient quantity and allocation of goods and services.[26] Economic efficiency means an allocation of resources that leads to a combination of production, consumption, and so on in which no individual can be made better off through a reallocation of economic resources without making some other individual worse off. Such outcomes are known as Pareto-efficient or Pareto-optimal. A fundamental theorem in welfare economics is that under well-specified conditions—including perfect competition and information—the "invisible hand" of market forces will lead to economically efficient (Pareto-efficient) outcomes.

Within this context, market imperfections occur because of the existence of five deviations from the definition of a perfectly competitive economy: externalities, public goods, incomplete information, incomplete markets, and a lack of competition.[27]

When a market imperfection occurs, the price established in the market will not equal the marginal *social* benefit of a good and it will not equal the marginal *social* cost of producing the good. As a result, the good in question will be consumed or produced (or both) in quantities that are economically inefficient. This can occur even when the market price equals both the marginal *private* cost and marginal *private* benefit that meets the economists' definition of an equilibrium price. That is, even in what economists consider to be an equilibrium, there can be deviations from a socially optimal outcome. This is the true import of a market failure—a situation in which a sustainable equilibrium is economically inefficient and socially suboptimal.

Note that a market failure is defined in terms of the economic efficiency of a price and resource allocation outcome, not in terms of the stability properties of equilibrium. Thus, a market failure need not pose a threat to market stability. Also note, however, that a market failure—particularly in finance—can lead to imbalances, which in turn could create a potential threat to stability.

---

[26]Some of this discussion is adapted from Sandler (1992) and Stiglitz (2000). In this chapter, the terms "market imperfections" and "market failures" are interchangeable.

[27]See Box 3.2.

Externalities

An *externality* is a secondary or an unintended consequence. In finance, externalities arise when a financial activity imposes benefits or costs on third parties or in markets that are not directly involved in the activity. If the externality provides benefits, it is a positive externality; if it increases costs, it is a negative externality.[28] If the activity imposes costs on a suffi-ciently large number of counterparts or markets, it could potentially become systemic, and pose systemic risk. If an externality provides benefits to society at large, it may also be a public good (see next subsection).[29]

In general, an externality—negative or positive—drives a wedge between private costs and benefits and social costs and benefits. Thus, the market-determined price, quantity, and allocation between counterparts of a finan-cial activity may not be socially optimal, implying that the activity would not be produced and consumed to the point that the social marginal costs and benefits exactly match the private costs and benefits. The less-than-optimal outcome is reached because the external costs or benefits of goods are not factored into individual and market demands and supplies, because individual consumers and producers do not directly bear the external costs or reap the external benefits. Looking at this from the demand side only, goods that convey positive externalities will be underdemanded and, given rising marginal costs of production, underproduced. Similarly, goods that convey negative externalities will be overdemanded and overproduced.

Some aspects of finance are simultaneously associated with the potential for both positive and negative externalities. Banks funded by short-term deposits provide liquidity to potential borrowers and superior opportuni-ties for risk sharing. At the same time, however, in a completely unregulated environment—even in equilibrium situations—individual banks could be exposed to bank runs and panics as a result of imperfect or incomplete infor-mation, as banks were in the early part of the twentieth century. While the provision of liquidity and opportunities for risk sharing are positive exter-nalities, bank runs and panics are negative externalities; in some circum-stances, there are significant net social costs associated with bank failures and collateral damage. As noted earlier, social arrangements and mechanisms have been implemented to rule out this possibility (deposit insurance, for example) but they themselves are costly to society, thus there are both pri-vate and public trade-offs.

---

[28]A classic example of a negative externality is the production of pollution as a by-product in producing private goods.

[29]In this sense, externalities are a form of impure public goods; alternatively, public goods can be seen as an extreme form of externalities.

Box 3.2. Sources of Market Failure in Finance

Public good

- Finance provides unit-of-account services to financial balances (+)
- Finance extends universal acceptability benefits of fiat money to financial system (+)

Externalities

- Trust in finance enhances efficiency in intertemporal and interspatial allocations (+)
- Financial system creates network benefits (+)
- Finance subject to contagion and systemic risks (−)

Incomplete information

- Incomplete information in finance leads to price misalignment, resource misallocation, and multiple equilibria, possibly resulting in liquidity and credit runs (−)
- Asymmetric information between borrowers and lenders leads to adverse selection, moral hazard, and credit rationing (−)

Incomplete markets

- Uninsurable liquidity risks (lender-of-last-resort financing) increase economic uncertainty (−)
- Nonprice discrimination in provision of finance leads to missed exchange opportunities (−)

Imperfect competition

- Single money issuer improves services provided by fiat money and economizes on transaction balances (+)
- Monopoly of money supply generates seignorage revenues with incentives for overissue (−)
- Economies of scale and too-big-to-fail considerations lead to insufficient or excessive competition between financial institutions and with new entrants (−)

Note: (+) and (−) indicate a positive or negative contribution to market efficiency.

Externalities may also arise in finance in situations in which many individual market participants take independent actions that would benefit them separately and collectively only if a small number were engaged in the activity, and would be harmful to everyone if a large number engaged in the activity simultaneously. Consider the classic bank runs during the global financial panics that occurred in 1931 when many banking systems needed to be closed for several days. Bank depositors began withdrawing cash from particular banks thought by some to be experiencing difficulties. Ultimately, a bank would run out of liquid assets and close its doors, which led to concerns about solvency. Once the word spread, third-party depositors with deposits in other (also third-party) banks started questioning whether their banks would be able to make good on deposits. As the process continued, even good banks were experiencing runs, thus, even good banks ran into solvency problems as their depositor base dwindled. In this case, individually rational decisions—to withdraw deposits from the banking system—collectively created the negative externality of driving the banking system into the ground, which imposed costs on everyone (Diamond and Dybvig, 1983).

Liquidity runs can also occur in markets. Consider a market with many traders, each exposed to most other traders in the market. Even in highly efficient and liquid markets, liquidity problems can arise when traders withdraw from trading because they receive "news" that one of the traders is having difficulties obtaining financing. In reaction, all other traders pursue their self-interest and stop trading, perhaps with all other traders. This creates a chain reaction in which liquidity is reduced in the market. To the extent that liquidity in one market affects liquidity in another, there might be *contagion* or systemic effects from the initial liquidity pressures in the one market.[30]

Network externalities can also capture some of the benefits of scale in finance. A network externality exists when a product's value to the user increases as the number of users of the product grows. Each new user of the product derives private benefits, but also confers external benefits (network externalities) on existing users. Network externalities can cause market failures—for example, a network may not reach its optimal size because users fail to take external benefits into account. Network externalities can also be negative and in the extreme become systemic.

Public Goods

A *public good* (or *common good*) the extreme form of a positive externality. A public good has two defining characteristics: (1) the producer of the good is unable to control who benefits from consuming the good (nonexcludability in supply); and (2) consumption of the good by one person does not affect the benefits received in consuming the good by others (nonrivalry in consumption). Nonrivalry in consumption means that the marginal cost

---

[30]Diamond and Rajan (2002) examine the conditions under which a bank run can, through contagion, create aggregate liquidity shortages.

of providing the benefit to an additional consumer is zero. Nonexcludability in supply means that no one would be willing voluntarily to help supply the good or to pay for using it. Briefly stated, a pure public good conveys benefits that are both nonexcludable in supply and nonrival in consumption.[31]

Examples of goods that possess these properties are the provision of national defense against aggression, the maintenance of social law and order, the redistribution of resources to achieve a collectively chosen norm of social justice, and traffic monitoring and enforcement at intersections. Taking the first example, the security of national defense is a nonexcludable good: in providing national defense against aggression, the government (the supplier) cannot exclude citizens from enjoying its benefits and the marginal cost of an additional citizen enjoying the benefit is zero. In fact, it is impossible to exclude any citizen from enjoying these benefits; such a good is defined as a pure public good. In addition, the fact that one person receives the benefit does not diminish the ability of another citizen to also receive the benefit, and the marginal cost of providing the good does not increase as more individuals reap the benefits. Thus, national defense is a good that is nonrival in consumption. Although national security could, in principle, be provided by the private sector, there are incentives to be a *free rider,* defined as the reluctance of individuals to contribute voluntarily to the production of a public good.[32]

Table 3.1 presents a typology showing how private and public goods differ in the two characteristics of public goods. (See Sandler, 1992.) Note that even if a good is rival in consumption, it can still have a public-good character if the benefits it provides are nonexcludable. An example is the natural clean air we breathe—it is a *pure* public good, until there is rivalry in its use, such as when a company pollutes the air in a community. The company's actions cannot alter the supply of air to the citizens in the community, but the company's consumption of clean air (its pollution) reduces the ability of the citizens in the community to consume clean air.

With the development of the joint field of law and economics, a new practical insight emerged: the assignment of property rights can be used to "internalize" (that is, make private) the costs of the negative externality.[33] The introduction of property rights, therefore, tends to reduce the need for

---

[31]According to Cornes and Sandler (1996), nonexcludability is the crucial factor in determining which goods must be publicly provided.

[32]The free-rider problem arises because a public good can be consumed without paying for it. This originates in the nonexcludability-in-supply characteristic of public goods.

[33]Ronald Coase received the Nobel Prize in economics for this insight and his related seminal work. See Coase (1960).

Table 3.1. Typology of Benefits from Goods, Based on Characteristics of the Goods

	Excludable	Nonexcludable[1]
Rival	Pure private goods	Impure public goods Private externalities Common-pool resources
Nonrival[2,3] (zero marginal cost of consumption)	Impure public goods Local public goods Club goods	Pure public goods

Source: Sandler, 1992.

[1]According to Sandler (1992, p. 5), "Benefits of a good, available to all once the good is provided, are called nonexcludable. If the benefits of a good can be withheld costlessly by the owner or provider, then benefits are excludable."

[2]According to Sandler (1992, p. 6), "A good is *nonrival* or indivisible when a *unit* of the good can be consumed by one individual without detracting, in the slightest, from the consumption opportunities still available for others from that *same unit*." For nonrival goods, exclusion is possible (by charging fees or club membership) but undesirable because it results in underconsumption; but without exclusion (that is, without charging for the good), there is the problem of undersupply (because there is no incentive to supply it).

[3]Partially rival means one's consumption of the benefit diminishes the benefits of others but does not eliminate or preclude others from receiving some benefit from consumption—for instance, a crowded park or fishing stream, both of which are nonexcludable.

an outside agent (government) to create the conditions necessary for eliminating or reducing the adverse consequences of an externality. For instance, in the clean air example, if the community was granted property rights over the air in its boundaries, the citizens could collectively produce a private solution by imposing a user fee on the company, or restricting its activities to lower the level of pollution. This can occur in finance. For instance, a government could grant the authority to privately exchange financial instruments to a set of private agents provided they conformed to certain rules and regulations. Stock exchanges are an example.

A pure public good is produced in optimal quantities when the marginal cost of producing an extra unit of that good equals the marginal social benefit from the consumption of one more unit of that good. Public goods can be produced by both private and public sectors.

Public goods create market imperfections because in a completely unregulated market, public goods would be either underconsumed or underproduced, or even not produced at all. Underproduction occurs because the good would be produced only up to the point that the private marginal cost to the producer would exactly match the private marginal benefit to the producer (which is the portion of the social benefit that the producer is able to internalize by producing). Thus, it is difficult to provide incentives for private individuals to produce public goods in sufficient quantities. Goods that are nonrival in consumption but excludable in supply will be underconsumed, but when they are also nonexcludable they will be under-produced. It is worth noting again that the underproduction or undercon-sumption of a good is defined by the economic efficiency of an equilibrium and not by its stability properties.

As will be discussed in further detail in the next two sections, both fiat money and finance can and should be seen as having significant positive externalities and can also be seen as public goods. This suggests that both private-collective and public sector actions could enhance the private and social benefits of finance beyond what market forces alone would attain.

Incomplete Information

When counterparts in financial transactions (in formal and informal markets, and in bilateral or multilateral over-the-counter exchanges) are not well informed, free-market outcomes will tend to allocate resources ineffi-ciently. For example, because of imperfect information about a company within a particular industry, a local bank may underestimate or overesti-mate the risks associated with lending to firms in that industry. Moreover, the industry might be particularly sensitive to macroeconomic conditions in a neighboring town or state, which might be about to experience a boom or a bust. As a result of not having perfect, or even sufficient, information on firms and the industry, the bank might tend to take on a suboptimal amount of risk, either too much or too little. The outcome might be, there-fore, that the industry would receive more or less capital than it could rea-sonably efficiently utilize, and the bank and its depositors would end up owning more or less credit risk than is optimal for the bank and its finan-cial stakeholders.

When information is incomplete, adverse selection and moral hazard can lead to situations in which economically desirable goods are driven out of the market by economically undesirable goods. Consider the classic case of the "market for lemons": the case of the sale of a used car (or a loan orig-inated years ago by a bank) in which the owner of the used car (loan) knows almost everything about the performance of the car (loan) and the poten-tial buyer knows next to nothing (Akerlof, 1970). Because there is a risk of buying a dysfunctional automobile in this secondary market—that is, of buying a lemon—buyers tend to price the risk of a car being a lemon into their offer prices, which tends to lower all prices, even for good cars. The result is that fewer suppliers of cars are willing to sell, especially suppliers of good cars. This also means that more lemons are sold than is beneficial, which further reduces welfare.

Adverse selection in the credit derivatives market, which is a market for buying and selling insurance protection against the risk of a default on a loan, illustrates the same effect.[34] Adverse selection results from the fact that lenders who issued credits to borrowers with a higher risk of default are more likely to want to be insured than those who issued credit to borrowers with lower risks. This skewed demand encourages the insurer to raise premiums above the socially efficient price, which reduces the overall amount of insurance provided to a point below the social optimum. A situation can arise in which low-risk insurees are priced out of the market, so there would be a large number of high-risk insurees in the insured pool. In the extreme case, only owners of high-risk credits will be able to obtain insurance, which is highly inefficient. A similar situation can occur in credit markets in which riskier borrowers crowd out less risky borrowers.

One solution to this kind of adverse selection is to monitor. For example, insurance providers—both private and public—have a strong incentive to require inspections. Another solution is to offer co-insurance rather than full insurance. Still another is to insure large groups to capture the diversity of risks. In the extreme, this would mean insuring the entire population of depositors, which would appear to be optimal if it could be properly priced and monitored; but then there is the moral hazard.[35]

Incomplete Markets

Market forces often fail to provide a good for which the private cost of production is less than what private individuals are willing to pay. This market imperfection is referred to as *incomplete markets*. Economists have suggested several reasons for incomplete markets, including high transactions costs in running markets, enforcing contracts, and introducing new products; asymmetries in information concerning financial risks; enforcement costs on defaulted contracts; and adverse selection. Thus, incomplete markets often are the result of the existence of other market imperfections, such as incomplete information or insufficient competition.

---

[34]Adverse selection occurs when two parties in a negotiation have different amounts of information—asymmetric information—and the outcome restricts the quality of the good traded. This typically occurs because the party with more information is able to negotiate a favorable exchange.

[35]Moral hazard is the risk that one party to a contract can change its behavior to the detriment of the other party once the contract has been concluded. It occurs, for example, when an insured agent takes less than the efficient amount of precaution against the insured event. For example, a bank depositor who is fully insured takes no precaution against insolvency of the bank, such as monitoring the bank's ability to assess and manage credit risk.

Finance is thought to be an area where this market imperfection is prevalent, particularly with regard to loans, insurance contracts, and capital-market instruments. An example in lending and capital markets is the market for college student loans. In principle, lending to students is no more risky than lending to small and medium-size businesses. It can even be argued that lending to college students, whose incomes are likely to be higher than average, would be less risky. Until government guarantee programs were put in place, no market developed to offer loans to college students who were willing to pay even market rates for them. Now many major banks have student loan portfolios. A similar analysis can be made for U.S. home-mortgage loans: once quasi-government agencies stepped in to underwrite them, the market for home mortgages expanded at a more rapid pace. Another example is deposit insurance. Even though banks would have been willing to pay for insurance to keep a steady stream of deposits flowing, no such market was created until the government stepped in during the Great Depression to provide deposit insurance.

Fiat Money As a Public Good?

In private exchanges, the use of specific units of currency is rival in consumption and thus conveys private benefits. It is rival in consumption because in bilateral or multilateral trades and exchanges, only the parties to the exchanges benefit from the value obtained in them. To the extent that the supply of fiat money (or another form of legal tender) is fixed at any time, it is also excludable in supply, even though the issuer does not specifically restrict its use to one set of individuals.

More generally, the more that people use fiat money in their exchanges, the more efficient multilateral exchange becomes; likewise, the more efficient other economic processes that rely on exchange also become. Once the use of fiat money extends beyond a certain critical social threshold, *the widespread use of money as legal tender provides positive externalities* to others not necessarily involved in every exchange using specific units of currency. As the universality of use of fiat money grows, there is a greater pool of potential transactors and liquidity in using fiat money. In terms of the characteristics of rivalry and excludability, as universality of use expands, the pool of transactors and liquidity surrounding the fixed supply of fiat money becomes nonexcludable. In the literature on public goods, this is known as a common-pool resource. It is similar to a lake or stream in which there is nonexcludable access to fish but in which the benefit of consumption of the good (catching fish) is rival because once a fish is caught it can no longer be consumed by someone else—unless there is a catch-and-release policy at the lake or stream.[36] This common-pool resource is a nonpure public good, as defined in the upper right corner of Table 3.1 (rival but nonexcludable goods). Note that fiat money itself is not the public good, in part because the marginal cost of providing it to a growing population is not zero (in the way the marginal cost of another person benefiting from national defense would be)—the public good is the efficiency-enhancing pool of transactors and liquidity that develops because of the existence of fiat money and its characteristics and services.

However, once fiat money reaches the point of *universal acceptability* in providing finality-of-payment services, the positive externality extends to all members of society. In this way, the services provided by fiat money are public goods. In fact, the universal acceptability of fiat money as society's means of payment satisfies the two defining requirements of a pure public good: nonexcludability in supply and nonrivalry in consumption. The first property is satisfied because in a society in which there is a universally accepted means of payment, the fiat issuer cannot exclude anyone from benefiting from one of its most important services, that of universal acceptability. The second property is satisfied because the fact that one agent receives the benefit of having access to a universally accepted means of payment does not reduce the ability of others to enjoy the benefits of universal acceptability.[37] Moreover, the universal use of a common means of payment facilitates more efficient multilateral trade and exchange among members of an economy.[38]

The idea that fiat money is a public good is ancient, and has been exploited by sovereigns throughout human history. According to Kindleberger (1993, p. 22),

> The public good character of money was early recognized by rulers who laid down standards for mints within their jurisdictions and tried to see that they were maintained. The Holy Roman Empire, for example, decreed ordinances for regulating the number of mints within its constituent elements and the weight and

---

[36]See Maier-Rigaud and Apesteguia (2004). They show differences in rivalry for nonexcludable goods lead to differences in aggregate investment behavior in a neighborhood of the Nash equilibrium. More specifically, the authors demonstrate that public goods and common pools are distinct rather than identical Nash-equilibrium games: the public-goods game leads to private investment above the Nash-equilibrium level of investments while the common-pool game leads to private investment above the Nash equilibrium. However, over time, both games converge to the same Nash equilibrium. Thus, "aggregate behavior in both games is surprisingly similar in the sense that it starts in the neighborhood of the Pareto optimum and moves to the respective aggregate Nash equilibrium" (Maier-Rigaud and Apesteguia, 2004, p. 12).

[37]Tobin (1980, p. 83; 1992) writes, "Social institutions like fiat money are public goods."

[38]Note that these same arguments apply to the unit-of-account service of fiat money.

fineness of the coins struck, and it sent imperial assayers on visits to see that its standards were adhered to. The lesser governments had their own interests in raising funds—for consumption, for building palaces, and, when war broke out, for hiring mercenaries—and these often clashed with the overall public interest. The principalities, duchies, bishoprics, imperial cities, and the like were tempted from time to time to debase the currency issued by their mints, to earn income by minting more coins for a given amount of metal, and then to encourage the taking of debased coins across the border and exchanging them for good coins. If a coin were not too badly worn, sweated (i.e., rubbed), clipped or adulterated, it could pass at its nominal value, especially if it were a subsidiary coin used in retail trade and the payment of wages. If, on the other hand, it was badly deteriorated or was a large silver or a gold coin, it had to be weighed and tested before the recipient would be willing to accept it. The 12 million escudos paid by Francis I of France in 1529 to ransom his two sons, who had been substituted for him as hostages when he was captured in the war between France and Spain, took four months to count and test, and 40,000 coins were rejected by the Spanish as below standard.

Finance and Financial Stability as Public Goods?

As the universally accepted means of payment, fiat money is a public good because it conveys external benefits that are nonrival and nonexcludable, for example, in the way that it facilitates multilateral trade and exchange. Without it, Jevons' "double coincidence of wants" would constrain the efficiency and amount of trade and exchange, and economic activity more generally. Fiat money accomplishes this because it eliminates the need for human trust, and is the economy's surrogate for trust, in trade and exchange.

Finance is an exchange of one service for another with a promise to reverse the exchange; it involves a temporary exchange of fiat money for a promissory note. Within a particular exchange, finance provides rival and excludable benefits to the counterparts of the bilateral or multilateral exchange. That is, individual financial transactions occur among private individuals and provide private benefits.

As a critical mass of financial activity is reached, finance both provides positive externalities and conveys public goods. The positive externalities are associated with the efficiency gains that finance provides over fiat money in facilitating the more efficient intertemporal allocation of resources (such as borrowing against future earnings) and in providing greater and more effective opportunities for all members of society to store value and accumulate wealth. In effect, finance enhances, or leverages, the public good function of fiat money; it amplifies the universally accepted finality-of-payment services of fiat money, both spatially and intertemporally. If the services of fiat money are a public good, some of the services of finance are also a public good.

Moreover, when the level and effectiveness of finance as a process or system reaches a critical mass, the process or system itself provides the opportunity for all to have access to effective and superior stores of value—*the process* that provides these services becomes a public good.[39] It does so because it begins providing benefits to society that reach well beyond the aggregation of the benefits of private individual transactions, and because such transactions also become both nonrival in consumption and nonexcludable in supply. Access to the efficiency benefits of a well-functioning financial system is nonrival because one person's access to (and consumption of) the benefits of the process does not diminish another's access to the benefits of the process. Indeed, it can be argued that the more everyone accesses these benefits, the greater is the benefit to all. Access to the efficiency benefits is nonexcludable because no one can be excluded from reaping the broader social benefits of finance's contributions to the efficiency of economic processes. Finance provides other positive externalities as well, because it enhances the services of fiat money by facilitating a greater number of transactions than fiat money alone could support, and does so intertemporally.

Just as the introduction of fiat money allows for the timing of receipt of income to be separated from the timing of of expenditures, finance—borrowing and lending—allows individuals to shift purchasing power forward in time. This intertemporal separation allows societies to achieve a more efficient allocation of resources, greater production from available resources, and, in the end, greater consumption. These services are public goods and so, too, is finance.

Similar externality and public good arguments can be made for preserving financial stability. Everyone would like to see financial stability preserved because there are both private and public costs associated with bank failures, market dysfunctions, and systemic financial problems. However, no one individual or small group of individuals can do much to prevent problems from arising beyond engaging in prudent portfolio and risk management. Moreover, because the private cost of doing something about systemic risk is too high, and the rewards too low, on balance everyone has the incentive to let someone else worry about it. The provision and maintenance of financial stability would provide benefits to all individuals, and the fact that one person incurs these benefits does not prevent others from doing so. Thus, the principles of nonexcludability and nonrivalry would apply to financial stability just as it does to other public goods such as national defense.

---

[39]For another reason to see finance as a public good, see Box 3.3.

Market Imperfections in Practice: Some Produce Too Little of a Good Thing and Others Too Much of a Bad Thing

Some market imperfections in finance are positive in the sense that they do not produce private or social "bads." Instead, the market failure is that private incentives and market forces alone lead to the underproduction or underconsumption of financial activities with desirable characteristics and potential private and social benefits. Sources of market imperfections that lead to this kind of outcome are positive externalities, public goods, some forms of incomplete information, incomplete markets, and a lack of competition. A specific example is the lack of competition in supplying student loans, which would tend to lead to an overpricing of the risk of lending to students and therefore to an undersupply of loans to this class of borrower. The challenge in these cases is to provide incentives to supply and consume more of the goods that provide positive externalities and public benefits, that tend to open up new markets, and that increase competition unless there are natural monopolies. (See Box 3.2.)

The introduction of fiat money in the mid-seventeenth century (but which did not come into its own until the early part of the twentieth century with the disappearance of commodity monies and standards) may have been the first "socially collective" push to increase the beneficial aspects of financial activity. The advent of banking and other financial arrangements also helped to increase the potential benefits of finance to individuals and society at large. As financial systems continue to evolve, new arrangements are likely to be created, and existing arrangements improved. One aim of financial-system policies is to ensure that this process of innovation and evolution continues to increase overall economic efficiency and therefore the public as well as private benefits of finance.

However, there is another side to finance. Some market imperfections in finance can be seen as negative in the sense that they lead to outcomes in which private and social "bads" are produced. The market failure in these cases is that private incentives and market forces alone lead to the overproduction or overconsumption of financial activities that have undesirable characteristics and potential social costs. Sources of these market imperfections include negative externalities, some kinds of information failures, and excessive competition. Here the challenge is to provide incentives to minimize the production and consumption of financial activities that result from these imperfections. A specific example is excess competition in particular segments of the market for loans—for example, credit card loans—which can lead to underpricing of the risks (and therefore oversupply of this particular class of loans).

Both sides of market failures in finance can be illustrated in many ways. The most direct is to consider the characteristics of bank money, the closest finance substitute for fiat money (or other forms of legal tender). To the extent that bank money (bank notes or demand deposits that promise to pay fiat money on demand) provides superior store-of-value services to society at large and also enhances (by literally leveraging) the real economic benefits of the universally accepted means-of-payment services of fiat money, it both conveys positive externalities and is a public good. However, if completely left to market forces, because of the inherent uncertainty about trust, the future, and information, the demand for bank money would be less than what is considered socially optimal. Individual private demands for bank deposits would focus exclusively on the private benefits and risks, and not incorporate the external benefits of leveraging the finality-of-payment services of money as legal tender.

A potential *negative externality* can also be associated with bank deposits, however, similar to the negative externalities of traffic jams. Individuals lend their fiat money to banks in return for a promise to get it back on demand. Meanwhile, banks invest these funds in risky assets, which the banks understand better than the depositors. Thus, these bank notes are risky. If banking was left entirely to market forces, when banks become suspected of mismanaging their assets, individuals have the incentive to withdraw their funds. If a large number of depositors withdrew their funds simultaneously, the bank would quickly run out of liquid funds, become insolvent, and most individuals would lose their deposits. That is, when left to market forces alone, bank deposits can be subject to runs from time to time, as uncertainty about trust ebbs and flows. Knowledge of this possibility would tend to reduce the amount of deposits in the financial system below the economically and socially desirable amount. The introduction of deposit insurance—either privately or publicly funded—would eliminate these sources of market failure and help moderate demand around the socially optimal level, provided the deposit insurance scheme was appropriately priced and monitored for abuse and moral hazard.

Policy Implications and Conclusions

Modern finance is a dynamic network of a large number of individual private financial contracts seeking exclusive private gains. Accordingly, the net social benefits of finance are the aggregate of (albeit difficult to measure) individual private net benefits.

However, it would be an illusion to consider the effectiveness of private finance and its enormous real economic benefits either entirely as private or exclusively as the result of individual private actions and unrestrained market forces. Regardless of opinions about the necessity and efficacy of public policies, obtaining the full extent of the private net benefits of modern finance requires, at a minimum, the existence and effectiveness of many private-collective, publicly sanctioned, publicly mandated, and taxpayer-financed social conventions and arrangements.

Many of these important social arrangements are taken for granted. For example, modern private financial contracts are predominantly written in terms of the social convention of a legally sanctioned unit of account. This unit-of-account service has the properties of a pure public good, and is part of every financial transaction. All receive benefits and none pay a private cost, except as taxpayers. The service could be provided and financed privately, but most attempts to do so throughout history have neither succeeded nor endured. A second example is that settlement and delivery of payments for financial transactions typically require a universally accepted legal tender (a fiat money), which, as argued earlier, also has the characteristics of a public good. Third, transactors presume the availability of legal recourse in the absence of financial contract performance, which relies on the effectiveness of a publicly financed and enforced legal system. Other aspects of social-collective action underlie the effectiveness and efficiency of private finance, including well-run and well-supervised financial institutions, effective micro- and macro-financial system policies, and effective micro- and macro-economic policies.[40]

Although finance would no doubt exist and bestow benefits without these particular social arrangements, there would most likely be significantly less of it, and it would be significantly less efficient and supportive of economic activity, wealth accumulation, growth, and ultimately social prosperity. In short, the enormous and pervasive private benefits of modern finance and financial systems are possible because the existence of an effective financial system has long been understood and supported as a

---

[40]Levine (1999) finds that the legal and regulatory environment of financial intermediaries is positively associated with economic growth. More specifically, Leahy and others (2001) show that the transparency and enforcement of these legal and regulatory frameworks, in particular in terms of investor protection, accounting, and auditing requirements, is broadly linked to innovation and investment in new enterprises. Beck, Demirgüç-Kunt, and Levine (2003) establish that countries with better developed national institutions and policies governing issues such as property rights, the rule of law, and competition are less likely to suffer systemic banking crises.

Box 3.3. Samuelson's Store of Value As a "Social Contrivance" Providing a Public Good

Although the public-good nature of fiat money has been well understood—both historically and conceptually—and widely accepted, it was not until the beginning of the post–Second World War period that a rigorous economic-the-oretic demonstration proved that "money" provided public goods. "Providing public goods" means that the introduction of money allowed a stylized economy to move to a more beneficial outcome for society as a whole. It was not the intro-duction of fiat money as a means of payment that provided the lubrication to move the economy to the best outcome, but instead money as a store of value.

Samuelson's Model

The seminal paper that considered this issue was Paul Samuelson's, "An Exact Consumption-Loan Model of Interest With or Without the Social Contrivance of Money."[1] In that paper, Samuelson considers a model of a highly stylized economy that produces and consumes only a single perish-able good, that exists indefinitely into the future, and that has three overlap-ping generations (OLG) of finite-lived economic actors: the working young, the middle-aged worker facing retirement, and the retired old. In this model, all actors must consume the single perishable good available in the econ-omy to survive. Because retired workers no longer receive income, they have to find some other way—a *contract* with the young and middle-aged—to obtain the consumption good during their retirement; otherwise they would die after they became unable to produce.

Individuals could, in principle, enter into private contracts to secure *promises* to receive goods in retirement. However, the various equilibria con-sidered in the model turn out to be socially suboptimal. The equilibria are suboptimal because to avoid starvation in retirement, *consumption loans* necessary for survival would lose a significant share of their value in one period. That is, in the consumption-loan model, the equilibrium interest rate would either be negative if population growth were zero, or fall well short of

---

[1]See Samuelson (1958) and Allais (1947).

public good. (This is not meant to imply that all public policy involvement in private finance is appropriate, beneficial, or acceptable.)

Thus, more realistically, while modern finance is primarily a private affair, the private net benefits originate in two inseparable sources. First are the direct individual private net benefits derived from private finan-cial transactions. Second are the indirect private and collective net bene-

society's biological growth rate, which would be undesirable from a social point of view. As Samuelson emphasized,

> It [the model] points up a fundamental and intrinsic deficiency in a free pricing system, namely, that free pricing gets you on the Pareto-efficiency frontier but by itself has no tendency to get you to positions on the frontier that are ethically optimal in terms of a social welfare function; only by *social collusion*—of tax, expenditure, fiat, or other type—can an ethical observer hope to end up where he wants to be (Samuelson, 1958, p. 479).

To try to overcome the suboptimality, Samuelson introduced the "social contrivance of money," as a "social compact" to achieve the socially optimal Pareto-efficient equilibrium. In Samuelson's words,

> The present model enables us to see one 'function' of money from a new slant—as a social compact that can provide optimal old age social security. . . . If each man insists on a quid pro quo, we apparently continue until the end of time, with each worse off than in the social optimum. . . . Yet how easy it is by a simple change in the rules of the game to get to the optimum. Let mankind enter into a Hobbes-Rousseau social contract in which the young are assured of their retirement subsistence if they will today support the aged, such support to be gua\ranteed by a draft on the yet-unborn. Then the social optimum can be achieved within one lifetime (p. 479).

The social compact introduced comprises valueless pieces of paper and the understanding—and more important, the trust—that these pieces of paper could be used to buy goods *now and forever in the future*. Samuelson's money constitutes bot]h a universally acceptable means of payment and, more important, a *store of value* of no intrinsic value other than its exchangeability for goods in the future. Young and middle-aged workers accept this paper in return for goods they produce because the social contract would hold for them in retirement as well. All of this occurs by social decree, trust, and acceptance by all present and future generations.

Samuelson proved that the introduction of this social compact—this store of value—moved the economy to the socially optimal Pareto-efficient equilibrium. In Samuelson's own words,

fits associated with having access to an effective process of finance and sharing in the enormous collective efficiency gains finance creates for the economic system as a whole. All citizens do not benefit equally or have equal access to these private and social benefits, but the social benefits are there for the taking, especially in the more democratic societies with liberalized economies.

Box 3.3. (*concluded*)

Once social coercion or contracting is admitted into the picture, the present problem disappears. The reluctance of the young to give to the old what the old can never themselves directly or indirectly repay is overcome. Yet the young never suffer, since their successors come under the same requirement. Everybody ends better off. It is as simple as that (p. 480).

In effect, the introduction of Samuelson's money as a "social contrivance" moved the OLG barter economy to a more Pareto-efficient resource allocation.

Samuelson's "Social Contrivance" Is Not Just Money: It Is Finance

Within the model, Samuelson's money is not just a means of payment. It represents a store of value that facilitates intertemporal transfers of purchasing power and thereby creates both a private and a social-welfare improvement.

This is finance as it has been discussed in the chapter.[2] The social contract works in the model because it removes the element of human trust between generations, which no doubt accounts for the decline in loan value after the first period. In effect, within the OLG model without the social contract, there is a negative externality that prevents the emergence of the socially optimal outcome. The negative externality is that the economy lacks an important market—a financial market. The retired citizens have no way of establishing a contract with the young that would make the young feel comfortable that they themselves would be repaid. While the model did not explicitly model the frailty of human trust, this is the negative externality. Introducing the "social contrivance of money" as the social compact allows the young and old to enter into private contracts using a vehicle that permits them to internalize in private transactions the negative externality.

---

[2]Cass and Yaari (1966) demonstrate that when durable goods are introduced into Samuelson's framework both government and private *finance* in the form of promissory notes (debt) can, under different conditions, produce the social optimum.

Despite the current consensus that many of the social conventions and arrangements developed over time are essential prerequisites for effective finance, this reflects a relatively new and modern understanding of the role of finance. Less than 75 years ago, society's mismanagement of both money and finance played an important and devastating role in the Great Depression.[41] More recently, some of these lessons had to be learned again, in both

---

[41]Bordo (2000) discusses some of the connections between, and historical experience of, unsound money and finance.

mature markets and in an increasing number of emerging- and developing-market countries. For example, in the aftermath of recent corporate scandals in some mature markets, improvements are being advocated and implemented for accounting standards and their enforcement and the efficacy of existing corporate governance procedures and accountability. Likewise, as the result of recent financial crises in emerging-market countries, many of these social arrangements are being aggressively advocated for adoption in less advanced as well as least developed economies and financial systems.

Viewed from the perspective of public-sector economics (and as discussed earlier in the chapter), if finance did not produce positive externalities, public goods, and other sources of market imperfections, the best public policy approach would be to leave finance completely to individual actions and market forces. As observed, however, finance inherently embodies uncertainty about trust and several other market imperfections:

- Some financial services provide positive externalities, and are therefore underproduced or underconsumed, while others provide negative externalities and are therefore overproduced or overconsumed.
- Some financial services are public goods and are therefore underproduced or underconsumed.
- There are information failures, which can work both ways.
- Financial markets are incomplete, which leads to underproduction of financial products and services.
- Competition is not always perfectly balanced, and when there is not enough of it goods are underproduced; when there is too much of it goods are overproduced.

In practical terms, market imperfections in finance may lead to the underconsumption and underproduction of some socially desirable financial activities, and the overconsumption and overproduction of some socially undesirable ones. This is a compelling practical motivation for private-collective action and public policy.

The overall objective for collective action would be to move the economic and financial systems toward a more economically efficient and socially optimal level, mix, and allocation of finance, measured in part by the ability of finance to facilitate real economic processes. In this way, collective action in finance could enhance both private and social welfare.

It would seem reasonable to think that private-collective and public actions could be designed and implemented to address each source of market imperfection in finance, depending on how significant the efficiency losses associated with each one might be. In considering this, the effectiveness of policies could be improved if they were designed and implemented in a cohesive fashion so that a policy designed to eliminate the negative impact of one kind of market imperfection does not offset the benefits of a policy designed to deal with another. It is not clear to what extent such policy cohesiveness and coordination is actually achieved in practice by countries or across borders.

When a market imperfection inhibits consumption and production of desirable goods, the challenge is to provide incentives to supply and consume more of the goods that provide public benefits and positive externalities, that tend to open up new markets, and that increase competition unless there are natural monopolies. When a market imperfection encourages consumption and production of undesirable goods, the challenge is to minimize the production and consumption of financial activities that result from these market failures. Because both tendencies exist simultaneously, financial-system policies would be more effective if they strove to strike a socially optimal balance between maximizing the net social benefits of the positive externalities and public goods and minimizing the net social costs of the other market imperfections in finance. As noted already, this will most likely encompass a combination of both private-collective and public policy involvement, which should also be striving to achieve some kind of social optimum. Striving to achieve the social optimum will undoubtedly entail difficult choices, including trading off some of the individual private benefits for the greater good, if and when this can be justified.

As noted earlier, not each and every loss of efficiency requires intervention. It is much clearer that when a market imperfection in finance leads to an inefficiency that is potentially destabilizing, either for financial institutions or for markets or for both, that some form of collective action might be desirable or necessary. Unfortunately, in the financial-system policy literature, often no clear distinction is made between sources of market imperfections that tend to lead to instability and those that do not. Likewise, no framework now exists either for measuring the efficiency losses associated with market imperfections in finance or for assessing the risks to financial stability associated with market imperfections. These are some of the challenges in the period ahead for which an analytical framework for financial stability would be useful for policy purposes.

4

Efficiency and Stability

This chapter distinguishes briefly between the concepts of efficiency and stability. It then discusses three situations that help put observed financial dynamics into perspective.

Economic, or Financial, Efficiency

What is meant by efficiency, in more rigorous terms than were used in Chapter 3? Take a simple example of a market for a financial instrument—credit, for instance. The market demand for credit can be represented by a demand schedule that plots the various combinations of the cost of a unit of credit against the aggregate demand for credit forthcoming for each unit cost. Under normal conditions, the demand curve would be downward sloping indicating that as cost per unit of credit declines, more and more individuals want to borrow, and some want to borrow more units as the cost per unit declines. One can also envision a market supply curve that plots the combinations of cost and aggregate supply of credit. Under normal conditions this supply curve would be upward sloping indicating that as the cost of a unit of credit rises it becomes more profitable to supply, so a greater aggregate supply is forthcoming. Market equilibrium occurs at the price and quantity pair for which demand equals supply. This concept can be expanded to cover many markets simultaneously, including for goods and services as well as other asset prices.

When considering efficiency, the key issue is whether the aggregate demand and supply curves represent private benefits and costs or social benefits and costs or both simultaneously. If the curves represent both simultaneously, the equilibrium is efficient—both the price and quantity of credit match the private and social price of credit and the socially desirable

Figure 4.1. Private Demand and Supply Equal to Social Demand and Supply

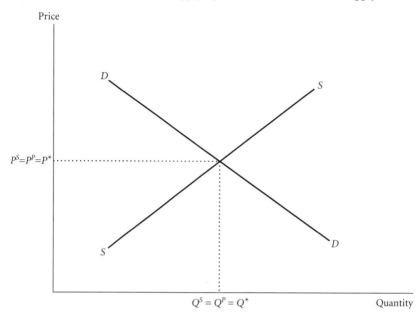

Note: P^S and Q^S represent social price and quantity, respectively. P^P and Q^P represent private price and quantity, respectively. P^* and Q^* represent equilibrium price and quantity, respectively.

quantity of credit. This is illustrated in Figure 4.1, in which schedule DD is the demand curve representing both the private and social benefits that would be obtained per unit of credit for each aggregate quantity or amount of credit demanded. Likewise, schedule SS is the supply curve with the cost per unit of credit representing both the private and social costs of producing the aggregate quantity or amount of credit.

Now consider a situation, depicted in Figure 4.2, in which the private market demand—the dotted demand schedule—lies below the social demand curve. The fact that the private demand curve lies below the social demand curve means that for each quantity demanded the private benefit is less then the social benefit. This occurs because individual private demanders only consider their personal benefit and not the potential benefits to others not consuming the good directly. In this case, the unfettered market outcome would lead to a quantity of credit Q^P that falls short of the socially desirable amount of credit Q^S. In addition, the price paid per unit of credit would be P^P, which is below the price that would be paid along the demand curve that represents social benefits or P^S.

Figure 4.2. Private Marginal Benefit Below Social Marginal Benefit

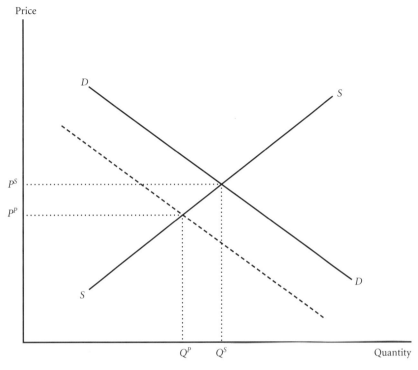

Note: P^S and Q^S represent social price and quantity, respectively. P^P and Q^P represent private price and quantity, respectively.

Figure 4.3 illustrates an example in which the market supply curve is below society's supply curve meaning that for each aggregate quantity supplied, the market is only considering the lower private cost of a unit of credit and not the social cost (for example, the additional social cost of the pollution created in the production process). This means that private outcomes would result in a quantity of credit in excess of the socially desirable amount, reflecting the underpricing of a unit of credit risk—at $P^P < P^S$.

Stability

Under normal conditions—with the demand curve downward sloping, the supply curve upward sloping, and excess demand implying a price increase—the market-clearing (equilibrium) price and quantity of credit

Figure 4.3. Private Marginal Cost Below Social Marginal Cost

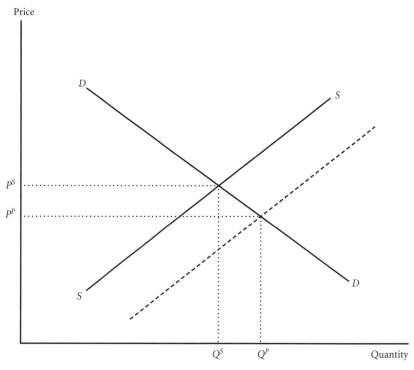

Note: P^S and Q^S represent social price and quantity, respectively. P^P and Q^P represent private price and quantity, respectively.

would be stable. Here stability is defined as the following situation: if at any given price (such as at P^1 in Figure 4.4) the quantity demanded exceeds supply, the price and quantity supplied would rise back toward the market equilibrium—for example, along the supply curve in Figure 4.4. Symmetrically, if at some given price (say P^2) demand falls short of supply, the price would decline and the quantity demanded would rise along the demand schedule. This is what is typically meant by stability in economics—a tendency for price and supply to rise when demand exceeds supply; and a tendency for price to fall and demand to rise when supply exceeds demand. This concept of stability can be extended to deal with a set of markets, and is an application of the stability analysis often applied in Newtonian physics and other sciences.

In the example used above, the demand and supply curves are linear, so the dynamics are uncomplicated. With nonlinear demand and supply

Figure 4.4. Stable Disequilibrium

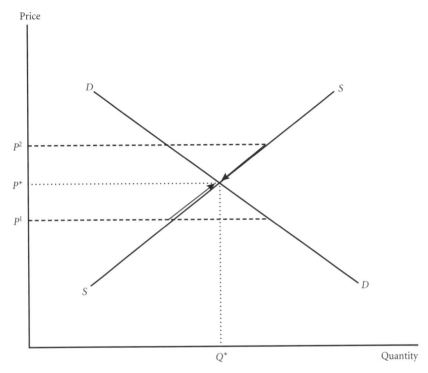

Note: P* and Q* together represent a "Stable Disequilibrium" when either P* is not equal to the socially optimal price or Q* is not equal to the socially optimal quantity or both.

curves, or by specifying more complicated and multidimensional demand and supply processes, the dynamics can become quite complex. An extensive discussion of these complexities is beyond the scope of this book, but such complexities obviously exist in the real world, particularly in financial systems and in financial-stability analysis. Some of these complexities and their implications for financial-stability assessments will be discussed briefly in Chapter 6, where measurement and modeling issues are examined.

Considering Efficiency and Stability

Three situations illustrate efficiency and stability in financial markets.

The first situation to consider is that of perpetual stability and efficiency, where the social equilibrium and private equilibrium are identical and stable.

In such a situation, the equilibrium price reflects both the private and social costs and benefits, and the market is stable in the sense that if price deviates from the equilibrium for some unforeseen reason, prices and quantities will tend to gravitate back to the social equilibrium.

A second situation is one of perpetual stability with inefficiency. In this case, the market finds an equilibrium at the intersection of private demand and supply, which is stable. Although a social equilibrium exists, it would be unstable and therefore unsustainable, which implies that while a socially optimal outcome in the financial system exists, it cannot be maintained because it is unstable. Thus, in this second instance, while the financial system can remain in equilibrium—that is, stable—it is also inefficient.

A third situation is one of intermittent instability with inefficiency. Both private and social equilibria exist, but both are unstable and therefore unsustainable. Unless the financial system starts off in equilibrium and remains undisturbed, the financial system will tend to wander in ways that are determined by its internal structure and the external forces that impinge on it.

The real world is probably most accurately characterized as lying somewhere between the second and third situations. This is consistent with what has been observed in the international financial system (see Table 1.6), which recently experienced periods of stability with intermittent periods of

- high volatility and market turbulence, as experienced during the bond-market turbulence of 1994 and again in 1996;
- persistent asset-price misalignments, as experienced in the behavior of the dollar-yen exchange rate in the mid-1990s, and the dollar-euro rate in 2002–2004;
- asset-price bubbles, as experienced during the build-up and then bursting of the dot-com bubble in 1999–2000;
- financial fragility, as experienced in Russia during the aftermath of the Russian debt default and in global markets during the near collapse of the hedge fund Long-Term Capital Management;
- financial crises, as experienced in Asia in 1997–98 and in some Latin American economies in the early 2000s.[42]

---

[42]See Davis (2002) for a useful classification of deviations from stability and a more thorough examination of recent periods of such deviations. Also see various issues of the IMF's *International Capital Markets: Developments, Prospects, and Key Issues* for the years 1993–2001 for descriptions and analyses of many of these episodes.

PART II

TOWARD A FRAMEWORK FOR FINANCIAL STABILITY

Chapter 1 expressed in detail the growing importance of safeguarding financial stability, and the absence of a widely accepted definition and framework for analyzing financial-stability issues. In addition, Part I argued that financial stability is a public good that requires private-collective and public policy involvement. Lacking a framework, a set of models, or even a concept of equilibrium, it is difficult to envision a definition of financial stability and a system for safeguarding it akin to what economists normally demand and use. Nevertheless, it would be useful to have a guide that allows for the development of policy frameworks and analytical tools for safeguarding financial stability. The framework proposed in this part of the study is one step in this direction, and is offered for wider debate.

The Meaning of Framework

The notion of a framework, as used in this part of the book, is a set of definitions, concepts, and organizing principles that impose discipline on the analysis of the financial system. As will be discussed and examined in more detail, an important component of safeguarding financial stability is the early identification of risks and vulnerabilities that might threaten the maintenance of stability.

An effective framework requires three important standards:

- First, there must be rigorous definitions and understandings of key concepts, such as what is meant by the terms financial system, financial stability and instability, and systemic risk, among others.
- Second, to be most useful for monitoring and policymaking, the framework's concepts and definitions ultimately must be either

directly measurable or correlated with measures—concepts and definitions must have useful and policy-relevant empirical counterparts.
- Third, the set of definitions, concepts, and organizing principles, along
  with their empirical counterparts, must ensure internal consistency in
  the identification of sources of risk and vulnerability and in the design
  and implementation of policies aimed at resolving difficulties should
  they emerge.

Many of the relevant concepts of finance and economics necessary for
developing the framework were introduced and analyzed in Part I, drawing
on the wide range of literature in finance and economics. Many of the links
between finance and economics have been highlighted, and in having done
so, many of the organizing principles for how to think about financial stability issues and how to design a framework for safeguarding financial-
stability have been examined. Thus, much of the necessary conceptual and
logical development of the framework has already been provided.

Organization of Part II

What remains to be accomplished in Part II is the development of the
basic framework for safeguarding financial stability and an examination of
many of its most important parts and features so that it can be applied
effectively. To accomplish this, Part II is divided into three chapters.

Chapter 5 proposes working definitions of financial system, financial
stability, and systemic risk. It then draws out the important characteristics
of the proposed definition of financial stability so as to set the stage for
using the definition in setting up the framework and then introducing its
main features and objectives.

Chapter 6 develops a comprehensive and practical framework for safeguarding financial stability, particularly for organizing the work for preventing and resolving financial imbalances and crises. It defines the
financial-stability challenge, and then places financial-stability work in the
context of the broader economic and social system. The chapter then provides an overview of the framework in the form of a schematic representation, then further develops its main features in some detail. The chapter
also examines the important measurement and modeling issues in making
financial-stability assessments. The final section examines the most difficult remaining challenges, many of them involving analytical and measurement research.

Chapter 7 examines the responsibilities of central banks in ensuring
financial stability. While central banks are not the only authority involved

in safeguarding financial stability (there are also supervisory and regulatory authorities) the chapter argues that they do have a natural interest, and role to play, in safeguarding financial stability. The chapter draws on some of the experiences in certain advanced countries, particularly in the euro zone, Japan, the United Kingdom, and the United States.

5

Defining Financial Stability

This chapter proposes a definition of financial-system stability that has practical and operational relevance and that encompasses many of the relevant features of the existing policy literature.[43] Financial stability is defined as the ability of the financial system to facilitate and enhance economic processes, manage risks, and absorb shocks. Moreover, financial stability is considered a continuum, changeable over time and consistent with multiple combinations of finance's constituent elements.

As noted, there is, as yet, no general agreement on what financial stability exactly means.[44] Some have defined it in terms of what it is not—a situation in which financial imbalances impair the real economy,[45] for example, when information problems undermine the financial system's ability to allocate funds to productive investment opportunities.[46] A similar approach is taken by those focusing on systemic risk, specifically with regard to financial problems that stem from links between financial institutions or markets and that have a potentially large adverse impact on the real economy.[47] Haldane (2004) defines financial stability using a simple model in which asset prices serve to secure the optimal level of savings and investment. Others take a macro prudential viewpoint and specify financial stability as limiting risks of significant real output losses associated with episodes of systemwide financial distress.[48]

---

[43]Attempts to define financial stability have been made recently, but most accommodate a particular theme of a paper or speech. In addition, most authors prefer to define financial instability or systemic risk. See the annex to this chapter for a selection of these definitions.

[44]Oosterloo and de Haan, 2003.

[45]Crockett, 1997; Davis, 2002.

[46]Mishkin, 1999.

[47]De Bandt and Hartmann, 2000; Group of Ten, 2001; Hoelscher and Quintyn, 2003; Summer, 2003.

[48]Borio, 2003.

This chapter first briefly collects some of the main conclusions from the previous chapters that are relevant for designing a framework for safe-guarding financial stability, in particular some of finance's strengths and weaknesses. These attributes serve as both practical and analytical focal points for developing a concept of what the financial-stability challenge is, especially in the absence of a widely accepted definition of financial stability, a concept of equilibrium, and an analytical framework for safeguard-ing stability. Explanations of "financial system" and "systemic risk" follow. After this groundwork, the chapter provides a broad definition of financial stability and discusses the meaning of some of the language in the defini-tion. The chapter also makes the case that financial stability occurs along a changeable continuum or range of conditions of the constituent parts of the financial system, as opposed to a single configuration or state of these parts as is most often used in microeconomic and macroeconomic models. Sev-eral complexities of the definition are identified in the succeeding section. The final section explains why it is more productive to anchor the analysis in a definition of financial stability rather than financial instability.

The Strengths and Weaknesses of Finance

In developing a framework for safeguarding financial stability and espe-cially in developing a working definition of financial stability, it is useful to review some of the ideas developed and observations made in Part I of this study. These particular ideas can be understood either as prerequisites or as relevant concepts for designing and implementing a framework.

First, a barter economy is less effective and efficient in allocating scarce resources than is an economy that incorporates the ability to use financial claims on future real resources. A discussion of financial stability must nec-essarily take place within the context of a monetary economy in which a legal tender as money is universally accepted as the economy's unit of account and means of payment.

Second, fiat money (or any other legal tender) is not necessarily the most desirable store of value—except in the very short run or during episodes of financial distress and dysfunction. As suggested in Chapter 2, throughout recorded history, human ingenuity has driven an evolutionary process of finance to overcome this persistent deficiency. Modern finance provides substitutes for legal tender, including the various derivative forms of money such as bank demand deposits, that provide temporary and reversible intertemporal means-of-payment and store-of-value services. These substitutes are promises to pay legal tender in the future, and are designed in part to facilitate intertemporal resource allocations.

Third, as discussed in Chapter 3, many of the services provided by money (as legal tender) and finance are both private and public goods. Their private-good nature arises out of the provision of benefits to individuals in their private affairs, benefits that convey only to the counterparts engaged in specific transactions. Money and finance separately and jointly provide public goods as well, because they allow multilateral trade and exchange to be more efficient, in part by eliminating the need for Jevons' "double coincidence of wants," both sectorally at moments in time and intertemporally. In addition, finance provides public goods beyond those of money as legal tender: by enhancing and distributing the public-good characteristics of legal tender, finance enlarges society's opportunities for, and efficiency in, intertemporal economic processes such as trade, production, wealth accumulation, economic development and growth, and social prosperity. In sum, the universal acceptability of money as legal tender and the existence of an effective process of finance together create an environment that provides collective benefits to all members of society.

Fourth, an alternative and useful way of understanding finance is to bring to the surface one of its defining characteristics. Unlike money as legal tender—which eliminates the element of human trust in trade and exchange—finance involves human promises to pay back specific amounts of money as legal tender in the future. In this way, finance intrinsically embodies uncertainty (about human trust). Modern financial systems have evolved to provide beneficial and necessarily imperfect ways of transforming this fundamental uncertainty into quantifiable and priceable risks, such as default risk; and, through social arrangements (both markets and financial institutions), this uncertainty is transformed into market risk, liquidity risk, and so on. In less traditional but no less appropriate terms, modern finance provides societies with effective, albeit imperfect, mechanisms for transforming, pricing, and allocating economic and financial uncertainties and risks.

Finally, there are both potential benefits and costs associated with finance because finance intrinsically embodies uncertainty.[49] On the one hand, finance enhances the private and social benefits of money, in part by enlarging the pool of liquidity available for production, consumption, and exchange, and in part by facilitating and enhancing the efficiency of intertemporal economic processes. In effect, the willingness to engage in finance (that is, to take the leap of faith) and accept the uncertainty of trust has created social welfare gains far beyond what fiat money alone could provide.

---

[49]Diamond and Dybvig (1983) and Diamond and Rajan (2001) explore this in the context of bank intermediation.

On the other hand, trust is fragile: it can, and often enough does, become a source of potential financial instability, which can in the wrong circumstances affect both individual and social welfare. To the extent that doubts about human trust are transformed by the financial system into market and other financial risks, they too can become companion sources of instability—even more so if a society's financial market mechanisms are impaired and unable to effectively reallocate and price such doubts. How such doubts propagate through the financial system is an important determinant of whether they either self-correct and remain isolated and harmless or become widespread, harmful, and perhaps even systemic. Because finance supports and facilitates real economic processes, these potential instabilities may well extend to the real economy.

Bringing "Financial System" and "Systemic Risk" into Focus

Recall from Part I that the key functions of a financial system are to facilitate and enhance economic processes; to price, manage, and allocate risks; and to help the economy absorb and dissipate shocks from both within and outside the economic system. But what do we mean by "financial system" and "systemic risk?"

Financial System

Broadly, the financial system comprises three separable but closely related components.

First are financial intermediaries that pool funds and risks, then allocate them to their competing uses. Increasingly, financial institutions provide a range of services, not just the traditional banking services of taking deposits and making loans. Now institutions such as insurance companies, pension funds, hedge funds, and financial-nonfinancial hybrids (such as General Electric) each supply diverse financial services.

Second are financial markets that directly match savers and investors, for example, through the initial issuance and sale of bonds or equities directly to investors. Financial markets also allow investors to rebalance their portfolios continuously as economic and financial conditions change, to achieve a more desirable balance of risk and return. This rebalancing of portfolios in and across financial markets facilitates the repricing and redistribution of assets and risks within the economic system.

Third is the financial infrastructure, including both privately and publicly owned and operated institutions—such as clearance, payment, and settlement systems for financial transactions—as well as monetary, legal, accounting, regulatory, supervisory, and surveillance infrastructures.[50]

Notably, both private and public persons own and invest in financial institutions; participate in financial markets; and either own, regulate, or participate in vital components of the financial infrastructure. Governments borrow in markets, hedge risks, operate through markets to conduct monetary policy and maintain monetary stability, and own and operate payment and settlement systems.

Accordingly, *the financial system consists of the monetary system with its official understandings, agreements, conventions, and institutions as well as the processes, institutions, and conventions of private financial activities.*[51] Any analysis of how the financial system works and how well it is performing its key functions requires an understanding of these components.

Systemic Risk

According to the Group of Ten report (Group of Ten, 2001, pp. 126–127) on financial consolidation and risk,

> Systemic financial risk is the risk that an event will trigger a loss of economic value or confidence in, and attendant increases in uncertainty about, a substantial portion of the financial system that is serious enough to quite probably have significant adverse effects on the real economy. Systemic risk events can be sudden and unexpected, or the likelihood of their occurrence can build up through time in the absence of appropriate policy responses. The adverse real economic effects from systemic problems are generally seen as arising from disruptions to the payment system, to credit flows, and from the destruction of asset values.

The Group of Ten study notes that this definition encompasses much of what is in the literature but is stricter in two respects. First, the negative externalities of a systemic event extend into the real economy. They are not confined to the financial system. Second, this extension into the real economy occurs with relatively high probability. The emphasis on real effects reflects the view that it is the output of real goods and services and the accompanying employment implications that are the primary concern of economic policymakers. "In this definition, a financial disruption that does not have a high probability of causing a significant disruption of real economic activity is not a systemic risk event" (p. 127).

---

[50]On the role of the legal system see, for example, Levine (1999), Leahy and others (2001), and Beck, Demirgüç-Kunt, and Levine (2003).

[51]This particular formulation is an adaptation of "international financial system" from Truman (2003).

Defining Financial Stability and Examining Its Key Implications

As noted earlier, there is no widespread agreement on a useful working definition of financial stability. Some authors define financial instability instead of stability, and others prefer to define the problem as one of managing systemic risk rather than as maintaining or safeguarding financial stability.[52]

This book takes a positive approach in that it focuses on safeguarding financial stability while recognizing that understanding and trying to identify the boundary between stability and instability is the essence of both maintaining stability and managing systemic risk. The justification for taking this approach is discussed later in this chapter.

Definition of Financial Stability

With this in mind, financial stability can be defined as follows:

Financial stability is a situation in which the financial system is capable of satisfactorily performing its three key functions simultaneously. First, the financial system is efficiently and smoothly facilitating the intertemporal allocation of resources from savers to investors and the allocation of economic resources generally. Second, forward-looking financial risks are being assessed and priced reasonably accurately and are being relatively well managed. Third, the financial system is in such condition that it can comfortably if not smoothly absorb financial and real economic surprises and shocks.

If any one or more of these key functions is not being satisfactorily achieved and maintained, it is likely that the financial system is moving in the direction of becoming less stable, and at some point might exhibit instability. For example, inefficiencies in the allocation of capital or shortcomings in the pricing of risk can, by laying the foundations for imbalances and vulnerabilities, compromise future financial system stability.

All three of these aspects of the definition can and do encompass both endogenous and exogenous elements. For example, surprises that can impinge on financial stability can emanate both from within and from outside the financial system. Moreover, the intertemporal and forward-looking aspects of this particular definition of financial stability emphasize that threats to financial stability arise not only from shocks or surprises but also from the possibility of disorderly adjustments of imbalances that have built

---

[52]See, for example, the definitions surveyed in the annex to this chapter. Davis (2002) develops a taxonomy of instability.

up endogenously over time—because, for example, expectations of future returns were misperceived and therefore mispriced.[53]

A more compact way of defining financial stability that is still consistent with the inclusion of endogenous and exogenous elements follows:

> *A financial system is in a range of stability whenever it is capable of facilitating (rather than impeding) the performance of an economy, and of dissipating financial imbalances that arise endogenously or as a result of significant adverse and unanticipated events.*

Note three important features of the fuller definition that are expressed more explicitly in this compact definition. First, the phrase "range of stability" signifies that financial stability (and instability) occurs along a continuum. As will be described more fully later in this section, the continuum can be conceived of, and in principle measured, as a *corridor* representing the many different ways in which the constituent parts of the financial system (institutions, markets, and infrastructure) can satisfactorily perform their key functions (facilitating real economic processes, pricing and managing risks, and absorbing and dissipating economic shocks).

Second, the phrase "facilitating (rather than impeding) the performance of an economy" means, among other things, that finance is contributing to (not hampering) the efficient allocation of real resources, the rate of growth of output, and the processes of saving, investment, and wealth creation—and may also include other observable and measurable aspects of economic performance.

Third, the term "dissipate financial imbalances" signifies a movement along the continuum in the direction of stability (away from boundaries) through self-corrective mechanisms—through asset price adjustments and portfolio flows, for instance. Such corrections could include the exit and entry of market participants (financial institutions or nonfinancial entities acting on behalf of others or individuals acting directly in the markets).

A more general definition that does not require the specification of what constitutes a financial system follows:

> *Financial stability is a condition in which an economy's mechanisms for pricing, allocating, and managing financial risks (credit, liquidity, counterparty, market, and so forth) are functioning well enough to contribute to the performance of the economy.*

---

[53]That financial stability should not be thought of simply as a static concept of shock-absorption capacity has been emphasized by, among others, Minsky (1982) and Kindleberger (1996).

Analytical Features and Implications

Several important analytical features or implications of this definition of financial stability merit further consideration. In effect, these analytical characteristics provide the conceptual muscle needed to better understand the nature of the financial-stability challenge; they are also essential for designing the practical framework for safeguarding financial stability that is developed and examined in Chapter 6.

Facilitation of real economic processes

Judgments about the performance of the financial system must be based on how well the financial system is facilitating economic resource allocation, the savings and investment process, and, ultimately, economic growth. The links go both ways—the real economy can be affected by the financial system, and the performance of the financial system can be affected by the performance of the real economy. A framework useful for assessing financial stability must take heed of these two-way links.

Disturbances in financial markets or at individual financial institutions need not be considered threats to financial stability if they are not expected to damage economic activity at large. In fact, the incidental closing of a minor financial institution, a rise in asset-price volatility, and sharp and even turbulent corrections in financial markets may be the result of competitive forces, the efficient incorporation of new information, and the economic system's self-correcting and self-disciplining mechanisms. By implication, in the absence of contagion and the high likelihood of systemic effects, such developments are welcome—even healthy—from a financial-stability perspective. Just as in Schumpeterian business cycles (Schumpeter, 1934), where the adoption of new technologies and recessions have both constructive and destructive implications, a certain amount of instability can be tolerated from time to time because it may encourage long-term financial system efficiency.

Systemic perspective

Financial stability is a broad concept, encompassing the different parts of the financial system—infrastructure, institutions, and markets. Because of the links between these components, expectations of disturbances in any one component can affect overall stability, thus requiring a systemic perspective. Consistent with the definition of the financial system, at any given time stability or instability could be the result of either private institutions and actions, or official institutions and actions, or both simultaneously or iteratively.

Mutual dependence of financial and monetary stability

Financial stability not only requires the financial system to adequately fulfill its role in allocating resources, transforming and managing risks, mobilizing savings, and facilitating wealth accumulation and growth, but also requires that within this system the flow of payments throughout the economy functions smoothly (across official and private, retail and wholesale, and formal and informal payment mechanisms). Smooth functioning requires that money—both central bank money and derivative monies, such as demand deposits and other bank accounts—adequately fulfills its roles as means of payment and unit of account and, when appropriate, as a short-term store of value. In other words, financial stability and monetary stability overlap to a large extent.[54]

Preventive and remedial dimensions of financial stability

Financial stability requires the absence of financial crises and the ability of the financial system to limit and deal with the emergence of imbalances before they constitute a threat to stability. In a well-functioning and stable financial system, this occurs in part through self-corrective, market-disciplining mechanisms that create resilience and that endogenously prevent problems from festering and growing into systemwide risks. In this respect, there may be a policy choice between allowing market mechanisms to work to resolve potential difficulties and intervening quickly and effectively—through liquidity injections via markets, for example—to restore risk-taking or to restore stability. Thus, financial stability has both preventive and remedial dimensions.

The continuum of financial stability

Given that finance is dynamic—involving intertemporal transactions and innovations—financial stability can be considered to occur along a continuum that is changeable over time and that dynamically reflects different possible combinations of conditions of the financial system's constituent parts. Along this continuum, a multidimensional range or corridor of stability may be identified within which the financial system broadly performs its key tasks. In observable states outside this range, aggregate production is substantially below its potential because funds are not being

---

[54]See Padoa-Schioppa (2003), Schinasi (2003), and Chapter 7 of this book for discussions of the role of central banks in financial stability.

channeled to profitable activities, risks are not being managed, and shocks are not being absorbed.

This continuum for financial stability is multidimensional and occurs, in principle, across a multitude of observable and measurable variables. The set of variables must encompass a subset that quantifies, however imperfectly, how well finance is facilitating economic and financial processes such as savings and investment, lending and borrowing, liquidity creation and distribution, asset pricing, and, ultimately, wealth accumulation and growth.

As a continuum, financial stability is broad and imprecise—the financial system may not return to a single and sustainable position or path after a shock or perturbation such as might result with other (Newtonian) concepts of equilibrium and stability used in economic or financial analysis and models, and in many other disciplines. The proposed definition is consistent with a financial system in a perpetual state of flux and transformation while its ability to perform its key functions remains well within a set of tolerable boundaries—within a corridor defined over a set of measurable variables—that are consistent with it successfully carrying out its important facilitative and efficiency-enhancing roles. Observable states approaching these boundaries would indicate that the financial system is losing some of its ability to perform. Observations outside these boundaries would indicate that the system is no longer effectively facilitating economic processes, perhaps because aggregate production is substantially below its potential if funds are not being channeled to profitable activities, if risks are not being managed, and if shocks are not being absorbed. In such cases, remedial action would be called for, which in the extreme would mean crisis resolution and restoration.

To illustrate the multidimensional nature of the definition and the continuum, consider a simple two-dimensional example. In assessing the joint stability of financial markets and financial institutions, one might be able to identify combinations of interest rate spread volatility (as a possible market source of instability) and banking system capital (as an institutional source of shock-absorptive capacity) that are consistent with the financial system continuing effectively to facilitate efficient resource allocation. Likewise, other combinations could be identified that would not be consistent with stability. The former would constitute the range of stability and the latter would fall outside this range.

A more comprehensive set of factors could be envisioned for determining a grid over which a continuum is defined. In principle, this multidimensional approach could be generalized and made amenable to theoretical and empirical model building. For example, one could define a set of n variables that encompass all relevant measures of the components of financial stability. The range of stability could be defined as a subset of

n-tuples bounded by n functions (most likely nonlinear) defining the limits of stability in terms of n variables. Statistical tools could be used to select such factors by considering historical episodes of both stability and instability, in part by using forward-looking, market-determined expectations of future outcomes and matching them with actual outcomes. This methodology could, theoretically, also help to establish estimates of boundaries or zones separating stability from potential instability.

To illustrate further the concept of a continuum, consider the health of an organism, which also occurs along a continuum. A healthy organism can usually reach for a greater level of health and well-being, and the range of what is normal is broad and multidimensional. In addition, not all states of un-health (or illness) are significant, systemic, or life threatening. Some illnesses, even temporarily serious ones, allow the organism to continue to function reasonably productively and return to a state of health without permanent damage. One implication of the financial-stability continuum is that maintaining financial stability does not necessarily require that each part of the financial system operate persistently at peak performance; the financial system can operate on a "spare tire" from time to time (Greenspan, 1999).

The concept of a continuum is relevant because finance fundamentally involves uncertainty, is dynamic (that is, it is both intertemporal and innovative), and is composed of many interlinked and evolutionary elements (infrastructure, institutions, markets). Accordingly, financial stability is expectations based, dynamic, and dependent on many parts of the system working reasonably well. What might represent stability at one time might be more stable or less stable at some other time, depending on other aspects of the economic system—such as technological, political, and social developments. Moreover, financial stability is consistent with various combinations of the conditions of its constituent parts, such as the soundness of financial institutions, financial market conditions, and the effectiveness of the various components of the financial infrastructure.

Endogenous threats to financial stability

The proposed definition leaves open the possibility that the financial system could impede the performance of the economy endogenously, even in the absence of unanticipated events or shocks, for example, through the accumulation of imbalances caused by asset mispricing or other market imperfections. This is consistent with ample historical evidence that financial systems, particularly banking systems, are prone to the build-up of imbalances (credit-risk concentrations or illiquidity, for example) and even instability. Banks internalize the fragilities associated with the properties of liquidity, and are therefore prone to instability themselves.[55] Banks, other financial institutions, and even markets can be regarded as social arrangements—or as clearinghouses—for assessing, pricing, and trading human promises necessarily involving uncertainty and risk, including uncertainty about the fundamental element of trust in financial contracts. Social arrangements and institutional features of economic systems try to internalize the potential adverse consequences of negative externalities associated with the frailties of human trust. A tangible example is that banks internalize the potential adverse consequences of failures of trust by economizing on information about large pools of debtors and their ability to pay future claims or promissory notes. In internalizing these elements of financial risk and uncertainty, financial institutions and markets themselves embody the potential for financial fragility, which ultimately finds its source in a failure of human trust in some meaningful way (for example, a default).

Embodiment of externalities in finance

The definition of financial stability accommodates the idea examined in Chapter 3 that certain aspects of finance embody either negative or positive externalities. Thus, improvements in the ability of finance to facilitate rather than impede economic processes—including providing greater financial stability—is welfare improving because it enhances the efficiency of resource allocation (and pricing), especially intertemporally. Some points along the continuum of financial stability are more welfare improving (and efficiency enhancing) than others, and some points along the continuum of instability are to be avoided, seemingly at all costs.[56] Thus, in moving from a condition of stability to instability, the contribution of the financial system to aggregate economic welfare is reduced.

Normative implications

The concept of financial stability encompasses the normative property that the process of finance functions well enough to perform its main facilitative purposes successfully. A stable financial system enhances economic performance in many dimensions, whereas an unstable financial

---

[55]See Diamond and Rajan (2001, 2002).

[56]There would seem to be a trade-off in financial systems between financial stability and efficiency, but this is difficult to analyze given that there are different concepts of both stability and efficiency. The theoretical banking literature includes some work on this, but none could be found applicable to the financial-system level.

system detracts from economic performance. In this sense the definition is "normative." Ultimately, financial instability (unlike physical instabilities such as earthquakes, floods, and sunspots) can be dealt with through massive intervention by authorities, including by redefining the rules of the marketplace. Such measures would be "last resort" reforms to prevent the economic system from collapsing—as it did, for example, during the Great Depression in the 1930s and more recently in Asia during 1997–98.

Corollary Definitions

To illustrate the broad nature of this definition of financial stability, two corollary definitions are useful:

> A financial system **is entering a range of instability** whenever it is threatening to impede the performance of an economy.

> A financial system **is in a range of instability** when it is impeding performance and threatening to continue to do so.

Taken together, a good understanding of financial stability and instability can serve to define boundaries around the scope of the analysis. The safeguarding of financial stability should not be understood as zero tolerance of bank failures or as avoidance of market volatility but it should avoid financial disruptions that lead to real economic costs.[57]

Practical Implications of Financial-System Complexities

The definition of financial stability involves several complexities with practical significance for assessing risks to the smooth functioning of the financial system and for the contribution public policy can make to ensuring financial stability.

First, *developments in financial stability cannot be summarized in a single quantitative measure.* Most economic policy objectives (price stability, unemployment, external or budgetary equilibrium, and so on) have a generally accepted measure, even if still subject to methodological and analytical controversy. By contrast, no unequivocal unit of measurement for financial stability yet exists.[58] This reflects the multifaceted nature of financial stability—it relates to both the stability and resilience of financial institutions, and to the smooth functioning of financial markets and settlement systems

---

[57]Papers that focus on aspects of systemic risk are: De Bandt and Hartmann (2000); Hoelscher and Quintyn (2003); and Summer (2003).

[58]See Haldane (2004), which sets out how this might be done for financial stability.

over time. Moreover, these diverse factors also need to be evaluated for their potential ultimate influence on real economic activity. Although this may fall short of specifying a multidimensional financial-stability continuum, much progress can be made in developing composite indicators or benchmarks for financial stability, especially by considering historical episodes of both stability and instability and by comparing market-determined expectations with actual outcomes. However, the establishment of measures is further complicated by the fact that policy actions have actually been successful in preserving financial stability—disturbances are not observed and the actual value of any indicator, or for that matter, of relevant policies is difficult to establish empirically.[59]

Second, *changes in financial stability are inherently difficult to forecast.* Assessing the state of financial stability should not only take stock of disturbances as they emerge, but also indicate the risks and vulnerabilities that could lead to such disturbances in the future. A forward-looking approach is therefore needed to establish the buildup of risks and imbalances and to take account of the transmission lags in policy instruments. The challenge is that financial crises are inherently difficult to predict because of many factors—contagion effects and nonlinearities in the relationships between the constituent parts of finance, for instance. In addition, risks to financial stability often reflect the far-reaching consequences of unlikely events, implying that the focus of attention should not be the mean, median, or mode of possible outcomes or states but the entire distribution of them, and in particular the left "tail," composed of very low probability and negative, high-cost events, such as a major financial crisis. Beyond this, the distribution of possible outcomes may be subject to greater fundamental uncertainty (in the sense of Knight [1921]) than traditional macroeconomic projections, reflecting lack of knowledge about the actual shape of the probability distribution governing relevant factors (such as operational, reputation, or contagion risk). Thus, forecasts of financial stability might be inherently less reliable than forecasts of monetary or macroeconomic stability, for which there are well-worked and more reliable models and more timely and useful data. In the large sets of financial indicators now being used by central banks and international financial institutions, the relationships between indicators and financial-stability conditions may not be strong or robust enough to be reliable for assessments and predictions. Nevertheless, in looking at a broader array of indicators, in developing better analytical frameworks, and in using sophisticated statistical tools, there

---

[59]Measurement and modeling issues are discussed more fully in Chapter 6.

may be scope for improving the ability to monitor and assess financial stability in the future.

Third, as a policy objective, *financial stability is only partly controllable.* The policy instruments that can be used to safeguard financial stability generally have other primary objectives, such as protecting the interests of deposit holders (prudential instruments), fostering price stability (monetary policy), or promoting a swift settlement of financial transactions (policies governing payment and settlement systems). In addition to timing lags, the impact of these policy instruments on financial stability is thus often indirect; in some cases, financial-stability objectives may cause friction with the instrument's initial objective. Moreover, changes in financial stability are highly susceptible to exogenous shocks—ranging from natural catastrophes to abrupt swings in market sentiment—further limiting their controllability.

Fourth, *policies aimed at financial stability often involve a trade-off between resilience and efficiency.* Measures to enhance financial stability often require weighing the pursuit of an efficient allocation of financial resources against the ability to exclude or absorb shocks to the financial system. This implies a risk-return judgment that is difficult to make in a fully objective manner. For instance, in the sphere of prudential policies, higher solvency requirements will reduce the risk of a bank not being able to absorb an adverse shock, but will also imply capital costs and forgone investment opportunities. Similarly, exchange restrictions may reduce or exclude certain risks related to international capital flows, but may also limit the efficiency of the domestic financial market.

Finally, *policy requirements for financial stability may be time inconsistent.* Because some public policy instruments to safeguard financial stability circumvent market forces, the short-term stability gain may come at the cost of a longer-term stability loss. In particular, measures such as the provision of lender-of-last-resort finance or deposit guarantee may undermine market discipline, thereby creating moral hazard or adverse selection. This intertemporal trade-off is a fundamental issue in financial-system policy making.

In Defense of a Positive Approach: Why Focus on Stability and Not on Instability?

In defining the relevant concepts and in designing financial-system policies, policymakers and their respective institutions typically concentrate efforts on identifying, monitoring, and analyzing the sources of financial *instability.* The primary objective of doing so is to prevent instability, and failing this, at least to understand it sufficiently to minimize its adverse consequences for markets, the economy, and society more broadly. Indeed, an important part of the framework for safeguarding financial stability developed in Chapter 6 is a process of identifying sources of risks and vulnerabilities within the financial system that could threaten stability.

Such an approach is justified on two grounds, one political and the other practical. First, if instability were to arise without forewarning and impose severe costs on society at large, politicians and policymaking institutions would most likely be held accountable. Second, if the history of finance has taught us any great lessons, the most indelible is that finance is prone to instability. This lesson was reinforced in the logic presented in Part I. What better reasons could there be for policymakers to desire a framework in which they could strive to understand the sources and costs of financial instability, and the possible means to prevent these sources from occurring?

The incentive to think in terms of instability rather than stability has led to a rich menu of alleged sources of financial instability. The most often cited include natural tendencies of financial institutions toward excessive competition, concentrations of power, and oligopoly or near-monopoly; inherent negative externalities; information asymmetries; and related or resulting occurrences of adverse selection, resource misallocation, risk mispricing, and market failures. Given this list, it is not surprising that financial-system policies inevitably devolve into measures to ward off the potential negative consequences of these alleged deficiencies of finance.

Most systematic treatments of financial-stability issues, in fact, take this negativist approach. While useful, this focus on instabilities fails in one important respect, resulting in consequences for how one thinks about the financial system and how one designs financial-system policies.

The negativist approach conceals in the background an important and defining feature of finance—that finance is a public good (and not a public bad). Finance, when properly scaled to the needs of society, bestows both tangible and intangible benefits—in the large to society and in the small to individuals—on almost all aspects of political, economic, social, and cultural life. Without it, what are now modern economies and societies would be far less advanced, effective, and efficient organisms.

That deficiencies and limitations of finance might from time to time reduce the potential benefits of this public good clearly needs to be reckoned with. Should these deficiencies, though, be the defining focus of policy and the core elements of an analytical framework for understanding how the benefits of finance can be enhanced and not just preserved? Or is there a better alternative, one that leverages the truism—tempered by historical experience—that finance is a process that produces allocative efficiency and critically supports other important processes such as economic growth, wealth accumulation, and, ultimately, human well-being?

The operational implications of shifting the emphasis toward the positive aspects of finance, and away from factors that detract from its effectiveness, may not be obvious. Accentuating the positive aspects of finance and financial systems—the public goods provided by them—leads to an analysis of financial systems that tries to answer questions such as the following:

- From a social, systemic point of view, what is most important and beneficial about finance?
- How should policies be designed to produce the highest probability of preserving these important and useful features, and thereby maintain the benefits of finance?
- How can the benefits of finance be optimized for the economic system and society as a whole?

This represents a positive approach to analyzing financial stability issues.

Regarding finance and an effective and robust financial system as a public good means that policy's role is to ensure, in a positive way, that private incentives and rules of the game encourage and support the production by society of at least an adequate supply of the public good. This contrasts sharply with the approaches now taken, which cast the main objective of financial policies to be placing limits on finance in ways that can ultimately undermine the ability of finance to provide the optimal amount of public good.

It might be that these two approaches in practice lead to the same place— a policy framework and set of institutional arrangements that provide the mechanisms for ensuring financial stability. But the positive approach is a more constructive one because financial stability is something that needs to be nurtured, protected, and preserved, stemming in part from its intimate connection to money, but also from the great improvements in allocative efficiency it permits. It seems that the negative approach regards the management of market imperfections and other market failures as the immediate objective, perhaps leading to complacency and no full appreciation for the beneficial role of finance in fostering growth in modern economies and in raising living standards in developing economies.

Annex. Alternative Definitions of Financial Stability

This annex provides an overview of definitions or descriptions of financial stability by a selected group of officials, central banks, and academics.[60]

---

[60]Some authors choose not to define financial stability and instead use the concept of systemic risk. See Oosterloo and de Haan (2003) for a discussion of this concept.

Most of these definitions envision financial stability as the absence of instability, and thus can be associated with the negativist approach discussed in the chapter.

John Chant (Bank of Canada)

Financial instability refers to conditions in financial markets that harm, or threaten to harm, an economy's performance through their impact on the working of the financial system . . . Such instability harms the working of the economy in various ways. It can impair the financial condition of non-financial units such as households, enterprises, and governments to the degree that the flow of finance to them becomes restricted. It can also disrupt the operations of particular financial institutions and markets so that they are less able to continue financing the rest of the economy . . . It differs from time to time and from place to place according to its initiating impulse, the parts of the financial system affected, and its consequences. Threats to financial stability have come from such diverse sources as the default on the bonds of a distant government; the insolvency of a small, specialized, foreign exchange bank; computer breakdown at a major bank; and the lending activities of a little-known bank in the U.S. Midwest. (Chant, 2003, pp. 3–4)

Andrew Crockett (Bank for International Settlements and Financial Stability Forum)

[We can] define financial stability as an absence of instability . . . a situation in which economic performance is potentially impaired by fluctuations in the price of financial assets or by an inability of financial institutions to meet their contractual obligations. I would like to focus on four aspects of this definition.

Firstly, there should be real economic costs . . . Secondly, it is the potential for damage rather than actual damage which matters . . . Thirdly, my definition refers . . . not just to banks but to non-banks, and to markets as well as to institutions . . . Fourth, my definition allows me to address the question of whether banks are special . . . [A]ll institutions that have large exposures—all institutions that are largely interconnected whether or not they are themselves directly involved in the payments system—have the capacity, if they fail, to cause much widespread damage in the system. (Crockett, 1997, pp.1–2)

Deutsche Bundesbank

The term financial stability broadly describes a steady state in which the financial system efficiently performs its key economic functions, such as allocating resources and spreading risk as well as settling payments, and is able to do so even in the event of shocks, stress situations and periods of profound structural change. (Deutsche Bundesbank, 2003, p. 8)

Wim Duisenberg (European Central Bank)

[M]onetary stability is defined as stability in the general level of prices, or as an absence of inflation or deflation. Financial stability does not have as easy or universally accepted a definition. Nevertheless, there seems to be a broad consensus that financial stability refers to the smooth functioning of the key elements that make up the financial system. (Duisenberg, 2001, p. 39)

Roger Ferguson (Board of Governors of the U.S. Federal Reserve System)

It seems useful . . . to define financial stability . . . by defining its opposite, financial instability. In my view, the most useful concept of financial instability for central banks and other authorities involves some notion of market failure or externalities that can potentially impinge on real economic activity.

Thus, for the purposes of this paper, I'll define financial instability as a situation characterized by these three basic criteria: (1) some important set of financial asset prices seem to have diverged sharply from fundamentals; and/ or (2) market functioning and credit availability, domestically and perhaps internationally, have been significantly distorted; with the result that (3) aggregate spending deviates (or is likely to deviate) significantly, either above or below, from the economy's ability to produce. (Ferguson, 2002, p. 2)

Michael Foot (U.K. Financial Services Authority)

[W]e have financial stability where there is: (a) monetary stability; (b) employment levels close to the economy's natural rate; (c) confidence in the operation of the generality of key financial institutions and markets in the economy; and (d) where there are no relative price movements of either real or financial assets within the economy that will undermine (a) or (b).

The first three elements of this definition are, I hope, non-contentious. In respect of (a) and (b), it seems implausible to define financial stability as occurring in a period of rapid inflation, or in a mid-1930s style period of low inflation but high unemployment.

Similarly in respect of (c), it would be strange to argue that there was financial stability in a period when banks were failing, or when normal conduits for long-term savings and borrowing in either the personal or corporate sectors were seriously malfunctioning. Such circumstances would mean the participants had lost confidence in financial intermediaries. It would mean, almost certainly, that economic growth was being damaged by the unavailability or relatively high cost of financial intermediation.

This leaves us with (d) . . . I would say that there are four main channels by which changes in asset prices might affect the real economy: by changing household wealth and thereby consumption . . . ; by a change in equity prices . . . ; by their impact on firms' balance sheets which can then affect corporate spending . . . ; by their impact on capital flows, with for example inflows of capital— as during the dot.com boom in the US—strengthening the domestic currency. (Foot, 2003, pp. 2–3)

Andrew Large

In a broad sense ... think of financial stability in terms of maintaining confidence in the financial system. Threats to that stability can come from shocks of one sort or another. These can spread through contagion, so that liquidity or the honoring of contracts becomes questioned. And symptoms of financial instability can include volatile and unpredictable changes in prices. Preventing this from happening is the real challenge. (Large, 2003, p. 170)

Frederick Mishkin (Columbia University)

Financial instability occurs when shocks to the financial system interfere with information flow so that the financial system can no longer do its job of channeling funds to those with productive investment opportunities. (Mishkin, 1999, p. 7)

Norges Bank

Financial stability means that the financial system is robust to disturbances in the economy, so that it is able to mediate financing, carry out payments and redistribute risk in a satisfactory manner. (Norwegian Central Bank, 2003)

Tommaso Padoa-Schioppa (European Central Bank)

[Financial stability is] a condition where the financial system is able to withstand shocks without giving way to cumulative processes which impair the allocation of savings to investment opportunities and the processing of payments in the economy.

The definition immediately raises the related question of defining the financial system ... [which] consists of all financial intermediaries, organized and informal markets, payments and settlement circuits, technical infrastructures supporting financial activity, legal and regulatory provisions, and supervisory agencies. This definition permits a complete view of the ways in which savings are channeled towards investment opportunities, information is disseminated and processed, risk is shared among economic agents, and payments are facilitated across the economy. (Padoa-Schioppa, 2003, p. 22)

Anna Schwartz (National Bureau of Economic Research)

A financial crisis is fueled by fears that the means of payment will be unobtainable at any price and, in a fractional reserve banking system leads to a scramble for high-powered money. It is precipitated by actions of the public that suddenly squeeze the reserves of the banking system ... The essence of a financial crisis is that it is short-lived, ending with a slackening of the public's demand for additional currency. (Schwartz, 1986, p. 11)

Nout Wellink (De Nederlandsche Bank)

According to our own definition at the Nederlandsche Bank, a stable financial system is capable of efficiently allocating resources and absorbing shocks, preventing these from having a disruptive effect on the real economy or on other financial systems. Also, the system itself should not be a source of shocks. Our definition thus implies that money can properly carry out its functions as a means of payment and as a unit of account, while the financial system as a whole can adequately perform its role of mobilizing savings, diversifying risks and allocating resources. Financial stability is a vital condition for economic growth, as most transactions in the real economy are settled through the financial system. The importance of financial stability is perhaps most visible in situations of financial instability. For example, banks may be reluctant to finance profitable projects, asset prices may deviate excessively from their underlying intrinsic values, or payments may not be settled in time. In extreme cases, financial instability may even lead to bank runs, hyperinflation, or a stock market crash. (Wellink, 2002, p. 2)

6

A Framework for Financial Stability

The framework developed in this chapter seeks to integrate the analytical and policy elements of financial stability, building on the characteristics of finance and the definition of financial stability developed in earlier chapters. A key part of the framework is an assessment that brings together macroeconomic, monetary, financial market, supervisory, and regulatory input. The purpose of this framework is to provide a coherent structure for the analysis of financial stability issues to

- foster early identification of potential risks and vulnerabilities;
- promote preventive and timely remedial policies to avoid financial instability;
- resolve instabilities when preventive and remedial measures fail.

The ultimate goal of the framework is to *prevent* problems from occurring or to *resolve* problems if prevention fails. While this chapter touches on resolution, its main focus is prevention.

The framework is designed to go beyond the traditional "shock-transmission" approach that is the basis of many existing policy-oriented frameworks. In this shock-transmission approach, the system would either be presumed to remain in a state (or path) of equilibrium if undisturbed or adjust to a different, perhaps less desirable, state (or path) of equilibrium if and when it experiences a shock. Instead, the focus here is on identifying and dealing with the buildup of vulnerabilities prior to downward corrections in markets, prior to problems within institutions, or prior to failures in financial infrastructure. This approach implicitly assumes that a shock that may eventually trigger such adjustments is usually less relevant itself when compared to the actual imbalances that were present in the financial system when the shock occurred. This approach also accords with the view that financial stability should be viewed as a continuum, in which imbalances may develop and either dissipate through self-corrective mechanisms or accumulate to the point of moving the financial system outside the range of stability.

As will be discussed in this chapter, the key to prevention is the early identification and analysis of risks to stability and of potential sources of vulnerability in the financial system before they lead to unsustainable and potentially damaging imbalances and consequences. Along with identifying potential sources of risks and vulnerabilities, it is also necessary to attempt to calibrate their intensity and potential for leading to financial-system problems and possible systemic effects.

The key to resolution is to have mechanisms in place and policy tools available to remedy situations in which the financial system seems to be in the early stages of moving toward instability. Such tools might include moral suasion and intensified supervision or market surveillance or both. Should remedial measures fail, or undetected endogenous factors or unanticipated exogenous factors lead to instability, tools should be available for resolving problems and instabilities quickly and with minimum collateral damage, either to the financial system or the economy. Such tools would include emergency liquidity assistance.

Various works have tried to tackle some or all of these issues in the past, but none of these approaches has gained wide acceptance within the profession.[61] An increasing number of central banks and other policymaking institutions, including the IMF, cover financial stability issues in periodicals published once or twice a year, and some of them provide a rudimentary discussion of their analytical structure.[62] At the international level, the IMF and the World Bank have launched the Financial Sector Assessment Program (FSAP), which examines selected countries' financial soundness and assesses their compliance with financial system standards and codes (see International Monetary Fund and World Bank, 2003).

The next section of this chapter discusses the financial-stability challenge more precisely than in previous chapters, and examines the possible relationship between efficiency and stability and the need for a systemwide approach. The succeeding section outlines an overarching framework for

---

[61]Crockett (1996) undertook an early and extensive survey of the underlying literature. Some analyses are formulated in academic or theoretical terms, paying only limited attention to policy implications (Davis, 2002; Mishkin, 1999). Other studies take an institutional approach, by discussing regulatory regimes (Das, Quintyn, and Chenard, 2003; Llewellyn, 2001), or investigating specific responsibilities of central banks (Oosterloo and de Haan, 2003).

[62]Bank of England, 1999; Deutsche Bundesbank, 2003; National Bank of Belgium, 2002; Sveriges Riksbank, 2003.

safeguarding financial stability in which both prevention and resolution of financial problems and crises are key objectives. This section first places financial-stability work in a broader economic and financial context, then sketches out the vital parts of the framework, focuses on the prevention and resolution parts of the framework, and finishes by examining policy implications. This is followed by a discussion of some of the more practical challenges in making financial-stability assessments, first by outlining criteria for disciplining the process of information gathering, monitoring, and assessing, and then by examining the formidable measurement and modeling issues in making assessments. The final two sections briefly outline some of the immediate and difficult challenges ahead in assessing financial stability, and draw conclusions.

What Is the Financial-Stability Challenge?

There are many ways to characterize the challenges faced in achieving and maintaining financial stability. Moreover, the nature of the challenge will depend to some extent on the structure and maturity of the economic system. Although what follows can be adapted to all financial systems, for mature financial systems the financial-stability challenge can be characterized as

> *maintaining the smooth functioning of the financial system and maintaining the system's ability to facilitate and support the efficient functioning and performance of the economy; and having in place the mechanisms to prevent financial problems from becoming systemic or from threatening the stability of the financial and economic system, but without undermining the economy's ability to sustain growth and perform its other important functions.*

The challenge is not to prevent all financial problems from arising. First, it is not practical to expect that a dynamic and effective financial system would avoid instances of market volatility and turbulence, or that all financial institutions would be capable of perfectly managing the uncertainties and risks involved in providing financial services and enhancing financial stakeholder value.

Second, it would be undesirable to create and impose mechanisms that are overly protective of market stability or that overly constrain risk-taking by financial institutions. Constraints could be so intrusive and inhibiting that risk-taking could be reduced to the point where economic efficiency is inhibited. Moreover, the mechanisms of protection or insurance could, if poorly designed and implemented, create the moral hazard of even greater risk-taking.

The phrase "but without undermining the economy's ability to sustain growth and perform its other important functions" is an important component of the challenge of financial stability. The achievement and maintenance of financial stability should be balanced against other, perhaps higher-priority objectives such as economic efficiency. This balance reflects the notion that finance is not an end in itself but plays a supporting role in improving the ability of the economic system to perform its functions.

Efficiency and Stability

That the challenge is a balancing act can be seen by considering that the likelihood of systemic problems could be limited by a set of rules and regulations that restrict financial activities in such a way that the incidence or likelihood of destabilizing asset-price volatility, asset market turbulence, or individual bank failures could be reduced if not eliminated. However, this type of "stability" would likely only be achieved at the expense of economic and financial efficiency.

This reasoning leads to the impression that there is a trade-off between achieving economic and financial efficiency on the one hand, and economic and financial stability on the other. That is, if one is concerned solely with stability, it may be possible to achieve and maintain it by trading off some efficiency.

The possibility of a trade-off can be illustrated by narrowing the definitions of stability and efficiency. Consider a market for a good whose price is sensitive to incoming information, a condition that applies to many asset prices. The variability of the asset price could, in principle, be limited by the imposition of restrictions in the market that would inhibit the ability of traders to price-in every small piece of information. However, from a trader's and investor's perspective, such restrictions would be inhibiting the efficiency of the market's ability to price and allocate resources in the presence of uncertainty.

It is possible, however, to try to maintain efficiency, and even enhance it, while at the same time allowing the financial system room to innovate, evolve, and better support the economic system. If the cost of these dual objectives is greater asset-price volatility or capital flow volatility, it is up to society to choose a point along this trade-off.

Some have characterized the difference between the U.S. financial system and the European financial system as the choice of different points along this trade-off. The U.S. system is more market oriented in that the financing of both household and corporate activities is accomplished more through markets than in Europe, where there is much greater reliance on bank funding than on tradable securities (although this is changing). While one might argue that the U.S. system of finance has led to greater economic productivity and efficiency, this "greater efficiency" is accompanied by greater asset market volatility and turbulence, and a greater observed tendency to financial stress.

The Need for a Systemic Approach

From a broader perspective, the challenge of achieving and maintaining financial stability goes well beyond the stability of asset prices, or prices more generally. Authorities, central banks in particular, should still be concerned with asset-price volatility, and price volatility more generally, because they do determine the value of money. However, the challenge of financial stability is broader than, and in fact encompasses, the need to limit the impact of price instability on the functioning of the overall financial system. In fact, if the financial system is stable, it will be able to tolerate higher levels of asset-price volatility, as well as other financial problems, including problems in financial institutions. To jump immediately to the highest level of generality, the challenge of financial stability is to manage the risk of the occurrence of a systemwide problem, that is, to manage systemic financial risk (defined in Chapter 5).

Defining and Operationalizing a Financial Stability Framework

A financial system is one part of a larger economic, social, and political system. It is affected by economic, social, and political developments, and in turn affects the performance of the economy and the well-being of society more generally. That is, finance takes place within a context. So, too, does the work of safeguarding financial stability, and so, too, does the framework developed here.

To illustrate the financial-stability framework's context, Figure 6.1 presents a stylized view of factors affecting financial system performance. As observed in Part I of this book, finance helps the economic system allocate resources, manage risks, and absorb shocks, while the presence of market imperfections implies a role for public sector policy. In the figure, this is indicated by the financial system's links with the real economy and policy. An explicit distinction is made between imbalances that arise within the financial system and those that may originate or be exacerbated by disturbances from outside the system. This distinction is primarily motivated by

Figure 6.1. Stylized View of Factors Affecting Financial System Performance

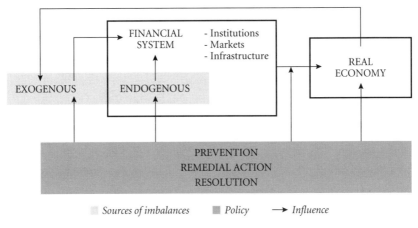

Source: Houben, Kakes, and Schinasi, 2004.

differences in policy implications, as explained below. A crucial element of the financial-stability framework is the interaction between analysis and policy formulation and implementation.

Overview of Framework

A natural point of departure in defining and operationalizing a framework is the analysis of potential risks and vulnerabilities in the financial system, guided by the definition of financial stability as a continuum. This analysis of risks and vulnerabilities should be comprehensive and ongoing, examining all factors that influence the workings of the financial system—covering the macro-economy, financial markets, financial institutions, and financial infrastructure—and should be aimed at early identification of financial vulnerabilities. Subsequently, an assessment should be made indicating to what extent these vulnerabilities pose a threat to financial stability and what policy responses may be appropriate.

The financial system's position within the continuum of financial stability (discussed in Chapter 5) might rest within any of three zones, with resulting implications for policy. First, the financial system may be assessed to be broadly in a zone or corridor of stability and likely to remain so in the near future. In this case, the appropriate policy is mainly preventive, aimed at maintaining stability by relying on both private sector market-disciplining mechanisms and official supervision and surveillance.

Second, the financial system may be within a corridor of stability but moving toward a boundary with instability, for instance, because imbalances are starting to develop or because of changes outside the financial system. Safeguarding the stability of the system may then call for remedial action—through moral suasion and more intense supervision, for example.

Third, the financial system may be outside the corridor of financial stability and unable to perform its functions adequately. In that case, policies should be reactive (possibly including crisis resolution) and aimed at restoring stability. Within this third category, the financial system could be further judged either to be in a position in which self-corrective processes and mechanisms are likely to move the system back toward the corridor of stability or, alternatively, to need prompt remedial and even emergency measures to move it back to a zone of stability.[63]

The main elements of this financial-stability framework—the analysis, assessment, and three possible policy stances—are summarized in Figure 6.2. Obviously, owing to the multifaceted nature of financial stability, the distinction between the policy categories will seldom be clear-cut, as illustrated by the gradual change from light (passive) to dark (active).

Assessments could be classified a number of other ways. Financial conditions and potential difficulties could be delineated according to their intensity, scope, and potential threat to systemic stability. For example, potential financial difficulties can be thought of as falling into one of the following fairly broad categories:

- difficulties in a single institution or market not likely to have system-wide consequences for either the banking or financial system;
- difficulties experienced by several relatively important institutions involved in market activities with the real possibility of spillovers and contagion to other institutions and markets;
- problems likely to spread to a significant number and different types of financial institutions and across usually unrelated markets for managing liquidity needs, such as forward, inter-bank, and even equity markets.

Problems occurring within each of these categories would overlap to some extent and also occur along a continuum. They would also require dif-

---

[63]As Kindleberger (1996, p. 4) puts it: "markets work well, on the whole, and can normally be relied upon to decide the allocation of resources and, within limits, the distribution of income, but . . . occasionally markets will be overwhelmed and need help."

ferent diagnostic tools and policy responses, ranging from doing nothing, to intensifying supervision or surveillance of a specific institution or market, to liquidity injections into the markets to dissipate strains, to interventions into particular institutions.

Prevention: Financial-Stability Analysis and Assessment

Because prevention is one of its main objectives, the analysis of financial stability involves a continuous examination of potential risks and vulnerabilities that may threaten the health of the financial system and the flow of economic activity. To prevent problems from occurring or becoming significant enough to pose a risk to financial stability, the approach taken should be a continuous process of information gathering, technical analysis, monitoring, and assessment. Because of the links between the real economy and the financial system, and between the various components of the financial system, this continuous process is most useful if it encompasses both economic and financial dimensions, and institutional knowledge about institutions, markets, and the financial infrastructure. As already noted, the process needs to be comprehensive and analytical (see the top bar in Figure 6.2). Ongoing and more fundamental research into the changing structure of the financial system and its changing links to the real economy, as well as the further development of measurement techniques for detecting growing imbalances and calibrating risks and vulnerabilities, are vital for keeping the critical monitoring function up to date.

The analytical process involves gathering and monitoring information about the macro-economy (and, at times, microeconomic functions) and about various aspects of the financial system through supervisory, regulatory, and surveillance mechanisms. Each of the financial-system monitoring components could involve both macro- and micro-prudential characteristics. For example, in gathering information about and monitoring individual institutions, the supervisory process could be aided by knowledge about the economy's position in the business and credit cycles and about how markets have been performing overall, because the macro-economy and markets provide the background against which the operational performance of individual institutions should be assessed. Likewise, an assessment of the condition of financial markets depends on whether the major institutions operating in the markets are well capitalized and profitable. Trade-offs again emerge, even in the assessment process, in safeguarding financial stability.

The reason for gathering and analyzing information, and for continuously monitoring the various components of, and influences on, the

Figure 6.2. Framework for Maintaining Financial System Stability

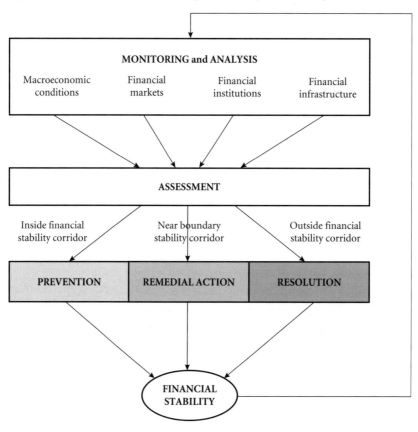

Source: Houben, Kakes, and Schinasi, 2004.

financial system is to systematically and periodically make assessments about whether the financial system is performing its main functions within the corridor of financial stability. As noted in the previous section, such an assessment could lead to three conclusions, each of which has quite different implications for action (see Figure 6.2).

The assessment of risks and vulnerabilities should be comprehensive, as described in Table 6.1. An operationally significant distinction can be made between sources of risk that are present or may develop within the financial system, and sources of risk that may originate in and emanate from the real economy and be transmitted to the financial system. These different sources

Table 6.1. Sources of Risk to Financial Stability

Endogenous	Exogenous

Institutions based
  • Financial risks
    Credit
    Market
    Liquidity
    Interest rate
    Currency
  • Operational risk
  • Information technology weaknesses
  • Legal or integrity risk
  • Reputation risk
  • Business strategy risk
  • Concentration risk
  • Capital adequacy risk
	Macroeconomic disturbances
	  • Economic environment risk
	  • Policy imbalances
	
	Event risk
	  • Natural disaster
	  • Political events
	  • Large business failures

Market based
  • Counterparty risk
  • Asset price misalignment
  • Run on markets
    Credit
    Liquidity
  • Contagion	

Infrastructure based
  • Clearance, payment, and settlement system risk
  • Infrastructure fragilities
    Legal
    Regulatory
    Accounting
    Supervisory
  • Collapse of confidence leading to runs
  • Domino effects	

Source: Houben, Kakes, and Schinasi, 2004.

of risks tend to have different policy implications. The size and likelihood of endogenous imbalances can typically be influenced by the financial authorities through regulation, supervision, or adequate crisis management. By contrast, aside from macroeconomic policies that are subject to long, varying, and uncertain lags, external disturbances can hardly be influenced. Rather, the scope for policy is mostly limited to reducing the impact of external disturbances on the financial system, for instance, by maintaining the capacity to absorb shocks and establishing backup systems to protect vital information.

In keeping with the broad definition of the financial system and its main constituent components outlined in Chapter 5, endogenous sources of risk can arise either in financial institutions, or in financial markets, or in the infrastructure, or in any combination. The endogenous and exogenous sources of risks and vulnerabilities outlined in Table 6.1 are summarized in the following sections.

Risks in financial institutions

First, risks and vulnerabilities may develop in financial institutions. For instance, problems may initially arise at a single institution and subsequently spread to other parts of the financial system, or several institutions may be affected simultaneously because of similar exposures. Traditional financial risks such as credit, market, and liquidity risks, and interest rate and foreign currency exposure may be present in financial institutions, and if they materialize could hamper the process of reallocating financial resources between savers and investors.[64] Institutions are also prone to operational, legal, and reputation risks. Furthermore, business strategy and a concentration of exposures can make financial institutions sensitive to adverse developments in particular areas, while a decline in economic capital reduces institutions' absorption capacity.

Financial market risk

Financial markets are a second source of endogenous risk, not only because they offer alternative sources of finance to nonfinancial sectors but because they systemically link financial institutions and, more directly, savers and investors. Obvious examples of risks emanating from market activities are counterparty risk and asset-price misalignments. Financial markets are also vulnerable to runs and contagion. During the 1990s and the early years of the 2000s, financial systems and the global financial system became more market oriented, through both an increase in financial institutions' market activities and exposures, and greater participation by nonfinancial corporations and households in markets. Hence, market-based risks are becoming more relevant for financial stability. At the same time, the role and relative importance of safety nets is also changing. Traditionally, deposit insurance and lender-of-last-resort facilities address problems arising at individual institutions and prevent these from spreading through the financial system. Because market-based vulnerabilities immediately

---

[64]Interest-rate and foreign-currency exposures may also be seen as examples of market risk and be subsumed within this category of risk.

affect a substantial part of the financial sector, the appropriate instruments are also becoming more generalized, for instance, through liquidity injections in the financial system (White, 2003). A thorough understanding of market vulnerabilities is important for effective implementation of such instruments.

Financial infrastructure risk

Financial infrastructures are a third important endogenous source of risk, in part because they link market participants, but also because they provide the institutional framework in which financial institutions and markets operate. In payment systems, several risks may develop related to clearing and settlement. These often originate in the financial institutions participating in the system, and are in that sense related to institutions-based vulnerabilities. Examples are operational failures, concentration risk, and domino effects. To the extent that financial infrastructure is itself generally run by a financial institution, infrastructural vulnerabilities may also stem from institution-specific financial risks. Other examples of infrastructure-based risks are weaknesses in the legal system and the accounting system. Such vulnerabilities may directly affect a large part of the financial sector.

Exogenous risks

Finally, vulnerabilities may be exogenous, that is, originate outside the financial system. For instance, disturbances may arise at the macroeconomic level, such as oil price shocks, technological innovations, and macroeconomic policy imbalances. These exogenous macroeconomic disturbances can pose risks for financial stability because they can directly influence the ability of economic and financial actors (households, companies, and even the government) to honor their financial obligations. More generally, coherent and consistent macroeconomic (that is, monetary and fiscal) policies are critical requirements for achieving and maintaining financial stability. Furthermore, microeconomic events, such as a failure of a large company, may undermine market confidence and create imbalances that affect the whole financial system. Other examples of exogenous disturbances are a sudden introduction or withdrawal of trade restrictions, political events (including terrorist actions and wars), and natural disasters (earthquakes, floods).

Financial-stability analysis covers all these endogenous and exogenous sources of risks and vulnerabilities, and thus requires that individual parts of the financial system (financial markets, institutions, and infrastructure) and the real economy (households, firms, the public sector) be systematically monitored. The analysis must also take into account cross-sector and cross-border links, because imbalances often arise due to a combination of weaknesses from different sources. For instance, operational failures in payment systems may be caused by problems in financial institutions, and a large business failure (such as Enron) may be linked to weaknesses in the accounting system. The number and importance of cross-links is increasing as a result of the main trends—financial deepening, integration, and complexity—described in Chapter 1. Financial institutions are becoming more exposed to financial markets and other sectors, which increases the scope for contagion and underscores the importance of a comprehensive approach to the financial system as a whole.

Judging the scope and impact of vulnerabilities

Along with endogenous and exogenous sources of risk, another policy-relevant issue is the initial scope of vulnerabilities and their eventual impact on the greater financial system. Two extreme cases serve as examples. First, financial stress may initially arise at the micro level and subsequently spread over the financial system. The most obvious examples are a bankruptcy of a large nonfinancial company, or a bank failure, which can affect other parts of the financial system through interbank exposures and confidence effects. At the other extreme, developments may immediately have the potential to affect a major part of the economy—a systemic problem, for instance, such as the destruction of a vital part of an economy's payments and settlement infrastructure as might have occurred in the absence of swift remedial measures in the aftermath of the events of September 11, 2001. Investors can often protect themselves against micro-level disturbances through insurance or diversification of exposures, which also reduce the risk of contagion and systemic crises. For systemic risks, however, insurance either does not exist or tends to be prohibitively expensive, implying that official intervention may have a role in reducing the impact of systemic crises.

Although Table 6.1 provides a long list of sources of risks to financial stability, it is not exhaustive and would need to be updated as the structure of finance changes over time. For example, the liberalization, integration, and globalization of financial systems experienced in recent decades probably changed the nature of systemic risk, meaning that a broader, more comprehensive set of indicators is required to assess systemic risk. Specifically, the increasing market orientation of financial systems and the improvement of risk diversification instruments—through activities such as hedging, credit risk transfers, and securitization of bank loans—may have lowered risk concentrations and thereby reduced the likelihood of individual bank failures and related traditional domino-effect systemic risks. After all, banking institutions now shed risk more easily into a more complete set of markets and across a more diversified group of nonbank institutional and individual investors. However, the systemic benefits of this greater sharing of risks may be somewhat offset by a greater vulnerability to systemwide shocks, because the aggregate exposure to financial markets has surged, implying a potentially larger simultaneous influence of extreme adverse events in these markets.

The analysis of financial stability corresponds somewhat to macroprudential analysis (see, for example, Evans and others, 2000). Standard indicators are

- balance sheet data reflecting sectoral (household and corporate) financial positions;
- ratios between net debt and income;
- measures of counterparty risk (such as credit spreads);
- measures of liquidity and asset quality (such as nonperforming loans);
- open foreign exchange positions;
- exposures within individual sectors with special attention to measures of concentration.

These are mostly micro-prudential indicators, aggregated to the macro level. Thus, dispersions within these aggregates warrant analysis.

To cover the entire financial system, a broader set of indicators would also monitor conditions in important markets, including interbank money, repurchase, bond, equity, and derivatives markets. Relevant indicators include

- measures of market liquidity (such as bid-ask spreads);
- asset price expectations (as embedded in futures, forward, and other derivative prices);
- uncertainty and risk (as reflected in historical and implied asset-price volatilities);
- asset-price sustainability (as indicated by market depth and breadth as well as deviations in asset-pricing models, fundamentals-based models of equilibrium prices, or price-earnings ratios).

A basic compilation of some of these variables is provided by the Core and Encouraged Set of Financial Soundness Indicators promoted by the IMF (Table 6.2). Complementary indicators may also be derived for how well the financial infrastructure is functioning, including payment system

Table 6.2. IMF Financial Soundness Indicators: Core and Encouraged

Core Set
Deposit-taking institutions

Capital adequacy	Regulatory capital to risk-weighted assets
	Regulatory Tier I capital to risk-weighted assets
Asset quality	Nonperforming loans to total gross loans
	Nonperforming loans net of provisions to capital
	Sectoral distribution of loans to total loans
Earnings and profitability	Return on assets
	Return on equity
	Interest margin to gross income
	Noninterest expenses to gross income
Liquidity	Liquid assets to total assets (liquid asset ratio)
	Liquid assets to short-term liabilities
Sensitivity to market risk	Net open position in foreign exchange to capital

Encouraged Set

Deposit-taking institutions	Capital to assets
	Large exposures to capital
	Geographical distribution of loans to total loans
	Gross asset positions in financial derivatives to capital
	Gross liability positions in financial derivatives to capital
	Trading income to total income
	Personnel expenses to noninterest expenses
	Spread between reference lending and deposit rates
	Spread between highest and lowest interbank rate
	Customer deposits to total (non-interbank) loans
	Foreign currency–denominated loans to total loans
	Foreign currency–denominated liabilities to total liabilities
	Net open position in equities to capital
Other financial corporations	Assets to total financial system assets
	Assets to GDP
Nonfinancial corporate sector	Total debt to equity
	Return on equity
	Earnings to interest and principal expenses
	Net foreign exchange exposure to equity
	Number of applications for protection from creditors
Households	Household debt to GDP
	Household debt service and principal payments to income
Market liquidity	Average bid-ask spread in the securities market[1]
	Average daily turnover ratio in the securities market[1]
Real estate markets	Real estate prices
	Residential real estate loans to total loans
	Commercial real estate loans to total loans

Source: IMF and World Bank, 2003.
[1]Or in other markets that are most relevant to bank liquidity, such as foreign exchange markets.

figures for incidents (failures due to hardware, software, or connectivity problems), stop sendings, slowdowns, and queuing, as well as nonsettlements. In addition to conditions these indicators might highlight, infrastructural issues relating to the legal, regulatory, accounting, or supervisory fields may primarily arise in reaction to situations of financial tension.

Finally, macroeconomic variables such as economic growth, investment, inflation, the balance of payments, and nonfinancial asset prices may indicate a buildup of imbalances.

Developing analytical and measurement tools

Greater understanding and analysis of sources of imbalances and the mechanisms through which they can be magnified could significantly improve the process of assessing financial stability in several other important areas, all of which are discussed in greater detail in the next two sections of this chapter (on practical challenges in making assessments and remaining challenges in designing and implementing the framework). First, early warning systems composed of sets of financial-market indicators can play a role in weighing the importance of different indicators for financial stability and in anticipating financial stress, both within and across classes of financial institutions and within and across the various securities markets. Second, financial stability analyses need to examine not only potential disturbances, but also the degree to which such disturbances can be absorbed by the financial system. In particular, the different factors that can cushion or contain a shock need to be taken into account, such as the size of capital buffers, the reliability of reinsurance facilities, and the presence and functioning of fire walls, safety nets, and backup systems. Third, because the development of analytical tools for financial stability assessments is still in a formative stage, the assessment function must also involve the continuous improvement of methods for monitoring and assessing the sustainability of developments in financial markets and institutions, and for bringing together separate, partial analyses. Fourth, financial stability assessments are complicated by nonlinearities and the need to focus on exceptional but nonetheless plausible events. Hence, it is often necessary to consider distributions of variables (especially the left tail) and to analyze what happens if risks manifest themselves simultaneously. Finally, and within this context, stress tests are becoming a useful tool to give an overall picture of the resilience of parts of the economy under extreme conditions. As discussed further in the next section, while stress tests may be carried out for individual financial institutions, perhaps the banking system, and perhaps even individual sectors, the use of stress tests for the financial system as a whole would be difficult at this stage. The difficulty stems from a scarcity of appropriate data and empirical models. The remaining challenge ahead is to develop systemwide stress tests that take account of financial sector interconnections and of second-round effects that financial institutions have on each other and the real economy.

Policy Implications: Prevention, Remedial Action, and Resolution

The three stages of policy implications presented in Figure 6.2 are somewhat similar to the way a doctor examines a patient. Imagine someone who is in good health with no indications of illness. Within the framework, the health of this person would be in the prevention mode, meaning that he or she should try to maintain a healthy condition by continuing to consume balanced meals, do enough exercise, refrain from smoking, and so on. Signs that the patient's condition is deteriorating (increasing weight or shortness of breath, for example) change the situation. This is the remedial stage: even though the patient is not yet ill, preemptive action may be needed to ensure that he or she remains healthy. The doctor will intensify regular checkups, recommend a better diet and exercise, and use moral suasion to improve the patient's lifestyle. If the patient nonetheless falls ill, intervention (intensive care, medicine, surgery) will be needed. Just as a doctor's actions range from pure prevention to remedial action and, in the ultimate case, serious intervention, financial authorities' policies will intensify as the financial system moves toward—or eventually crosses—the boundary of stability.

As with a healthy patient, the financial system is in the preventive mode in the absence of significant indications that it may become unstable in the near future. Existing policies should be maintained and updated for structural changes to prevent future imbalances. In itself, the surveillance of financial markets, institutions, and infrastructure constitutes an important element of preventive policy (in the health metaphor, this is similar to regularly checking one's weight, blood pressure, and pulse, or going to the dentist). Specifically, tight surveillance will stimulate a judicious management of financial risks. Obviously, surveillance must be coupled with the overall financial-stability assessment. For instance, innovative financial trends such as securitization and the development of derivatives markets are changing the way risks are spread over financial market participants, and may therefore require timely adjustments in both how risks and vulnerabilities are analyzed and assessed, and how existing policy instruments are designed and implemented.

In this context, surveillance and other policy instruments, such as supervision, regulation, official communication, and macroeconomic policies, are key to sustaining a situation of financial stability (as summarized in the Prevention column of Table 6.3). By way of illustration, the trend toward greater complexity implies that transparency deserves more attention, while level playing field problems due to cross-sector and cross-border integration may be addressed by international standards and codes (prominent examples being the Basel Accord[65] for banking supervision and the Lamfalussy Standards[66] for payment systems). Furthermore, support may be given to private sector initiatives that enhance financial stability, for example, through self-regulation or improvement of the financial infrastructure. A recent example of an improvement to the financial infrastructure, with central bank involvement, is the creation of the Continuous Linked Settlement (CLS) bank, which has significantly lowered the risks related to foreign currency transactions (Herstatt risks[67]).

The situation changes if the financial system is close to, or at the boundary of, the range of stability. For instance, imbalances may be building up because of rapid credit growth in combination with excessive asset-price inflation and declining banking system capital; even if immediate risks are absent, problems may become acute if such imbalances continue to expand. Another example is a sudden change in the financial system's domestic or external environment, for instance, due to a sovereign default by a neighboring country. Because of such changes, an initially robust financial system may soon be near the boundary of the financial stability corridor.

In such a situation, the appropriate policies are not just preventive but should also influence or correct actual developments (see Table 6.3, Remedial action column). Policy instruments such as surveillance and supervision need to be intensified to get a firmer grip on these developments. Furthermore, to avoid risks related to bank and liquidity runs and to contagion, it may be useful to strengthen instruments such as safety nets. Other policy tools such as moral suasion and adjustments in macroeconomic

---

[65]The Basel Committee was formed in 1974 under the auspices of the Bank for International Settlements. Its members are the central bank authorities of the Group of Ten countries. The first Basel Accord, published in 1988, called for banks to hold minimum capital of 8 percent of risk-weighted assets as a cushion against credit risk and market risk. Basel II, announced in 2004, refines those minimum capital requirements, calls for supervisory review of an institution's internal assessment process and capital adequacy, and requires disclosure to strengthen market discipline as a complement to supervisory efforts.

[66]The Lamfalussy Standards were established in 1990 by the Committee for Interbank Netting Systems of the Central Banks of the Group of Ten Countries (chaired by Alexandre Lamfalussy). The Lamfalussy Standards attempt to reduce risk in bank settlement (netting) systems by setting forth procedural, legal, and operational goals. The need for such standards was precipitated by the growing number of settlement transactions, the growing size of electronic net fund transfer systems, and the growing worldwide interdependencies between the systems, all of which contributed to a growing risk within the systems.

[67]Settlement risk is sometimes called Herstatt risk, after the circumstances surrounding the failure of the Herstatt Bank, in Germany. One day in 1974, Herstatt Bank had taken in all its foreign currency receipts in Europe, but had yet to make any of its U.S. dollar payments. At the end of the business day in Germany, German banking regulators closed down the bank. Counterparties were left holding unsecured claims against the insolvent bank's assets.

Table 6.3. Policy Instruments for Financial Stability

Tools	Prevention Implementing existing policies to safeguard financial stability	Remedial action Implementing preemptive measures to reduce emerging risks to financial stability	Resolution Reactive policy interventions aimed at restoring financial stability
Market disciplining mechanisms	Maintain, update	Strengthen	Discretionary measures
Self-regulation	Maintain, update	Strengthen	Discretionary measures
Financial safety nets	Maintain, update	Strengthen	Lender of last resort, deposit insurance
Surveillance	Maintain, update	Intensify	Further intensify
Supervision and regulation	Maintain, update	Intensify	Discretionary measures
Official communication	Existing policies	Moral suasion	Restore confidence
Macroeconomic policies	Maintain, update	Reduce imbalances	Discretionary measures
Legal system	Maintain, update	Strengthen	Discretionary measures

Source: Houben, Kakes, and Schinasi, 2004.

policies may also be beneficial. In practice, this intermediate stage of remedial policy is probably the most ambiguous one. It is inherently difficult to assess vulnerabilities that have not yet manifested themselves, and perhaps even harder to identify, motivate, and implement the appropriate remedial instruments in the absence of financial instability. The buoyant Dutch housing market in the mid-1990s is a good example of the remedial action phase (see Box 6.1).

The final stage of policy relates to situations of financial instability—the financial system cannot adequately perform its functions (in terms of the health metaphor, the patient is seriously ill). In particular, banks may not finance profitable projects, asset prices may be far removed from their intrinsic values, or payments may not be settled in a timely manner or at all. In extreme cases, financial instability may even spark a run on financial institutions and markets or lead to hyperinflation, a currency crisis, or a stock market crash.

In such situations, policies are generally reactive or, in the case of a financial crisis, focused on crisis resolution. Surveillance and supervision are further intensified, while more activist policies may be needed to restore the system's capacities and to boost confidence (Table 6.3, Resolution column). These situations typically call for discretionary measures that are dif-

Box 6.1. Remedial Action: Dutch Housing Market Boom in the 1990s

In the second half of the 1990s, both house prices and mortgage lending roughly doubled in the Netherlands. Of primary importance among the various factors causing the boom, households' borrowing capacity had been augmented by historically low interest rates and strong income growth, in combination with a significant loosening of mortgage lending criteria. Demographic developments (the number of households increased), greater use of the very generous tax treatment of mortgage interest payments (fully deductible from income tax, leading to low, or even negative real interest rates), and an insufficient supply of new dwellings all contributed. Furthermore, these factors mutually reinforced each other, as loan-to-value (LTV) ratios typically rose to above 100 percent, implying that higher house prices were accommodated by higher borrowing capacity and vice versa.

Given the adverse repercussions of the housing market collapse in the early 1980s in the Netherlands as well as in other countries, an important issue was whether this development could become a threat to financial stability. The unbridled credit growth prompted the central bank—which is also the banking supervisor—to investigate the underlying causes and possible risks. In the period 1999–2000, an intensive survey was carried out among Dutch banks (DNB, 2000). The assessment that was made on the basis of this survey, and the policy conclusions that were drawn, fit under the "remedial action" category in Figure 6.2. While the financial sector's solidity was considered beyond dispute, it was also stressed that the Dutch economy had become more vulnerable and that some developments were leading to further imbalances. Hence, in terms of the framework, the financial system was considered within the range of financial stability, but moving toward its boundary.

A variety of remedial policies were implemented. The surveillance of the housing market and mortgage market was intensified. Banks' regular reporting requirements on mortgages were extended and financial institutions were encouraged to develop stress tests to assess more precisely potential risks in their mortgage portfolios. By publicizing its concerns about the sustainability of housing market developments, the central bank also exercised moral suasion. Moreover, De Nederlandsche Bank launched regular surveys among households to gain a better insight into their uses of mortgage loans and possible risks. Several measures were also taken to get a better grip on the dynamics underlying the rapid increase in mortgage lending. In some cases, supervisors gave banks' administrative organizations and internal controls extra attention. In addition, the generous fiscal treatment of mortgage payments was put to discussion and a maximum LTV limit of 100 percent was proposed to break the self-reinforcing spiral of credit growth and higher house prices. These steps were clearly remedial—they were aimed at preemptively reducing the buildup of imbalances, rather than at directly intervening to resolve a crisis.

Source: Houben, Kakes, and Schinasi, 2004.

ficult to specify deductively and that authorities may be reluctant to detail for strategic reasons (for example, to avoid moral hazard through constructive ambiguity). Examples are forbearance, the activation of financial safety nets, and both institution-targeted or systemwide liquidity injections. In addition, official communication and macroeconomic policies can help prevent excessive financial market turbulence. An illustration of policies in the crisis resolution phase is provided by the financial authorities' reactions to the September 11, 2001, terrorist attacks (see Box 6.2).

Practical Challenges in Making Financial-Stability Assessments

The potential measures and possible states of stability and instability are innumerable, thus, some practical boundaries need to be set to ensure the utility of the assessment process. In addition, models of stability or instability are complex, of necessity. These two issues are addressed in the following discussion.

Disciplining the Assessment Process

While categories of possible assessments may be easy to discuss in principle, they are difficult to identify in actual practice. For example, how should the boundary of stability be defined and measured? When does an isolated small problem threaten to become a systemic one? A bias to be prudent and overreach in identifying potential sources of both risk and vulnerability may intrude, leading to an overestimation of their likelihood and importance. Thus, some ground rules or guidelines must be established for disciplining the continuous process of information gathering, analysis, and monitoring, and most important, for identifying sources of risks and vulnerabilities. A checklist of disciplining principles for identifying risks and vulnerabilities and for assessing where along the stability spectrum the financial system might be could include the following:

- Is the process systematic?
- Are the identified risks plausible?
- Are the identified risks systemically relevant?
- Can links and transmission (or contagion) channels be identified?
- Have risks and links been cross-checked?
- Have the identification of risks and the assessment been time consistent?

In practice, and as discussed somewhat in the previous section on prevention, the process of assessing financial stability entails a *systematic* iden-

---

Box 6.2. Crisis Resolution: Terrorist Attacks on September 11, 2001

Policy actions taken in response to the terrorist attacks on the Twin Towers are a good example of crisis resolution. Because the attacks hit the world's main financial center, the stability of the international financial system was at stake. In addition to the damage in New York itself, the problems could have easily spread due to financial links and behavioral reactions in financial markets.

Policymakers immediately needed to assess the situation and the threats to financial stability. While the international payments systems continued to work smoothly, money markets were not operating properly, as reflected by insufficient liquidity. Given the crucial role of these markets, this risked causing serious damage to the financial system as a whole. Hence, in terms of the framework advanced in this book, the financial system was crossing the boundary of financial stability, implying that intervention was needed to resolve the crisis.

The following corrective measures were taken: First, central banks communicated that, if necessary, almost unlimited liquidity would be made available. Large liquidity injections by the U.S. Federal Reserve (about US$80 billion) and the Eurosystem (70 billion euro) were sufficient to keep the system afloat. Second, a swap agreement was arranged between the European Central Bank and the Federal Reserve—making another US$50 billion available in the subsequent days—in part to reduce the potential for cross-border contagion. Third, the New York Stock Exchange was closed for a week. Finally, both the Federal Reserve and the Eurosystem decided to cut their main interest rates by 50 basis points, which also gave relief to financial markets.

These measures successfully and promptly restored financial stability. The liquidity injections were only temporarily necessary and were easily reversed afterward. In many respects, the policy reactions to the terrorist attacks were similar to official responses to earlier financial crises (Neely, 2004). The next step, in line with Figure 6.2, was to insert the feedback from restored financial stability into the analysis and assessment phase. Several initiatives were subsequently launched to strengthen the financial system's ability to react to and prevent future disturbances, including measures to combat the financing of terrorism.

Source: Houben, Kakes, and Schinasi, 2004.

---

tification and analysis of the sources of risk and vulnerability that could impinge on stability in the circumstances in which the assessment is being made. For example, the comprehensive inventory of sources of risks in Table 6.1 provides a preliminary checklist that can be examined each time an assessment is to be made. Financial-stability assessments should systematically and periodically monitor each of these sources of risks, both individually and collectively, by including cross-sector and cross-border links.

Calling attention to the main sources of financial-stability risk and vulnerability does not necessarily aim at identifying the most likely future scenarios. Instead, it entails the identification of all potential sources of risk and negative events, even if these are remote and unlikely. To preserve discipline in an exercise that essentially involves determining what could go wrong, a key consideration is the *plausibility* of the risks identified. For example, an analysis of conditions in the household and corporate sectors might reveal that a sizable drop in the rate of output growth could, by significantly lowering income and profits, cause a significant rise in household and corporate loan default rates, and thereby threaten the smooth functioning of the financial system. However, if the constellation of economic fundamentals underpinning the pace of economic activity suggests that the likelihood of recession is very low, such an assessment would carry limited value. Ideally, a rigorous determination of the plausibility of a source of risk would be achieved if the probability of a disruptive event occurring could be reasonably estimated. In current practice, given data, measurement, and methodological limitations (discussed later in this chapter), in most cases a ranking of the plausibility of the various identified risks must be based on qualitative judgments derived from very limited information.

While it is desirable to consider seriously all plausible sources of risk to financial stability, it is also desirable to distinguish sources that could prove to be *systemically relevant* from sources that are unlikely to prove costly. For example, the plausible risk of an asset market correction would be regarded as relatively benign if it posed only a minor threat to the financial condition of the household, corporate, and financial sectors. However, if the risk was judged to threaten the solvency of a significant portion of any one of these sectors it could prove to be more costly from a systemic perspective. The challenge is to distinguish between those threats to financial stability that, should they crystallize, carry a high probability of a significant disruption to real economic activity from those that are likely to prove self-correcting without having a material impact either on the level of activity or the process of resource allocation. As implied by the examples, determining the systemic relevance of a particular set of risks can be achieved if a reasonable judgment—quantitatively supported, if possible—can be made about the likely real economic costs, given materialization of the risks. Ideally, the expected losses (for example, resulting from the product of the probability of the event and the cost, given materialization) could lead to a ranking of the importance of the various plausible risks identified. Realistically, formidable practical challenges remain in assessing and estimating the likelihoods of typically low-probability events actually occurring and in measuring the associated costs. As discussed later, costs are also difficult to estimate, but at least the history of financial events could, in principle, allow for the calibration of potential costs.

Once plausible and systemically relevant sources of financial-stability risk and vulnerability have been identified, it is important to *avoid partial equilibrium analysis*. For example, in calibrating the financial-stability implications of the risk of a sharp drop in equity prices, the analysis needs to go far beyond its potential impact on financial markets: it would need to examine the implications for household balance sheets, future corporate funding, and so on. More generally, an internally consistent framework for financial-stability analysis requires an identification of the links and the channels of contagion within the financial sector and also between financial and nonfinancial sectors. Because a financial system comprises many parts (markets, institutions, and infrastructure), the overall degree of financial stability will depend not only on the degree of stability of each of its constituent parts but also on their links and channels of contagion. This calls for a comprehensive approach to collecting and processing information on all the important sectors of the economy and the financial system.

Because the process of identifying sources of risks and vulnerabilities is to some extent contrarian—it identifies what could go wrong—the burden of proof should arguably be higher than that required for the prediction of the most likely outcome. Hence, financial-stability analysis should involve rigorous *cross-checking* of the assessment through the use of a wide range of alternative analytical tools, models, and data sources, including a continuous dialogue with market participants.

Concerning *time consistency,* further discipline in the process of identifying risks and vulnerabilities can be achieved if the horizon over which a given risk is most likely to materialize can be assessed. The empirical literature has shown that it can be a challenging, if not impossible, task to predict the timing of crises. This should not preclude attempts to determine whether a given plausible source of risk has a near-, medium- or long-term likelihood of materializing. Making such determinations systematically and periodically for the same sets of risks can serve to improve accountability in the financial-stability assessment process. Some risks may ultimately prove to be self-correcting without posing any systemic threat, and it is important to understand why. If the "false signal" resulted from a more orderly than predicted unwinding of an imbalance or from a structural change such as better risk management that strengthened the financial system thereby mitigating the risk, this information can serve to improve future assessments.

Measurement and Modeling Issues

So far, the discussion has dwelled on three important aspects of producing a comprehensive assessment of financial stability. The first entails forming a judgment about the individual and collective strength and robustness of the constituent parts of the financial system—institutions, markets, and infrastructures. The second involves systematically identifying the plausible and systemically important sources of risks and vulnerabilities that could pose challenges to financial stability in the future. The third is an appraisal of the potential costs—that is, the ability of the financial system to cope—should some combination of the identified risks and vulnerabilities materialize.

Thus far, the ability to measure and model strength and robustness, or to calibrate the plausibility and importance of the various risks, or to appraise quantitatively the potential costs should risks materialize have been ignored. Each of these areas poses formidable measurement and modeling challenges, so much so that in actual practice many shortcuts and qualitative judgments must be made to produce an overall assessment. This section discusses some of the remaining challenges of measurement and modeling; however, it barely scratches the surface in this important and uncharted territory.

For most macroeconomic or monetary policy objectives (low unemployment, external or budgetary equilibrium, price inflation, and so forth) there is a widely accepted, measurable indicator or set of indicators that define and measure deviations from the objective, even if still subject to methodological and analytical debate, or outright controversy. Both macroeconomics and monetary economics took some 20 to 30 years of practice, trial-and-error, measurement-and-modeling development, and fundamental research to arrive at this point. As noted in the first chapter, financial-stability analysis is still in its infancy. Thus, by contrast, there are no widely accepted measurable indicators of financial stability that can be monitored and assessed over time. In part, this reflects the multifaceted nature of financial stability, because it relates to both the stability and resilience of financial institutions, and to the smooth functioning of financial markets and settlement systems over time.[68] Moreover, these diverse factors need to be weighed in terms of their potential ultimate influence on real economic

---

[68]Sets of indicators have been developed, and are widely used, for assessing the soundness of banking institutions. See, for example, the IMF Soundness Indicators, both core and encouraged sets in IMF and World Bank, 2003, and the IMF's guide on financial soundness indicators in IMF, 2004.

activity. The lack of measurable indicators reflects the relatively young age of the discipline of assessing financial stability. Because measurement is not highly developed yet, it is reasonable to view the current practice of assessing financial stability as more of an art form than as a rigorous discipline or science.

Each of the three main conceptual aspects of the notion of financial stability—resource allocation, risk pricing and management, and absorptive capacity—poses challenges for measurement. Take the simple example of measures of solvency for judging the potential resilience and absorptive capacity of an individual financial institution or bank. Even if balance sheet capital (that is, the difference between assets and liabilities) provides a good indication of near-term shock absorption capacity, bank solvency may not be a sufficient measure for capturing the forward-looking dimensions of financial stability. If high solvency reflects forgone lending opportunities in a highly competitive industry, then, through future profit erosion and loss of market share, the foundations may be laid for future weaknesses in the bank. To take a financial market example, while low asset-price volatility could be indicative of stable conditions in a financial market, it may alternatively signal a failure in the price discovery process. Should this lead to a misallocation of financial resources, it may sow the seeds of vulnerabilities that threaten financial stability in the future.

Challenges in measuring financial-system stability reach well beyond the challenges of measuring the degree of stability in each individual subcomponent of the financial system. Financial stability requires that the constituent components of the system—financial institutions, markets, and infrastructures—be jointly stable. Weaknesses and vulnerabilities in one component may or may not compromise the stability of the system as a whole, depending on size and links—including the degree and effectiveness of risk sharing between different components. Moreover, because different parts of the system perform different tasks, aggregating information across the system poses challenges. For example, in diversified financial systems—in which both financial institutions and markets are important providers of finance—no commonly accepted way has been developed to aggregate information on the degree of stability in both the banking system and financial markets to form an overall assessment of system stability. If the banking system is functioning well but financial markets exhibit signs of strain, the overall assessment of financial-system stability is likely to be ambiguous, particularly if the respective shares of the two components as providers of finance are similar. The more complex and sophisticated a financial system, the more complex the task is likely to be of precisely measuring overall stability.

Measurement challenges in identifying risks and boundaries to financial stability can be illustrated by examining the Minsky (1977) *financial instability hypothesis*. In this hypothesis, as an economy enters an upswing, risk premiums are steadily eroded as managers of firms and banks discover that the majority of conservatively financed projects are succeeding. Gradually, two characteristics emerge: "Existing debts are easily validated and units that were heavily in debt prospered: it paid to lever" (Minsky, 1977, p. 12). As a result, prevailing risk premiums begin to be considered excessive. Lenders and borrowers begin to take on greater risks and, fueled by credit and optimism about future profits, both growth in investment and exponential increases in asset prices occur. At some point, excesses occur, and the conditions that underpinned the boom eventually trigger its collapse. Overinvestment begins to reduce the return on capital, bankruptcy rates begin to rise, firms scale back on investment, and consumers reassess their capacity to repay debt. As optimism gives way to pessimism, aggregate demand in the economy falls sharply and asset prices plummet, possibly inducing a financial crisis.

An implication of this hypothesis is that the inferences for risks to financial stability that can be drawn from some imbalance indicators may, at certain points in the cycle, be rather benign but, for a small change in the same direction, suddenly pose a significant threat following the breach of a key threshold. In practice, the challenges to mapping such hypotheses into empirical frameworks for measurement can be significant. For instance, theory may not offer good answers to questions such as, at what pace of growth does robust and productive investment become overinvestment? Ultimately, the answers to such questions are likely to be settled not theoretically but empirically.

Analytical frameworks are required to help guide measurement, for example, by identifying and suggesting the sets of variables and conditions that could underpin threats to financial stability. Presently, no general-equilibrium models or comprehensive systemwide approaches exist for identifying measures of, and risks to, financial stability.[69] Alternatively, some practitioners employ partial approaches, relying on the analysis of individual indicators of financial imbalances. Sometimes such assessments are based on "rule of thumb" thresholds derived from longer-term historical averages or from cross-country comparisons. Here, too, important measurement (and modeling) issues can arise. Many imbalance indicators

---

[69]A rare exception can be found in Haldane (2004), who develops a general-equilibrium model for deriving a simple financial stability "indicator" that is related to monetary stability.

can be interpreted in either of two ways, each one of which has different implications (perhaps cycle-dependent) for financial-stability assessments. As discussed, high bank solvency, while possibly indicating a stable bank, could instead be the harbinger of emerging vulnerabilities. Narrow spreads across a wide range of fixed income markets could indicate perceptions of low credit risks in these markets but also may reflect a mispricing of risks— as proved to be the case prior to, and following, the near collapse of Long-Term Capital Management in 1998. High price-earnings ratios in equity markets might indicate a stock price bubble but could alternatively reflect an accurate expectation for future strengthening of corporate sector profitability. Similarly, while high non–financial sector debt ratios might be indicative of heightened credit risks facing banks they could also be a reflection of a welfare-enhancing relaxation of liquidity constraints together with a favorable assessment of long-term economic prospects by private economic agents. These examples serve to illustrate that in the absence of a broad range of indicators and an understanding of the broader economic and financial environment in which indicators are being measured, excessive reliance on single-indicator analyses can lead to unsound financial-stability assessments.

Ambiguities that can arise in single-indicator analyses of risks and vulnerabilities can be remedied. While identifying financial imbalances ex ante can be challenging, progress can be made by combining the information contained in individual indicators such as credit growth and asset prices (see Schinasi and Hargraves, 1993a and, more recently and rigorously, Borio and Lowe, 2002). Other cross-checking approaches can involve looking beneath the surface of aggregate data by examining micro data. For instance, a question of whether abnormally high aggregate household debt ratios pose acute credit risks for banks may be easily settled if micro data on households reveal that the most indebted households also have sufficient financial buffers to protect them from sharp changes in interest costs or employment income.[70] Overall, the best assurance of a robust financial-stability assessment is to base it on a wide range of data sources.

An important component of a financial-stability assessment is an appraisal of the ability of the financial system to cope with problems, should plausible risks materialize. Stress testing is a common way to perform such appraisals. Stress testing can be based on a range of techniques, including sensitivity and scenario analyses. These approaches—increasingly used by

---

[70]See, for instance, Sveriges Riksbank (2004).

individual financial institutions[71]—are also being used at an aggregated macro level for assessing systemic stability. The IMF has introduced macroeconomic stress testing as a key element in its Financial Sector Assessment Program (FSAP).[72] Sensitivity tests are ordinarily designed to isolate the likely impact of selected risk factors such as changes in interest or exchange rates. Scenario analyses tend to be richer, involving simultaneous moves in a number of risk factors. The scenarios can be based on historical episodes of financial stress or on hypothetical events that are considered plausible, or on sets of such events. Because such approaches often have a high degree of internal consistency, they can make an important contribution to the understanding of the systemic relevance of financial risks.

While methodological advances have been made, macro stress-testing techniques as currently practiced have several limitations. The impacts of scenarios can be gauged both through bottom-up approaches—aggregating information on how a range of institutions would weather a plausible but challenging scenario—or at an aggregate level, perhaps employing a macro-econometric model. Combining the two approaches can facilitate cross-checking and more reliable assessment. However, a limitation of both approaches is that potential second-round effects of scenarios tend to be ignored because the underlying models pay insufficient attention to macro-financial interaction (as discussed in Hoggarth and Whitley, 2003). Thus, the overall impacts of adverse disturbances could well be underestimated. For instance, during a decline in the pace of economic activity sufficiently large to challenge the robustness of the banking system, weakened banks might face an increase in funding costs or a withdrawal of deposits (or both) that put further downward pressure on profits. At the same time, faced with deterioration in the creditworthiness of their customers, banks might be inclined to tighten lending terms and conditions. These events would most likely have second-round effects on aggregate demand and output, potentially leading to further losses in the banking system. Moreover, a disturbance sufficiently large to cause the failure of a large financial institution might have a direct impact on the capital, or even solvency, of other counterparty banks. Macro stress testing is generally not capable of assessing the importance or gauging the magnitude of these second-round effects.

---

[71]See Committee on the Global Financial System (2005).
[72]See IMF and World Bank (2003); Blaschke and others (2001).

Financial-stability assessments carry a higher degree of uncertainty than that ordinarily associated with forecasts based on macro-econometric models. This higher uncertainty results from the formidable practical challenges to measuring, modeling, and assessing the consequences of rare events. First, if past crises were prevented or tackled by policy actions, assessments of the likely costs of a selected scenario, based on simulations drawn from historical data sets, will likely prove to be biased unless sufficient account is taken of policy reaction functions. It is doubtful that past policy responses to episodes of financial stress could be summarized by a mechanical reaction function, particularly if the authorities were mindful of avoiding the moral hazards that typically follow from predictable behavior. Moreover, even in cases that did not prompt policy responses, the frequency of crises in historical data sets may be too low to facilitate precision in estimating the likely "policy neutral" consequences of a stylized scenario.

Second, confidence intervals around the expected output losses associated with the materialization of a specified scenario may either be not well defined statistically, or not defined at all. For instance, simulations based on historical episodes tend to be founded on statistical relationships that reflect the central tendency of, rather than the tails of, probability distributions. Moreover, for hypothetical scenarios with no basis in the past, it may not be possible to compute a confidence interval around the simulation because the events themselves may be subject to so-called Knightian uncertainty (Knight, 1921), or unquantifiable risk.

Third, most macro-econometric models used for stress testing tend to be built on the basis of log-linear relationships. For simulations, this means that a doubling of the size of a shock will result in a proportionate change in the effect. However, in reality, unpredictable nonlinearities may surface, for instance, due to threshold effects.

Fourth, as witnessed during the near collapse of Long-Term Capital Management in 1998, unexpected links—such as correlations between financial markets that do not ordinarily tend to be correlated—may surface during crises. Given such uncertainties, the real economic costs associated with a particular scenario could well prove to be larger than those predicted by an empirical model. Such considerations would suggest that the output of any stress-testing exercise should only be viewed as indicative of how, or if, the financial system would endure adverse disturbances, as opposed to an accurate quantitative assessment of actual effects on the system or its constituent parts. To avoid complacency, a high degree of caution and judgment is called for in forming financial assessments and in uncovering links.

The literature concerning measurement of the costs of financial instability is just in its formative stage and has tended to focus on the rising incidence of bank crises and their considerable costs.[73] Even defining a
systemic financial crisis is not straightforward and, once defined, several
elements must be taken into account in assessing the costs (as shown by
Hoggarth and Saporta, 2003). In measuring costs, it is particularly important to be mindful of feedback: banking crises can be caused by sluggishness in the pace of economic activity but they can, in turn, be the cause of
an economic slowdown or recession. A challenge for measurement is to
disentangle the feedback effects and isolate the quantitative impact of the
crisis on the economy. The costs associated with banking crises can include
losses faced by stakeholders—including shareholders, depositors, and other
creditors—in the banks that have failed. Taxpayers may face costs if there is
public sector resolution of the crisis. If, because of rising risk aversion or
the rationing of credit, borrowers lose access to funds or face difficulties in
accessing other sources of finance, economic activity may be adversely
affected. The incomes of depositors may also be adversely affected if banks
seek to widen spreads by lowering deposit interest rates to recoup loan
losses. Finally, if the payments system is impaired because consumers
become reluctant to make deposits with banks, the overall adverse impact
on economic activity may be magnified. For measurement, whether the
overall costs should be gauged by losses in GDP, the fiscal costs, or some
combination of the two is not clear cut. The impact on the broader macro-
economy of some crises may have been avoided because of early resolution,
resulting in the incurrence of fiscal costs. For other crises there may have
been no direct fiscal implication but a significant impact on economic
activity.

Although the wealth effects and costs of the bursting of asset-price bubbles can be gauged, less progress has been made in determining the costs of
financial market turbulence and dislocation. Possible channels would
include the direct and indirect effects of loss of access to funds for borrowers in capital markets, or the costs of refunding short-term obligations at
higher cost with financial institutions, as well as the redistributional effects
of asset-price changes, which could, in extreme situations, have direct
impacts on the capital, or even solvency, of banks.

---

[73]See Bordo and others (2001), and Garcia-Herrero and Del Rio (2003) for work on
increasing numbers of bank crises. See Lindgren, Garcia, and Saal (1996), Hoggarth and
Saporta (2003), and Barrell, Davis, and Pomerantz (2005) on the costs of bank crises.

Remaining Challenges in Design and Implementation

To advance the practice of financial-stability assessment from an art to a science, progress is needed on at least three fronts: data, models, and the understanding of links.

Data

A priority for data gathering must be micro balance sheet data covering financial institutions, households, and firms. While a picture of the aggregate risks borne within each of these sectors can be useful for financial-stability analysis, far more important is an understanding of the way in which the risks are distributed across sectors and especially whether pockets of vulnerabilities can be pinpointed. In mature economies, the availability and comprehensiveness of such data is mixed, particularly for the household sector.

It has become fashionable to employ financial-stability assessment indicators that are based on the prices of securities. In principle, if markets are efficient, indicators derived from securities prices—such as credit spreads, distances-to-default, volatilities implied by options prices, and so on—should contain invaluable information for such purposes. Securities prices should contain the collective expectations of the multitude of market participants for the underlying fundamentals governing valuations. If those market participants also have an eye on the possible impacts of the same risks and vulnerabilities that the public authorities are watching market indicators could reveal information on the ability of the financial system to weather plausible adverse disturbances. For instance, using risk-neutral densities, options prices can even facilitate the extraction of market-based probabilities of the occurrence of prespecified asset-price movements over prespecified horizons. However, the analysis risks circularity because a comprehensive financial-stability assessment should attempt to gauge whether there are plausible risks of market dislocations resulting from mispricing while inferences on market expectations are built on the assumption that prices are always "correct." More and better data on quantity indicators, such as indicators of liquidity, leverage, market positioning, and so forth, would shed light not only on the indicator properties of securities prices for financial-stability assessments but also on the vulnerabilities prevailing within financial markets.

Models

Two areas where more and better analytical research on financial-stability modeling appears necessary include models for identifying risks and vulnerabilities (early warning systems) and models for assessing the consequences of adverse disturbances.[74] The literature raises doubts that models will ever be capable of predicting crises, particularly when it comes to the precise timing. Nevertheless, this should not inhibit the development of models for assessing vulnerabilities. For example, early warning systems can play a role in weighing the importance of different indicators for financial stability and in anticipating financial stress, both within and across classes of financial institutions and within and across the various securities markets. Sets of financial market indicators provide important information that captures developments beyond these markets themselves. Various potential risks in large parts of the economic and financial system are immediately reflected in variables such as bond spreads and stock prices. Moreover, based on past experience, even simple single indicator approaches can be useful for gauging risks to financial stability (Campbell and Shiller, 2001). Ongoing work also holds promise for the development of more comprehensive frameworks for pinpointing the sets of variables (see International Monetary Fund, 2004a) and the conditions that raise the likelihood of financial stress (see, for example, Borio and Lowe, 2002). As for the prediction of crises, advances in other disciplines in the modeling of discontinuous processes, such as the prediction of earthquakes, may offer insights for financial-stability assessment.

Ideally, to accurately assess the likely impacts of adverse disturbances, dynamic general equilibrium modeling frameworks capable of measuring possibly nonlinear interaction within and between financial and nonfinancial sectors of the economy, including at the global level, would be needed. Although current tools fall far short of such a model, the implementation of macroeconomic stress-testing frameworks, such as those increasingly applied in the context of IMF FSAPs, have undoubtedly advanced the development of internally consistent frameworks for assessing the resilience of financial systems to adverse disturbances.[75] Sources of risk and vulnerability can be quantitatively mapped into their impacts on bank balance sheets,

---

[74]See Sahajwala and van den Berg (2000) for an overview of early warning systems used by some Group of Ten authorities, and Persson and Blåvarg (2003) on the use of financial market indicators.

[75]Blaschke and others (2001) review issues of measurement and methodology in stress testing, as well IMF FSAP experiences.

both individually and on a systemwide basis. However, reflecting the limitations of underlying models, current practices tend to ignore the second-round effects of financial crises. Current practices also tend to focus exclusively on the banking system when a broader definition of the financial system requires an understanding of the likely impacts on other financial institutions and on the functioning of financial markets and infrastructures. Further work needs to be conducted not only on the modeling of economic-financial interactions, the complexity of which exhibits a tendency to increase over time, but also on interactions within the financial system itself.

Links

Finally, a good understanding of links is crucial for financial-stability analysis. To ensure that important links are not missed in a financial-stability assessment, both the financial system and the sources of potential risk and vulnerability should be defined broadly. For instance, although alertness grew in the late 1990s and in 2000 of the vulnerability of the U.S. stock market to an abrupt correction, the general awareness of the possible impact on the European insurance industry—one of the places where the subsequent market tumble hurt the most—was rather limited. Little macro-prudential surveillance of the industry was being undertaken at the time. Micro balance sheet data, especially on exposures, can be helpful for identifying the relevance of links both between economic and financial sectors and within the financial system itself. As financial institutions strengthen disclosure, data availability in this area may improve over time. Cross-correlation analysis of securities prices can also be helpful for making inferences on links and channels of contagion, although sight should not be lost of the fact that during crisis periods correlations may differ markedly from those prevailing when markets are operating smoothly.

Conclusion

In recent years, financial stability has explicitly become a key objective for public policy. It is argued that finance fosters the processes of consumption, production, wealth accumulation, and risk diversification, but is subject to market failures that justify a public sector role. In this context, financial stability is defined as a situation in which the financial system efficiently allocates resources between activities and across time, assesses and manages financial risks, and absorbs shocks.

In practical terms, finance was shown in Chapter 1 to have become more important over the past decades, both quantitatively and relative to money. In addition, the financial system has become more interwoven and complex. Driving factors are the deregulation, liberalization, and globalization of financial markets. As a result, financial innovation has surged, as evidenced by the spectacular rise in securitization and derivatives, and financial activities have increasingly taken on cross-sector and cross-border dimensions. These developments have strengthened the links between financial institutions and markets, but have also complicated the analysis of financial vulnerabilities.

The analytical framework presented in this chapter takes these developments into account. An important part of the framework is the assessment of financial stability, which is considered as a continuum of possible states with ambiguous boundaries. The process of assessment should be based on a wide-ranging analysis of the system's different constituent elements (financial institutions, markets, and infrastructure) as well as on the interaction among these elements and with the external environment (the macro-economy). Depending on the assessment's outcome, policy implications fall into three broad categories—prevention, remediation, resolution—each aimed at maintaining or restoring financial stability, that is, aimed at keeping the financial system within the corridor of stability. While many of these elements relate to activities that have always been part and parcel of the work of central banks and supervisory bodies, the framework emphasizes the importance of undertaking these activities using a systemwide viewpoint.

Indeed, policymakers' approaches to financial stability as an objective in itself are changing. Monitoring, analysis, assessment, and policymaking are becoming more encompassing, focusing on the financial system as a whole rather than its individual segments, as the system itself becomes more interwoven and interdependent. The change in approach is also reflected in changes to the institutional organization of supervisory tasks, as many countries are integrating supervision into broader, cross-sectoral structures. In addition, considerable emphasis is being placed on international cooperation, for instance, the development of international codes for the supervision of banks and insurance firms (under the Basel and Solvency Accords) and for payment systems (the Lamfalussy Standards). A related initiative is the recent establishment of the Financial Stability Forum, which brings together the relevant national authorities from mature financial markets to identify and discuss weak spots in the international financial system.

The challenges that lie ahead for financial-stability analysis concern both measurement and theory, although this chapter has focused more on the former. The challenges are formidable, in part because financial-stability assessments must not only take stock of disturbances as they emerge, but also identify and examine the vulnerabilities that could lead to such disturbances in the future. A forward-looking approach is required to identify the potential buildup of financial imbalances and to account for transmission lags in policy instruments. The real difficulty is that financial crises are inherently difficult to predict, in part because of contagion effects and likely nonlinearities in both the buildup of imbalances and their transmission to the real economy. In addition, financial-stability risks often reflect the far-reaching consequences of unlikely events, implying that the focus is not the mean, median, or mode of possible outcomes but the entire distribution of outcomes, in particular the "left tail."

While macro stress-testing techniques are improving knowledge in determining the systemic relevance of plausible risks to financial stability, these techniques have important limitations, including shortcomings in the modeling of economic-financial interaction and feedback as well as the uncertainty that surrounds estimates of potential costs. Until these limitations are sufficiently addressed, the best and most pragmatic assurance of robust financial-stability assessment is to use an eclectic approach that draws upon inputs from a wide range of data sources, indicators, and models.

Looking forward, the rapid pace of financial structural changes evident since the mid-1980s is likely to continue. The shift to a larger, more integrated, leveraged, complex, and market-based financial system will continue to change the nature of financial risks. In this respect, the framework proposed in this book should be seen as a flexible tool that can be used to interpret changes and translate these into policy implications. A major challenge is to develop a deeper understanding of how the different dimensions of financial stability interact with each other and the real economy, and how these interactions are influenced by policy actions. More specifically, efforts should be focused on broadening the available data, improving the empirical tools (methodologically and analytically), and developing wide groups of indicators from which some predictive power can be derived, while also linking developments under these indicators to specific instruments. This is a heavy agenda. Undoubtedly, practical experiences will also show the way.

7

The Role of Central Banks in Ensuring Financial Stability

This chapter[76] addresses three questions:

- Do central banks have a natural role in ensuring financial stability?
- If there is a role, what does a central bank need (in the way of information, authority, and tools) to execute it effectively?
- What have central banks actually done to safeguard financial stability?

Despite a long history of central banking and of the management of financial crises, considerable controversy remains over the role of central banks in ensuring financial stability. The following two examples illustrate this point.

First, in 2000 the United Kingdom moved responsibility for banking supervision from the Bank of England to the Financial Services Authority as part of the process of creating a single financial regulator. The creation of a single financial regulator is one way of rationalizing or merging disparate organizations that are responsible for parts of the financial regulatory or supervisory framework. With the creation of the Financial Services Authority, the Bank of England, which is the lender of last resort and the ensurer of financial as well as monetary stability, relinquished its responsibility for banking supervision. An important issue raised by this example is, what kind of information does a central bank need to fulfill its mandate for ensuring financial stability and effectively providing lender-of-last-resort protection against instability?

---

[76]This chapter is based on Schinasi (2003), which was adopted from a recorded transcript of a one-hour lecture to a group of legal counselors from the central banks of selected emerging-market and transition countries.

A second example is the European Central Bank (ECB). This central bank (newly created in 1998), which is supranational, manages the monetary policy of the euro zone, composed of 12 countries. In many ways, Deutsche Bundesbank was the model for designing the ECB, both in statute and in practice. As explained more fully later in the chapter, the Bundesbank, as it existed prior to the creation of the euro zone, could be characterized as a central bank based on a "narrow" concept of central banking. The Bundesbank had a single objective—the stability of the deutsche mark—which, in domestic terms, meant price stability. In practice, the Bundesbank was a bank supervisor as well, even though there was a separate Federal Supervisory Office. The Bundesbank was responsible for collecting all the information required for good banking supervision, and it provided that information to the Federal Supervisory Office, which legally was the supervisor. The Bundesbank had a very direct and central role in banking supervision. By contrast, the ECB does not. The ECB appears to be the ultimate narrow central bank; it has a mandate for price stability only and a very small role in ensuring financial stability, confined to ensuring the smooth functioning of the TARGET[77] payments system, not the whole financial system.

Do Central Banks Have a Natural Role in Ensuring Financial Stability?

This section argues that central banks do have a natural role in ensuring financial stability. Specific features of central banking make central banks a natural contender. Consider the traditional definition of monetary stability from Henry Thornton's classic monograph, *An Enquiry into the Nature and Effects of the Paper Credit of Great Britain,* published in 1802:[78]

> To limit the amount of paper issued, and to resort for this purpose, whenever the temptation to borrow is strong, to some effectual principle of restriction; in no case, however, materially to diminish the sum in circulation, but to let it vibrate only within certain limits; to afford a slow and cautious extension of it, as the general trade of the kingdom enlarges itself; to allow of some special, though temporary, enquiries in the event of any extraordinary alarm or difficulty, as the best means of preventing a great demand at home for guineas; and to lean to the side of diminution, in the case of gold going abroad, and of the general exchanges continuing long unfavorable; this seems to be the true policy

---

[77]TARGET stands for the Trans-European Automated Real-time Gross Settlement Express Transfer System—the real-time gross settlement system for the euro.

[78]See also Capie (2000).

of the directors of an institution circumstanced like that of the Bank of Eng-land. To suffer either the solicitations of merchants, or the wishes of govern-ment, to determine the measure of the bank issues, is unquestionably to adopt a very false principle of conduct (Thornton, 1802, p. 259).

In this definition, one can see the traditional monetary policy role of a central bank. It has all the ingredients of managing monetary aggregates and interest rates. It has embedded in it the monetary transmission mech-anism and references to monetary targets.

Turning to Thornton's views on what may be interpreted as the role of the Bank of England in ensuring financial stability at that time, three pas-sages from his classic work appear relevant:

If any one bank fails, a general run upon the neighboring ones is apt to take place, which if not checked in the beginning by pouring into the circulation a large quantity of gold, leads to very extensive mischief (p. 180).

[I]f the Bank of England, in future seasons of alarm, should be disposed to extend its discounts in a greater degree than heretofore, then the threatened calamity may be averted through the generosity of that institution (p. 188).

It is by no means intended to imply that it would become the Bank of England to relieve every distress which the rashness of country banks may bring upon them: the bank, by doing this, might encourage their improvidence. There seems to be a medium at which a public bank should aim in granting aid to inferior establishments, and which it often must find it very difficult to be observed. The relief should neither be so prompt and liberal as to exempt those who misconduct their business from all the natural consequences of their fault, nor so scanty and slow as deeply to involve the general interests. These interests, nevertheless, are sure to be pleaded by every distressed person whose affairs are large, however indifferent or even ruinous may be their state (p. 188).

The first passage describes a process of contagion that is likely to occur with a run on one bank. The second describes the role of the Bank of Eng-land in a crisis. The third passage describes the concept of moral hazard, which is taken up in Chapter 8 of this volume. The three passages together show clearly that Thornton had a working definition of the role of central banks in financial stability.

Consider a more modern view of the role of central banks in ensuring financial stability, which is consistent with Thornton's view. The following view was expressed by Paul Volcker in 1984, when he was Chairman of the Board of Governors of the U.S. Federal Reserve System:

A basic continuing responsibility of any central bank—and the principal reason for the founding of the Federal Reserve—is to assure stable and smoothly func-tioning financial and payments systems. These are prerequisites for, and complementary to, the central bank's responsibility for conducting monetary policy as it is more narrowly conceived . . . To these ends, the U.S. Congress has over the last 70 years authorized the Federal Reserve (1) to be a major participant in the nation's payments mechanism; (2) to lend at the discount window as the ultimate source of liquidity for the economy; and (3) to regulate and supervise key sectors of the financial markets, both domestic and international. These functions are in addition to, and largely predate, the more purely "monetary" functions of engaging in open market and foreign exchange operations and setting reserve requirements; historically, in fact, the "monetary" functions were largely grafted onto the "supervisory" functions, not the reverse (Volcker, 1984, p. 548).

According to Volcker, the Federal Reserve System was first the ensurer of financial stability and secondarily the manager of monetary stability. Certain key points made by Thornton and Volcker establish the reasons for central banks to have a natural role in financial stability.

First, the central bank is the only provider of the legal means of payment and of immediate liquidity. That is, only the central bank provides "finality of payment."

The second natural role for the central bank is to ensure the smooth functioning of the national payments system. It is within the context of the soundness and stability of national payments systems that policymakers have traditionally and naturally considered systemic risk. Traditionally, systemic risk has been viewed as the possibility that problems at one bank would create problems at other banks, in particular, banks that make up the core of the national payments system. In this view, problems at one bank would cascade through the payments system and perhaps lead to bottlenecks in payments and the possibility of a widespread domino effect. The payments system, being the core of the financial market, has been the subject of much discussion, policy, and reform. Through Group of Ten efforts, there now exist real-time gross payments settlements systems that try to prevent the failure of one institution from cascading through the payments system and affecting other institutions within the payments system. So, again, the central bank has a natural role to play in financial stability—even if it is confined to the payments system.

The third natural role relates to the fact that the banking system is the transmission mechanism through which monetary policy has its effect, in the first instance, on the real economy. If the banking system is experiencing distress, the central bank will find it difficult to provide the liquidity necessary to achieve its monetary objectives. For this reason alone, central banks have a natural interest in sound financial institutions and stable financial markets. Central banks have, therefore, an interest in maintaining the stability of the banking system, in having the ability to see problems at an early stage, and in being in a position to influence corrective actions.

Finally, monetary stability and financial stability are explicitly linked. In Anna Schwartz's definition of a financial crisis, she refers to the propensity for the money supply to collapse (Schwartz, 1986). One simple equation makes this clear. Basic money-and-banking courses often begin with an equation called the money multiplier, which establishes a relationship (some would even say an identity, if these parameters are fixed) between central bank money B held as bank reserves by the banking system and the money supply M. Formally,

$$M = mB$$

that is, the money stock (M) is equal to high-powered money or the monetary base (B) times the money multiplier (m). This can be written explicitly as follows:

$$M = \left[\frac{1 + \dfrac{C}{D}}{\dfrac{C}{D} + \dfrac{R}{D}} \right] B,$$

where C/D is the currency to deposit ratio of the public, and R/D is the cash (or reserves) to deposit ratio of the banks.

It has not been made clear in the above discussion whether M is a narrow monetary aggregate (comprised only of base money and demand deposits) or a broad monetary aggregate (comprised of base money, demand deposits, and time deposits, and perhaps even money-market mutual funds): that will depend on what the ratios C/D and R/D are. Regardless, the money supply of the economy is directly linked to what the central bank provides in the way of central bank money. In the midst of a financial crisis, a run on liquidity could occur. Everyone will demand liquidity (and the finality of payment), and everyone in the system understands that the only liquidity that really exists is central bank money, that is, base money B. In this rush for central bank money, the money supply shrinks because the ratio C/D increases very rapidly as everyone increases C and reduces D. If the money supply (M) is shrinking very rapidly in the presence of financial instability, it will not take long before the central bank will have to supply liquidity, or (B), to restore monetary stability as the monetary aggregates collapse, because monetary stability objectives (unquestionably the central bank's responsibility) are less likely to be achieved, even in the short run, without more central bank money. So when financial instability occurs, monetary instability is likely to follow. This establishes a link between the natural role of the central bank as the provider of payment finality and its role in financial stability.

What Does the Central Bank Need to Execute This Role Effectively?

There are competing views on the question of what the central bank needs to execute its role. The first view might be characterized as the "open market operations view," which holds that the conduct of monetary policy inherently conflicts with the conduct of broader financial policies. If a central bank has responsibility for achieving monetary objectives (keeping inflation in some target range, for example) and also has responsibility for banking supervision, the question that arises is whether the central bank will face a situation in which the viability of several large banks critically depends on interest rates but at the same time the central bank needs to tighten monetary policy to achieve its monetary objectives. What then does the central bank do? Does it raise interest rates by 300 basis points to achieve its monetary objectives, thereby risking the viability of some large banks? Or does it relax its commitment to its monetary objectives, thereby saving these banks and presumably the financial system?

The open market operations view argues that the central bank should maintain its commitment to its monetary objectives (for example, a monetary-aggregate or interest-rate target), because it contends that the tools the central bank has to implement monetary policy—open market operations—can also be used to inject liquidity into the financial system appropriate for safeguarding the financial system from the collapse of large banks and from any contagion that might occur.[79] The argument rests on first, the central banks' ability to obtain good collateral in return for the central bank money it provides to banks through its market operations, and second, the belief that the market itself can distinguish quickly between solvent and insolvent institutions; that is, the market can distinguish between those institutions that have liquidity needs but are otherwise solvent and viable institutions, and those institutions that are having difficulties obtaining liquidity because they truly are insolvent. The relevance of collateral in this argument is that if a bank has good collateral, it is not illiquid, and if it is insolvent it will not have good collateral.

---

[79]See Prati and Schinasi (1999a) for a fuller discussion of these views and references to original sources.

The alternative view is the "banking policy view." The banking policy view also recognizes this inherent conflict between achieving both monetary objectives and broader financial policy objectives. However, it is more transparent, and therefore more pragmatic, about how difficult it is to distinguish illiquid from insolvent institutions and, in particular, how difficult it is for private stakeholders with limited information to discriminate between illiquid and insolvent institutions. For example, a bank may have assets it could use as collateral but they may be illiquid collateral, such as a commercial builiding. In this case, even a solvent bank may not be able to trade its collateral for the cash it needs to conduct its business. Therefore, the banking policy view holds that the central bank has a role to play by helping the market to distinguish between illiquid and insolvent institutions. In the banking policy view, the central bank has a banking supervisory function. This function helps the central bank know the banking system and know the banks through which it conducts its monetary policy so that when uncertainty arises about the liquidity or solvency of a large (systemically important) bank, it has current and useful information about the strength and soundness of each of the institutions it supervises. In this view, the distribution of liquidity injections matters as well. Open market operations may not be sufficient to deal with bank runs and financial crises and the central bank does have a natural role in banking supervision and the broader financial policy–financial stability function.

The Central Bank and Prevention

Regardless of what role the central bank plays, as examined in previous chapters of this study, a financial system should have in place both self-correcting market mechanisms—which work mostly because of effective market discipline—and an infrastructure for identifying vulnerabilities, preventing those vulnerabilities from leading to crises, and dealing with crises should these other safeguards of financial stability fail. The key elements of prevention consist of the following:

- market discipline
  internal incentive systems within financial institutions
  risk management and control systems
  market transparency and effective disclosure of financial information
  stakeholder governance (shareholders, counterparties)
- banking supervision
- market surveillance (both on-exchange and over-the-counter markets)

Market discipline is one of the first lines of defense against systemic problems. If market discipline is working, individual financial institutions that make mistakes will pay for those mistakes early on. The four critical components to market discipline identified above all play an important role.

Are there reasons to believe that private market discipline alone would be insufficient to prevent problems from arising? Yes, and one of the most important of these reasons is the existence of a financial safety net. In return for access to the financial safety net, each institution is subject to banking supervision and required to hold a minimum amount of capital and conform to regulatory requirements, including best practices regarding accounting standards and business conduct. The required capital acts as a cushion to absorb losses—losses that the taxpayer will not have to bear. Prudent management also requires adherence to strict accounting standards. The accounting standards are in place so that whatever losses are suffered will be reported and disclosed quickly. In some cases, disclosure occurs within a month, in most cases, within a quarter. Shareholders have access to that information and can act as a disciplining force on the institution.

An example of market discipline at work is the way in which some financial institutions were affected after the near collapse of Long-Term Capital Management (LTCM) in the autumn of 1998. (A more extensive explanation of the LTCM crisis can be found in Box 9.1.) Internationally active financial institutions were the major counterparties of the hedge fund LTCM in the autumn of 1998. Even though no one fully understood how large or small the losses of these institutions would be, the behavior of stock prices was telling. The share prices of some of these institutions declined by up to 40 percent within a week. The institutions that suffered those equity price losses received a clear message that shareholders disapproved of their behavior in the period leading up to the LTCM problem. Thus, shareholders have a role and the only way that shareholders can really exact an accurate penalty on firms is if there is good accounting disclosure—which circles back to the best practices requirements for access to the financial safety net.

Banking supervision and market surveillance also provide important defenses against systemic problems and are part of the infrastructure that facilitates effective market discipline. As noted in Part I, because finance is a fragile process owing to its dependence on trust and confidence, there are negative externalities associated with it. But because finance facilitates important economic processes (such as resource allocation, savings and investment, and growth), there are also positive externalities, and finance provides public goods. Financial infrastructures (rules, laws, and regulations) are required to ensure that finance provides a maximum of benefits and a minimum of costs to the economy. Financial safety nets, such as deposit insurance and taxpayer-financed payments and settlement systems, are an important part of this infrastructure and are designed to encourage risk-taking and financial activity beyond a certain minimum threshold to create efficiency gains for society at large.

The supervision of individual financial institutions, especially banks, and the surveillance of markets together help to ensure that the incentives for risk-taking and financial activity provided by safety nets do not lead to excesses. Such excesses can occur, in part, because they can be exploited by the institutions and market participants that benefit directly from them. Banking supervision provides safeguards against a bank exploiting deposit insurance by taking undue risks with government-insured deposits. Market surveillance helps ensure that market rules and regulations are enforced, that financial institutions with direct access to payments systems do not exploit them to the detriment of their clients or counterparts, and that market forces do not lead to the accumulation of detrimental market imbalances. In effect, banking supervision and market surveillance are vehicles through which the authorities can detect weaknesses in institutions and markets before they become significant enough to threaten the stability of the banking system, financial markets, and the financial system as a whole.

The IMF's 1999 *International Capital Markets* report includes a chapter on managing global finance, in which the authors tried to step back from the turbulence in the mature markets in the fall of 1998 to draw lessons. There were certainly failures in private risk management and shortcomings in disclosure and other aspects of market discipline. However, weaknesses in banking supervision and market surveillance also contributed. How could the kind of vulnerabilities that built up in the two years preceding the LTCM crisis not be detected at individual institutions through internal risk management and control systems and banking supervision, and in the markets through market surveillance? The report does not provide definitive answers, but it does provide analyses about what banking supervision and market surveillance can do to identify these vulnerabilities before they build up to the point where a crisis occurs. In particular, more proactive (but not necessarily more intrusive) banking supervision and more proactive market surveillance can be useful in identifying vulnerabilities before they become financial crises.

The Central Bank and Crisis Resolution

Key elements for crisis resolution include the following:

- a legal framework for bankruptcy and closeout procedures for financial contracts

- exit strategies for insolvent institutions (large and small)
- lender-of-last-resort function in the central bank

First, crisis resolution requires a clear and effective legal framework for bankruptcy, and requires closeout procedures for financial markets and contracts. Closeout procedures are, in effect, a last resort, credit-risk mitigation technique. If all else fails, closeout procedures allow a claimant to make good on at least part of the claim against a defaulting party. One of the lessons from LTCM was that even in the most advanced financial markets in the world, closeout procedures could not be relied on. Nor could netting arrangements.

The second part of crisis resolution is an exit strategy for insolvent institutions. To the extent that fiscal and monetary authorities become engaged with insolvent institutions, exit strategies for public agencies are required as well. As is well known, Japan has supplied a significant amount of public funds to its banking system in return for restructuring. It has structured those injections of public monies so that it can exact governance, either by ultimately taking over the banks and their management or by selling the banks' shares in the market. Whenever a government intervenes in a bank directly, it needs to have an exit strategy. One of the most practical exit strategies would be holding publicly traded shares in the company (which can be sold, to exit).

Another key element of crisis resolution is the lender-of-last-resort function of the central bank. As suggested earlier in this chapter, and as examined in detail in Part I of this book, financial crises often involve a loss of trust in counterparty relationships, a loss of confidence in the stability of markets, and a significant increase in the demand for central bank money—the surrogate for trust and the source of liquidity in an economy. The central bank is the ultimate and immediate provider of liquidity either through its market operations or directly to institutions that are deemed to be illiquid but solvent. Market participants must feel confident that when a crisis occurs, that either self-correcting market mechanisms will continue to function or the central bank will stand ready to help facilitate market activities until confidence is restored and self-correcting market mechanisms are able to function normally again. In having the ability—and in most countries, the obligation—to help maintain smoothly functioning markets, in part through the provision of liquidity when it is needed, the central bank is a vital element of crisis resolution. When providing temporary liquidity during a crisis, the central bank must also be aware of the implications of these temporary actions on its ability to continue to achieve its monetary objectives. This often requires "mopping up" the liquidity once confidence is restored.

Evolving Issues about the Role of the Central Bank and Financial Stability

Several issues are still evolving regarding prevention and resolution of financial crises and the role of the central bank. These issues include the role of the European Central Bank in ensuring financial stability in the euro zone; the relationship between the Bank of England as lender of last resort and the U.K. Financial Services Authority as the relatively new single regulator and supervisor; and the 1999 U.S. banking law, the Gramm-Leach-Bliley Act, which shifted the emphasis of supervision and regulation for U.S. financial conglomerates in the direction of the Federal Reserve System.

Issues concerning the role of the central bank focus on three key elements. One is, can market participants who are the agents of market discipline distinguish illiquid from insolvent institutions during a crisis and thereby continue to perform a useful market disciplining role during that crisis? A conclusion that can be drawn from the turbulence that followed the collapse and private rescue of LTCM is that in a panic, there is no market discipline. It is a situation akin to a panic in a full movie theater that has only three or four exit doors, and when all patrons smell smoke and rush for the exits at the same time. Even if there is no fire, some people get hurt because everyone is rushing for the exits simultaneously. During the LTCM crisis, there was good reason for everyone to try to exit the markets.

Given that there is a role for some official participation in crisis resolution, and given that the central bank is the only provider of payment finality—of central bank money—the central bank is the only practical lender of last resort. Even if it is not the lender of last resort (which might ultimately be a Treasury), it is the immediate provider of liquidity during a crisis. This leads to the second key issue. In fulfilling its role as lender of last resort, can the central bank clearly distinguish illiquid from insolvent institutions while in the middle of a crisis (and while market participants fail to provide market discipline)?[80] A corollary to that question is whether the central bank really needs to distinguish between illiquid and insolvent institutions. Going back to the open market operations view, the central bank often only needs to provide liquidity to the market, rather than to specific institutions. The market will then sort out how to distribute that liquidity. It can be argued that this would be the case if a relatively limited

---

[80]As discussed earlier, whether the central bank can distinguish illiquidity from insolvency depends importantly on whether or not the central bank has timely access to the information necessary for analyzing the soundness of a financial institution.

number of smaller institutions are experiencing difficulties, in which case liquidity provided to the market might be sufficient. If larger institutions are involved, institution-specific injections of liquidity (not capital) might be required. In these cases the central bank would need to have information to distinguish illiquid from insolvent. If it is known that a bank is insolvent, the authorities would probably use an alternative mechanism to resolve the problem. The central bank would not want to rely on a lender-of-last-resort role.

The third key element is what kind of information a central bank needs to effectively execute its role as lender of last resort and whether it needs to be directly involved in banking supervision. In considering this question it is helpful to study the actual practices of central banks, which vary across countries. First is the concept of central banking adopted by the U.S. Federal Reserve System (as discussed in the Volcker quote). The U.S. Federal Reserve's responsibilities could be identified, in both its monetary policy and financial policymaking mandates, to be those of a broadly conceived central bank. It has many mandates, only one of which is the conduct of monetary policy.

At the other extreme is the role of the European System of Central Banks (ESCB) in financial stability in the euro zone, which is difficult to discuss concretely because the euro zone has only been in existence since January 4, 1999. The ESCB is composed of the ECB and 12 national central banks. Some of these national central banks have responsibility for banking supervision, and some do not. Separate national agencies are responsible for banking supervision in the countries in which the central bank does not have that authority. The ESCB decision-making body has 18 votes, 12 of which are distributed among the national authorities, and six of which are retained by the ECB Executive Board. Even if all national central banks had responsibility for banking supervision, there might be a conflict in the presence of a crisis. What to do? Who gets the information? How quickly does the ECB get information, so that its votes can carry accurate information to the board table?

If one takes the ECB as the central body of the ESCB, the ECB has little responsibility for ensuring financial stability. The following four passages describe the ESCB's functions related to prudential supervision and the stability of the payments and financial systems:

- First, Article 25(1) of the ESCB Statute envisions a specific advisory function for the ECB in the field of European Community legislation relating to the prudential supervision of credit institutions and the stability of the financial system. Whenever the European Union proposes legislation that directly bears on financial stability issues, a draft of the legislation goes to the ECB for comment. The ECB can exert whatever influence it has, but it has no specific role.

- Second, Article 105(5) of the Maastricht Treaty stipulates that "the ESCB shall *contribute* to the smooth conduct of policies *pursued by the competent authorities* relating to the prudential supervision of credit institutions and the stability of the financial system" [emphasis added]. Thus, the Maastricht Treaty establishes that the ESCB is not the competent authority, either for prudential supervision of credit institutions or for the stability of the financial system.
- Third, Article 105(6) of the Maastricht Treaty states that "the Council may, acting unanimously on a proposal from the Commission and after consulting the ECB and after receiving the assent of the European Parliament, confer upon the ECB specific tasks concerning policies relating to the prudential supervision of credit institutions and other financial institutions with the exception of insurance undertakings." This mechanism allows the EU Commission to recommend to national parliaments and the European Parliament (in consultation with the ECB) to provide responsibilities for banking supervision to the ECB, thereby confirming that the ECB has no banking supervision or financial-stability mandate.
- Fourth, the ECB is given a more explicit role in relation to the working of the payments system. Article 105(2) of the Maastricht Treaty stipulates that one of the basic tasks of the ESCB "shall be to promote the smooth functioning of the payments system." Article 22 of the ESCB Statute is more specific, stating that "the ECB and national central banks may provide facilities, and the ECB may issue ECB regulations to ensure efficient and sound clearing and payments systems within the Community and with other countries." As this passage indicates, the ECB has a mandate for ensuring the smooth functioning of the target payments system within Europe. A rigorous reading of the Maastricht Treaty and the ECB Statute or the ESCB Statute would suggest that this is the ECB's only tangible mandate in the financial stability area—to ensure the smooth functioning of the payments system. This mandate is not insignificant, but it does not truly encompass financial markets stability.

To summarize, the broad central bank as in the United States contrasts sharply with a narrow central bank as in the European Monetary Union. The U.K. system lies somewhere in between, in that the central bank has the lender-of-last-resort role and has a role in ensuring financial stability, but has no mandate for banking supervision. A memorandum of understanding between the Bank of England, the U.K. supervisor, and Her Majesty's Treasury ensures that the Bank of England will have free and open access to whatever information it needs to carry out its mandates (Bank of England, 1997).

How Far Have Central Banks Gone to Ensure Financial Stability?

The final question is to what extent central banks have exercised their powers in safeguarding financial stability. As noted, these powers might be limited to market surveillance, or might be as broad as encompassing responsibility for banking supervision. In most cases, central banks are the immediate provider of liquidity to institutions with adequate collateral (if not the lender of last resort). In deciding whether collateral is adequate, central banks may have to decide, on behalf of taxpayers, whether it is necessary to incur financial risk—such as liquidity and credit risk—when it lends to financial institutions in need of lender-of-last-resort assistance. Three examples serve to shed some light on this question.

Barings plc

Barings plc, the oldest merchant banking group in the United Kingdom (established in 1762), was placed in "administration" (a court-supervised reorganization) by the Bank of England on February 27, 1995, because it experienced losses exceeding its entire equity capital—estimated to be around US$850 million at the time. The losses resulted from, among other things, inadequate risk-management controls surrounding very large accumulated unhedged trading positions in futures contracts on the Nikkei 225 stock index.[81] In this case, the Bank of England, along with other official bodies including Her Majesty's Treasury, probably decided that Barings was not systemically important. It was a small, at best medium-size bank, and it was not central to the U.K. payments system. The Bank of England, because of its banking supervisory role at the time, apparently understood the relationships Barings had with U.K. counterparts and with other European counterparts and over a weekend was able to determine, and then to decide, that Barings could be allowed to fail. If a ready and able buyer would have acquired Barings over the weekend, the Bank of England probably would have been very receptive, but that did not occur. In this case, the financial-stability role of the central bank was to decide how important the institution

---

[81]For further details and analyses see IMF (1995).

was for the U.K. financial system and the European financial system, and the central bank decided Barings was not important enough to save.

Long-Term Capital Management

LTCM was a $4 billion hedge fund—relatively small for advanced markets, certainly small for the U.S. financial market. (The notional value of outstanding derivative contracts in the world, as of the end of 1998, was estimated to be $80 trillion. The U.S. repurchase market had an outstanding daily value of $1 trillion.) LTCM was not federally "bailed out" because no public monies were used; it was a private rescue. A coordination failure among 17 major counterparty financial institutions of LTCM prompted the U.S. Federal Reserve to become involved to facilitate the rescue. As it turned out, 17 institutions did not participate in the rescue, only 14 institutions did. There appear to be two main reasons for the Fed's actions. One was to maintain financial stability; even with the private rescue and the 75 basis point reduction in interest rate, tremendous turbulence occurred in the deepest and most liquid markets in the world. The second reason the Fed may have intervened and, in particular, the reason the Fed lowered the interest rate 75 basis points, was that there was a real future threat to monetary stability—if risk-taking was not restored to at least a normal level, it is conceivable that even small businesses, viable businesses, thriving businesses, would not have been able to receive the credit needed to conduct day-to-day operations, posing a threat to monetary stability. In short, one can make the argument that the Fed acted for both monetary and financial-stability reasons. (See Box 9.1 for a detailed explanation of the events surrounding the near failure of LTCM.)

Hong Kong Equity Markets

The third example is that of the Hong Kong Monetary Authority (HKMA) intervening in the Hong Kong SAR equity markets during the Asian crisis in 1997. It is extremely unusual for a central bank to intervene in an equity market, especially in a sophisticated international financial center such as Hong Kong SAR. But the HKMA was confronted with very unusual circumstances, which it apparently viewed to be near life threatening for the Hong Kong SAR economy. This assessment was based on objective factors at the time, but was also influenced by the experiences of other countries in Asia that had suffered severe financial and economic distress during the Asian crises in 1997–98.

In particular, beginning in mid-1997, Thailand, Indonesia, and the Republic of Korea in rapid succession all experienced the beginnings of severe financial crises and economic crises. By the end of 1997 all three countries were in the throes of economic depressions. Other economies in the Asian region also experienced pressures in financial markets and on their economies, in part because of the financial and economic links within Asia. In addition, global investors were running for financial security, cutting their losses, and rebalancing their portfolios in light of perceived heightened risks. As in all episodes of market turbulence, there were, allegedly, speculators who were trying to profit from the asset-price declines occurring on some of the currency markets and equity markets, including the HK$, which came under severe pressure.

Between August 14 and 28, 1998, the HKMA bought a total of some US$15 billion in stocks and futures in the Hong Kong SAR equity market, constituting 7 percent of the capitalization and between 20 percent and 35 percent of the free float of the Hang Seng index. The authorities explained their intervention as being targeted toward a specific group of speculators that were manipulating equity and foreign exchange markets for profit in what was then called a "double-play," that is, a simultaneous attack on equity and currency markets. One possible reason for the intervention was for financial stability; the second reason was for monetary stability. The Hong Kong SAR economy was likely to be subject to widespread systemic problems if the equity market collapsed, and the HKMA came to the decision that it was necessary to take some risk and intervene in the equity market to restore stability to markets and sustain the stability of the Honk Kong SAR economy.

Conclusion

The experience of the advanced countries drawn on in this chapter suggest that in the realm of financial stability—as opposed to monetary stability—central banks

- have a natural role to play in ensuring financial stability;
- at times may require supervisory information to execute this natural role;
- have incurred risks to their balance sheets to ensure financial stability.

A key issue in deciding how far central banks can go in intervening in financial markets to ensure financial stability is the amount of risk a central bank should shoulder in its activities with the market, either on its balance sheet or in its off-balance sheet pursuits.

PART III

THE BENEFITS AND CHALLENGES OF MODERN FINANCE

This part of the study is a series of four essays examining the ongoing challenges to financial efficiency and stability posed by recent structural changes in national and global finance. Many of the changes began some 20 years or so ago, and have accelerated in importance in the past few years. Others are relatively more current.

Each of these essays examines structural changes that are no doubt improving financial and economic efficiency, but may also be posing new risks or redistributing existing risks in ways that are poorly understood and that may have systemic implications.

The chapters are sequenced so that they progress from a very high level of generality and broadness (the globalization of finance) to successively lower levels of generality (the financial market activities of insurance and reinsurance companies).

Chapter 8 addresses the challenges of the globalization of finance and risk, both at the national and international levels. In many ways, the broad challenges discussed in Chapter 8 encompass all the other challenges examined in subsequent chapters, so it serves as an introduction and summary of the remaining challenges in ensuring financial stability—many of which are discussed in more detail later.

Chapter 9 examines the over-the-counter (OTC) derivatives markets and how they have changed the nature of finance and banking in our modern world. Both benefits and challenges are discussed, with more focus on the latter.

Chapter 10 examines the implications for financial stability of the increased reliance on efficiency-enhancing risk transfer mechanisms; it focuses in particular on credit derivatives.

Chapter 11 discusses the supervisory, regulatory, and perhaps systemic challenges raised by the now greater role of insurance companies (and implicitly of other institutional investors) in financial and capital market activities.

Chapter 12 summarizes the broad areas identified throughout the book, and particularly in Part III, where reforms are most needed.

8

Challenges Posed by the Globalization of Finance and Risk

While it is reasonable to presume that the structural financial changes that occurred in international markets since the mid- to late 1970s have been beneficial overall, it would be complacent to ignore, and not try to reduce, the costs and adverse consequences of these changes. The structural features that now characterize the modern international financial system seem to have simultaneously increased the efficiency, volume, and volatility of international financial activity. They have also been associated with an increase in the complexity of financial transactions, the integration of national financial markets, the creation of large internationally active financial institutions, and the redistribution of financial risk ownership. Based on experiences in the 1990s and early 2000s—with asset-price volatility and bubbles, dramatic shifts in asset allocations and international capital flows, financial market turbulence, and financial crises—a lack of understanding about these structural changes might have increased the potential for mispricing and misallocating capital within the international financial system, and for financial turbulence and instability. This chapter examines several challenges to financial stability associated with these structural changes, with a view to identifying areas in which improvements can be made in the ability to maintain both financial efficiency and international financial stability. In the remainder of the chapter, these structural financial changes taken together will be referred to as the *globalization of finance*.

The first section of the chapter briefly discusses the globalization of finance (encompassing financial modernization and internationalization, greater securitization, and market integration) and identifies the key structural financial changes that have occurred since the mid- to late 1970s. These structural financial changes are posing a number of challenges to

Table 8.1. Cross-Border Transactions in Bonds and Equities
(Percent of GDP)

	1975–79	1980–84	1985–89	1990–94	1995–99	2000–03	2001	2002	2003
United States									
Bonds	4.0	9.4	63.6	93.9	139.0	188.0	161.4	208.4	262.1
Equities	1.9	3.6	9.9	14.7	45.0	90.8	87.4	85.0	82.1
Japan									
Bonds	2.2	9.8	115.3	72.9	63.7	70.2	73.7	73.8	77.8
Equities	1.1	4.4	14.9	9.6	17.2	36.5	36.7	33.1	35.3
Germany									
Bonds	5.3	9.7	37.8	86.5	208.7	350.5	378.7	351.1	394.0
Equities	1.9	3.4	11.7	14.9	48.6	132.6	133.6	115.6	112.2
France									
Bonds	...	6.8	21.9	108.6	233.5	293.9	288.1	299.3	362.0
Equities	...	2.4	12.1	16.9	56.1	150.7	140.2	138.1	154.0
Canada									
Bonds	1.2	3.9	29.3	104.5	216.6	149.5	135.6	157.0	175.8
Equities	3.3	6.5	14.8	19.2	52.3	122.8	101.9	151.5	132.1
Italy¹	0.9	1.4	9.4	114.7	518.8	1,126.5	821.9	1,197.0	1,705.2

Sources: Bank for International Settlements; and national balance of payments data.
Note: Gross purchases and sales of securities between residents and nonresidents.
¹No breakdown in bonds and equities is available.

both private market participants and national authorities responsible for prudential oversight. The second section of the chapter examines challenges in four broad areas that might have financial-stability implications: transparency and disclosure, market dynamics, moral hazard, and systemic risk. In each of these areas, the main challenges are either directly or indirectly related to the actual structural financial changes that have come to characterize the modern international financial system. One common theme is that the existing frameworks for ensuring international financial stability— a composite of private market discipline and nationally oriented prudential oversight—do not appear to have kept sufficient pace with structural changes. A final section suggests ways forward in dealing with some of these challenges. Two presumptions are maintained throughout the analysis: first, international financial stability is a global public good, one that needs to be nurtured collectively and continuously if it is to be preserved; and second, as the international financial system evolves, so, too, will the collective challenges of ensuring its stability.

The Process of Globalization and Its Impact on the International Financial System

The structural changes that occurred in national and international finance since the mid- to late 1970s—when financial liberalization began in earnest—are part of a complex process best described as the globalization (and modernization) of finance. Financial globalization has been a necessary counterpart to the expansion of international trade and payments, the growing financing needs of countries and market participants, the globalization of national economies, and the expanding opportunities for international investments. While each of these processes has driven economic and financial developments during much of recent history, the processes themselves as well as their consequences have accelerated along with recent advances in information and computer technologies. In many ways, the 1990s was the first full decade in which a critical mass of these structural changes manifested themselves in international financial markets.

Key elements of this ongoing transformation are

- the integration of national financial markets, investor bases, and borrowers into a global financial marketplace, with greater diversity in the quality, sophistication, and geographic origin of borrowers and lenders (Tables 8.1, 8.2, and 8.3);

Table 8.2. International Equity Issues by Selected Industrial and Developing Countries and Regions
(Millions of U.S. dollars)

	1990	1991	1992	1993	1994	1995	1996	1997	1998	1999	2000	2001	2002	2003	2004
Industrial countries															
Belgium	0.0	0.0	0.0	266.2	96.5	169.1	1,498.2	1,192.8	349.2	1,529.7	3,727.3	406.1	211.9	1,197.4	4,633.7
Canada	83.5	467.3	268.2	528.5	360.5	1,761.6	1,377.3	3,228.8	1,237.9	5,443.0	5,286.1	1,983.6	4,302.8	1,430.9	10,783.9
France	896.2	1,273.7	1,553.9	4,198.1	6,895.4	2,492.6	5,965.7	9,810.3	12,003.2	12,347.3	14,200.1	15,471.2	8,787.9	13,248.7	24,104.4
Germany	251.1	437.6	261.8	314.2	4,482.0	4,023.1	6,952.1	5,644.8	4,918.7	13,919.1	23,090.1	4,313.5	4,456.6	14,553.5	18,657.8
Italy	132.3	521.8	755.6	631.9	2,643.8	3,328.9	3,504.9	8,448.1	6,901.6	6,181.0	3,883.6	3,766.4	1,757.8	2,341.8	11,843.7
Japan	872.4	0.0	47.2	0.0	444.9	153.9	841.2	1,872.1	9,908.1	10,413.8	9,375.0	6,761.6	2,268.3	4,780.3	7,169.5
Luxembourg	0.0	0.0	0.0	62.1	362.6	115.0	160.1	85.0	972.1	10.2	613.6	93.5	162.5	99.4	2,929.7
Netherlands	667.2	628.4	32.4	1,283.7	3,847.2	4,876.8	6,581.7	5,270.0	4,746.9	17,425.8	22,248.4	8,590.2	6,538.6	7,091.2	3,394.9
Sweden	308.5	6.5	130.1	1,129.8	2,841.0	1,120.8	2,444.8	2,631.6	575.4	753.9	6,057.9	1,545.9	4,518.3	363.2	4,466.6
Switzerland	148.3	0.0	517.7	0.0	74.9	817.2	502.6	2,648.2	5,461.2	5,208.7	6,935.1	5,099.0	6,602.6	4,553.4	3,887.9
United Kingdom	2,904.2	4,024.9	3,691.2	3,260.2	3,776.5	4,735.2	7,202.4	8,021.1	6,386.3	12,431.4	18,041.1	17,616.1	4,913.5	4,698.3	16,137.6
United States	1,698.8	5,740.4	7,852.8	10,323.2	5,278.8	8,110.1	8,968.9	10,239.8	11,273.0	16,392.8	19,554.5	6,536.1	1,603.2	481.8	409.9
Developing countries and regions															
Africa															
South Africa	0.0	143.4	144.3	57.1	206.8	379.0	641.0	984.9	409.0	601.1	1,971.9	277.3	329.8	1,083.3	1,571.1

Asia															
Hong Kong SAR	0.0	287.8	313.8	844.3	410.7	1,546.9	6,716.6	4,968.2	1,460.4	5,245.2	11,546.0	1,605.5	3,867.1	6,086.3	7,551.8
Indonesia	586.0	109.6	118.7	344.9	1,321.5	1,162.2	1,310.1	1,290.6	0.0	810.3	27.8	305.8	238.9	1,166.6	726.1
Korea, Rep. of	40.0	200.0	150.0	328.2	1,167.9	1,310.0	1,150.9	630.0	495.5	6,870.7	964.7	3,676.4	1,553.7	1,222.6	4,855.3
Malaysia	0.0	0.0	384.9	0.0	0.0	568.9	599.8	424.3	161.8	0.0	194.5	26.7	1,065.6	555.6	786.0
Philippines	31.6	97.9	333.1	125.9	948.9	808.7	1,000.7	265.1	462.9	228.4	194.6	0.0	43.5	103.9	97.2
Singapore	151.9	184.2	274.4	564.0	327.6	474.7	421.0	712.3	765.3	4,527.0	3,501.6	1,657.6	1,746.7	1,494.0	2,163.5
Thailand	82.5	134.3	13.0	458.8	759.2	531.5	170.3	28.3	2,265.2	1,697.1	44.0	225.3	56.3	1,483.2	1,024.8
Europe															
Czech Republic	0.0	0.0	0.0	0.0	9.9	32.0	104.0	0.0	123.9	0.0	0.0	0.0	0.0	815.1	174.4
Hungary	69.1	87.4	11.9	7.7	200.3	258.8	351.1	1,668.8	157.4	479.0	19.1	0.0	0.0	13.2	860.2
Poland	0.0	0.0	0.0	0.0	0.0	68.5	17.3	765.5	926.9	628.7	384.2	0.0	217.3	667.0	778.9
Turkey	45.6	0.0	0.0	178.3	374.7	142.5	11.8	409.6	837.6	0.0	2,437.1	0.0	54.7	50.9	686.3
Latin America															
Argentina	0.0	360.1	391.8	2,717.3	734.8	0.0	383.3	2,043.0	0.0	349.6	228.9	34.4	0.0	0.0	0.0
Brazil	0.0	0.0	132.5	0.0	1,051.7	295.6	444.8	2,397.4	138.7	161.4	3,095.3	1,228.1	1,083.9	460.3	1,735.9
Chile	98.3	0.0	129.2	287.6	798.9	224.2	296.8	563.3	72.4	0.0	0.0	0.0	0.0	115.6	105.4
Mexico	0.0	3,531.4	3,077.3	2,912.9	1,678.9	13.4	715.0	768.2	0.0	162.0	3,275.5	0.0	846.6	540.0	189.4
Venezuela	0.0	0.0	145.6	41.6	0.0	0.0	915.9	94.6	0.0	0.0	0.0	0.0	0.0	0.0	0.0
Middle East															
Israel	0.0	505.6	281.3	336.0	74.9	278.3	825.4	709.6	717.2	3,623.3	2,771.4	489.6	14.1	139.6	1,359.5

Source: Dialogic Bondware.

Table 8.3. Outstanding International Debt Securities by Nationality of Issuer for Selected Industrial and Developing Countries and Regions
(Billions of U.S. dollars)

	1993	1994	1995	1996	1997	1998	1999	2000	2001	2002	2003	2004
All countries	2,022.3	2,389.2	2,700.1	3,111.2	3,479.7	4,284.3	5,353.2	6,362.5	7,502.2	9,189.6	11,661.8	13,928.0
Industrial countries	1,644.4	1,937.4	2,202.1	2,519.8	2,797.6	3,476.6	4,492.8	5,454.1	6,532.9	8,097.3	10,382.9	12,474.8
Belgium	51.1	62.7	81.1	93.8	96.9	100.5	116.7	131.1	145.4	187.9	251.5	302.5
Canada	145.5	162.2	172.5	177.2	181.6	206.3	218.1	202.4	217.7	235.2	270.7	297.4
France	131.1	155.0	167.2	174.5	180.5	220.9	265.7	315.9	394.0	516.4	743.2	926.0
Germany	121.3	186.8	262.4	341.0	394.5	511.9	697.7	898.2	1,068.2	1,449.3	1,938.1	2,338.5
Italy	66.3	81.0	88.1	90.5	93.1	110.4	154.3	209.5	279.6	371.4	527.0	683.2
Japan	335.2	347.8	344.1	337.2	314.4	317.4	335.0	285.0	253.4	248.0	269.6	298.3
Luxembourg	1.3	2.2	4.2	6.7	7.7	8.7	9.0	11.9	18.0	27.0	38.5	46.9
Netherlands	55.1	79.7	100.8	119.1	137.2	187.3	228.5	295.0	330.2	430.1	578.4	685.4
Sweden	77.1	100.0	106.8	111.4	104.2	104.6	108.0	106.9	106.1	131.0	158.3	181.5
Switzerland	19.8	25.4	34.3	41.1	64.0	79.6	85.1	101.5	105.6	127.6	157.9	260.9
United Kingdom	185.8	212.8	229.3	274.0	312.8	373.2	488.3	588.4	656.0	825.0	1,134.0	1,446.3
United States	174.1	203.3	261.3	383.6	545.1	834.5	1,301.1	1,748.6	2,324.7	2,716.8	3,073.4	3,358.8
Developing countries and regions												
Africa												
South Africa	1.1	2.5	3.7	4.3	4.5	5.2	5.9	6.9	8.2	11.6	15.4	17.2

Asia												
Hong Kong SAR	6.2	12.3	13.0	15.3	22.6	21.6	25.6	30.9	38.2	41.7	51.4	54.3
Indonesia	2.4	4.3	4.4	10.9	17.7	17.2	13.1	11.1	9.3	9.0	9.0	10.0
Korea, Rep. of	14.9	19.5	27.5	43.7	51.2	53.0	49.7	49.4	48.5	54.6	63.9	74.5
Malaysia	4.9	5.2	6.9	9.4	12.7	12.2	14.8	16.0	17.4	23.4	23.4	28.7
Philippines	1.3	2.4	3.3	7.0	10.0	10.7	15.2	16.3	16.6	20.9	25.2	27.0
Singapore	1.0	1.3	1.2	3.4	4.7	5.6	7.2	11.3	18.0	16.8	22.4	31.1
Thailand	3.3	6.0	7.4	12.5	14.5	14.4	14.9	13.8	11.0	10.9	10.0	10.1
Europe												
Czech Republic	0.6	1.1	1.0	1.2	1.6	2.5	2.3	1.9	1.6	1.9	2.0	5.1
Hungary	10.2	13.6	15.7	13.3	11.4	12.2	12.5	10.3	10.1	10.3	11.9	15.8
Poland	0.0	0.0	0.3	0.6	2.3	3.4	4.8	5.2	7.6	11.0	18.6	23.5
Latin America												
Argentina	8.2	12.8	18.3	28.9	40.7	54.2	61.9	70.9	84.5	85.4	89.0	90.5
Brazil	9.8	12.6	16.8	27.5	36.7	40.4	44.7	55.9	62.8	70.1	88.3	90.2
Chile	0.8	0.8	0.7	2.0	3.1	3.4	4.8	5.0	6.6	8.8	10.3	11.0
Mexico	24.7	31.0	29.2	41.9	49.4	53.2	62.5	66.2	65.4	65.7	73.6	80.9
Venezuela	4.3	4.1	3.6	3.3	8.3	10.7	11.8	10.9	12.5	12.5	14.8	16.8
Middle East												
Israel	1.5	1.2	1.3	1.9	3.3	4.3	6.6	8.7	10.6	11.7	14.1	18.1

Source: Bank for International Settlements.

- an increase in the technical capability (and the use of information and computer technologies) to unbundle, price, trade, distribute, and manage financial (credit, counterparty, market, liquidity, operational) risks;
- greater reliance on securitized, market-oriented forms of finance, and less on traditional bank-intermediated finance;
- rapid growth in, and predominance of, derivatives markets, and the increasing reliance of financial and nonfinancial entities on them, most recently in the form of new vehicles for transferring credit risks—through markets, special purpose vehicles, and instruments—from original owners to different owners;
- the continued blurring of distinctions between financial institutions, and more recently, nonfinancial entities, and the activities and markets they engage in;
- diversification of banking from lending into fee- and service-based businesses, and transformation of balance-sheet activities into more tradable and off-balance-sheet positions, along with the associated bank disintermediation (Tables 8.4, 8.5, and 8.6);
- rapid growth and increasing importance of nonbank financial institutions—institutional investors such as pension funds, insurance companies, mutual funds, and hedge funds—with different governance structures and motives (Table 8.7) (resulting in significant consolidation in the banking industry as a competitive reaction);
- consolidation of financial activities into large, complex internationally active financial institutions—some as conglomerates combining traditional commercial and investment banking, insurance, and asset management—that provide a menu of financial products and services in a range of wholesale and retail markets and countries;

Table 8.4. Major Industrial Countries: Bank Deposits of Commercial Banks
(Percent of total bank liabilities)

	1980	1990	1995	2000	2001
United States	75.5	78.1	70.1	67.2	67.1
Japan	71.8	76.2	77.8	74.4	78.1
Germany	73.9	76.4	72.0	70.3	70.5
France	...	63.9	67.0	58.4	57.1
Italy[1]	46.3	50.4	44.0	35.2	34.9
United Kingdom	86.5	87.9	68.5	61.8	60.6
Canada	79.7	85.8	78.6	71.4	68.5

Source: OECD, *Bank Profitability: Financial Statements of Banks,* various years.
Note: Interbank deposits and nonbank deposits.
[1]All banks.

Table 8.5. Major Industrial Countries: Bank Loans of Commercial Banks
(*Percent of total bank assets*)

	1980	1990	1995	2000	2001
United States	63.3	65.0	63.4	64.7	63.1
Japan	55.3	57.5	66.8	60.3	62.1
Germany	83.6	58.9	57.4	50.2	48.7
France	. . .	37.2	20.1	20.1	21.3
Italy[1]	35.7	45.6	41.8	45.2	47.2
United Kingdom	43.6	62.1	52.1	53.9	52.6
Canada	70.4	77.7	66.5	60.4	58.1

Source: OECD, *Bank Profitability: Financial Statements of Banks,* various years.
[1]All banks.

- emergence of hybrid entities engaged in both nonfinancial and financial activities, operating in the same financial instruments and markets as commercial and investment banks, mostly as their counterparties.

These key structural changes have transformed the international financial system by opening it up to

- an accelerated expansion of cross-border financial activity;
- new interdependencies among market participants, markets, and financial systems;
- greater international mobility of capital and market liquidity;
- enhancements in efficiency in international markets;
- greater complexity of financial instruments and trading strategies and tactics;
- faster adjustments of financial flows and asset prices.

This transformation in the international financial system has increased investor and borrower awareness of financial risks and rewards around

Table 8.6. Major Industrial Countries: Tradable Securities Holdings
(*Percent of total bank assets*)

	1980	1990	1995	2000	2001
United States	18.0	19.2	21.4	19.8	20.2
Japan	14.7	13.6	14.3	21.5	20.2
Germany	10.2	12.2	17.0	22.5	22.4
France	. . .	9.1	18.8	23.4	22.9
Italy[1]	20.4	13.0	14.6	8.9	8.1
United Kingdom	9.2	7.5	18.5	19.7	21.1
Canada	. . .	10.2	19.6	23.5	24.1

Source: OECD, *Bank Profitability: Financial Statements of Banks,* various years.
[1]All banks.

Table 8.7. Major Industrial Countries: Financial Assets of Institutional Investors
(*Billions of U.S. dollars, unless otherwise noted*)

	1993	1994	1995	1996	1997	1998	1999	2000	2001
Insurance companies[1]									
United States	2,397.4	2,541.0	2,803.9	3,016.3	3,358.3	3,645.9	3,943.0	4,001.8	4,087.6
Japan	2,182.8	2,518.8	2,707.1	2,488.1	2,279.0	2,604.2	3,041.2	2,695.8	2,321.4
Germany	453.7	555.8	678.8	691.3	665.3	781.0	732.9	728.7	753.4
France	398.1	457.0	655.6	728.4	764.9	917.8	918.9	912.9	890.4
Italy	76.3	100.0	120.3	146.0	151.8	196.9	205.5	225.8	239.2
United Kingdom	669.2	660.1	817.1	1,021.6	1,204.1	1,387.3	1,588.4	1,459.7	1,394.8
Canada	150.3	147.4	163.0	173.1	180.0	176.0	200.5	204.4	199.4
Total	6,177.5	6,832.7	7,782.8	8,091.7	8,423.4	9,533.1	10,429.9	10,024.7	9,686.8
Pension funds									
United States	3,354.9	3,547.9	4,226.7	4,745.7	5,563.6	6,231.9	6,857.3	6,805.0	6,351.3
Japan	591.6	672.4	735.1	663.3	623.9	722.2	923.9	825.8	710.7
Germany	47.6	55.5	65.3	64.8	60.5	69.3	63.3	62.2	60.5
France	...	...	...	...	...	...	...	...	...
Italy	33.9	35.5	39.0	39.2	34.4	38.7	51.3	48.8	47.3
United Kingdom	683.2	660.5	759.7	893.2	1,058.4	1,136.2	1,281.5	1,116.3	954.0
Canada	203.1	207.2	229.8	254.9	272.1	283.7	313.9	342.6	330.9
Total	4,914.3	5,179.0	6,055.6	6,661.1	7,612.9	8,482.0	9,491.2	9,200.7	8,454.7
Investment companies									
United States	2,051.1	2,195.3	2,725.8	3,372.8	4,182.1	5,103.7	6,298.2	6,447.8	6,596.6
Japan	412.4	388.9	425.6	380.7	299.4	372.8	562.6	501.7	366.1
Germany	228.4	293.6	369.1	411.8	474.7	646.0	732.8	716.0	664.5
France	508.3	549.2	574.3	586.5	564.7	711.4	772.2	824.2	811.0
Italy	64.6	79.9	80.0	129.0	209.3	436.6	478.9	420.8	358.9
United Kingdom	191.1	201.5	238.1	310.7	341.7	369.3	451.4	442.0	394.5
Canada	82.5	94.1	107.0	141.6	174.2	198.3	242.8	260.6	264.0
Total	3,538.4	3,802.5	4,519.9	5,333.1	6,246.1	7,838.1	9,538.9	9,613.1	9,455.6

Other forms of institutional saving

United States	1,248.3	1,300.7	1,480.6	1,594.0	1,739.4	1,874.7	2,175.5	2,267.9	2,222.2
Japan	424.0	438.4	429.4	371.3	288.4	305.3	400.5	344.2	246.6
Germany	...	...	...	...	...	...	...	...	...
France	...	...	...	...	...	...	...	...	...
Italy	83.9	111.1	121.4	170.2	213.3	328.6	372.0	364.9	362.2
United Kingdom	...	...	...	...	...	...	...	...	...
Canada	...	...	...	...	...	...	...	...	...
Total	1,756.2	1,850.2	2,031.4	2,135.5	2,241.1	2,508.6	2,948.0	2,977.0	2,831.0

All investors

United States	9,051.7	9,584.9	11,237.0	12,728.8	14,843.4	16,856.2	19,274.0	19,522.5	19,257.7
Japan	3,610.7	4,018.5	4,297.2	3,903.3	3,490.8	4,004.5	4,928.2	4,367.5	3,644.8
Germany	729.8	904.8	1,113.2	1,167.9	1,200.6	1,496.3	1,529.0	1,506.9	1,478.4
France	906.3	1,006.2	1,230.0	1,314.9	1,329.6	1,629.2	1,691.1	1,737.1	1,701.3
Italy	258.7	326.6	360.7	484.4	608.7	1,000.8	1,107.6	1,060.3	1,007.5
United Kingdom	1,543.6	1,522.1	1,814.9	2,225.5	2,604.2	2,893.1	3,321.3	3,017.9	2,743.3
Canada	435.9	448.7	499.8	569.6	626.4	658.1	757.3	807.5	794.3
Total	16,536.7	17,811.8	20,552.8	22,394.4	24,703.7	28,538.2	32,608.5	32,019.7	30,627.3

Total assets of all investors (percent of GDP)

United States	136.3	135.9	151.8	162.9	178.4	192.0	207.8	198.7	191.0
Japan	83.0	81.5	88.6	88.4	86.7	89.6	98.9	97.8	94.7
Germany	38.9	41.3	45.3	50.6	58.8	66.3	76.9	79.8	81.0
France	73.9	71.7	77.7	86.6	97.0	106.9	124.2	131.8	131.8
Italy	28.2	32.2	32.0	39.0	53.9	79.6	99.5	97.8	94.0
United Kingdom	162.2	143.0	162.8	172.0	194.2	202.0	227.7	212.8	190.9
Canada	79.4	81.7	84.2	93.2	101.4	110.1	111.5	113.8	115.8

Source: OECD, *Institutional Investors Statistical Yearbook*, 2003.

[1]Life and nonlife insurance companies.

the world. It has also made the maintenance of financial stability more challenging.

Global financial markets directly and indirectly serve a large number of globally diverse end users, including countries, multinational corporations, financial and nonfinancial businesses, and ultimately individual savers and investors. However, the bulk of this international financial market activity occurs within a complex and sophisticated network of international financial relationships among the world's largest and most active financial institutions, although smaller internationally active financial institutions, as well as nonfinancial entities (such as General Electric, General Motors, and others), continue to compete in providing financial services.[82] The worldwide reach and domestic penetration of some of the global banks and financial services conglomerates, and the speed with which they have attained this reach and penetration, are staggering; some financial brand names now rival the name recognition enjoyed by Coca-Cola, Mercedes-Benz, and Sony.

Many of these global institutions derive a large share of their net earnings and returns on capital from their cross-border activities. Moreover, many of them operate in all of the major international markets on a 24-hour basis, by passing their trading activity and risk management systems between their subsidiaries operating in one international financial center as it closes to subsidiaries in another center as it opens. This relatively small group of international institutions (numbering perhaps no more than 50 institutions and probably fewer) intermediate the bulk of transactions in global currency, bond, equity, derivative, and interbank money markets. They also intermediate the bulk of cross-border capital flows between the major financial centers and play a major role in placing most of the funds invested in the emerging capital markets. These institutions and their financial relationships transcend national borders and markets, legal jurisdictions, and supervisory and regulatory frameworks.

There is little reason to doubt that over the years, and as a result of the globalization of finance, the international allocation of capital and asset pricing efficiency within the mature markets and across international financial markets improved significantly. In addition, by gaining access to international capital and lower cost financing alternatives, and, ultimately,

---

[82]For example, General Motors and other U.S. automobile manufacturers routinely provide credit to purchase an automobile, and thereby incur credit risk. Likewise, many large retailers provide credit cards to purchase goods in their stores. This is a significant change because, more so than nonbank financial institutions, the financial activities of nonfinancial entities generally are not subject to financial regulation and supervision.

through higher growth and improved living standards, developing countries as a group also benefited from these structural changes.

While the benefits are clear, the extent to which individual countries, both advanced and emerging, have been able to balance those benefits against the costs of this dramatic transformation has not been uniform, as demonstrated by the increased volatility, turbulence, and financial crises of the 1990s. In addition, even where the net benefits have been obviously positive, negative side effects—such as increased financial-asset price volatility, an apparent increased tendency toward liquidity pressures, and sharp asset price adjustments—have persisted. Thus, even in countries and markets where the net benefits are positive, consideration of some adjustments is desirable.[83]

Challenges Posed by Financial Globalization

In the 1990s, adequately comprehending the complexity of the international financial system became increasingly challenging. It is now significantly more challenging, and in many cases more costly to

- assess financial risks (counterparty, market, liquidity, and operational);
- anticipate market dynamics and the way in which financial disturbances will be transmitted from one counterparty, market, or country to another;
- understand how financial risks are distributed across institutions within national and across international markets;
- assess financial risks and vulnerabilities, and national and international systemic risk.

In the private sector, these challenges were the driving force behind financial consolidation and conglomeration, undertaken in part to capture perceived (if not actual) economies of scale and scope in providing financial services to a more internationally focused group of clients. Unexploited economies of scale and scope in supervising financial institutions and in international financial market surveillance may also exist.

This section examines four broad areas posing significant challenges related to aspects of the globalization of finance:

---

[83]See Volker (1998 and 1999).

- reduced transparency and, by implication, less effective market discipline;
- more rapid and volatile market dynamics;
- increased moral hazard;
- the changed nature of systemic financial risk.

Reduced Transparency and the Effectiveness of Market Discipline and Official Oversight

The ability of globally active, highly integrated financial services firms to engage in modern techniques of finance in a diverse set of markets and countries has been associated with a corresponding separation between the initial allocation of capital and the distribution of financial risks and rewards. For example, a European global bank operating in Hong Kong SAR can take a stake in a Chinese company, unbundle the cash flows, the capital appreciation of the investment, and the counterparty risk, and sell these pieces separately to investors residing in a variety of locations and legal jurisdictions. Globalization has accordingly reduced the informational content of balance sheets and reduced the transparency of international financial activities. At the same time, financial risks have been redistributed internationally and among different classes of institutions, and financial markets have become more complex and complete, in the sense that opportunities for raising funds, investing, and engaging in financial risk-taking more generally have expanded significantly.

Because of this reduced transparency about who owns financial risks, financial stakeholders (both private and public) find it more difficult to evaluate risks and risk concentrations. Existing financial disclosure rules might not have kept pace with the globalization of finance, particularly the complexity and completeness of markets, and may be inadequate for ensuring effective private market discipline. Additional disclosure requirements may be necessary for classes of financial entities (hedge funds and other nonbanks) and hybrid entities (such as GE and GM) engaged in intermediation and market making now subject to few, if any, disclosure requirements and little supervision.

In market-based economies and financial systems, the primary market mechanisms for constraining private risk-taking and leverage from reaching too far beyond prudent levels are firms' internal private discipline (set by internal incentives and enforced by top management in financial firms) and market discipline (provided by external incentives from creditors, equity holders, and counterparties). Internal and market disciplining mechanisms are intended to detect growing financial imbalances within firms and penalize them—the former through internal management controls (such as credit and concentration limits, value-at-risk limits, and so forth) and the latter through market mechanisms (appropriate incentive structures, arbitrage opportunities, profit and loss statements, and market-related governance such as the threats of takeovers and bankruptcies)—before they become large and threatening to a particular financial institution, market, or set of markets.

Presumably, the development of an unsustainable risk profile by a single financial institution will become known and will be reflected either in the institution's share price or in its ability to raise capital or attract deposits. Reliance on private market discipline as a line of defense against systemic problems rests on the fundamental assumption that sufficient and appropriate information is available, on a timely basis, to investors and counterparts so they can assess reasonably accurately the risk profiles of their counterparts and their relationships with them. Without sufficient and timely information, the market disciplining mechanisms relied upon to address financial imbalances before they become vulnerabilities might not produce the appropriate self-corrective adjustments.

In addition to reducing the effectiveness of market discipline, lower transparency may also diminish the effectiveness of financial supervision and surveillance. Most supervisory and regulatory frameworks evolved around the traditional functions of commercial banking (lending and deposit taking) and nationally oriented financial markets. However, banks now engage in less of this traditional activity while providing a much broader menu of financial services to a more internationally diverse clientele in global markets. Moreover, many institutional investors now engage in commercial banking–type activities even though they are neither regulated nor supervised as banks.

As a result, credit and market risk exposures now reside either in other institutions not necessarily regulated as banks, or across the wide diversity of participants in securities markets for which surveillance is not always effective or even possible. Thus, large classes of market participants now own credit risk but are not closely regulated or supervised for this kind of financial risk-taking. In recent years, banks have sold much of the credit risk embodied in their loan books to insurance companies and pension funds through credit derivatives and other vehicles for securitizing risks, motivated in part by regulatory arbitrage: bank loans are subject to capital requirements, whereas charges for credit risk are lower for insurance companies and do not exist for pension funds. Although banking supervision has evolved to some extent along with the transformation of finance, it has not done so completely. Moreover, the regulation of other financial institutions—insurance companies, for example—has not kept pace with globalization, bank disintermediation, diversification of financial businesses, and increased use of direct finance in securities markets. The bottom line is that without the right kind of timely information, those in charge of official market surveillance and systemic risk management will find it difficult to know where all of the risks and vulnerabilities reside within the international financial system and where and how they might be concentrated.

Regulators and supervisors around the globe have been aware of these challenges for some time now, and have been pursuing efforts to deal with them. For example, with the adoption in 2005 of the Basel II framework for capital adequacy (Basel Committee on Banking Supervision, 2004), financial institutions worldwide and supervisors of internationally active financial institutions began making a transition likely to last several years, from a rules-based to a risk-based capital adequacy framework. Moreover, before the ink was dry on this international agreement, supervisors and more generally policymakers in many Group of Ten countries were continuing to consider how to put in place mechanisms for evaluating the governance and internal management control structures of globally active banks and securities firms. Given the breakdowns in corporate governance and accounting in the early 2000s and even continuing into mid-2005, and the prospect for continued rapid financial innovation and structural change, supervisors and the financial institutions themselves should consider redoubling these efforts, and possibly accelerate them.

At a more general level, the Group of Ten and Group of Seven have, as collective official bodies, also made progress in improving the amount of information they share and their surveillance of the global economy and financial system, working closely with the IMF and Bank for International Settlements. Despite these efforts, however, there is little doubt that globally consolidated surveillance of the global economy and financial system, and also of the global financial institutions that make up its financial core, can be improved significantly, in part through closer coordination between the responsible authorities. Moreover, financial institutions and financial market participants more generally, including global corporations, can be provided more direct and transparent incentives to manage the risks they face through the involvement of the highest levels of policymaking in these important issues.

Overall, the objective of enhancing the degree of transparency and disclosure is to improve financial market efficiency through greater market discipline. To be effective, policy changes to enhance market transparency and improve disclosure requirements must be designed to strike the appropriate balance between (1) requiring the provision of the appropriate kind and amount of information (publicly to the markets and confidentially to the authorities), and (2) encouraging rather than inhibiting efficiency-enhancing financial activity. Finding the correct balance entails providing the appropriate kind of information that, on the one hand, private counterparts require to assess counterparty risk accurately and that, on the other hand, allows systemic risk managers to assess market imbalances and vulnerabilities soon enough to take preemptive actions against potential turbulence. Ideally, information to both private and official stakeholders would be provided without impeding the efficient production and allocation of financial products and services.

Impact of Globalization on Market Dynamics

The greater securitization and globalization of finance has dramatically altered the structure of market dynamics, measured by the magnitude of changes in financial asset prices and transactions flows, and the time scales over which they occur. Transactions costs have been reduced to a minimum, and markets are now electronically linked, have a greater diversity of borrowers and lenders, and can accommodate large volumes of transactions over a short span of time. The high degree of capital mobility, the growing volume of cross-border transactions, and the links between trading exchanges and clearinghouses have tended to reduce the time it takes to rebalance portfolios and to reallocate large volumes of capital internationally. This increased speed has been facilitated by the large financial intermediaries with global reach that manage large, geographically dispersed portfolios of diverse asset classes for a wide variety of classes of investors. The broad experience in international markets since the early 1990s seems to suggest that markets have become more subject to periods of "feast and famine," in which the amplitudes (and perhaps the frequency) of financial cycles have increased as a result of structural changes. Indeed, the increased frequency of sharp price movements[84] and the apparent increase in the ability to shift capital and market liquidity reflects the roles played by global financial institutions and the ways they manage their portfolios and risks.

Four closely related aspects of the modernization and globalization of finance are influencing the structure of market dynamics at the same time that they are enhancing efficiency. First, nonfinancial firms, investors, and

---

[84]Examples of sharp price movements include U.S. equity markets in 1987 and 1997; bond market turbulence in 1994 and 1996; major currency swings throughout the 1990s; Mexican (1994–95), Asian (1997), Russian (1998), and Long-Term Capital Management (1998) crises; and global equity markets in 2000 and 2001 (see Table 1.6).

financial institutions rely to a much greater extent on securities markets rather than bank loans for obtaining funding. Securities are actively traded and repriced, and financial institutions are relying increasingly on global markets to fund and risk-manage their exposures.

Second, the large, internationally active financial institutions, which intermediate the bulk of capital internationally, rely heavily on modern portfolio risk management and control systems to manage portfolios (including those of their clients) and inventories of risks they own to provide financial services to clients. Financial positions and risks are actively managed and hedged by relying on sophisticated trading strategies involving both underlying assets and derivatives across a range of markets. Mark-to-market risk management and accounting, stop loss orders, collateral calls, and dynamic hedging are all used to limit losses when prices move counter to expectations. While extremely beneficial for managing risk, enhancing efficiency, and safeguarding the soundness of individual institutions, the widespread use of these techniques can lead to massive and persistent selling (or buying) pressures in already declining (or rising) markets, which exacerbates price movements (which results in under- or overshooting). Markets also show an increased tendency to become more highly correlated during times of heightened financial activity, in part because investors hedge positions in geographically distinct markets. For instance, prior to the Russian default in 1998, investors in Russian investments hedged their credit exposures by taking short positions in Brazilian paper on a highly liquid futures exchange, because Russian and Brazilian credit risk seemed to be correlated. Because of this proxy hedging, turbulence in Russia created turbulence on Brazil's exchanges.

Third, large, internationally active financial institutions (many of them conglomerates) engage simultaneously in market making and position taking. Their market-making activities have them holding inventories of risks (financial positions) for which they try to minimize their risk exposures by hedging in repurchase and derivatives markets. Hedging and rehedging is a continuous process, and involves sophisticated trading and risk control systems.

Fourth, as a result of the previous three conditions, the financial activities of the major international financial institutions are liquidity hungry and are predicated on readily available liquidity and the ability to put on or liquidate positions quickly. Thus, liquidity and speed have become hallmarks of modern finance and key underlying attributes of the international financial system.

Market psychology also plays a role. Financial markets have long been subject to cycles of market sentiment, in which excessive optimism suddenly gives way to excessive pessimism. This phenomenon is sometimes attributed to market irrationality, but it can have fundamental underlying causes. Early in the cycle, a critical mass of market participants begins to view some investment opportunity in a more attractive light than in the past. This belief might be triggered by a new paradigm, a strong track record of returns, or the observation that those market participants that are viewed as having "inside information" or special expertise are pursuing that opportunity and profiting from it. Any of these reasons can cause trend-following behavior by market participants who extrapolate past returns, and "copycat" behavior by those that attempt to "free ride" on the superior information of "insiders" and "experts." Eventually, some event puts the initial optimism in question; in response, risk is reassessed and portfolios are rebalanced. Sentiment deteriorates rapidly, capital is withdrawn, and prices fall further, potentially creating a cycle of price declines and eroding sentiment that feeds upon itself.

These psychological dynamics are common to financial markets, and may have been at work during some of the episodes of volatility and turbulence in the 1990s and in the first half of the first decade of the 2000s. For example, in retrospect, many of the elements of market psychology and the associated market dynamics were evident in U.S. and other equity markets during the inflating and then dramatic bursting of the "dot-com" bubble in the late 1990s and early 2000s. Suggestions that the economic structure changed in the 1990s may have led market participants to overweight the unusually favorable experience and invest in new and unknown companies and industries. In emerging-market countries, the short price history of markets most likely provided a potentially distorted favorable picture of the risks of investing in those markets during the early 1990s. After a pause following the Asian crises in 1997–98, the Russian default in 1998, and problems surrounding Argentina, Brazil, and Turkey in the early years of the 2000s, this trend may have reappeared more recently and continuing into 2005, where many emerging markets are borrowing on very favorable terms. Finally, as this book goes to press in mid-2005, financial journalists around the globe are openly speculating in print about whether the generous liquidity in international financial markets—and a presumption that it will continue to be provided on generous terms—may still be boosting asset prices in a wide variety of markets. If so, this would be a continuation of what likely occurred throughout the later years of the 1990s in many markets and countries, which culminated in the spectacular bursting of the equity bubble in 2000.

As a result of all the factors outlined above, market dynamics have changed in two important ways. First, modern finance allows risks to be priced and traded more actively, more continuously, in larger quantities, and ideally more safely. Changes in fundamental economic value once hidden on bank balance sheets are now recognized more quickly and more frequently in a mark-to-market environment through market prices. In addition, as market prices provide continuous (albeit noisy) signals about value, market participants reappraise risk, rebalance portfolios, and deploy or withdraw capital. This reassessment and rebalancing can, in turn, feed back to market prices. Thus, along with potential improvements in efficiency have come more frequent changes in asset prices and financial flows, and possibly more rapid and complicated market dynamics.

Second, because the market makers that provide critical market liquidity (the globally active financial institutioins) are often also traders and investors, large price shocks can result in the withdrawal of capital from market making, a decline in market liquidity, and sharp and disruptive price declines (not only in the market that originally experienced the shock, but in any market where market makers might have been active).

Many of these features of modern finance are efficiency enhancing most of the time, and even in times of stress when used in moderation. However, when a critical mass of these features are pushed simultaneously to their limits, turbulent market dynamics can result, particularly where there is high leverage, similar position-taking (herding), and excessive reliance on—and presumption of—continuous market making and ample liquidity. The number of episodes of turbulence in the 1990s and early 2000s with these characteristics suggests that market dynamics have been altered significantly during the process of financial modernization and globalization. This is most evidenced by (1) the frequency of sharp and rapid price movements in both mature and emerging markets; (2) the at-times sharp changes in correlations across markets, sometimes from negative to positive; and (3) the increased ability to shift capital and local market liquidity. These changes are posing challenges to private market participants in their attempts to maintain steady profit margins and to manage financial risks. They are also challenging the ability of national and international authorities to prevent, manage, and resolve financial-system problems.

If effective market discipline is practiced, the fast pace of market dynamics alone should be sufficient encouragement for private market participants to insulate their business activities, net incomes, and balance sheets from the sharp price movements and changes in market liquidity. One factor inhibiting market discipline is moral hazard: some of the most important market participants are, in fact, a vital part of the public financial infrastructure (payments systems), and are therefore, at times, subject to several forms of moral hazard.

Role of Moral Hazard

The existence of financial safety nets (for depositors, financial institutions, and markets) creates the presumption that when market discipline is not sufficient to prevent systemic problems, the public sector will manage and resolve the crisis through supervision and market surveillance, and occasionally through more direct means of financial support. As discussed in Part I, financial stability is a public good that can be adversely affected by a collection of private actions. Without financial safety nets—for example, deposit insurance to protect depositors against bank failures—private market participants might collectively lack the willingness or ability to undertake optimal levels of financial risk, and they might therefore engage in suboptimal levels of financial intermediation. Massive withdrawals from intermediation, market making, and risk-taking occurred frequently in the 1990s, during episodes when the widespread fear of private losses disrupted the normal operation of financial markets, to an extent that raised systemic problems—as, for example, at the height of market turbulence in the autumn of 1998 and more recently in 2001 when the "dot-com" equity bubble deflated. The threat of massive withdrawals from private financial risk-taking was seen as possibly affecting economic growth and financial stability, which is one reason central banks intervened to reduce the cost of liquidity and financial risk-taking.

Prudential oversight and other elements of official involvement constitute preventive and corrective mechanisms that—like market discipline—provide a degree of insurance and stability to national financial systems and more broadly to the international financial system. However, official involvement must remain within reasonable boundaries and not lead market participants into thinking they can engage in imprudent risk-taking without suffering the consequences of bad outcomes. The presumption should be that official involvement occurs only up to the point that it encourages normal and prudent risk-taking.

This poses a difficult balancing act for policymakers who are responsible for encouraging normal risk-taking and at the same time insuring the financial system against systemic problems. The challenge is for banking supervision, market surveillance, and financial policymaking more generally to balance efforts to maintain financial stability and manage systemic risks against efforts to ensure that market participants, especially systemically important institutions, bear the costs of imprudent risk-taking and accordingly have the right incentives to avoid imprudence. Accountability may also need to be bolstered in some cases, to foster and promote discipline in the exercise of official supervision and surveillance. Overall, the ideal set of reforms would create a composite of private and regulatory incentives that encourages financial institutions and market participants to internalize the potential for systemic risk in their private risk-taking.

The Changed Nature of Threats to Financial Stability and Systemic Risk

As previous sections have suggested, the evolving character of the global financial system raises challenges for maintaining financial stability and systemic risk management, too. Over the past several decades, in efforts to safeguard financial stability, countries have put in place private and official lines of defense against systemic problems as well as mechanisms for managing and resolving financial problems when these lines of defense are breached. Efforts to maintain financial stability and manage systemic risk necessarily rely on a combination of private market discipline and taxpayer-financed financial safety nets, supplemented by official prudential oversight and monitoring in the form of financial supervision, regulation, and surveillance. These defenses are built on the presumption that a systemic financial event is one in which the problems at one institution might cascade through a payments system, interbank relationships, or depositor runs and infect other institutions to the point of posing risks for the financial system itself. This concept may have become too narrow, given the expanded opportunities for risk-taking and reliance on markets for financing.

As financial systems have been transformed from nationally oriented bank-based systems to internationally integrated market-based systems, financial infrastructures, including official national payments systems, have also been reformed to reduce systemic risk. Market-based financial systems—in which securities are traded in markets—have lower potential for *traditional* systemic risk than bank-intermediated systems. Securities firms hold tradable, liquid assets and have a higher proportion of longer-term funding; economic shocks are often absorbed by price changes, and the effects of the shocks are spread and dispersed more widely (in fact, almost globally).

However, the greater reliance on securitized finance in national financial systems and the international financial system appears to have created a more market-oriented form of systemic risk, involving an array of markets and their underlying infrastructures, which are primarily privately owned and operated. As a result, systemic risk may now be more highly concentrated in capital and derivatives markets (as discussed in Chapters 9 through 11), and involve private settlement systems and quasi-private clearinghouses.

As noted, in addition to relying on private market discipline, current financial regulatory frameworks generally provide a financial safety net supported by prudential regulations requiring banks to maintain sufficient capital and to adhere to reporting and accounting standards and best business practices. Regulations are designed to ensure that financial institutions—particularly systemically important ones—have sufficient capital to absorb internally any losses sustained so that taxpayer costs are minimized. Adherence to standards and best practices helps to ensure that losses are quickly and adequately reflected in profit and loss statements so that private stakeholders can exercise market discipline on financial institutions to implement changes that prevent future losses. This general approach has worked reasonably well in the mature financial systems in limiting collateral systemic damage from private financial excesses (imprudent risk-taking) and problems throughout the 1990s and so far in the 2000s.

Nevertheless, this approach is not without tensions. It creates potential conflicts between the objectives of regulators and those of regulated institutions. Regulators—by providing insurance—underwrite private risk-taking beyond some prudent limit that might not otherwise be taken; and regulated institutions have incentives to find ways to take greater risks within (and sometimes beyond) the boundaries of market discipline and official rules of the game, including regulatory capital constraints. A danger in imposing further constraining regulations is that the regulatory environment might then tend to inhibit efficiency-enhancing risk-taking. Alternatively, the danger in not adequately enforcing existing regulations and perhaps reforming them is that financial institutions will take risks not usually considered worth taking.

A complicating factor is the element of dynamic competition—a dynamic game—between the regulated and the regulator. Because of the combination of technological advances, private incentive structures, and increased competition in providing financial services, private financial practices tend to adapt quickly and dynamically to structural changes, more so than it is possible for supervisory and regulatory frameworks to adapt to monitor them. In part because of differences in resources and incentives, the ability of the private sector to capture the gains from technological advances may have exceeded the ability of officials to learn how these technologies can be applied to the measurement, calibration, and management of systemic risk. As noted by one former senior regulator, this dynamic game can be likened to that of a "bloodhound chasing a greyhound": regulators have trouble keeping pace with the ability of internationally active financial institutions, and the gap between them may be widening.

These challenges may have no perfect or final solution. It is neither possible nor desirable for supervisory authorities to know as much about a financial institution and its risk-taking activities as the financial institution's own management. Nevertheless, financial authorities necessarily must continuously reassess policy instruments intended to encourage prudent financial activity, behavior, and risk management, recognizing that some instruments are likely to be imperfect and blunt. The policy challenge is to develop instruments that are effective in encouraging prudent behavior and management but that do not inhibit efficiency-enhancing activities. As markets evolve and become more complex, regulatory frameworks need to be continuously adapted to the changing nature of private financial risk and systemic risk.

Summarizing these observations, the transformation of the modern financial system is changing the nature of systemic risk.[85] A fundamental concern and challenge is that existing private incentives may no longer be strong enough to prevent excesses and that the existing lines of defense presently inadequately address some aspects of the transformed, more market-oriented systemic risk. Reforming existing private and public mechanisms (including crisis prevention and management mechanisms) to deal adequately with all these evolving elements of the international financial system may be desirable. In addition to encouraging and monitoring reforms of private risk management and control systems of the major financial institutions, Group of Ten financial policymakers may also need to consider reforming systemic risk management systems to more effectively deal with the evolving nature of systemic risk and events. This most likely will entail development of a more global orientation and approach, as has taken place so far in the policy discussion on, and reform of, financial standards and codes, under the rubric of reforms of the international financial architecture in the aftermath of the Asian, Russian, and Long-Term Capital Management crises and more recently in changes in legislation (in the United States and Europe) introduced in the early 2000s to address some of the breaches of corporate governance and accountability.

---

[85]This was noted most clearly by Hans Tietmeyer in 1999 when he was President of the Deutsche Bundesbank: ". . . systemic risk is not a given quantity. To a large extent, it is an endogenous variable which depends on the structures of the financial markets, on the supervisory framework at the national and international levels and on the decisions taken by the political and monetary authorities" (Tietmeyer, 1999, p.1).

Ways Forward

Looking back on the past several decades, the cumulative processes of globalization appear to have transformed the international financial system into a fast-paced, global mechanism for distributing both risk ownership and financial distress, a system in which a relatively large number of episodes involving financial turbulence and crises occurred. A key question is, do the volatility, turbulence, and crises experienced since the early 1990s accurately represent what can be expected in international financial markets in the future or was some of the turbulence part of a still ongoing transitional phase of globalization?

In the private sector in mature markets toward the end of the 1990s, the large internationally active financial institutions had already learned lessons, and incorporated them into their institutional memories in the form of new risk management and control systems, and greater attention to diversifying their portfolios of businesses and not just their portfolios. Likewise, some national authorities—many of them surprised by much of the turbulence—reexamined and reformed their banking regulations and supervisory frameworks during the 1990s, particularly toward the end of the decade. Similarly, the international (mostly official) community undertook initiatives, some under the umbrella of reforming the international financial architecture (mostly for dealing with crises in emerging markets), but also many initiatives involving international supervisory, regulatory, and other bodies—including international financial institutions—addressing the issue of how to improve supervision, regulation, market surveillance, and crisis management and resolution.

The apparent resilience of the advanced countries' financial systems during the second half of the 1990s—and more recently during, and in the aftermath of, the bursting of the global equity "dot-com" bubble in March 2000, the record levels of corporate bond defaults in 2000–2001, the related series of breaches of corporate governance and accountability, and the financial fallout of the events of September 11, 2001—suggests that these efforts have enhanced the financial systems' ability to diversify private and national risks sufficiently to reduce potential, and realized, private and systemic financial losses to a manageable level. All concerned also seem to have a greater appreciation of the interdependencies between macroeconomic stability and financial stability, especially the importance of central bank policies (including monetary and financial-stability policies) in balancing these two important aspects of stability. Because of all these factors, advanced-country financial systems have become more insulated from, and better able to cope with, shock waves in international markets, even with financial system problems in Japan, the second largest banking system in the world, and other systemically important events that at times seemed fundamentally to threaten international financial stability. However, financial activity has become significantly more complex and less transparent, and containing financial excesses before they become large enough to produce the potential for volatility and turbulence is even more difficult.

By contrast, financial systems in many emerging-market countries do not seem to have acquired the same degree of insulation and resilience. Many developing countries have access to global finance but have not yet been able to effectively manage the risks associated with it. For a number of reasons they have not fully kept up with structural changes and fully prepared themselves for a world of modern finance and modern financial markets. In many cases, fundamental and enduring macroeconomic and microeconomic structural reforms have not been achieved, or if achieved, not maintained. In addition, financial structural reforms have not been achieved—such as transparent and effective legal systems; guaranteed contract performance and collateral collection; financial infrastructure building, including financial supervision and regulation, and well-designed, monitored, and enforced safety nets; and corporate governance structures—even in the high, sustained-growth countries. For many emerging markets, the globalization of finance has been a double-edged sword: during good times, the flows aid their economic and financial development but during bad times, the setbacks can be highly disruptive. The propensity for country crises seems to have increased for these countries as a result of their accessing global financial markets without also having achieved the necessary reforms.

Looking forward, and in considering further reform efforts, it is prudent to presume that while the international financial system has become more efficient and resilient than it was before the 1990s, it may also have become more likely to experience sharp asset-price and capital movements, market turbulence, crisis situations, and perhaps even the potential for systemic risk. Accordingly, national and international authorities alike must focus more attention on building better financial infrastructures; improving national and international financial surveillance, supervision, and regulation; and establishing clear mechanisms and rules of coordinating reforms and interventions when such interventions are necessary. Key to any reform efforts would be a reconsideration of the balance of reliance placed on private market discipline and on official oversight in ensuring financial stability. Greater reliance on the former and less on the latter should be strongly considered, but would require significant enhancements to market transparency, financial disclosure, and governance and accountability.

In improving supervisory and regulatory frameworks, appropriate attention should be paid to three lessons learned from the turbulence and crises of the 1990s (and since then), each lesson applying equally to mature, international, and emerging markets. The first is that greater supervisory attention to internal risk management and control systems, to the capability and involvement of senior management in these processes, and to corporate governance mechanisms is crucial for the future. One way to preserve the financial efficiency gains, to safeguard financial stability, and to protect the public interest in providing a financial safety net, may be to penalize errant institutions by requiring them to hold more capital than the minimum required by existing international agreements (the policy of super-equivalency that has been followed for some time by some countries, such as the United Kingdom). The strategy of this approach is to better insulate the less responsible institutions from negative outcomes. This would be one step in the direction of creating an incentive structure that encourages financial institutions and market participants to internalize, privately and individually, the financial-stability implications of their collective private risk-taking.

The second lesson is to make better use of market discipline. An important feature of having strong and, if possible, failsafe infrastructures—in particular, real time gross settlement payments systems—is that financial institutions, even large ones, can be allowed to fail and be liquidated without necessarily threatening the stability, or even the effectiveness, of national payments systems. Accordingly, the benefit of improving transparency and both regulatory and public disclosure is that the probability will be higher that both market participants and supervisors will see hints of errant investment strategies or financial problems as they begin. Greater transparency and disclosure also make it easier for supervisors and policymakers to come to more informed judgments about the potential collateral damage that other institutions or markets might suffer if one institution is allowed to fail. Moral hazard also inhibits the effectiveness of market discipline as a deterrent to systemic financial problems. In these cases, national and international risk management can be improved, and financial supervision and regulation can play a more proactive role to ensure that access to the financial safety net is not being exploited. Some combination of transparency and disclosure, effective supervision, and market discipline will aid tremendously in safeguarding national financial systems and in so doing safeguard the efficiency and smooth functioning of the international financial system.

A third lesson for all countries—but particularly the Group of Ten countries—is to more fully recognize and operationalize the principle that, because of the globalization of finance, international financial stability is a global public good transcending national objectives and interests. As the experience in the 1990s demonstrated, mature financial markets—in Europe, Japan, and the United States—can be both affected by, and sources of, international financial instability and international systemic risk. While all countries can contribute to international financial stability by achieving and maintaining national financial stability, financial system policies designed exclusively to achieve national objectives can create problems in other countries or in international financial markets.

The private financial sector provides a relevant example. Just as a global orientation to risk management and control is required to be profitable in providing private financial services in global financial markets, a global approach may also be required to effectively supervise, regulate, and provide surveillance of international financial activity in global markets and thereby preserve international financial stability. In this regard, a key implication of the globalization of finance is that without some fully recognized and operationally binding international coordination mechanisms, nationally focused financial system policy frameworks may not be able to provide the type of global orientation necessary for promoting and ensuring enduring international financial stability.

9

Systemic Challenges Posed by Greater Reliance on Over-the-Counter Derivatives Markets

Rapid growth, development, and widespread use of over-the-counter (OTC) derivatives markets have accompanied the modernization of commercial and investment banking and the globalization of finance. Both modernization and globalization have been driven by recent advances in information and computer technologies, and have contributed significantly and positively to the effectiveness of national and global finance, particularly to the effectiveness of international financial markets. Much has been written about derivatives as financial instruments and about the role of highly leveraged institutions. By contrast, less has been written about the markets for OTC derivatives and the heavy reliance on them by the small group of internationally active financial institutions. This chapter attempts to fill part of this gap.[86]

Derivatives bestow considerable benefits by allowing financial risks to be more precisely tailored to risk preferences and tolerances; they contribute to more complete financial markets, improve market liquidity, and increase the capacity of the financial system to bear risk and intermediate capital. Derivatives instruments, the structures for trading and risk-managing them, and the infrastructures for ensuring their smooth functioning play a central role in the smooth functioning of the major financial and capital markets. These instruments and markets have been designed and developed by the internationally active financial institutions that derive a large

---

[86]This chapter draws on material in Schinasi and others (2000), some of which was also published in IMF (2000). The author is grateful to his colleagues for the joint effort at the time, and for their permission to draw on this publication.

share of their earnings from these activities. These are the same financial institutions that make up the core of the international financial system and have access to financial safety nets.

While derivatives instruments and markets have improved the effectiveness of intermediation and finance generally, and are likely to continue to do so, as crises in the 1990s demonstrated OTC derivatives activities can contribute to the buildup of vulnerabilities and adverse market dynamics in some circumstances. The severity of repeated episodes of turbulence in the 1990s and early 2000s suggested at that time that OTC derivatives activities were capable of producing fragility and of threatening stability, in some cases akin to a modern form of traditional bank runs. A most relevant example occurred in the autumn of 1998 as revealed in the contours of the market dynamics in the aftermath of the near-collapse of Long-Term Capital Management (LTCM). A substantial buildup in derivatives credit exposures and leverage contributed significantly to this turbulence. This substantial leverage—LTCM accumulated $1.2 trillion in notional positions on equity of $5 billion—was possible primarily because of the existence of large, liquid OTC derivatives markets. The virulence of the 1998 turbulence in the mature financial markets took market participants and authorities by surprise, and some—including U.S. Federal Reserve System Chairman Alan Greenspan (Greenspan, 1998) and former Bundesbank President Hans Teitmeyer (Teitmeyer, 1999)—acknowledged at that time that they did not fully understand the rapidly changing structure and dynamics of global financial markets.[87]

While some progress has been made since then, market structures have continued to change and evolve, leading to a growing recognition that understanding markets is a never-ending challenge and that these dynamic markets require vigilant surveillance and supervision. The issue has remained so important that the systemic implications of, and challenges posed by, continuing structural change in finance was discussed years after the events of 1998 by the President of the Federal Reserve Bank of New York, Tim Geithner (Geithner, 2004). On July 27, 2005, as this book was being completed, the Counterparty Risk Management Group II (CRMPG II), led by Gerald Corrigan—a managing director at the investment bank Goldman Sachs and former president of the Federal Reserve Bank of New York (FRBNY)—called for "urgent" action by the financial industry to strengthen the market infrastructure for confirming and processing com-

---

[87]See Box 9.1 "LTCM and Turbulence in Global Financial Markets," for a description of the problems encountered by the hedge fund and the market turbulence associated with it.

plex financial transactions, including credit derivatives.[88] Moreover, in late August 2005, the FRBNY invited 14 key derivatives market participants (including Citigroup, Deutsche Bank, Goldman Sachs, JPMorgan, Merrill Lynch, and Barclays Capital) and other regulators (including the U.S. Federal Reserve Board, the U.S. Securities and Exchange Commission, the U.K. Financial Services Authority, and both German and Swiss market regulators) to attend a meeting (on September 14, 2005) to discuss what it called "important" issues in the credit derivatives market.[89] The issues to be discussed apparently include problems that surfaced during a sharp increase in trading volumes in credit derivatives markets following sharp credit-rating downgrades of bond issues of General Motors and Ford during the summer of 2005.

While difficult to measure, there can be little doubt that the net private and social benefits of OTC derivatives markets are overwhelmingly positive. If these markets are so overwhelmingly beneficial, why is it necessary to focus attention on the potential downside risks? Three reasons follow:

- OTC derivatives markets are mostly unregulated, except indirectly through the regulation and supervision of financial institutions.
- Disclosure is poor and market transparency is an issue.
- OTC derivatives markets are often a flashpoint for problems early in the process of fragility, yet conducting surveillance of these markets is difficult because of their limited transparency.

In short, because of their importance in global finance, it is important to understand more fully the potential capacity for the OTC derivatives activities of internationally active financial institutions to contribute to international financial volatility and perhaps fragility and thereby threaten international financial stability.

The chapter is organized as follows: Taking the benefits and efficiency-enhancing characteristics of OTC derivatives as a given, the next section of this chapter begins with a brief discussion of modern financial intermediation. It reveals that internationally active financial institutions have become exposed to additional sources of fragility because of their large and dynamic exposures to the counterparty credit risks embodied in their OTC derivatives activities. Before identifying these sources of fragility, potential volatility, and threats to stability, the succeeding section compares OTC with exchange-traded derivatives, including their respective trading

---

[88]See Corrigan, 2005, and CRMPG II, 2005.
[89]See Beales and Hughes, 2005.

environments. This comparison reveals significant differences in the way in which private and collective risks are managed and suggests that OTC activity may be more prone to producing systemic risks. The next section discusses that certain features of OTC instruments, modern financial institutions, and the underlying OTC infrastructures can pose risks to stability, separately and jointly, that in some circumstances create the tendency toward volatility, fragility, and instability in global financial markets. It is easier to identify potential threats to stability in OTC derivatives markets than it is to find remedies, which can only be pragmatically formulated and implemented by private and official practitioners in these markets. Nevertheless, in the concluding section the chapter points to both private efforts (more effective market discipline, risk management, and disclosure) and public efforts (strengthened incentives for market discipline, removal of legal and regulatory uncertainties, and improvement of effectiveness of OTC market surveillance) required if the risks to stability are to be contained in modern OTC derivatives markets.

OTC Derivatives Markets and Modern Banking

Large internationally active financial institutions have transformed the business of finance dramatically since the late 1980s. In doing so, they have improved the ability to manage, price, trade, and intermediate capital worldwide. Many of these benefits come from the development, broadening, and deepening of OTC derivatives and a greater reliance on OTC derivatives activities and markets. Although modern financial institutions still derive most of their earnings from intermediating, pricing, and managing credit risk, they are doing increasingly more of it off balance sheet, and in less transparent and potentially riskier ways. This transformation accelerated during the 1990s and the early 2000s.

A brief examination of the difference between traditional banking and modern banking provides a sense of the importance and extent of this transformation. Traditional banking involves extending loans on borrowed funds (deposits) of different maturities. Each side of this ledger has different financial risks. A simple loan is for a fixed sum, term, and interest rate; in return the bank is promised a known schedule of fixed payments. The risk in lending, of course, is that the borrower may become unable or unwilling to make each fixed payment on schedule. This is credit (or counterparty) risk,[90] composed of both the risk of default (missing one or all

---

[90]See Glossary for definitions of special terms.

payments) and the expected loss given default (that less than is promised is paid). Loans are funded by deposits with much shorter maturities than most bank loans, a situation that imparts liquidity risk. The basic business of banking is to manage these two sets of cash flows, each having a different, stochastic structure. As the history of bank runs and failures indicates, managing these cash flows is inherently risky and banking is prone to fragility and, at times, instability. (See Bryant, 1980; Diamond and Dybvig, 1983; and Kindleberger, 1996.)

This tendency toward fragility may have increased with the further development and more widespread use of OTC derivatives markets in the 1990s and early 2000s, including in emerging markets (Mathieson and others, 2004). In modern finance, financial institutions' off-balance-sheet business involves extensions of credit. For example, a simple swap transaction is a two-way credit instrument in which each counterparty promises to make a schedule of payments over the life of the contract. Each counterparty is both a creditor and debtor and, as in traditional banking, the modern financial institution has to manage the cash inflows (the creditor position) and outflows (the debtor position) associated with the derivatives contract. There are important differences, however. First, the embedded credit risk is considerably more complicated and less predictable than the credit risk in a simple loan, because the credit exposures associated with derivatives vary with time and depend on the prices of underlying assets. Traditional bank lending is largely insulated from market risk because banks carry loans on the balance sheet at book value, which means that they may not recognize and need not respond to market shocks. Nevertheless, market developments can contribute to unrecognized losses that can accumulate over time. By contrast, OTC credit exposures are subject to volatile market risk and are, as a matter of course, marked to market every day. This creates highly variable profit and loss performance, but imparts market discipline and prevents undetected accumulations of losses. Day-to-day shifts in the constellation of asset prices can have a considerable impact on credit risk exposures—both the exposures borne by any particular financial institution and the distribution and concentration of such exposures throughout the international financial system.

Second, the liquidity dynamics of modern finance are considerably more complex than those of deposit markets. Deposit flows have a degree of regularity associated with the flow of underlying business. By contrast, flows associated with OTC derivatives and liquidity conditions in these markets, and in related markets, can be highly irregular and difficult to predict, even for the most technically advanced dealers with state-of-the-art risk management systems. Overall, the stochastic processes that govern the

Table 9.1. Top 20 Derivatives Dealers in 2004 and Their Corresponding Ranks in 2003

Derivatives Dealers	Rank		Members of Exchanges					
	2004	2003	CME	LIFFE	EUREX	HKFE	TSE	TIFFE
J. P. Morgan	1	2	x	x	x	x	x	
Deutsche Bank Securities	2	4	x	x	x	x	x	
UBS	3	6	x	x	x	x	x	
Citigroup	4	1	x	x	x	x	x	
Goldman, Sachs & Co.	5	3	x	x	x	x	x	
Morgan Stanley	6	5		x	x			x
Credit Suisse First Boston	7	8	x	x	x	x	x	
Merrill Lynch	8	9	x	x	x	x	x	
Bank of America Securities	9	10	x	x	x			x
Lehman Brothers	10	7	x	x	x	x	x	
HSBC	11	12	x	x	x	x	x	
Royal Bank of Scotland	12	11	x	x	x	x	x	x
Barclays Capital	13	14		x	x	x	x	x
Société Générale	14	13		x	x		x	
BNP Paribas	15	19	x	x	x	x	x	
ABN Amro	16	15	x	x	x	x	x	
Bear, Stearns & Co.	17	17	x	x	x		x	
Credit Agricole Indosuez	18	n.a.	x	x	x			
Dresdner Kleinwort Wasserstein	19	n.a.	x	x	x		x	x
Banc One Capital Markets	20	n.a.	x	x	x	x	x	

Source: *Institutional Investor* (January, 2004)
Note: n.a. = Not applicable. CME = Chicago Mercantile Exchange. LIFFE = London International Financial Futures and Options Exchange.
EUREX = European Derivatives Market. HKFE = Hong Kong Futures Exchange. TSE = Tokyo Stock Exchange. TIFFE = Tokyo International Financial Futures Exchange.

cash flows associated with OTC derivatives are inherently more difficult to understand and are more unstable during periods of extreme volatility in underlying asset prices.

Thus, in addition to assessing and managing the risk of default and the expected loss given default, the modern financial institution has to assess the potential change in the value of the credit extended and form expectations about the future path of underlying asset prices. This, in turn, requires an understanding of the underlying asset markets and establishes a link between derivatives and underlying asset markets.

The unpredictable nature of OTC derivatives markets would merit little concern if OTC derivatives were an insignificant part of the world of global finance. They are not, and they are increasingly central to global finance. OTC derivatives markets are large, at end-2004 consisting of nearly $248 trillion in notional principal, the reference amount for payments; nearly $9.1 trillion in gross market value; and nearly $2.1 trillion in off-balance-sheet gross credit exposures after controlling gross market values for legally enforceable netting and other risk reducing arrangements (Tables 9.1 and 9.2). The markets are composed of systemically important financial institutions, and together the instruments and markets interconnect the array of global financial markets through a variety of channels.[91]

Since the late 1980s, the major internationally active financial institutions significantly increased the share of their earnings coming from derivatives activities, including from trading fees and proprietary trading profits. These institutions manage portfolios of derivatives involving tens of thousands of positions and daily aggregate global turnover was roughly $2.4 trillion at end-June 2004. The market is an informal network of bilateral counterparty relationships and dynamic, time-varying credit exposures whose size and distribution are intimately tied to important asset markets. Because each derivatives portfolio is composed of positions in a wide variety of markets, the network of credit exposures is inherently complex and difficult to manage. During periods in which financial market conditions stay within historical norms, credit exposures exhibit a predictable level of volatility and risk management systems can, within a tolerable range of uncertainty, assess the riskiness of exposures. Risk management systems guide the rebalancing of the large OTC derivatives portfolios. In normal periods risk management systems can enhance the efficient allocation of risks among firms, but—especially in times of financial stress—they can be a source of trading and price variability that feeds back into the stochastic nature of the cash flows.

---

[91]See the discussion of spillovers and contagion in IMF (1998a).

Table 9.2. Global Over-the-Counter Derivatives Markets: Notional Amounts and Gross Market Values of Outstanding Contracts by Counterparty, Remaining Maturity, and Currency
(Billions of U.S. dollars)

	Notional Amounts					Gross Market Values				
	End-Dec. 2002	End-June 2003	End-Dec. 2003	End-June 2004	End-Dec. 2004	End-Dec. 2002	End-June 2003	End-Dec. 2003	End-June 2004	End-Dec. 2004
Total	141,665	169,658	197,167	220,058	248,288	6,360	7,896	6,987	6,395	9,133
Foreign exchange[1]	18,448	22,071	24,475	26,997	29,575	881	996	1,301	867	1,562
By counterparty[1]										
With other reporting dealers	6,842	7,954	8,660	10,796	11,664	285	284	395	247	485
With other financial institutions	7,597	8,948	9,450	10,113	11,640	377	427	535	352	665
With nonfinancial customers	4,009	5,168	6,365	6,088	6,271	220	286	370	267	412
By remaining maturity[1]										
Up to one year	14,522	17,543	18,840	21,252	23,115	…	…	…	…	…
One to five years	2,719	3,128	3,901	3,912	4,386	…	…	…	…	…
Over five years	1,208	1,399	1,734	1,834	2,073	…	…	…	…	…
By major currency[2]										
U.S. dollar	16,500	19,401	21,429	24,551	25,998	813	891	1,212	808	1,441
Euro[2]	7,794	9,879	10,145	10,312	11,936	429	526	665	380	751
Japanese yen	4,791	4,907	5,500	6,516	7,083	189	165	217	178	257
Pound sterling	2,462	3,093	4,286	4,614	4,349	98	114	179	130	220
Other	5,349	6,862	7,590	8,001	9,783	233	296	329	238	454
Interest rate[3]	101,658	121,799	141,991	164,626	187,340	4,266	5,459	4,328	3,951	5,306
By counterparty										
With other reporting dealers	46,722	53,622	63,579	72,550	82,190	1,848	2,266	1,872	1,606	2,146
With other financial institutions	43,607	53,133	57,564	70,219	86,256	1,845	2,482	1,768	1,707	2,655
With nonfinancial customers	11,328	15,044	20,847	21,857	18,894	573	710	687	638	505

By remaining maturity[3]									
Up to one year	36,938	44,927	46,474	57,157	62,185	⋯	⋯	⋯	⋯
One to five years	40,137	46,646	58,914	66,093	76,444	⋯	⋯	⋯	⋯
Over five years	24,583	30,226	36,603	41,376	48,711	⋯	⋯	⋯	⋯
By major currency									
U.S. dollar	34,399	40,110	46,178	57,827	59,724	1,917	2,286	1,734	1,464	1,508
Euro	38,429	50,000	55,793	63,006	75,443	1,499	2,178	1,730	1,774	2,920
Japanese yen	14,650	15,270	19,526	21,103	23,276	378	405	358	324	336
Pound sterling	7,442	8,322	9,884	11,867	15,166	252	315	228	188	237
Other	6,738	8,097	10,610	10,823	13,732	220	275	278	201	304
Equity-linked	2,309	2,799	3,787	4,521	4,385	255	260	274	294	501
Commodity[4]	923	1,040	1,406	1,270	1,439	86	100	128	166	170
Other	18,328	21,949	25,508	22,644	25,549	871	1,081	957	1,116	1,594
Memorandum item:									
Gross credit exposure[5]	n.a.	n.a.	n.a.	n.a.	n.a.	1,511	1,750	1,969	1,478	2,076

Source: Bank for International Settlements.

Note: All figures are adjusted for double counting. Notional amounts outstanding have been adjusted by halving positions *vis-à-vis* other reporting dealers. Gross market values have been calculated as the sum of the total gross positive market value of contracts and the absolute value of the gross negative market value of contracts with nonreporting counterparties.

[1]Residual maturity.

[2]Counting both currency sides of each foreign exchange transaction means that the currency breakdown sums to twice the aggregate.

[3]Single-currency contracts only.

[4]Adjustments for double counting are estimated.

[5]Gross market values after taking into account legally enforceable bilateral netting agreements.

Expansions and contractions in the level of OTC derivatives activities are a normal part of modern finance and typically occur in a nondisruptive manner even when volatility or isolated turbulence occurs in one underlying market. The potential for excessively rapid contractions and instability seems to emerge when credit exposures in OTC activities rise to levels that create hypersensitivity to sudden unanticipated changes in market conditions (such as interest rate spreads) and when new information becomes available, as in the emerging markets during the Russian default in July 1998 and later in the mature markets with the collapse of LTCM in September 1998. The creditor and debtor relationships implicit in OTC derivatives transactions between the internationally active financial institutions and their counterparts can create situations in which the possibility of isolated defaults can threaten the access to liquidity of key market participants—similar to a traditional bank run. This can significantly alter perceptions of market conditions, particularly perceptions of the riskiness and potential size of OTC derivatives credit exposures. The rapid unwinding of positions as all counterparties run for liquidity is characterized by creditors demanding payment, selling collateral, and putting on hedges, while debtors draw down capital and liquidate other assets. Until OTC derivatives exposures contract to a sustainable level, markets can remain distressed, giving rise to systemic problems. This is what happened in 1998: after it became known that Russia had defaulted, for example, investors and dealers were concerned that their counterparties were heavily exposed to Russian paper. The induced changes in market conditions quickly created a run for liquidity in seemingly unrelated markets such as the derivatives exchange in Brazil.

Greater asset-price volatility related to the rebalancing of portfolios may be a reasonable price to pay for the efficiency gains from global finance. However, in the 1990s OTC derivatives activities sometimes exhibited an unusual volatility, and added to the historical experience of the extremes that volatility can reach. For example, in the 1990s there were repeated periods of volatility and stress in different asset markets (exchange rate mechanism crises in Europe; bond market turbulence in 1994 and 1996; the Mexican, Asian, and Russian crises; LTCM; Brazil) as market participants searched for higher rates of return in the world's major bond, equity, foreign exchange, and derivatives markets. Some of these episodes suggest that the structure of market dynamics has been adversely affected by financial innovations and become more unpredictable, if not unstable. (See the IMF's *International Capital Markets* reports from 1994 to 2001.)

Examples of extreme market volatility include movements in the yen-dollar rate in both 1995 and 1998. In both cases the yen-dollar exchange rate exhibited extreme price dynamics—beyond what changes in fundamentals would suggest was appropriate—in what was, and is, one of the deepest and most liquid markets. The extreme nature of the price dynamics resulted in part from hedging positions involving the use of OTC derivatives contracts called knockout options (see Box 9.2). Knockout options are designed to insure against relatively small changes in an underlying asset price. Yet, once a certain threshold level of the yen-dollar rate was reached, the bunching of these OTC options drove the yen-dollar rate to extraordinary levels in a very short period—an event that the OTC options were not designed to insure against.

Such episodes of rapid and severe dynamics can also pose risks to systemic stability. In particular, the turbulence surrounding the near-collapse of LTCM in the autumn of 1998 posed the risk of systemic consequences for the international financial system, and seemed to have created consequences for real economic activity (see Box 9.1). This risk was real enough that major central banks reduced interest rates to restore risk-taking to a level supportive of more normal levels of financial intermediation and continued economic growth. LTCM's trading books were so complicated and its positions so large that the world's top derivatives traders and risk managers from three major derivatives houses could not determine how to unwind LTCM's derivatives books rapidly in an orderly fashion without retaining LTCM staff to assist in liquidating the large and complex portfolio of positions.

Derivatives have also featured in market dynamics in emerging-market countries, where markets for pricing and trading derivatives are significantly less well developed. While there is little doubt that emerging-market countries should continue to allow the development of derivatives market activities—in part to improve financial efficiency through price-discovery processes—allowing them to develop too rapidly can lead to unwanted adverse consequences. In particular, while the possibility to hedge the risks associated with emerging-market investments with derivative instruments clearly encourages a higher level of capital flows than would otherwise occur, derivative instruments also create the potential for severe market dynamics when circumstances change and foreign investors want to rebalance portfolios to reduce their exposures. Thus, a balance must be struck between allowing these activities to occur in local domestic markets in emerging-market countries and not allowing them to develop so rapidly that they outdistance the capacity of the country to deal with rapid outflows associated with the unwinding of derivatives positions (Mathieson and others, 2004). (See Box 9.3.)

Both private market participants and those responsible for banking supervision and official market surveillance are learning to adapt to the fast pace of innovation and structural change. This already-challenging learning process is even more difficult because OTC derivatives activities may have

Box 9.1. Long-Term Capital Management and Turbulence in Global Financial Markets

The turbulent dynamics in global capital markets in late 1998 were preceded by a steady buildup of positions and prices in the mature equity and bond markets during the years and months preceding the Russian crisis in mid-August 1998 and the near collapse of the hedge fund Long-Term Capital Management (LTCM) in September. The bullish conditions in the major financial markets continued through the early summer of 1998, amid earlier warning signs that many advanced country equity markets, not just those in the United States, were reaching record and perhaps unsustainable levels. As early as mid-1997, differences in the cost of borrowing between high- and low-risk borrowers began to narrow to the point where several advanced country central banks sounded warnings that credit spreads were reaching relatively low levels and that lending standards had been relaxed in some countries beyond a reasonable level. A complex network of derivatives counterparty exposures, encompassing a very high degree of leverage, had accumulated in the major markets through late summer 1998. The credit exposures and high degree of leverage both reflected the relatively low margin requirements on OTC derivatives transactions and the increasingly accepted practice of very low, or zero, "haircuts" on repurchase transactions.

Although the weakening of credit standards and complacency with overall risk management had benefited a large number of market participants, including a variety of highly leveraged institutions, LTCM's reputation for having the best technicians as well as its high profitability during its relatively brief history earned it a particularly highly valued counterparty status. Many of the major internationally active financial institutions actively courted LTCM, seeking to be LTCM's creditor, trader, and counterparty. By August 1998, and with less than $5 billion of equity capital, LTCM had assembled a trading book that involved nearly 60,000 trades, including on-balance-sheet positions totaling $125 billion and off-balance-sheet positions that included nearly $1 trillion of notional OTC derivatives positions and more than $500 billion more of notional exchange-traded derivatives positions. These large and highly leveraged trading positions spanned most of the major fixed income, securities, and foreign exchange markets, and involved as counterparties many of the financial institutions at the core of global financial markets.

Sentiment weakened generally throughout the summer of 1998 and deteriorated sharply in August when the devaluation and unilateral debt restructuring by Russia sparked a period of turmoil in mature markets that was virtually without precedent in the absence of a major inflationary or economic shock. The crisis in Russia sparked a broadly based reassessment and repricing of risk and large-scale deleveraging and portfolio rebalancing that cut across a range

Note: This box draws on the analysis in IMF (1998b; 1999).

of global financial markets. In September and early October, indications of heightened concern about liquidity and counterparty risk emerged in some of the world's deepest financial markets.

A key development was the news of difficulties in, and ultimately the near-failure of, LTCM, an important market maker and provider of liquidity in securities markets. LTCM's size and high leverage made it particularly exposed to the adverse shift in market sentiment following the Russian event. On July 31, 1998, LTCM had $4.1 billion in capital, down from just under $5 billion at the start of the year. During August alone, LTCM lost an additional $1.8 billion, and LTCM approached investors for an injection of capital.

In early September 1998, the possible default or bankruptcy of LTCM was a major concern in financial markets. Market reverberations intensified as major market participants scrambled to shed risk with LTCM and other counterparties, including in the commercial paper market, and to increase the liquidity of their positions. LTCM's previous preferred creditor status evaporated, its credit lines were withdrawn, and margin calls on the fund accelerated. The major concerns were the consequences—for asset prices and for the health of LTCM's main counterparties—of having to unwind LTCM's very large positions as well as how much longer LTCM would be able to meet mounting daily margin calls. As a result, LTCM's main counterparties, including Bear Stearns, LTCM's prime brokerage firm, demanded additional collateral. On September 21 Bear Stearns required LTCM to put up additional collateral to cover potential settlement exposures. Default by as early as September 23 was perceived as a real possibility for LTCM in the absence of an injection of capital.

In response to these developments and the rapid deleveraging, market volatility increased sharply, and there were some significant departures from normal pricing relationships among different asset classes. In the U.S. Treasury market, for example, the spread between the yields of "on-the-run" and "off-the-run" treasuries widened from less than 10 basis points to about 15 basis points in the wake of the Russian debt restructuring, and to a peak of over 35 basis points in mid-October, suggesting that investors were placing an unusually large premium on the liquidity of the on-the-run issue. Spreads between yields in the eurodollar market and on U.S. Treasury bills for similar maturities also widened to historically high levels, as did spreads between commercial paper and Treasury bills and those between the fixed leg of fixed-for-floating interest rate swaps and government bond yields, pointing to heightened concerns about counterparty risk. Interest rate swap spreads widened in currencies including the U.S. dollar, deutsche mark, and pound sterling. In the U.K. money markets, the spread of sterling interbank rates over general collateral repurchase rates rose sharply during the fourth quar-

Box 9.1. (*concluded*)

ter, partly owing to concerns about liquidity and counterparty risk (and also reflecting a desire for end-of-year liquidity).

As securities prices fell, market participants with leveraged securities positions sold those and other securities to meet margin calls, adding to the decline in prices. The decline in prices and rise in market volatility also led arbitrageurs and market makers in the securities markets to cut positions and inventories and withdraw from market making, reducing liquidity in securities markets and exacerbating the decline in prices. In this environment, considerable uncertainty about how much an unwinding of positions by LTCM and similar institutions might contribute to selling pressure fed concerns that the cycle of price declines and deleveraging might accelerate.

In response to these developments, central banks in major advanced economies cut official interest rates. In the United States, an initial cut on September 29 failed to significantly calm markets; spreads continued to widen, equity markets fell further, and volatility continued to increase. Against this background, the Federal Reserve followed up on October 15 with a cut in both the federal funds target rate and the discount rate, a key policy action that stemmed and ultimately helped reverse the deteriorating trend in market sentiment. The easing—coming so soon after the first rate cut and outside a regular Federal Open Market Committee meeting (the first such move since April 1994)—sent a clear signal that the U.S. monetary authorities were prepared to move aggressively if needed to ensure the normal functioning of financial markets.

Calm began to return to money and credit markets in mid-October. Money market spreads declined quickly to pre-crisis levels, while credit spreads declined more slowly and remained somewhat above pre-crisis levels, probably reflecting the deleveraging. The Federal Reserve cut both the federal funds target and the discount rate at the Federal Open Market Committee meeting on November 17, noting that although financial market conditions had settled down materially since mid-October, unusual strains remained. Short-term spreads subsequently declined. The calming effect of the rate cuts suggested that the turbulence stemmed primarily from a sudden and sharp increase in pressures on liquidity (broadly defined), including securities market liquidity, triggered by a reassessment of risk.

changed the nature of systemic risk in ways that are not yet fully understood (Greenspan, 1998; Tietmeyer, 1999; and Geithner, 2004a and 2004b). The heavy reliance on OTC derivatives appears to have created the possibility of systemic financial events that fall outside the more formal clearinghouse structures and official real time gross-payment settlement systems designed to contain and prevent such problems. Heavy reliance on new and even more innovative financial techniques, and the possibility that they may create volatile and extreme dynamics, raises the concern that OTC derivatives could yet produce even greater turbulence with consequences for real economic activity—perhaps reaching the proportions of real economic losses typically associated with financial panics and banking crises.

In sum, the internationally active financial institutions have increasingly nurtured the ability to profit from OTC derivatives activities and now benefit significantly from them. As a result, OTC derivatives activities play a central role in modern financial intermediation, raising the issue of whether this new, more modern form of banking fragility—that associated with modern finance and OTC derivatives markets—could give rise to systemic problems that potentially could affect national financial markets and, more generally, the international financial system. The remainder of this chapter discusses facets of these markets relevant for assessing their potential to create fragility or threaten financial stability.

Exchange versus OTC Derivatives Markets

Key differences between exchange-traded derivatives and OTC derivatives, including the different trading and risk-management environments, indicate why OTC derivatives activities are both efficiency enhancing and prone to problems. Compared to exchange-traded derivatives, OTC derivatives markets have the following features:

- Management of counterparty risk (credit risk) is decentralized and located within individual institutions.
- There are no formal centralized limits on individual positions, leverage, or margining.
- There are no formal rules for risk and burden sharing.
- There are no formal rules or mechanisms for ensuring market stability and integrity, and for safeguarding the collective interests of market participants.

Broad Similarities, but Important Differences, in Contract Structure

Derivatives offer significant benefits because they facilitate the unbundling and transformation of financial risks such as interest rate risk and currency risk (see the discussion of knockout options in Box 9.2). Individual components of risk can be isolated, individually priced, repackaged, and, if desired, traded. In this way, derivatives allow market participants to tailor more precisely the risk characteristics of financial instruments to their risk prefer-

---

Box 9.2. The Role of OTC Currency Options in the Dollar-Yen Market

OTC derivatives activities can exacerbate disturbances in underlying markets—even some of the largest markets, such as foreign exchange markets. Such a disturbance occurred in the dollar-yen market in March 1995 and again in October 1998; once the yen had appreciated beyond a certain level, the cancellation of OTC knockout options and the unwinding of associated hedging positions fueled the momentum toward further appreciation.[1] During these periods of heightened exchange rate volatility, OTC derivatives activities also significantly influenced exchange-traded option markets because standard exchange-traded options were used by derivatives dealers as hedging vehicles for OTC currency options.

In 1995, the yen appreciated against the dollar from 101 yen in early January to 80 yen in mid-April, strengthening by 7 percent in four trading sessions between March 2 and March 7. A combination of macroeconomic factors was widely cited as having contributed to the initial exchange rate move. The speed of the move also suggests that technical factors (such as the cancellation of knockout options) and short-term trading conditions (such as the unwinding of yen-carry trades, also involving OTC derivatives) reinforced the trend. In early 1995, relatively large volumes of down-and-out dollar put options were purchased by Japanese exporters to partially hedge the yen value of dollar receivables against a moderate yen appreciation.

In September and October 1998, the yen again appreciated sharply against the dollar from 135 yen to 120 yen per dollar. Of particular interest are the developments during October 6–9, 1998, when the yen strengthened by 15 percent against the dollar. Talk of an additional fiscal stimulus package in Japan and a reassessment of the relative monetary policy stances in Japan and the United States may have sparked the initial rally in the yen and corresponding weakening in the dollar. The initial spate of dollar selling, in turn, was viewed as having created the sentiment that the dollar's longstanding strengthening against the yen had run its course. However, as in March 1995, in addition to reversals of yen-carry trades, knockout options were

---

[1]See International Monetary Fund (1996, 1998b, Box 3.1) and Malz (1995).

---

ences and tolerances. By contributing to more complete financial markets, derivatives can improve market liquidity and increase the capacity of the financial system to bear risk and intermediate capital.

Both exchange-traded and OTC contracts offer these benefits in broadly similar ways. However, exchange-traded contracts have rigid structures compared with OTC derivatives contracts. For example, the Chicago Board of Trade's treasury bond futures contract dictates

widely viewed as having provided additional momentum that boosted demand for yen and contributed to the dollar selling.

Knockout options (a type of OTC barrier option) differ from standard options in that they are canceled if the exchange rate reaches certain knock-out levels; they therefore leave the investor unhedged against large exchange rate movements. Nonetheless, knockout options are widely used because they are less expensive than standard options. In 1995 and 1998, knockout options, particularly down-and-out put options on the dollar, amplified exchange rate dynamics through three separate channels:

- As the yen appreciated toward knockout levels, sellers of knockout options had an incentive to try to push the yen up through the knock-out levels to eliminate their obligations.
- Japanese exporters who bought knockout options to protect against a moderate depreciation of the dollar sold dollars into a declining market when the knockout options were canceled to prevent further losses on their dollar receivables.
- Dynamic hedging strategies employed by sellers of knockout options required the sudden sale of dollars after the knockout levels had been reached.

Ironically, OTC knockout options that protect only against moderate exchange rate fluctuations can sometimes increase the likelihood of large exchange rate movements—the very event they do not protect against.

Although knockout options represented a relatively small share of total outstanding currency options (between 2 percent and 12 percent), they had a profound effect on the market for standard exchange-traded options. It is easy to see why: knockout options are sometimes hedged by a portfolio of standard options. Dealers who employed this hedging technique needed to buy a huge amount of standard options at the same time as other market participants were trying to contain losses from canceled down-and-out puts. As a consequence, prices of exchange-traded put options (implied volatilities) doubled in March 1995 and almost doubled in October 1998.

- how many treasury bonds must be delivered on each futures contract;
- the types of treasury bonds acceptable for delivery;
- the way prices are quoted;
- the minimum trade-to-trade price change;
- the months in which contracts may expire;
- how treasury bonds may be delivered from the seller of the contract to the buyer.

Box 9.3. The Role of Derivatives in Crises in Emerging Markets

Derivatives played an important role in the financial crises experienced by several emerging markets. This discussion focuses mainly on two issues: (1) the types of financial derivatives used by market participants before the onset of a crisis and how the use of these instruments affected the stability of the domestic financial system; and (2) the impact of the unwinding of derivative positions on the crisis dynamics. While the Mexican and Asian crises highlighted the role of structured notes and swaps in magnifying balance sheet mismatches and the associated volatility in foreign exchange markets, the Russian and Argentine crises demonstrated the importance of counterparty risk and spillovers through credit markets. (The analysis of the role of derivatives in emerging-market crises is seriously hampered by data availability, because transactions in OTC derivatives are not reported systematically. Thus, in many cases, anecdotal evidence and reported losses on derivatives positions by major investment banks of the industrial countries are the main sources of information.)

The Mexican Crisis, 1994

In the early 1990s, the recently privatized Mexican banks aggressively built up their on- and off-balance-sheet positions, which increased their credit and market risk exposures well beyond prudent limits. In particular, they used various derivatives to achieve leveraged returns. One of the popular instruments that allowed local banks to leverage their holdings of exchange-rate-linked treasury bills (the tesobonos) was a tesobono swap (Garber, 1998). In a tesobono swap, a Mexican bank received the tesobono yield and paid U.S. dollar LIBOR plus a specified number of basis points to an offshore counterparty, which in turn hedged its swap position by purchasing tesobonos in the spot market. The only transactions that were recorded in the balance of payments were an outflow of bank deposits related to the payment of collateral by the Mexican bank, and a U.S. dollar inflow related to the purchase of tesobonos by the foreign investor. Thus, traditional balance of payments accounting provided a misguided representation of capital flows and associated risks—that is, although it appeared that the foreign investor had a long position in government bonds, it was, in fact, the local bank that bore the tesobono risk, while the foreign investor was effectively providing a short-term dollar loan. Tesobono swaps were not the only instruments that allowed

---

Another key difference is that exchange-traded contracts are regulated, often by both a regulatory authority and an exchange's self-regulatory organization. In the United States, the Securities and Exchange Commission (SEC) regulates exchange-traded derivatives that are legally "securities" (for example, certain options); the Commodity Futures Trading Commission

local banks to establish leveraged positions financed by short-term U.S. dollar loans from their offshore counterparties; structured notes and equity swaps were also used.[1]

At the onset of the crisis, the tesobono yields jumped from 8 percent to 24 percent and the U.S. dollar value of the collateral fell, triggering margin calls on Mexican banks. Quoting market sources, Garber (1998) suggested that the total of margin calls on tesobono and total return swaps was about $4 billion (compared to $6.1 billion in foreign exchange reserves of the Banco de Mexico at year end 1994). The continued pressure on the exchange rate forced the authorities to float the peso on December 21, 1994.

The Asian Crises, 1997–98

As in the Mexican crisis, unhedged currency and interest rate exposures were key determinants of the severity and scope of the Asian crises (IMF, 1998a). Banks and nonfinancial corporations in Asia left their exposures unhedged because (1) domestic interest rates were higher than foreign interest rates, (2) the pegged exchange rates were generally perceived as stable, and (3) domestic hedging products were underdeveloped, while offshore hedges were expensive. Because of these factors, foreign banks were eager to lend to East Asian banks that tried to capture carry profits on the interest rate differentials. However, local prudential regulations, such as restrictions on the net open foreign exchange exposures and risk-to-capital ratios, limited the amount of profitable arbitrage trade. Therefore, Asian financial institutions turned to derivatives "to avoid prudential regulations by taking their carry positions off balance sheet" (Dodd, 2001, p. 10).

According to market sources, the majority of losses reported by both U.S. and European banks on their Asian lending were listed as due to swaps contracts, presumably including both total return swaps and currency swaps (Kregel, 1998). In a total return swap, one counterparty pays the other the cash flows (both capital appreciation and interest payments computed on a mark-to-market basis) generated by some underlying asset (equity, bond, or loan) in exchange for dollar LIBOR plus a specified number of basis points.

---

[1]Equity swaps are a subset of total return swaps discussed in the Asian Crisis section of this box.

(CFTC) regulates those that are legally "commodities" (for example, financial futures). Regulations promote investor protection because exchange members act as agents for customers; promote market integrity against the potential for manipulation when supplies of underlying goods, securities, or commodities are limited; and promote efficient price discovery, an

Box 9.3. (*concluded*)

Thus, the flows between Asian financial institutions and foreign counterparties were similar to those in the Mexican tesobono swap. As in the case of tesobono swaps, offshore counterparties were buying the underlying assets to hedge their swaps positions, while local banks were left with short U.S. dollar positions. When the exchange rate peg collapsed and domestic interest rates rose, both counterparties had incentives to either unwind the swaps or hedge their foreign exchange exposures, which exacerbated the sell-off in Asian assets and currencies.[2]

Russia's Default and Devaluation, 1998

Although the poor state of Russia's fiscal accounts was well known by mid-1998, the announcement of a 90-day moratorium on external debt payments on August 17, 1998, caught most market participants by surprise. At the time of the default, the estimates of the outstanding notionals of the U.S. dollar–ruble nondeliverable forward (NDF) contracts ranged from $10 billion to $100 billion and the total foreign exposure to the domestic bond market (GKOs and OFZs) was around $20 billion. According to market sources, the U.S. dollar–ruble foreign exchange forwards with Russian firms as counterparties were the largest source of credit losses by major swap dealers during 1997–98, exceeding the losses made on their Asian lending. The events in Russia highlighted the presence of convertibility risk even when local currency positions in emerging markets were hedged, and raised the issue of the NDF valuation when an official rate was not available. In addition, Russia's default sent shock waves through the credit derivatives markets, with the cost of protection increasing in all sectors, including the investment-grade segment. Ambiguous and often misleading definitions of reference obligations, credit events, and settlement mechanics made it very difficult for protection

---

[2] Other structured instruments were also used in the run-up to the Asian crisis. For example, one of the well known instruments was called a PERL—principal exchange rate linked note. A PERL was a dollar-denominated instrument that generated cash flows linked to a long position in an emerging market currency. If the exchange rate remained stable, the return on the PERL was significantly higher than the return on the similarly rated dollar paper, but in the event of major depreciation, the return could become negative (Dodd, 2001).

important function of exchange-traded derivatives (United States, President's Working Group on Financial Markets, 1999b).

According to market participants, in the exchange environment, regulatory authorities evaluate proposed new contracts in a time-consuming and costly process. By contrast, OTC derivatives contracts can involve any underlying index, maturity, and payoff structure. OTC contracts can fill the

buyers to enforce the contracts. According to dealers, many credit default swap contracts were initially triggered under "failure to pay" clauses, but the attempts to enforce the contracts under such clauses were often frustrated by other credit events that appeared more significant and therefore had to carry more weight under contractual law. To address the legal issues highlighted during the Russian crisis, the International Swaps and Derivatives Association (ISDA) issued new credit derivative documentation guidelines in 1999.[3]

Argentina's Default and Devaluation, 2001

In contrast with the Russian crisis, the Argentine default and devaluation in December 2001 were widely anticipated and occurred at a time when the credit derivatives market was relatively more mature. The protracted recession and gradual deterioration of the sovereign's credit quality gave market participants sufficient time to exit the bond and credit protection markets and also allowed the main sellers of credit protection on Argentine sovereign bonds (broker-dealers) to hedge their books in the repurchase market. According to market sources, liquidity in the Argentine credit default swap (CDS) market dried up in August–September 2001, following a bout of volatility in July. The announcement of the moratorium on all debt payments on December 23, 2001, was unanimously accepted as a "repudiation/moratorium" credit event consistent with the ISDA definitions. Reportedly, some disputes occurred as to which bonds could be considered as "deliverable," but they were resolved fairly quickly. According to market sources, 95 percent of all CDSs were settled by mid-February 2002 and there were no reported failures to deliver, with the total sum of contingent payments from the protection sellers to the protection buyers estimated at $7 billion (Ranciere, 2002).

---

[3]The most recent (1999) ISDA guidelines include the following types of credit events: "failure to pay," "obligation acceleration," "obligation default," "repudiation/moratorium," and "restructuring."

Note: The author is grateful to Don Mathieson and Anna Ilyna, who allowed the use and adaptation of this material from Chapter IV of the December 2002 *Global Financial Stability Report* (IMF, 2002).

gaps where exchange-traded contracts do not exist, including exotic currencies and indexes, customized structures, and maturities that are tailored to other financial transactions. Nonetheless, some OTC derivatives instruments have become "commoditized," as market conventions and standards have developed over time for payment frequencies, maturities, and underlying indexes. About two-thirds of the gross market value of OTC deriva-

Figure 9.1. Structure of OTC Derivatives Markets, End-December 2004

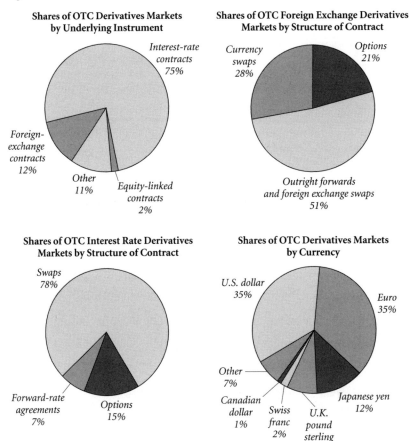

Source: Bank for International Settlements.

tives is accounted for by simple forwards and swaps, many of which could be traded on an exchange except for minor differences in maturity dates, notional amounts, and underlying indexes (Figure 9.1). In addition, OTC derivatives instruments are lightly and indirectly regulated, often because they fall into regulatory gaps. In the United States, for example, swaps contracts are classified neither as securities nor as commodities, so are regulated neither by the SEC nor the CFTC. Many justifications for regulating exchange-traded derivatives contracts are not relevant for OTC derivatives. As was recognized by U.S. courts (*Procter and Gamble v. Bankers Trust*), OTC derivatives are principal-to-principal agreements between sophisticated counterparties, and investor protection is not regarded as an important issue. In addition, the risk of manipulation in OTC derivatives markets is minimal, because contracts do not serve a price-discovery role as do exchange-traded derivatives (Greenspan, 2000).

OTC and exchange markets are viewed by market participants as existing in parallel, and OTC contracts are hedged by using standard, exchange-traded derivatives. The major participants who benefit most from OTC derivatives markets envision that exchange-traded derivatives will remain an important part of their risk-management toolbox, and that organized exchange markets will continue to exist alongside OTC markets.

Organization of Markets

Apart from contract flexibility, the most salient differences between OTC and exchange-traded derivatives lie in the organization of trading and the corresponding frameworks for promoting market stability. Trading, clearing and settlement, risk management, and contingency management (handling a clearing-member default, for example) are highly formalized and centralized in exchange markets, but are informal, bilateral, and comparatively decentralized in OTC markets.

Organized exchange markets: centralized, formal, regulated, rule-driven

Organized exchange trading has several standard features:

- membership requirements;
- rules governing conduct (including risk management);
- centralized trading, clearing, and settlement;
- rules that mutualize risk, including loss-sharing in case of defaults.

These features are designed to ensure market integrity, promote efficient price discovery, and safeguard the resources of the clearinghouse. A clearinghouse may be part of the exchange, or a separate legal entity. Exchange members normally commit capital or have an ownership interest in the clearinghouse.

To maintain market stability and financial integrity, exchanges impose soundness, disclosure, transparency, and prudential requirements on members. Typically, there are minimum capital requirements, rules governing protection of customer funds, reporting requirements, and compliance with other rules and regulations. Exchanges closely monitor trading activity to identify large customer positions or concentrations of positions. They also promote transparency by reporting positions, turnover, and price data, and determining settlement prices, usually on a daily basis. Following the collapse of Barings, some clearinghouses share information and assess members' net exposures across markets (Steinherr, 1998). (See p. 147 for more detail on Barings.)

The clearinghouse manages credit risk and is the central legal counter-party to every transaction; it has a matched market-risk position, but has current credit exposures. Credit risk arises because a change in the price of the underlying asset could cause one counterparty to owe a considerable amount on its position, particularly if the contract is highly leveraged. If an exchange member defaults, the clearinghouse normally has the right to liq-uidate the member's positions; take the member's security deposit, margin, and performance bonds; attach certain other member assets; and invoke any guarantee from the member's parent company. If the defaulting mem-ber's resources cannot cover the obligation, the exchange can normally turn to the resources of other clearing members by invoking loss-sharing rules. In the event of member default, most clearinghouses transfer the member's client positions to another member; a few close out the client positions and liquidate the margin. Exchanges also have backup credit lines (Kroszner, 1999). Overall, clearinghouse defaults have been exceedingly rare.

Most important, exchanges formalize risk-management and loss-sharing rules designed to protect the exchange's capital and the capital of its mem-bers. Members are usually, but not always, required to keep speculative posi-tions within strictly defined limits, mark to market at least daily, and post initial and variation margin to limit the exchange's net credit exposure to the member. Members are subject to surprise inspections and surveys of their financial condition, compliance with exchange rules, and risk-management abilities. Likewise, certain rules protect the exchange and its members from trading activities of nonmembers, which must trade through members. For example, on some exchanges, members of the exchange need not be mem-bers of the clearinghouse, but trades must be cleared through clearinghouse members. Exchanges also dictate minimum margin requirements for mem-ber exposures to clients (often higher than the requirements for members), as well as client position limits. In addition, clearing members handling clients' accounts may face more stringent capital requirements compared with those only trading on their own account.

OTC markets: decentralized, informal, lightly supervised and regulated, market-discipline driven

By contrast, OTC derivatives markets lack a formal structure. Because of the lack of membership criteria, counterparties prefer to deal only with highly rated and well-capitalized intermediaries to minimize counterparty risk. OTC derivatives markets are similar to interbank and interdealer mar-kets. They consist of an informal network of bilateral relationships; there is no physical central trading place. Instead, the OTC derivatives markets exist on the collective trading floors of the major financial institutions. No central mechanism limits individual or aggregate risk-taking, leverage, and credit extension, and risk management is completely decentralized. Market participants individually perform risk management, particularly management of the credit risk in the bilateral, principal-to-principal agreements, which is especially challenging because exposures vary with the price of the underlying security and can rise sharply.

The operational aspects of OTC derivatives markets are also decentralized. OTC markets have no centralized trading, clearing, or settlement mechanism. Transparency is generally limited as well. Except for semiannual central bank surveys, market participants do not report outstanding positions or prices for aggregation or dissemination. Information about market concentration and who owns which risks is generally unavailable; at best, a trading desk might know that some institutions are building up positions. This lack of transparency enabled LTCM to build up outsized positions during 1997 and 1998 (IMF, 1999).

OTC instruments and trading are essentially unregulated, although they are affected indirectly by national legal systems, regulations, banking supervision, and market surveillance. None of the major financial centers has an "OTC derivatives regulator" similar to a banking or a securities regulator.[92] Market participants create instruments to minimize regulatory burdens (including capital requirements), and in many jurisdictions, supervisory and regulatory frameworks geared toward traditional banking and securities activities impinge only indirectly on OTC derivatives markets. Institutional coverage is not comprehensive either, because while banks are regulated and heavily supervised, hedge funds and certain securities affiliates are not regulated. Because financial activities evolve more rapidly than official oversight, the gap between regulator and regulated seems to have widened. Official surveillance of these markets also is limited. Overall, the supervision of financial institutions (including of brokers and dealers) and market surveillance play a critical but limited role in ensuring the smooth functioning of OTC derivatives markets, primarily by seeking to ensure the overall soundness of the institutions that make up those markets.

Regulations are also highly fragmented, both nationally and internationally. In the United States, for example, there are at least three groups of regulators—securities, commodity futures, and banking—impinging, however slightly, on OTC derivatives activities. In addition, while the major market-making institutions flexibly book trades around the globe, super-

---

[92]Among the exceptions, in Brazil all OTC derivatives transactions must be centrally registered. See United States, Commodity Futures Trading Commission (1999).

vision and regulation are nationally oriented. Over time, efforts have been made to adapt the current framework, including through the 1995 amendment to the Basel Accord on Capital Adequacy.[93] Authorities acknowledge that significant gaps in coverage remain and new gaps will likely emerge between market practices and official frameworks.

Despite its limited role, the current regulatory framework has had a visible impact on the market. Existing regulation and concerns about possible regulation have influenced the choice of jurisdictions where trading takes place; the type of legal structure (including unregulated subsidiaries) used to handle dealer activities; the structure of trading, clearing, and settlement (including the degree of centralization and automation); and contract design. These choices reflect efforts to minimize or eliminate the impact of regulations (capital requirements, for example) and also reflect the effects of regulatory uncertainty, including whether regulators might construe types of OTC derivatives as falling under their purview and hence being subject to, for example, more burdensome disclosure and capital requirements.

This light regulation and supervision exists alongside a set of private mechanisms that facilitate smoothly functioning OTC derivatives markets. Market discipline, provided by shareholders and creditors, promotes market stability by rewarding financial institutions based on their performance and creditworthiness. Recent research finds market discipline to be strong only during periods of banking sector stress and volatile financial markets (Covitz, Hancock, and Kwast, 2000).

Market discipline is present when a firm's private sector financial stakeholders (shareholders, creditors, and counterparties) are at risk of financial loss from the firm's decisions and can take actions to "discipline" the firm and to influence its behavior. Market discipline may operate through share price movements, by constraints to the supply of credit, or through the willingness to do business through counterparty relationships. Market discipline in financial markets therefore rests on two key elements: investors' ability to accurately assess a firm's financial condition (monitoring) and the responsiveness of the firm's management to investor feedback (influence). (See United States, Board of Governors of the Federal Reserve System, 1999.) Institutions mark their trading books to market daily so that unprofitable decisions and poor risk management can be reflected immediately in measured performance (profits and losses). This informs senior management and, through disclosure, finan-

---

[93]In the Basel Accord, the credit equivalent of an off-balance-sheet item (the basis for capital requirements) has two components: current replacement cost and add-ons designed to capture potential future credit exposure. Add-on ratios to notional value are specified in a matrix of contract types and remaining maturity. See Basel Committee on Banking Supervision (1995).

cial stakeholders. These mechanisms have some influence, as demonstrated during the turbulence in 1998 when those institutions that appeared to manage well enjoyed the most buoyant stock prices, and creditors of institutions perceived to be less creditworthy refused to roll over credit lines or bond issues, and sold their credit instruments in the secondary market. The subsequent reductions in proprietary trading activity seem to have been largely motivated by financial stakeholders' desires for less risky earnings.

In OTC derivatives markets, special obstacles to effective market discipline (both monitoring and influence) tend to be related to information disclosure—one of the fundamental preconditions for effective market discipline. For example, the off-balance-sheet character of derivatives makes it difficult for outside financial stakeholders to evaluate the financial health of an institution and its contingent liabilities. Data on individual exposures is proprietary, and disclosure could diminish potential profits. In addition, competitive pressures and the desire to generate order flows can lead creditors to extend credit without insisting on adequate counterparty disclosure, as occurred, for example, with LTCM. Therefore, more emphasis may have to be placed on counterparty monitoring, because the application of broader market discipline for complex institutions active in the OTC derivatives markets may have significant limitations.

As a supplement to these mechanisms, a number of industry groups are involved in initiatives designed to support well-functioning OTC derivatives markets, notably the International Swaps and Derivatives Association (ISDA), the Counterparty Risk Management Policy Group II (reconstituted in February 2005 after completing its initial work in 1999), the Group of 30, and the Derivatives Policy Group.[94] Efforts include dissemination of

---

[94]The ISDA and the Group of 30 are ongoing organizations with at least two decades of history each. ISDA, with membership of about 625 financial institutions, develops standards and serves as a forum for the discussion of legal and documentation issues surrounding OTC derivatives contracts. The Group of 30 consists of senior representatives of the private and public sectors and academia and explores international economic and financial issues; its influence has been most felt in global clearings and settlement processes. The Counterparty Risk Management Policy Group (CRMPG) and the Derivatives Policy Group (DPG) were much smaller groups, formed to tackle a limited range of issues. DPG consisted of six nonbank OTC derivatives dealers, and worked closely with the CFTC and the SEC in the mid-1990s to develop voluntary procedures for risk management, internal controls, and external reporting. CRMPG initially came together in early 1999, following the market turbulence of 1998, as a group of 12 internationally active commercial and investment banks with the objective of improving internal counterparty credit and market risk management practices. The group was reconstituted, with the encouragement of the president of the New York Federal Reserve Bank, in 2005 with 15 members as a response to growing concerns about the market implications of the rapid growth of unregulated hedge funds.

best practices in risk management, standardization of documentation, identification of gaps in risk-management practices, and flaws in the operational infrastructure, assessments of legal and other operational risks, efforts to foster interindustry and public-private dialogues on key issues, and initiatives to voluntarily disclose information to regulatory authorities. The activities of these groups reflect the fact that market participants see it as in their best interests to encourage an orderly, effective, and efficient market—and to discourage regulation.

Corporate governance monitoring by financial stakeholders and other private initiatives impose discipline on OTC derivatives activities and increase incentives to reflect the degree of counterparty risk in pricing, margins, or collateral. Monitoring also creates benchmarks against which participants, end users, and regulators can measure progress in dealing with the issues raised in public and private forums. Paradoxically, some of the same factors that complicate market discipline (such as the opacity of OTC derivatives) are also the very factors that make market discipline desirable from the standpoint of financial regulators.

Sources of Volatility and Potential Fragility in OTC Derivatives Activities and Markets

As noted in the previous sections, some of the features of OTC derivatives contracts and markets that provide benefits and enhance efficiency either separately or jointly embody risks to financial market stability. OTC derivatives activities are governed almost exclusively by decentralized private infrastructures (including risk management and control systems, private netting arrangements, and closeout procedures) and market-disciplining mechanisms. By comparison, the more formal centralized rules of exchanges protect the stability and financial integrity of the exchange. In addition, the major financial intermediaries in OTC derivatives markets have access to financial safety nets. Because this can affect their behavior, they are required to adhere to prudential regulations and standards in the form of minimum risk-adjusted capital requirements and accounting and disclosure standards that inform financial stakeholders and, to some extent, support market discipline. The financial industry also has its own standards and best practices, which are promulgated by various industry groups.

Private, decentralized mechanisms have so far safeguarded the soundness of the internationally active financial institutions, in part because many of them have been well capitalized. However, these mechanisms have not adequately protected market stability, and markets and countries only remotely related to derivatives activities experienced instability because of spillovers and contagion. For example, while no major institution failed during the mature market turbulence of 1998 surrounding the near-collapse of LTCM, private, decentralized market-disciplining mechanisms did not prevent the buildup and concentration of counterparty risk exposures within the internationally active financial institutions.

The features of OTC derivatives markets that can give rise to instability in institutions, markets, and the international financial system include

- the dynamic nature of gross credit exposures;
- information asymmetries;
- the effects of OTC derivatives activities on available aggregate credit;
- the high concentration of OTC derivatives activities in the major institutions;
- the central role of OTC derivatives markets in the global financial system.

The first underlying source of market instability is the dynamic nature of gross credit exposures, which are sensitive to changes in information about counterparties and asset prices. This feature played an important role in most of the crises in the 1990s. A disruption that sharply raises credit exposures has the capacity to cause sudden and extreme liquidity demands (to meet margin calls, for example). Just as traditional banks were not always prepared for sudden, abnormally large liquidity demands and withdrawals of deposits during bank runs, today's derivatives market participants may not be prepared for sudden and abnormally large demands for cash that can and do arise in periods of market stress.

A second, well known and related source of market instability is information asymmetries, as in traditional banking (Diamond, 1984). Not having sufficient information on borrowers complicates the assessment of counterparty risks. This problem is exaggerated for the credit exposures associated with OTC instruments because of the price-dependent, time-varying nature of these credit exposures. A counterparty's risk profile can change quickly in OTC derivatives markets. As a result, information asymmetries in OTC derivatives markets can be more destabilizing than in traditional banking markets because they can quickly lead intermediaries and market makers to radically scale back exposures, risk-taking, and the amount of capital committed to intermediary and market-making functions.

Third, OTC derivatives activities contribute to the aggregate amount of credit available for financing, and to market liquidity in underlying asset markets. The capacity for the internationally active institutions to expand

and contract off-balance-sheet credit depends on the amount of capital they jointly devote to intermediation and market making in derivatives markets. This capital can support more or less activity depending on several factors, including the risk tolerances (amount of leveraging) of the intermediaries and market makers; the underlying cost of internal capital or external financing; and financial-sector policies (for example, capital requirements). A determinant of the cost of capital for OTC derivatives activities is the risk-free interest rate (such as on 10-year U.S. treasury bonds), which is also used for pricing contracts. When underlying financing conditions become favorable, the OTC-intermediation activities can become more profitable and more cheaply funded and the level of activity can expand relative to the base of equity capital in the financial system. This tendency for expansion (and, when conditions change, contraction) can become self-generating, and it can, and has, occasionally become hypersensitive to changes in market conditions.

Fourth, as noted, aggregate OTC derivatives activities are sizable and the trading activity ($2.4 trillion daily turnover) and counterparty exposures are highly concentrated in the internationally active financial institutions. This makes those institutions and the global markets susceptible to a range of shocks and dynamics that impinge on one or more major counterparties. The reason for this concentration is clear. Profitability requires large-scale investments in information technologies (such as sophisticated risk-management systems) and also requires a broad client base and the ability to deal in a wide variety of related cash products. Only the largest organizations with global reach and international networks of clients and distribution channels can effectively compete as the central players in OTC markets. As a result, intermediation and market making are performed by global institutions, which hold and manage the attendant risks through hedging and trading, among other mechanisms. The major intermediaries have access to financial safety nets, which may impart an element of subsidy in the pricing of credit and other risks, possibly contributing to an overextension of credit. This concentration makes OTC derivatives markets and the institutions trading in them potentially vulnerable to sudden changes in market prices for underlying assets (interest rates and exchange rates, for example) and in the general market appetite for risk.

Fifth, OTC derivatives activities closely link institutions, markets, and financial centers, making them possible vehicles for spillovers and contagion. About half of OTC derivatives trading in the largest segments takes place across national borders. Links arise from the contracts themselves (currency swaps mobilize liquidity across the major international financial centers) and through the international institutions that make up these markets. In addition, hedging, pricing, and arbitrage activities link OTC derivatives markets to the major cash and exchange-traded derivatives markets: for example, hedging and arbitrage activities link the market for interest rate swaps and the markets for bonds, interest rate and bond futures, and interest rate options. The interconnections and the opportunities for arbitrage the interconnections provide add to the efficiency and complexity of the international financial system. At the same time, links also mean that disruptions in OTC activities necessarily result in spillovers and contagion to these other markets.

To summarize, certain features of OTC derivatives and how they are traded and managed make OTC derivatives markets subject to instability if the wrong combination of circumstances arises. This instability occurs, in part, because OTC derivatives markets are centered around the internationally active financial institutions that each are counterparty to tens of thousands of bilateral, price-dependent, dynamic, credit exposures embodied in OTC derivatives contracts. OTC derivatives contracts bind institutions together in an opaque network of credit exposures, the size and characteristics of which can change rapidly and, moreover, are arguably not fully understood with a high degree of accuracy even by market participants themselves. These institutions allocate specific amounts of capital to support their perceived current and potential future credit exposures in their OTC derivatives business. However, risk assessments and management of these exposures are seriously complicated by a lack of solid information and analyses about the riskiness of both their own positions and those of their counterparties. As a result, this market is characterized by informational imperfections about current and potential future credit exposures and marketwide financial conditions.

The potential for instability arises when information shocks, especially counterparty credit events and sharp movements in asset prices that underlie derivative contracts, cause significant changes in perceptions of current and potential future credit exposures. Changes in perceptions, in turn, can cause dramatic movements in derivatives positions of the major participants. When asset prices adjust rapidly, the size and configuration of counterparty exposures can become unsustainably large and provoke a rapid unwinding of positions. The experience of the late 1990s and early 2000s strongly suggests that the ebb and flow of credit exposures among the large internationally active financial institutions can be severely affected by events that cannot be easily predicted and that can lead to potentially disruptive systemic consequences.

Weaknesses in the Infrastructure

Certain aspects of the infrastructure for OTC derivatives activities can also lead to a breakdown in the effectiveness of market discipline and ultimately produce unsustainable market conditions and affect market dynamics, including producing or exacerbating underlying instabilities:

- inadequate counterparty risk management;
- limited understanding of market dynamics and liquidity risk;
- legal and regulatory uncertainty.

Each of these areas can be improved through the efforts, separately or jointly, of financial institutions, supervisors, and those responsible for market surveillance.

Inadequate Counterparty Risk Management

One of the most important lessons of the near collapse of LTCM and the market turbulence that followed is that counterparty credit risk management by the major global financial institutions was inadequate.[95] Counterparty risk is now widely understood to be of primary importance for managing risk in OTC derivatives markets, and it is still actively under discussion.[96] While there have been some changes, only limited progress has been made in improving the management of credit risks associated with OTC derivatives. Progress has been particularly slow in developing techniques for managing the interactions of credit, market, and liquidity risks, the latter being particularly important and difficult to deal with. Even less well understood are the interactions with operational risk and legal risk.

Several factors explain this limited progress. First, while counterparty disclosure has improved, it has not done so significantly since 1998. The leading providers of intermediation and market-making services in OTC derivatives markets still have serious concerns about the dearth of information supplied by clients, including hedge funds.[97] Accordingly, regula-

---

[95]See Corrigan (1999), and Counterparty Risk Management Policy Group (1999), which discusses the problems that existed before the near collapse of LTCM and recommends several reforms.

[96]Federal Reserve Chairman Alan Greenspan noted (2005, p. 2), "To be sure, the benefits of derivatives, both to individual institutions and to the financial system and economy as a whole, could be diminished, and financial instability could result, if the risks associated with their use are not managed effectively. Of particular importance is the management of counterparty credit risks."

[97]See the section on counterparty exposures and risk management on pp. 49–58 in IMF (2004b).

tors and supervisors have similar concerns, in part because it affects the ability of the major OTC dealers to provide effective and timely market discipline, especially when competition increases. Second, the conceptual and measurement challenges involved in understanding counterparty risk and other risks are unlikely to be resolved soon. Even sophisticated institutions acknowledge that significant additional progress is necessary.

Consider what happened during the LTCM collapse, which exposed many sources of potential weaknesses that are still relevant (in 2005) and will remain so in the future.[98] Widespread problems with assumed counterparty risk assessments and pricing produced turbulence in OTC derivatives markets, in part because incentives for prudent risk-taking proved to be insufficient to prevent the buildup and concentration of counterparty risk exposures in the autumn of 1998. After the turbulence, however, some of these same incentives worked better, including the discipline from losses in shareholder value and the associated lower bonuses for managers, and the discipline imposed by senior management in determining the risk culture, in setting risk tolerances, and in implementing risk management and control systems. Thus, the LTCM affair appears to have taught some valuable lessons.

If information to assess creditworthiness is insufficient, collateral is generally a reasonable counterparty risk mitigation technique. However, the assets held as collateral are subject to market risk and their value can decline precipitously when the protection they offer is most needed, namely, during periods of turbulence when the probability of counterparty default can rise significantly. This risk may not have been adequately accounted for in the management of OTC derivatives trading books. In the aftermath of 1998, institutions acknowledged the inadequacies in collateral management and uncertainties about legal claims on collateral. Both contributed to market turbulence in the 1990s by encouraging financial institutions to liquidate collateral into declining markets. In addition, in the runup to the turbulence of the autumn of 1998, counterparties tended to demand low or no haircuts on collateral, because of competitive pressures and the relatively low cost of funding at that time. These measures could have offered protection against declines in collateral values and helped to reduce pressures to liquidate collateral into declining markets.

Limited Understanding of Market Dynamics and Liquidity Risks

As noted in Chapter 8, market participants and officials acknowledge their limited understanding of market dynamics in OTC derivatives markets

---

[98]See Corrigan (2005) and CRMPG II (2005).

and the implications of those dynamics for related markets. Views diverge on whether OTC markets absorb financial shocks or whether they amplify shocks and contribute to volatility. Some believe derivatives markets dissipate shocks by facilitating hedging, while others see these markets as a channel of contagion. Market participants also disagree about how OTC derivatives markets affect the distribution and mix of credit, market, liquidity, operational, and legal risks. One view is that they redistribute risks to those most willing to hold them. Another is that they transform risks in ways that are inherently more difficult to manage because, while reducing market risk, they create credit, operational, and legal risk. Views on relationships between liquidity in derivatives, secondary, and money markets vary considerably. Finally, there is widespread uncertainty about how monetary conditions influence prices and liquidity in OTC derivatives markets.

Market participants acknowledge their previous failures to realize the importance of liquidity risk in OTC derivatives, and that the capacity to manage it is still in an embryonic stage. One common mistake in 1998 was that risk management systems assumed markets would remain liquid and price changes would follow historical norms. Risk managers also failed to engage in stress testing to examine the implications of severe liquidity problems. Few firms were, for the purposes of risk management, marking credit exposures to estimated liquidation values instead of to current market values. Even these few firms seemed to rely on stress tests that did not fully capture the dynamics revealed in 1998. These challenges are still under active consideration as of mid-2005.

Marking positions to liquidation values is likely to become standard practice at sophisticated financial institutions. However, liquidation values may not be uniquely determined because asset prices behave in nonlinear ways at stress points. Thus, even sophisticated institutions will make modeling errors. Less sophisticated firms may rely on margining requirements and haircuts. These, too, have their limitations in times of stress. Reliance on margin calls to limit counterparty credit risk, normally an effective risk management tool, can contribute to liquidity pressures in apparently unrelated markets and can raise the likelihood of default by financial institutions that would be solvent under normal market conditions. Likewise, overreliance on value-at-risk and mark-to-market accounting and other rules that encourage frequent portfolio rebalancing can induce large-scale selling of positions (Schinasi and Smith, 2000).

To address the challenges posed by liquidity risks and market dynamics, sophisticated institutions are focusing on the total risk they face rather than on the individual risks (market, credit, liquidity, operational, and legal). Particularly challenging is the link between liquidity and counterparty risk, which may depend on the underlying trading, risk-mitigation, and legal infrastructure. Liquidity risk can become closely linked to credit risk, because a loss of liquidity can depress market prices and increase the credit exposure on OTC derivatives. Conversely, heightened concerns about counterparty credit risk can precipitate a loss of liquidity by causing market participants to pull back from markets. International financial institutions recognize the need to incorporate such links into risk management systems, and the formidable challenges of measuring and modeling them. The market turbulence in September 1998 may have been the first event that revealed the importance of these links. Seven years later, because of the difficulty of understanding and modeling these links, institutions may still lack sufficient experience to reliably incorporate these links into their stress tests. Future improvements in the management of total risk should contribute to the smooth functioning of OTC derivatives markets.

Legal and Regulatory Uncertainties

Another important source of weakness in the financial infrastructure is legal and regulatory uncertainty. This type of uncertainty encompasses the possibility that private arrangements to mitigate risks (such as definitions of default and legality of closeout and netting arrangements) may turn out to be ineffective. To the extent that risk mitigation fails to work as designed, misperceptions, mispricing, and misallocation of financial risk can result. Legal and regulatory uncertainties can also be important sources of liquidity risk, because they can contribute to adverse market dynamics.

Cumbersome closeout procedures and uncertain enforcement of security interests in collateral can be impractical and ineffective in protecting firms against default. Such concerns contributed to the rapid liquidation of collateral in the autumn of 1998, and of credit-default swaps during the U.S. recession and corporate governance irregularities during 2001 (see discussion in Chapter 10). However, closeout procedures for some contracts are as legally uncertain in 2005 as they were then. The uncertainty arises because of important differences in bankruptcy laws among countries. Specifically, a number of countries do not allow the termination of contracts upon the initiation of insolvency proceedings, thus giving the trustee the opportunity to continue those contracts favorable to the estate (known as cherry picking). Moreover, even among countries that allow for the termination of contracts, some do not allow for the automatic set-off of contractual claims, which is necessary for netting and closeout. An increasing number of national bankruptcy laws are allowing for stays on the enforcement of security interests in collateral. In these cases, the law will often provide that the interests of secured creditors must be protected during the stay (for example, by compensating for the depreciation of the value of the collateral). One uncertainty arising in many countries is whether such protection will be provided and, if so, whether it will be adequate.

When market participants cannot close out positions or reclaim collateral as specified in private contracts, collateral does not give the expected protection against credit risk. Once a counterparty realizes that protection is absent, credit risk can quickly cross a threshold and be perceived as a default event. With this kind of uncertainty, firms holding collateral with creditor-stay exemptions (which allow counterparties to close out exempt OTC derivatives transactions outside of bankruptcy procedures) have the incentive to exercise their legal right to sell collateral. Closeout valuations require three to five market quotes per contract, and a derivatives desk may have thousands of contracts with a single counterparty. A dealer attempting to close out the number of swaps with LTCM in 1998 might have had to collect 16,000 market quotes from other dealers at a time of market stress when every other major desk was attempting to do the same. Alternative valuation procedures, including good-faith estimates, internal valuations, or replacement value, would be an improvement; this possibility is still under discussion nearly seven years after the near-collapse of LTCM.

Widely used netting agreements (such as the ISDA master agreement) have limitations in mitigating risk. Netting arrangements can reduce the credit exposures on a large number of transactions between two counterparties to a single net figure. Thus, netting arrangements are a risk-mitigating technique with significant potential to reduce large gross credit exposures. If netting cannot be relied upon as legally enforceable, the hint of default can trigger the unwinding of gross exposures. The failure to recognize this possibility may be a source of misperceptions of risk in certain contracts and transactions. Several initiatives were introduced in the aftermath of the turbulence in the late 1990s and have helped to facilitate bilateral and multilateral netting, but they were for specific instruments (RepoClear, for example). Because finance is innovative and new instruments are created continually, market participants and officials will no doubt face related challenges from time to time. An example that has become increasingly relevant is the desirability of introducing netting arrangements for exposures associated with credit derivatives, for which there are a host of still unsettled legal-enforceability concerns (as discussed in Chapter 10).

The various legal and regulatory environments in which OTC derivatives transactions are conducted present uncertainties, too, owing to the high pace of innovation, the relatively limited extent of legal precedent, the cross-border nature of OTC derivatives markets, and the supervisory and regulatory framework. Legal risks include the possibility that a counter-party may walk away from obligations, or may cherry pick; it may dispute the terms of an agreement; it may claim that it did not understand the agreement; and it may claim that it did not have the authority to enter into the agreement.

In the United States, whether certain types of swaps are subject to CFTC approval and oversight was legally ambiguous (see Box 9.4 for reasons) until recently, when new legislation was introduced. This legal uncertainty contributed to reluctance to standardize swap contracts and to centralize clearing (Folkerts-Landau and Steinherr, 1994). Some market participants believed in the late 1990s that bankruptcy procedures needed to be modern-ized to strengthen the legal certainty of risk-mitigation methods and the def-initions of what constitutes a default, which is particularly relevant for the development of credit derivatives. For example, some saw the need to extend creditor-stay exemptions under U.S. bankruptcy law beyond swaps and repurchase transactions to other OTC derivatives contracts. Legislation is still pending in the U.S. Congress that would strengthen and clarify the enforceability of early termination and closeout netting provisions and related collateral arrangements in U.S. insolvency proceedings and is expected to be considered in mid-2005 (Cunningham and Cohn, 2005).

Many jurisdictions, other than the United States and the United King-dom, are ill-suited for effective modern risk management. For example, collateral may afford limited protection in bankruptcy (unless the collateral is held in the United States or the United Kingdom). Legal staffs at major dealer and market-making institutions see significant legal uncertainties associated with the use of collateral in advanced countries (Canada, Italy, and Japan). While the legal and regulatory environments for OTC deriva-tives are complex in the United States and the United Kingdom they are considerably more complicated elsewhere. The same instrument might be legally defined as a swap transaction in one country, an insurance contract in a second country, and a pari-mutuel betting instrument in a third coun-try. Market participants are making strong efforts to mitigate the legal risks, but the private sector can accomplish only so much because contracts must ultimately be enforceable in a legal system.

Strengthening the Stability of Modern Banking and OTC Derivatives Markets

Market participants and officials acknowledge that issues in OTC deriv-atives markets need to be dealt with, and proposals and initiatives have been advanced as a result of experiences in the late 1990s and the early

**Box 9.4. Sources of Legal Uncertainty in the U.S.
Regulatory Environment**

In the United States, legal uncertainties arise from concerns about (1) whether some OTC swap contracts (primarily those that are standardized) could be construed to be futures contracts and would thus be subject to the Commodity Exchange Act (CEA) and (2) whether certain types of mechanisms for executing and clearing OTC derivatives transactions could alter the status of otherwise exempted or excluded swaps. There are also ambiguities about which securities-based derivatives fall under the jurisdiction of the Securities and Exchange Commission (SEC) or Commodity Futures Trading Commission (CFTC), or may, in fact, be prohibited.

Uncertainties about the standing of swap agreements emerged in connection with the CFTC's Swap Exemption. The Futures Trading Practices Act of 1992 granted the CFTC authority to exempt certain instruments from the CEA (and from the requirement to trade on an exchange). In 1993, the CFTC issued the Swap Exemption, which excludes any swap agreement that meets certain criteria from the CEA. These criteria restrict the design and execution of transactions and are meant to prevent unregulated exchange-like markets for swaps. To qualify for the exemption, a swap (1) must be concluded between eligible swap participants; (2) cannot be standardized as to the material economic terms; (3) cannot be part of a central clearing arrangement; and (4) cannot be traded through a multilateral transaction execution facility.[1] Uncertainties in the interpretation of these conditions have, however, emerged. The rise of electronic trading has blurred the line between bilateral and multilateral trading, and the advantage of centralized clearing systems has become widely recognized as trading volumes have increased and a wider range of users have entered the market.[2] As a result, the limits of the swap

---

[1]For a detailed list of these swap conditions, see United States, President's Working Group on Financial Markets (1999).

[2]Folkerts-Landau and Steinherr, 1994; United States, President's Working Group on Financial Markets, 1999.

2000s. Some progress has already been made, and the lessons of recent experience are likely to motivate further actions. However, the available evidence suggests that many recognized problems have yet to be adequately addressed. Insufficient progress has been made in implementing reforms in risk management, including counterparty, liquidity, and operational risks.[99] Relatively less attention has been focused on removing legal and

---

[99]See Counterparty Risk Management Policy Group (1999) and Basel Committee on Banking Supervision (2000a and 2000b).

exemption have come to be viewed as impediments to further development of the swaps market and in particular seem to be inhibiting the introduction of electronic trading platforms and clearing arrangements to mitigate risks.

Regulatory uncertainties may have restricted the types of OTC derivatives contracts that are written. Ambiguities about the extent of CFTC or SEC jurisdiction to regulate certain securities-based derivatives, such as equity swaps, credit swaps, and emerging country debt swaps, are largely the legacy of the 1974 amendment to the CEA that gave the CFTC exclusive jurisdiction over all futures (on physical and financial commodities) without superseding or limiting the jurisdiction of the SEC. However, the broad definition of "commodity" in the CEA raised concerns that OTC markets for government securities and foreign currency would have been covered by the Act. Therefore—upon the Treasury's request—an amendment (the Treasury Amendment of 1974) was inserted into the Act that excluded from it, among other things, transactions in foreign currency, government securities, and mortgages, "unless such transactions involve the sale thereof for future delivery conducted on a board of trade." However, these amendments did not eliminate conflicts regarding each agency's jurisdiction. Ambiguities and potential overlaps of CFTC and SEC jurisdictions remained, in particular, over novel financial instruments that have elements of securities and futures or commodity option contracts. Therefore, the Shad-Johnson Accord between the SEC and the CFTC was concluded in 1983; it explicitly prohibits futures contracts based on the value of an individual security (other than certain exempt securities).[3] The Shad-Johnson Accord itself created some uncertainty, particularly about the status of swap agreements that reference "non-exempt securities," such as equity swaps, credit swaps, and emerging market debt swaps.

---

[3]Exempt securities include government securities and other securities that are exempt from many of the federal securities laws.

regulatory uncertainty. Given the limited progress to date, the implementation of further reforms is essential (Geithner, 2004a; 2004b).

Balancing Private and Official Roles

Many of the instabilities identified above result from three areas of imperfection: (1) market discipline; (2) risk-mitigating infrastructures; and (3) official rule making and oversight. Elements of all three failed to prevent the buildup and concentration of counterparty exposures in 1998 and the more general governance lapses in 2001–2004. Strengthening market stability requires improvements in each of these three areas, but consideration should also be given to altering the balance of the roles of the private and public sectors in ensuring market stability, in particular in tilting the balance toward greater reliance on effective market discipline. It is in the general public's interest to have these markets function as smoothly as possible most, if not all, of the time. More generally, what is the appropriate balance of market discipline on the one hand, and official oversight on the other, for ensuring the smooth functioning of OTC derivatives markets?

In attempting to strike this balance several factors are relevant. The authorities in the mature markets, primarily through Group of Ten efforts, have collectively adopted an approach that places as heavy a reliance on market discipline as is feasible, while recognizing the limits to private discipline, including those emanating from moral hazard, information asymmetries, and other externalities. The desirable degree of official involvement evokes less agreement. Nevertheless, a strong case can be made for relying more heavily on market disciplining mechanisms, provided they can be made more effective. There may also be areas of complementarities and scope for constructive engagement. One such area is disclosure; more voluntary and some involuntary disclosure might greatly improve the effectiveness of risk management and market discipline through greater financial stakeholder awareness. However, only the right kind of disclosure would improve matters, and the international community is not clear about the optimal kind or frequency of information. There are also trade-offs. For example, more official oversight or regulation, by creating the impression that officials are monitoring, can create moral hazard by diminishing private stakeholder incentives to monitor and influence business decisions and reduce management incentives for risk-taking. Striking the right balance needs to take these interrelated effects into account.

If market discipline should carry the heaviest load, the limits (natural or otherwise) to what the private sector can achieve on its own must be identified more precisely against the background of existing rules of the game (supervisory and regulatory frameworks, including financial safety nets). An example of such a limitation is the coordination failure that apparently occurred in organizing the private rescue of LTCM. By some accounts, in the days before it became clear that LTCM might default on some of its contracts, several large institutions apparently tried to organize a group of institutions to take over the hedge fund. While some were willing to put up substantial amounts of capital, in the end it was insufficient. Moreover, several institutions with financial interests nevertheless decided they would not be a party to such a partnership. This example of the free-rider problem rep-

resents a limit to the ability of the private sector to ensure the smooth functioning of markets—by coordinating private solutions—in the presence of
market stress.

Reductions in information asymmetries may also be limited. LTCM was
widely viewed as a large source of both trading revenues and information in
1996 and 1997. Each creditor institution essentially formulated an investment and trading strategy with LTCM that seemed desirable, given the limited information they had. In effect, institutions were involved in a dynamic
game with LTCM and within the OTC derivatives markets. The institutions
provided financing for LTCM's trades in return for trading activity and
a window on LTCM's order flow and investment strategy. Although it is
easy in retrospect to question why LTCM's counterparts did not demand
more information, in a competitive environment, cost considerations must
have weighed heavily. Clearly, LTCM's counterparties thought the cost of
more information was too high, and walking away from deals was not in
their interests. Moreover, they all thought they were receiving useful information from LTCM's orders for trades.

Thus, situations can arise in which institutions in pursuit of self-interest
can collectively produce market conditions that become unsustainable and
harmful to them individually and collectively. That is, in the absence of a central, coordinating mechanism that enforces collective self-interest in market
stability (such as on an exchange), individually desirable strategies, when
aggregated, can produce bad market outcomes (the Prisoner's Dilemma of
Chapter 3). Perhaps private information sharing and coordination could
have made the LTCM game end without a severe disruption, but so could
more effective official refereeing. The challenge is to have a framework that
more effectively prevents these situations from arising, thus the responsibilities for strengthening areas with potential instabilities need to be assigned.

Strengthening Incentives for More Effective Market Discipline

In some cases, the entity that should be responsible for strengthening a
vulnerable area is obvious. Clearly, private financial institutions are responsible for managing individual private risks, within the regulatory and supervisory framework. Well-known improvements (as discussed above and
documented in several reports issued since the LTCM crisis and more recent
Enron problems in commodity derivatives) can be made in risk-management
and control systems to enhance the likelihood that institutions will remain
well capitalized and profitable and thereby help to avoid instability, even in
times of stress. The fact that market participants have not moved as quickly
as might have been expected to improve risk management systems—given

the virulence of the turbulence in the autumn of 1998—suggests that designing and implementing new systems to deal with the complex and evolving
risks involved in OTC derivatives is a difficult challenge.

Moral hazard, perhaps associated with national histories of market
interventions, may be another factor hampering the effectiveness of market discipline. The risk to financial stability arising from banks' OTC derivatives activities may also be influenced by access to financial safety nets,
which, by imparting a subsidy element, can influence the pricing of risk
and thereby lead to overextensions of credit both on and off balance sheet.
Access to safety nets (including central bank financing) can give rise to
incentives to take additional risks that can lead to the buildup of large,
leveraged exposures that, when suddenly unwound, can precipitate a financial crisis of systemic proportions. Moreover, interventions during one
stressful episode that limit losses can sow the seeds of the next buildup of
exposures. These influences may have dampened the strong signal that
institutions might have received from the turbulence that followed the near
collapse of LTCM.

Official sector incentives encouraging the private sector to improve its
ability to monitor itself, and to improve the effectiveness of market discipline, may now be required. As emphasized in IMF (1999), one way of
improving the ability of private incentives to effectively discipline behavior
is for the private and public sectors to jointly identify possible inconsistencies arising from the complex interplay of both private and regulatory
incentives as they affect private decisions. Inconsistencies between private
and regulatory incentives—for example, inconsistencies between internal
models for allocating capital and regulatory capital requirements—could
thus be rectified to alter behavior in ways that preserve efficiency and promote market stability.

Reducing Legal and Regulatory Uncertainty

There also seems to be an obvious assignment of responsibilities in the
area of legal and regulatory uncertainty. The official sector and national
legislatures can reduce legal and regulatory uncertainty. Legal or regulatory uncertainties that can be clearly identified should be addressed as
soon as possible. Three areas immediately come to mind: the regulatory
treatment of swaps and the implications for using private clearinghouses;
closeout procedures; and netting. In each of these cases, reducing uncertainty could have the adverse consequence of actually increasing risk-taking.
To ensure that measures to reduce legal and regulatory uncertainty actually strengthen financial stability, the measures should be linked to measures to address those features of OTC derivatives, institutions, and

markets that most clearly pose risks to market stability. For example, legal certainty of closeout and netting would implicitly provide OTC derivatives creditors seniority over general creditors if a counterparty defaults, possibly giving rise to incentives to engage in riskier activities. To counteract such incentives, the extent of legally sanctioned closeout of contracts and permitted netting of exposures could be made contingent on key structural reforms that enhance stability. In this example, trading arrangements along the lines of a clearinghouse could be treated more favorably with respect to closeout or netting. More generally, the public sector should consider how steps to strengthen the legal infrastructure could help promote structural improvements in OTC derivatives markets. With these provisos in mind, the following proposals could potentially reduce the risk of market instability.

First, in the United States, the agencies supervising institutions and regulating markets (including the Federal Reserve System, the Treasury, the SEC, and the CFTC) agree that financial swaps should be exempt from CFTC supervision and regulation. The 1999 report by the President's Working Group on Financial Markets on regulation of OTC derivatives recommended removing this uncertainty through legislative reforms that would grant swaps an exemption from potential CFTC oversight.[100] This was well received by the private sector, and efforts led to revisions to legislation that would clear the way for serious private consideration of reorganizing OTC derivatives markets, including taking advantage of many of the risk-mitigating possibilities of a clearinghouse structure. In 2000, certain features of the legislation that was introduced and considered in the U.S. Congress raised some concerns from the U.S. Federal Reserve Board, the Treasury, and the SEC.[101] As of May 2005, legislation to address these issues was still pending.[102]

If the legal obstacles are removed, a clearinghouse arrangement for OTC derivatives could mitigate risks associated with simple swaps—by handling clearing and settlement, formalizing and standardizing the management of counterparty risk through margin requirements, and mutualizing the risk of counterparty default—and thereby reinforce market discipline and encourage self-regulation.[103] Would market participants need official

---

[100]See United States, President's Working Group on Financial Markets (1999b).

[101]See testimony by Federal Reserve Chairman Greenspan, SEC Chairman Levitt, and Treasury Secretary Summers (United States Joint Senate Committees on Agriculture, Nutrition, and Forestry and Banking, Housing, and Urban Affairs, 2000).

[102]See Cunningham and Cohn (2005).

[103]For discussion of issues surrounding clearinghouses, see Hills, Rule, Parkinson, and Young (1999); Hills and Rule (1999, pp. 111–112); and Bank of England (2000, pp. 77–78).

encouragement to use a private clearinghouse? On the one hand, some market participants have expressed considerable skepticism about such an arrangement, and the clearing arrangements attempted thus far (such as SwapClear) have attracted little activity, in part because they are perceived to be costly, and they impose regulatory capital requirements. On the other hand, some market participants see a central clearinghouse as inevitable in view of the considerable operational difficulties of managing an OTC derivatives business, the challenges of managing credit risk on a bilateral basis, and the legal uncertainty of the OTC environment. In any case, if the regulatory environment is liberalized and the legal environment is clarified, the adoption of private electronic trading arrangements for swaps and other OTC derivatives (already in evidence since 2000 and continuing in early 2005) may well give rise to private clearinghouses.

Second, closeout procedures for derivatives contracts have proven to be impractical and ineffective in some jurisdictions and under some market circumstances. Had they worked effectively, some of the adverse market dynamics precipitated by the LTCM crisis might have been avoided. The uncertainty of the applicability of closeout procedures might be clarified by the appropriate regulatory and legal bodies, including at the Group of Ten level if the contracts involve more than one legal jurisdiction. Inaction could mean that virulent dynamics will not be avoided the next time rumors of default in OTC derivatives markets surface.

Third, netting arrangements, another risk-mitigation technique, can help reduce gross creditor and debtor counterparty positions to a single bilateral credit or debit with each counterparty. Uncertainty about the legality and regulatory treatment of these arrangements can give rise to situations of heightened credit risk. Further and stronger efforts should be made to strengthen the legal basis for netting.

Coordinated Improvements in Disclosure

Coordination is particularly necessary in the area of information disclosure. In finance, information is a source of economic rents. Natural limits determine how much information will be voluntarily provided publicly, or even privately, to establish counterparty relationships. Therefore, the private sector is unlikely, on its own accord, to provide the right amount and kind of information to counterparties, the markets, and authorities, unless it has incentives to do so. Accounting standards and prudential rules require certain forms of disclosure. However, information in 1998 and the early 2000s was insufficient for private counterparts, supervisors, or those responsible for market surveillance to reach the judgment that vulnerabilities were growing in the global financial system. The public sector has a strong role to play in providing incentives for greater disclosure to the markets, and greater information on a confidential basis to the official sector.

While in principle creditors have incentives to demand adequate disclosure from their counterparties, these incentives can be undermined by competitive pressures and concerns by their counterparties that confidentiality might not be protected. To overcome this weakness, the primacy of credit risk management can be emphasized, along with the autonomy of risk management within organizations to make confidentiality credible, in line with proposals by both private and official groups. The public sector role could be limited to assessing and monitoring the quality of risk management and control systems more systematically and thoroughly, and to defining how information is used, plus ensuring that counterparty disclosure is adequate. The counterparty market discipline imposed by creditors could also be strengthened significantly through better pricing and control of the terms of access to credit.

The challenges in improving public disclosure are formidable. The shift in the boundary between private and public information could, by reducing the private information advantage, lessen intermediation activity. The potential consequences for market functioning need to be weighed against the benefits for market participants of more information on risk concentrations. In addition, it will be difficult to guarantee confidentiality, and even more difficult to develop a consensus on what can usefully be disclosed, in what form, to whom, and how often. For these reasons, an eclectic, innovative approach is needed to address these challenges and pitfalls. Supervisors might promote and facilitate more exchange-like OTC market structures, such as clearinghouses and electronic trading and settlement systems, which would support greater transparency and potentially serve as a nexus for information. Supervisors and regulators could facilitate the adoption of such facilities by regulating them lightly and by devising arrangements for multilateral clearing of contracts that are already covered under bilateral master agreements. Addressing this challenge requires a continuous and close process of cooperation between public and private sectors to strike the right balance between financial market efficiency and stability.

Private and Public Roles in Reducing Systemic Risk

Both the private and public sectors must work to reduce systemic risk. Private market participants can—by developing and implementing effective risk management and control systems and risk-mitigation tools—individually ensure their own viability and soundness even in extreme circumstances.

Well-managed and highly capitalized financial institutions are important components of the first lines of defense against systemic financial problems. Improved risk management and control would reduce the potential for excessive risk-taking and the buildup of vulnerabilities at individual institutions, and highly capitalized institutions are better able to absorb losses when they occur. If all institutions succeeded in accomplishing these objectives, the effectiveness of the first line of defense against systemic risk—market discipline—would be strengthened. If a chain is only as strong as its weakest link, no financial institution can be assured of dealing in OTC derivatives markets with counterparties that are managing their risks well unless all of the systemically important financial institutions substantially improve their risk management systems. Thus, there is some—albeit not strong—incentive for collective private action centered around improving risk management and the financial infrastructure of these systemically important markets. Such collective private action would support the efforts of the ISDA, the Group of Thirty, the Counterparty Risk Management Policy Group II (CRMPG II), and other groups dealing with corporate governance lapses.[104] These efforts should be intensified and accelerated.

In addition to private actions to reduce systemic risk, authorities are responsible for ensuring financial stability through prudential regulations, banking supervision, and market surveillance. One strong step forward in the arena of prudential regulations would be for the Basel Committee on Banking Supervision to reconsider capital requirements for off-balance-sheet credit risks. While the Committee's 2004 revised bank capital requirements (Basel Committee on Banking Supervision, 2004) go some way toward more effectively recognizing the risks in off-balance-sheet activities, the increasing sophistication of banks in arbitraging capital requirements and the dynamic nature of OTC derivatives exposures are likely to widen existing gaps in the measurement of banks' overall credit exposures, and consequently in setting appropriate capital levels. The Committee should consider ways in which capital charges on OTC derivatives positions could more closely reflect the significant changes (positive and negative) that occur in a bank's current and potential future credit exposures when market prices change. In this context, banks' internal credit risk systems could be required to quantify off-balance-sheet credit exposures (both current and potential) as a basis for appropriate capital charges—subject to verification through effective supervision.

More generally, authorities face the difficult challenge of helping to ensure financial stability without encouraging risk-taking beyond some rea-

---

[104]See CRMPG II (2005).

sonable prudent level, without impeding financial innovation, and without unduly distorting market incentives. In principle, safeguards (including the financial safety net) promote a more desirable equilibrium than would be obtained without them. Perversely, the safeguards may also encourage excessive risk-taking. The challenge of keeping moral hazard to a bare minimum in the first instance requires authorities to engage in sufficient monitoring to ensure that the insured institutions and markets take appropriate account of the risks inherent in their activities. Banking supervision and market surveillance need to keep abreast of the changing financial landscape and the institutions that change it, and need to invest in developing analytical frameworks for understanding the changes.

10

The Market for Credit Risk Transfer Vehicles: How Well Is It Functioning and What Are the Future Challenges?

The market for instruments that transfer credit risk from one investor to another—vehicles such as credit default swaps and collateralized debt obligations—has experienced tremendous growth since the mid-1990s.[105] According to the British Bankers' Association report for 2003–2004 (British Bankers' Association, 2004), the notional value of credit derivatives traded in the global marketplace expanded to $3.5 trillion, up from around $1.2 trillion in 2001 and $0.2 trillion in 1997.[106] Around 45 percent of this activity occurred in London and 41 percent in the United States. A variety of market participants—including commercial and investment banks, and institutional investors (such as mutual funds, insurance companies, pension funds, and hedge funds)—are now using the market to hedge or take on credit risk (Figures 10.1 and 10.2).

Measured in terms of notional principal—the reference amount on contracts—the credit risk transfer market is still small compared with the entire over-the-counter (OTC) derivatives market, which amounted to about $220 trillion at end-June 2004. This comparison significantly understates the relative amounts at risk in credit risk transfer contracts compared

---

[105]This chapter draws on material in IMF (2002b). The author is grateful to his colleagues for the joint effort at the time, and for their permission to draw on this publication.

[106]The U.S. Office of the Comptroller of the Currency (OCC), which regulates and supervises nationally chartered banks, reports similar growth for credit derivatives activity in the United States. The notional value of credit derivatives outstanding on the balance sheets of OCC-regulated banks expanded to $2.4 trillion at the end of 2004, up from $0.4 trillion in 2001 and $0.055 trillion in 1997 (U.S. Comptroller of the Currency, 2005).

Figure 10.1. Global Credit Derivatives Market Size and Structure

Protection Purchased by Market Participants[1]

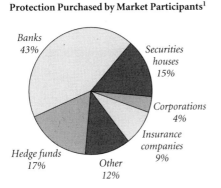

Protection Sold by Market Participants[1]

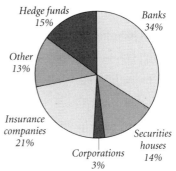

Net Protection Purchased by
Market Participants[1]
(Billions of U.S. dollars)

Breakdown by Instruments

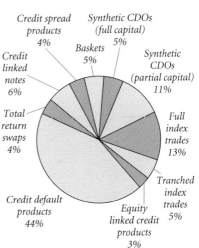

Source: British Bankers' Association (2004).
Note: Based on 2004 estimated market size and 2005 estimated shares of sales and purchases of protection.
CDO= Collateral debt obligation.
[1]"Other" includes government and export credit agencies, mutual funds, and pension funds.

with most OTC derivatives contracts. For a standardized contract such as an interest rate swap, credit exposure is typically equivalent to about 3 percent to 5 percent of the notional principal. By contrast, for a credit derivative, credit exposure could be up to 100 percent of the notional amount because some credit derivatives involve the exchange of a cash flow equiv-

Figure 10.2. Key Characteristics of Credit Derivatives Markets

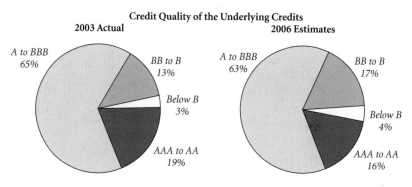

Credit Quality of the Underlying Credits

2003 Actual

2006 Estimates

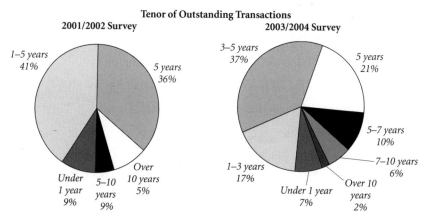

Tenor of Outstanding Transactions

2001/2002 Survey

2003/2004 Survey

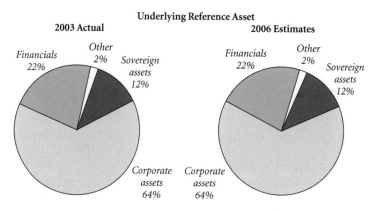

Underlying Reference Asset

2003 Actual

2006 Estimates

Source: British Bankers' Association, *Credit Derivatives Report 2003/2004.*

alent to the principal amount of the underlying credit instrument when they are exercised, whereas principal amounts are not exchanged in standardized interest rate swaps. Moreover, credit risk transfers will probably account for an increasing share of OTC derivatives markets owing to their rapid growth—which some market participants predict could range around 40 percent to 50 percent per year over coming years (see BBA, 2004).

As the markets mature and grow over time, credit risk transfers have the potential to enhance the efficiency and stability of credit markets overall and improve the allocation of capital. By separating credit origination from credit risk bearing, these instruments can make credit markets more efficient. They can also help to reduce the overall concentration of credit risk in financial systems by making it easier for nonbank institutions to take on the credit risks that banks traditionally hold. In addition, credit risk transfers allow banks and other financial institutions to diversify their credit exposures across markets and sectors. They also facilitate the trading of credit risk, which can help financial and nonfinancial institutions manage their credit exposures more flexibly. Finally, liquid credit risk transfer markets can augment price discovery and provide price information that usefully supplements the information available from more traditional credit markets.

At the same time, these instruments and markets are currently being driven by regulatory arbitrage, involve nontraditional players, and are adding to the complexity of financial transactions and markets. In this way—and as explained in more detail in the chapter—they have posed new challenges or intensified existing ones. Many of these challenges surfaced during the global credit derivatives markets' first serious test in 2001–2002 in the form of a U.S. recession and global economic slowdown following a relatively short period of very rapid growth. It was again tested in mid-2005 as two U.S. automobile manufacturers and traditional corporate stalwarts had their credit ratings downgraded significantly, creating turbulence in the market for corporate bonds and the global credit derivatives markets.[107]

Thus, alongside the potential benefits of these significant credit instruments, these market tests revealed several features about credit derivative contracts and markets that warrant further attention. First, they are reducing transparency of the institutional distribution of credit risk and its concentration. Second, while they are dispersing credit risk to a broader set of market participants, they may be creating or magnifying channels through which the distress associated with credit events could spread across institutions and markets (including through the web of rapidly shifting counter-

---

[107]See Beales and Hughes, 2005.

party exposures). Third, these instruments seem to have created demand for credit risk by a much larger and different set of market participants, generally less regulated than banks, or even not regulated, and not necessarily having the experience required for properly pricing or managing these risks. Finally, by their very nature, credit risk transfer mechanisms are leveraged instruments, and can add to the total amount of credit that is internally created within the financial system, thereby increasing the potential for mispricing and misallocation of capital. For these reasons, the market's ability to efficiently and effectively transfer credit risk potentially has implications for financial efficiency, if not financial stability.[108]

The Market's Tests During the Slowdown of 2001–2002 and Corporate Downgrades in 2005

During the slowdown in global growth in 2001 and 2002, financial strains on corporate and sovereign entities gave rise to a number of credit events, some of which triggered payments on—or legal disputes about—credit risk transfer instruments. In 2001, amid an unusually large cyclical erosion in U.S. corporate profits relative to GDP, corporate defaults rose to annual record levels, with 211 issuers defaulting on $115 billion in debt. In January 2002, corporate defaults reached new monthly highs, with 41 issuers defaulting on $31 billion in debt. Defaults were more clustered during this period than expected, and recovery rates were lower than expected. Accordingly, market participants reportedly began to adjust the pricing and collateral terms of contracts and scrutinize structured finan-

---

[108]As noted in Greenspan (2005, p. 2), "To be sure, the benefits of derivatives, both to individual institutions and to the financial system and economy as a whole, could be diminished, and financial instability could result, if the risks associated with their use are not managed effectively. Of particular importance is the management of counterparty credit risks. Risk transfer through derivatives is effective only if the parties to whom risk is transferred can perform their contractual obligations. These parties include both derivatives dealers that act as intermediaries in these markets and hedge funds and other nonbank financial entities that increasingly are the ultimate bearers of risk." This echoes concerns raised in Greenspan (2002), "derivatives have provided greater flexibility to our financial system. But their very complexity could leave counterparties vulnerable to significant risk that they do not currently recognize, and hence, these instruments potentially expose the overall system if mistakes are large. In that regard, the market's reaction to the revelations about Enron provides encouragement that the force of market discipline can be counted on over time to foster much greater transparency and increased clarity and completeness in the accounting treatment of derivatives."

cial instruments (involving underlying and derivatives instruments) more closely.

Some investors and credit-protection sellers sustained sharp losses. For example, American Express lost $370 million in June 2001 on a $1.4 billion collateralized debt obligation (CDO) portfolio. In addition, several internationally active financial institutions had already experienced losses on credit enhancement transactions with Enron while it was in the midst of bankruptcy proceedings, the full extent of which will not be known with certainty until the proceedings and related lawsuits are completed.[109] At the time there was also considerable uncertainty about the performance of some of the credit risk transfers used to hedge credit exposures to Enron.[110] According to credit analysts and market participants, except for Enron, no private counterparties to credit risk transfer vehicles had defaulted, and the markets were at that time judged as having worked reasonably effectively to insure credit risk. Dealers and credit rating agencies saw activities in credit risk transfer vehicles, which in the CDO market was reportedly fairly well-sustained through September 11, 2001, as reflecting continued investor and dealer appetite for credit risk.

As a result of the financial strains and credit events in 2001–2002, particularly the private default events involving Railtrack[111] and Enron, weaknesses in the legal and operational infrastructure of OTC derivatives markets resurfaced—as they had during the Long-Term Capital Management (LTCM) crisis in 1998—and raised concerns about the performance and enforceability of some credit risk transfers.[112] Three examples serve to

---

[109]As of mid-2005, Enron was still "in the midst of restructuring various businesses for distribution as ongoing companies to its creditors and liquidating its remaining operations." This quotation is from the banner on Enron's Web site, which can be accessed via the Internet at www.enron.com.

[110]See Hill and Silverman (2002); Hill and others (2002).

[111]Railtrack was a privately owned and publicly traded company that controlled Britain's rail infrastructure. It was put into administration (that is, under the control of government-appointed administrators) in October 2001. The company had just over a quarter million shareholders, and the vast majority of them (about 254,000) held less than 5,000 shares, controlling only about 17 percent of the company. (More information is available from the BBC Web site: http://news.bbc.co.uk/1/hi/business/1583675.stm)

[112]Earlier watershed credit events included the Conseco restructuring (September 2000), which raised issues about whether restructuring should be treated as a credit event, and the National Power demerger (November 2000), which raised issues about the treatment of credit derivatives involving obligations split between successor companies. These issues were subsequently addressed in supplements and user guides issued by the International Swaps and Derivatives Association. For a discussion of legal risks in OTC derivatives markets, including credit derivatives, see Box 3.6 in Schinasi and others (2000).

illustrate this. First, hedge funds had arranged credit default swaps[113] to hedge credit risk in convertible bonds issued by Railtrack, which was placed in administration in October 2001. Afterward, uncertainty prevailed about whether convertible bonds could be delivered for the swaps. Some of this uncertainty was addressed in November 2001 when the International Swaps and Derivatives Association (ISDA) issued supplementary documentation.[114]

Second, in December 2001, Enron's failure and its involvement in credit and other OTC derivatives markets highlighted longstanding uncertainties about the legal effectiveness in bankruptcy of "closeout netting" provisions in OTC derivatives documentation (Box 10.1).[115] Without closeout netting, OTC derivatives holders could be exposed to a defaulting counterpart on a gross, rather than net, basis (U.S. banks' gross OTC derivatives exposures are about four times larger than their net exposures). While there has been much discussion in both private and official forums on the importance of resolving some of this uncertainty, and even agreement on how to do so, as of May 2005, U.S. bankruptcy legislation that would resolve this uncertainty for U.S. contracts was still pending in the U.S. Congress.

Third, in early 2002, JP Morgan Chase sued insurance companies that failed to pay off on $965 million in surety bonds issued to JP Morgan as insurance against the failure of Enron to make good on forward contracts involving the delivery of natural gas and oil. Surety bonds typically are used as a general form of protection against nonperformance of delivery of goods.[116] The insurance companies alleged that JP Morgan had no intention of taking physical delivery and instead used the transactions as a way of

---

[113]Credit default swap contracts involve the payment of periodic premiums from a protection buyer to a protection seller. In the event that a predefined "credit event" such as default occurs, the protection seller makes a payment related to the market value of an underlying reference instrument such as a bond. For example, the protection seller might either buy the reference instrument at par value from the protection buyer, or make a payment that is equivalent to the difference between par and market value. For more technical details on these and other instruments see *Handbook of Credit Derivatives* (1999).

[114]ISDA develops standards and serves as a forum for the discussion of legal and documentation issues surrounding OTC derivatives contracts.

[115]Closeout netting—the settlement of net outstanding obligations by a single payment in the event of default—mitigates the risk that a bankrupt counterparty will cherry pick its obligations by attempting to enforce those that have positive value to it while repudiating the others. See Schinasi and others (2000).

[116]A surety bond is a bond issued by one party, the surety, guaranteeing that the party will perform certain acts promised by another or pay a stipulated sum, up to the bond limit, in lieu of performance should the principal fail to perform.

extending loans to Enron collateralized by the surety bonds. These examples together highlight, in actual practice, the opacity and legal uncertainties associated with credit risk transfers.[117]

Argentina's default in December 2001 also constituted a major test of the rapidly growing market for emerging-market credit default swaps. At that time, there were no reliable estimates or surveys of the total outstanding amount of Argentine default protection, but market observers suggested that the total could be in the range of $10 billion to $15 billion in notional amount covering a large number of contracts. Argentina concluded its global debt exchange on June 10, 2005, after some delays related to court proceedings in New York. Creditors holding about 76 percent of Argentina's external debt had agreed to the terms of Argentina's debt-restructuring offer. Notwithstanding the debt restructuring, there are still unresolved principal claims amounting to almost US$20 billion.

During the period following the experiences in 2001 and early 2002, and those at the end of 2004, derivatives markets encountered few if any difficulties. In mid-2005, the pending disputes involving the bankruptcy of Parmalat were coming to a critical point. In addition, markets were speculating whether General Motors (GM) would be able to avoid bankruptcy, and the credit rating agency Standard and Poors downgraded Ford's debt to the lowest rating for investment grade bonds and downgraded GM's debt to below–investment grade (or junk status). Because the debt of both of these companies is linked to credit derivatives—specifically, are included in tranches of CDOs—both the cash markets for corporate bonds and the credit derivatives markets experienced significant price movements and financial flows reflecting portfolio rebalancing. As noted in Chapter 9, both financial market participants and regulators have recently called for action to improve the stability of these markets.[118] It remains to be seen how well these still developing derivatives markets will withstand the financial market pressures surrounding these significant corporate events.

In sum, some progress has been made in addressing operational "teething problems" in the nascent credit risk transfer markets, particularly for standardized simple instruments such as credit default swaps. At the same time, some operational issues highlighted by the downturn in 2001–2002 and the breaches of corporate governance discussed above remain to be addressed. Moreover, there may be significant operational risks

---

[117]The suit was settled out of court in early 2003, with JP Morgan incurring a before-tax writeoff (loss) of about $400 million (see Chapter 11 for further details).

[118]See Corrigan (2005) and Geithner (2004a, 2004b).

Box 10.1. Financial Implications of Enron's Bankruptcy

Enron has come to symbolize the use of aggressive accounting techniques by major companies to mask excessive leverage and weak earnings. The company's collapse—the largest U.S. Chapter 11 bankruptcy to that time—also caused significant volatility in financial markets and led to substantial losses for financial institutions and institutional and retail investors. These effects did not have systemic financial consequences, because exposures to Enron were generally well diversified across institutions and markets. But at the time there were significant uncertainties, including the likelihood that hidden losses would be uncovered as Enron's highly complex financial operations were unwound; the magnitude of bank exposures to other energy companies that were also facing difficulties because of Enron's collapse; the size and structure of Enron's derivatives books; and the extent of insurance company exposure.

As described in the chapter, Enron's failure highlighted uncertainties about the effective functioning of credit risk transfer vehicles. It also underscored three broader capital-markets issues.

Inadequate oversight of financial activities of nonfinancial corporations. Enron was the main dealer, market maker, and liquidity provider in major segments of the OTC energy derivatives markets, and was also active in other derivatives markets segments (at the end of September 2001, its overall derivatives trading liabilities stood at about US$19 billion). Despite its size, complexity (including many off-balance-sheet special purpose vehicles), and central role in the energy derivatives markets, its OTC derivatives activities were essentially unregulated.[1] In particular, it was not required to disclose information about its risks to counterparties; disclose information about market prices or conditions, even in markets that it dominated; or set aside prudential capital against trading risks. These gaps contributed to its demise and the associated financial market implications. Because its trading unit's capital was not segregated from the parent company's capital, a loss of confidence in the parent company's soundness led its banks to withdraw credit lines, which in turn contributed to a collapse in its trading operation. Some

---

[1]Testimony of Vincent Viola, Chairman, New York Mercantile Exchange, before the Senate Energy and Natural Resources Committee, January 29, 2002. Energy derivatives are subject to the antifraud and antimanipulation provisions of the Commodity Exchange Act, however.

in the CDO market, which involves heterogeneous instruments and special purpose vehicles (SPVs) that can be complex and relatively nontransparent to investors. In addition, the potential for CDO investors to experience sudden and larger-than-anticipated losses (as in the case of American Express) observers have since called for revisions to the 2000 Commodity Futures Modernization Act that exempted energy derivatives activities from key regulatory provisions, and U.S. Congressional hearings have since discussed this issue. Nevertheless, even if these exemptions had not been made, Enron's activities in credit and other financial derivatives markets would still have been essentially unregulated.

Ineffective private market discipline, disclosure, corporate governance, and auditing. Enron's financial difficulties and vulnerabilities, including those associated with its extensive off-balance-sheet transactions, seemed to have gone undetected by analysts as well as its shareholders and creditors until it was on the brink of bankruptcy. In part, this reflected inadequate accounting rules and standards as well as errors by its auditors, who (among other oversights) did not uncover related-party transactions or require Enron to properly consolidate its many and complex off-balance-sheet special purpose vehicles (SPVs) in its financial statements. In October 2001, the correction of this and other errors resulted in a restatement of income since 1997 by US$600 million and a writedown of shareholder equity by US$1.2 billion. Questions also arose about the auditor's possible conflict of interest owing to its parent company's extensive consulting business with Enron (in 2000 Enron paid it US$25 million in auditing fees and US$27 million in consulting fees). Along with allegations that the auditor destroyed documents relevant to an SEC inquiry, these revelations led to widespread calls for a closer examination of auditing standards and practices.

Misallocation of retirement savings. More than 10,000 Enron employees held most of their retirement savings in Enron stock, including Enron's contributions (entirely in company stock)—which the company prohibited them from selling until age 50. In addition, for three weeks in October 2000, Enron required its employees to freeze their asset allocations as it switched plan administrators, during which time Enron stock fell by 35 percent. As a consequence of the pension plan's poor diversification and inflexibility, during 2001 a large share of employee savings were wiped out as Enron's stock price plummeted from about US$90 to less than US$1. In the early part of 2002, the U.S. authorities formed a working group to consider potential reforms to the Employee Retirement Income Security Act (ERISA) rules that govern private pension investments, and the U.S. Congress held hearings to discuss (among other topics) how to address gaps in ERISA that permitted a high concentration of Enron stock in the company's pension fund.

raises a question about whether such vehicles pose reputational risks to banks. An originating bank might prefer to compensate its investors for losses or buy back the product, rather than risk damage to its reputation that could prevent it from selling such products in the future. If this occurred, the bank would wind up with a loss on the underlying credit exposure despite having bought credit protection in what seemingly had been an arms-length transaction.

Remaining and Future Challenges

Markets for credit risk transfers are still in a developmental stage, typical of the product cycle for new markets. In 2001–2002, and again in 2004–2005, the market seemed to be able to cope with a series of credit events that emerged as the global economy slowed. Payments were made by credit risk protection sellers to protection buyers, even though in some cases this occurred only after arbitration. At the same time, these events revealed some challenges in using these instruments and in understanding their impact on financial stability.

Industry Challenges

First, credit derivatives can reduce the transparency about who owns credit risk, in part because the transfer of credit risk reduces the informational content of balance sheets without necessarily providing additional information about where the risk is transferred or even how it is priced. By reducing transparency about credit exposures, the growth in credit derivatives complicates the assessment of private credit risk and counterparty risk in individual institutions. It also makes it more difficult to assess the overall distribution of credit risk across institutions and markets, and to assess the challenges that credit risk transfers might pose to liquidity conditions in related underlying and derivatives markets (that is, it poses liquidity risks) and more generally to financial market stability. The fact that nontraditional entities—such as Enron—are now trading in these markets and not subject to the same disclosure rules and standards as regulated financial institutions further adds to the lack of transparency. Moreover, as illustrated by Enron, there are gaps in accounting rules and standards, particularly regarding SPVs, as well as in auditing practices, that apparently are also contributing to a lack of transparency.[119]

Second, regulatory arbitrage involving credit risk transfer vehicles is shifting credit risk exposures outside the banking system. Concern arises

---

[119]See Volker (2002).

because regulatory incentives appear to encourage banks to transfer credit risk to other institutions—such as hedge funds, pension funds, and insurance companies—that are not prudentially regulated as banks are, especially with regard to capital adequacy, and that have not traditionally had cultures or risk management systems attuned to credit risk. Nevertheless, these nonbank financial institutions manage a large volume of assets distributed across global markets and are part of the global network of counterparty risk exposures. Some believe they are the weak links in the chain of counterparty relationships. A string of unanticipated credit events causing those market participants to experience much larger than expected losses could lead them to reduce their willingness to supply credit protection when banks need it most. It could also lead to a withdrawal of capital devoted to market making in credit risk transfer vehicles. These reactions, if sharp and sustained, could significantly impair liquidity and create volatility in the credit derivatives and related markets, similar to the way in which the threat of default by LTCM affected credit markets in 1998.

Third, because the use of credit risk transfer vehicles tends to increase the links between markets and institutions, these new instruments tend to increase the potential for spillovers across markets or to intensify existing channels for spillovers. For example, unanticipated shocks to an underlying bond or loan transaction for which there is an associated credit derivative would give rise to increased demand for credit hedges. During a period of turbulence in the underlying market, situations could arise in which there would be one-sided, illiquid, and volatile credit derivatives markets that, through counterparty relationships, could spill over into connected markets. Likewise, in a market with relatively few very large counterparties, a cluster of credit events could trigger payments on many contracts at once and put considerable liquidity demands on one or more of the relatively small number of major market makers.[120] If these market makers had to sell a wide range of liquid securities from their portfolios to cover payments, volatility could rise sharply in a variety of markets at once. In addition, because a number of the institutions that sell protection—particularly insurance companies—typically have access to bank credit lines, they might tap these lines to fund payments on credit risk transfer contracts, potentially

---

[120]Global data are not available, but in the United States at end 2004, one U.S. bank held 45 percent of the banking system's outstanding notional credit derivatives; the top two banks held 67 percent, and the top three banks held 87 percent. (See Table 1 in U.S. Comptroller of the Currency, 2005.) As noted elsewhere, banks are net buyers of credit protection; it is unclear whether holdings of net protection sellers are similarly concentrated.

putting pressure on bank liquidity. Finally, credit hedges could fail to perform as expected if a major protection seller came under financial stress and either contested the legality of the contract or was unable to pay. This could leave banks with unhedged credit positions, give rise to an increase in the demand for credit hedges or unloading of credit positions, and potentially lead to an increase in credit market volatility.

These transmission mechanisms can be magnified by the leverage inherent in credit derivatives. As with other OTC derivatives, credit derivatives allow investors to take on exposure to an underlying credit instrument while committing much less in funds than would be required to actually buy the instrument. In addition, a single underlying credit transaction can give rise to multiple gross credit derivative transactions as dealers rehedge and lay exposures off on one another. The total gross credit exposures created through this process can, in principle, substantially exceed the exposure on the underlying instrument. For example, an initial $1 billion credit transaction might give rise to five rounds of hedging as dealers pass the exposure around the market. Each transaction involves the creation of another $1 billion in gross exposure to one counterparty; five such transactions therefore give rise to $5 billion in gross credit exposure.

A fourth challenge arises because these are relatively new instruments and markets, and investor access to credit risk markets is easier, so a significant amount of capital from nontraditional sources is flowing into credit risk transfers. Concerns have been raised that the costs and benefits of these instruments are not fully understood. More generally, the tendency for credit derivative spreads to be volatile and even decline below the spreads on the underlying bonds raises questions about whether participants in the credit derivatives markets—especially those that have not traditionally managed credit risks—have yet learned how to price these contracts appropriately. In early 2001, a strong supply of credit protection—including from institutional investors and money managers—compared with demand for credit protection from banks apparently contributed to narrow and sometimes even negative spreads between the credit default swap premium and the credit spread on the underlying security (Figure 10.3).[121] Whether

---

[121]The premium is the spread over the London Interbank Offered Rate (LIBOR) that is paid for credit protection. Although the analytical theory is still being developed, the difference between the premium on a credit derivative and the credit spread on the underlying instrument partly reflects differences in tax treatment, liquidity, and counterparty risks for a bond versus a credit default swap. These structural features might limit the extent to which market participants can arbitrage away the difference in spreads between the two markets. The sharp blowout in spreads during September 2001 probably reflected an increased demand for credit protection following the terrorist attacks.

Figure 10.3. Spread Between Credit Derivatives Premium and Underlying Bond Spread[1]
(In basis points)

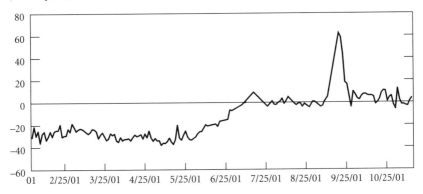

Source: Deutsche Bank.
[1]Average for credit default swaps on four investment grade U.S. corporations.

contracts are being properly priced is difficult to know, in part because the theory of credit derivatives pricing is still developing. If, in fact, credit derivatives prices "overshoot" and are excessively volatile relative to the price of the underlying credit, signals about credit risks would be distorted. Accordingly, it would also raise questions about whether credit risk transfer vehicles improve or reduce the efficiency of credit allocation in markets.

Looking ahead, improvements to the infrastructure for, and transparency of, credit risk transfers could help them to develop more fully, help market participants to manage the risks, and make the markets more efficient. This occurred in the OTC swaps markets during the 1990s, and there is good reason to expect the credit derivatives markets will mature through time as well. As of mid-2005 it is still too early to judge whether these markets have matured, in part because they are being tested once again with the downgrades of debt issued by GM and Ford, whose corporate bonds are widely held by institutional investors and are often within a tranche of collateralized debt obligations. As this book was being completed, various hedge funds were alleged to be in serious financial trouble as a result of their trading strategies involving GM and Ford bonds, and some counterparty major banks also were alleged to have experienced serious losses on their proprietary trading activities. Nevertheless, through mid-2005 the markets seem to have taken these quite remarkable events in stride. Infrastructure improvements in the future will no doubt include better documentation that further refines the definition of a credit event.

Bankruptcy legislation that would establish the legal effectiveness of close-out netting and a convergence in bankruptcy laws about what constitutes a default would also encourage further maturation of the market. Better information about the size and structure of the market and the exposures of bank and nonbank financial institutions active in the market would help market participants assess the attendant risks and gauge whether they are well managed by the institutions involved in the markets.

Implications for Retail Investors

Another issue that could become more important in the future is the small, but increasing, exposure of retail investors to the risks associated with credit risk transfers. Hard data on retail participation and exposures are not available, but retail investors are searching for higher-yielding alternatives to their traditional investment instruments such as stocks, government and corporate bonds, money-market mutual funds, and bank deposits in light of the low returns on such instruments through mid-2005. Retail demand may also reflect the longer-term, underlying trends of disintermediation and more direct retail investment in asset markets. In this environment, retail investors have increasingly invested in, and become exposed to the risks in, a variety of structured products, including guaranteed funds—providing downside protection by hedging exposures in derivatives markets—and mutual funds that own CDOs.

In mid-2005, credit analysts perceived that retail investors were participating in a relatively limited way in credit risk transfer markets through three main channels: investments by high net worth individuals, mutual funds, and hedge funds.[122] Although data are not available, in view of their recent proliferation, hedge funds may be a principal channel for direct or indirect retail participation in credit risk transfer markets. Hedge funds invest in CDOs and employ credit default swaps to hedge the credit risk in convertible bond arbitrage strategies. Retail investments in these strategies have become more accessible as hedge funds have reduced minimum investment requirements and instituted less restrictive "lock up" rules that allow investors to withdraw more quickly. Hedge funds that meet enhanced disclosure and regulatory requirements are allowed to increase the number of investors (thereby reducing their minimum investments), and are more

---

[122]Retail participation takes place through mutual funds investing in CDOs rather than credit derivatives, because credit derivatives trade only on OTC markets made up of financial institution counterparties.

readily accessible to pension funds and other institutional investors. Moreover, minimum investment rules are increasingly irrelevant, because one can invest any amount in recently created offshore-based funds, structured as closed-end funds, that invest 100 percent of their assets in hedge funds ("funds of funds"). It is estimated that about 482 funds of funds exist and account for about 20 percent to 25 percent of the hedge fund universe of about $950 billion in capital under management (in 2004).[123]

Even if direct involvement and exposure in credit risk transfer mechanisms is limited, retail investors can become exposed to credit risk in many less-transparent ways. For example, shareholders of American Express stock were adversely affected when it became known that American Express had taken significant losses on its investments in CDOs, which involved credit risk transfer mechanisms. Likewise, many retail investors may hold mutual funds that invest in riskier credit instruments to enhance their yields. One illustration of this is the unexpected impact of the collapse of Enron on Japanese mutual funds. These mutual funds invested in Enron's samurai bonds and marketed shares in their funds to Japanese retail investors as a high yield alternative to bank deposits. The collapse of Enron caused a run on these mutual funds, as investors withdrew 2 trillion yen (US$16 billion) from 27 mutual funds. This was well in excess of the funds' holdings of Enron samurai bonds (totaling 66 billion yen). The Bank of Japan had to intervene by injecting 6 trillion yen (US$49 billion) of liquidity to offset the potential adverse impact on the banking system. This injection followed an earlier injection of more than 8 trillion yen resulting from the impact of the liquidity effects in Japan following the events of September 11, 2001.

As a result of all these changes, the hedge fund industry, including the segment that is active in credit risk transfer markets, is widely considered to have been "democratized." For instance, many of the new retail investors are not the traditional high net worth individuals—minimum investments in hedge funds in Europe, Japan, and the United States are now as low as 20,000 euro (or $18,000). Reflecting this easier access, retail hedge fund investments surged from $8 billion in 2000 to over $22 billion in 2001 through September, and have continued to increase rapidly since then. The potential for retail participation will increase further as more hedge fund investment vehicles begin to be offered publicly.

The challenge for active retail participation in credit risk transfer markets seems to be mainly an investor protection issue. As noted above, even some

---

[123]The estimate of $950 billion in 2004 is from Van Hedge Fund Advisors International, 2005.

sophisticated market participants have encountered trials in investing in and understanding how best to use credit risk transfers. In this regard, there may be cause for concern about first, the ability of retail investors to understand fully the risks in credit risk transfer vehicles and price them accordingly and second, whether the disclosure and transparency standards developed for other instruments, such as mutual funds, need to be updated.

The activities of intermediaries that offer products such as guaranteed funds might be altering the distribution of credit risks in the financial system, adding a further complication. Internationally active financial institutions trade actively in global exchange-traded and OTC derivatives markets to hedge their exposures to the retail products they sell, in effect arbitraging between professional hedging markets and the retail markets. Because this activity effectively transfers credit risk from the guaranteed fund to its counterparties—which can include a wide range of financial institutions such as hedge funds and insurance companies—it both complicates an assessment of who bears the ultimate risks associated with the products and raises questions about whether the counterparties can manage these risks well.

As retail investor participation grows over time, the broader dispersion of credit risks across investors could improve the effectiveness of credit risk transfer markets in mitigating the financial effects of periods of economic stress. Nevertheless, the relatively limited sophistication of individual investors and questions about disclosure and transparency could have implications for financial efficiency and stability. For instance, herding or bandwagon effects could occur in credit risk transfer markets if retail investment decisions are driven primarily by investor sentiment rather than information about changing fundamentals. Similarly, if disclosure and transparency to retail investors about the risks in these vehicles are insufficient, the potential for investment mistakes to occur increases, as does the potential for rapid unwinding of investment positions when these mistakes are discovered. Both these effects would tend to increase volatility in credit prices and spreads, and might also adversely affect the efficient allocation of credit in the financial system.

11

Systemic Implications of the Financial Market Activities of Insurance and Reinsurance Companies

Insurance and reinsurance companies are an important and growing class of financial market participants. They insure a wide variety of business and household risks, thereby facilitating economic and financial activity. In addition, amid a drive to raise profitability they have become increasingly important investors and intermediaries in a broad range of financial markets around the globe. Such companies bring innovative insurance approaches to capital markets, providing insurance coverage for financial risks, intermediating their own insurance risks in the markets, and in the process developing new instruments that help bridge the gap between banking and insurance products. Insurers and reinsurers have broadened the range of available instruments, increased the diversity of market participants, created new opportunities for corporations and financial institutions to fund their activities and hedge risks, and contributed to liquidity and price discovery in primary and secondary markets.[124]

Compared with knowledge about commercial and investment banking activities, much less is known about the financial activities of insurance and reinsurance companies and the overarching environment in which these companies conduct their core businesses. The lack of information on insurers became known and of concern to policymakers after the bursting of the global equity-market bubble in early 2000. Many insurance companies in some countries, particularly in Europe, experienced large losses on their equity portfolios (in some cases driving them into insolvency), which

---

[124]This chapter draws on material in IMF (2002c). The author is grateful to his colleagues for the joint effort at the time, and for their permission to draw on this publication.

had grown substantially as a result of the heavy investments they made in equities during the mid- to late 1990s as the bubble was inflating. Insurance and other financial regulators then realized that they did not have sufficient information about the capital market activities of insurers, and that prudential regulations for insurers may not have kept pace with the growing market orientation of insurers' balance sheets.

This chapter fills part of the information and analysis gap by identifying issues likely to attract increasing attention and that may have medium-term implications for financial stability or efficiency. The first section of this chapter discusses the size and structure of insurers' and reinsurers' financial activities and how that size and structure have evolved in recent years. The second section explores some of the more forward-looking financial stability issues, including those surrounding a number of uncertainties about insurers' and reinsurers' financial market activities, and the attendant potential implications for financial efficiency and stability in the medium term.

Insurance and Reinsurance Companies' Financial Activities

Insurance companies' asset holdings grew substantially during the 1990s, even relative to banks'. Between 1990 and 2001 (the latest year for which there is complete and comparable data) the financial assets of insurers in six major countries grew by about 130 percent to $9.7 trillion, while the assets of banks in the same countries grew by 50 percent to $21.6 trillion (Figures 11.1 and 11.2).[125] In most countries, insurance companies hold larger amounts of financial securities than do banks (Figure 11.3). Moreover, their holdings of international and domestic securities are large relative to domestic markets (Figure 11.4).[126] For example, U.S. insurers are the largest domestic investors in corporate and foreign bonds (Figure 11.5). Insurance companies' large asset pools are invested conservatively, consistent with regulatory restrictions, although the composition of asset portfolios varies substantially across countries (Figures 11.6 and 11.7).[127]

In addition to investing, life insurance companies participate in financial markets by offering retail financial products in the form of hybrid

---

[125]The six countries are France, Germany, Italy, Japan, the United Kingdom, and the United States.

[126]For most countries, holdings of securities are not broken down into domestic and foreign. It is therefore impossible to make cross-country comparisons of domestic holdings relative to domestic market size.

[127]See Joint Forum (2001b) for more detailed explanations of regulatory restrictions.

Figure 11.1. Shares of Total Financial Assets of Institutional Investors and Banks: United States and Japan

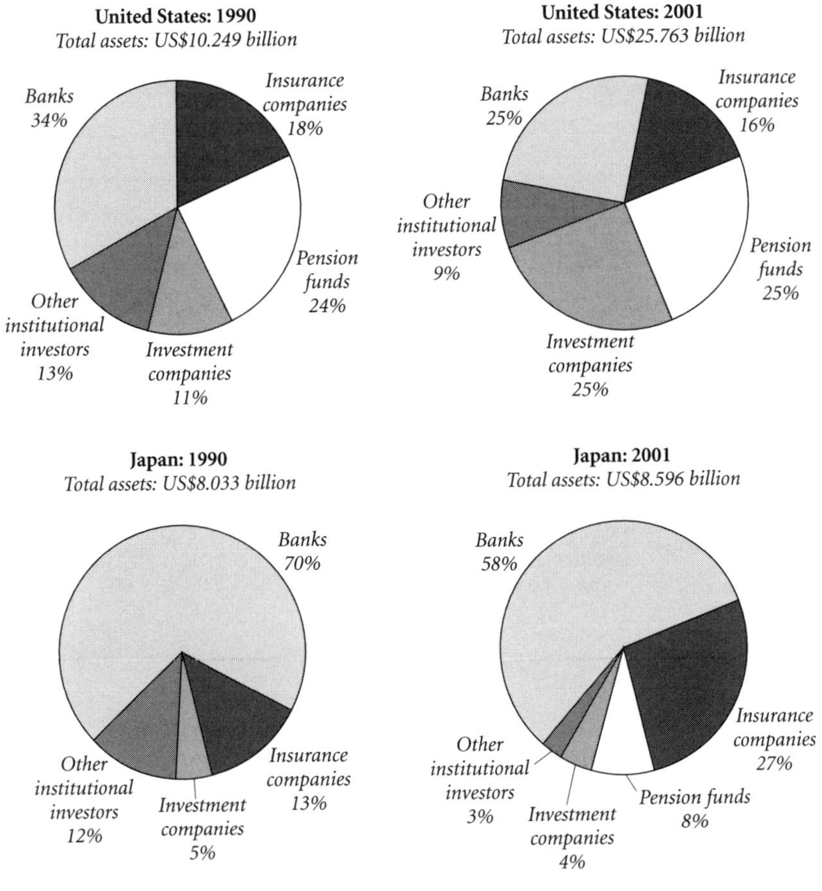

United States: 1990
Total assets: US$10.249 billion

- Banks 34%
- Insurance companies 18%
- Pension funds 24%
- Investment companies 11%
- Other institutional investors 13%

United States: 2001
Total assets: US$25.763 billion

- Banks 25%
- Insurance companies 16%
- Pension funds 25%
- Investment companies 25%
- Other institutional investors 9%

Japan: 1990
Total assets: US$8.033 billion

- Banks 70%
- Insurance companies 13%
- Investment companies 5%
- Other institutional investors 12%

Japan: 2001
Total assets: US$8.596 billion

- Banks 58%
- Insurance companies 27%
- Pension funds 8%
- Investment companies 4%
- Other institutional investors 3%

Sources: OECD, *Institutional Investors Yearbook*, various years; and OECD, *Bank Profitability: Financial Statements of Banks*, various years.

insurance contracts–mutual funds. These are growing rapidly in some countries. In the United States, about half of all new life insurance policies are unit-linked (linked to market returns). Such products are also popular in Europe, where they may have tax advantages over mutual funds. In Italy, single-premium, unit-linked products are offered; these products exchange a large up-front payment for a mutual fund that incorporates a life insurance policy. Such products are often sold through *bancassurance* groups, which are joint ventures between banks and insurance firms.

Figure 11.2. Shares of Financial Assets of Institutional Investors and Banks: Selected Euro Area Countries and the United Kingdom

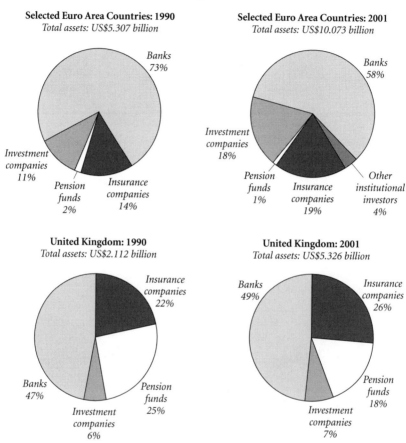

Sources: OECD, *Institutional Investors Yearbook*, various years; and OECD, *Bank Profitability: Financial Statements of Banks*, various years.
Note: Selected euro area countries are Germany, France, and Italy.

Investments As a Response to Underwriting Losses

The overall profitability of an insurance company depends on the net profitability of its insurance underwriting and financial activities. Three main factors influence this profitability:

- *The incidence and size of claims.* Notable increases in nonlife insured losses arose following Hurricane Andrew in 1992, the attacks of September 11 in 2001, and natural disasters in 2004 (Figure 11.8).

Figure 11.3. Holdings of Financial Securities by Insurance Companies and Banks
(Billions of U.S. dollars)

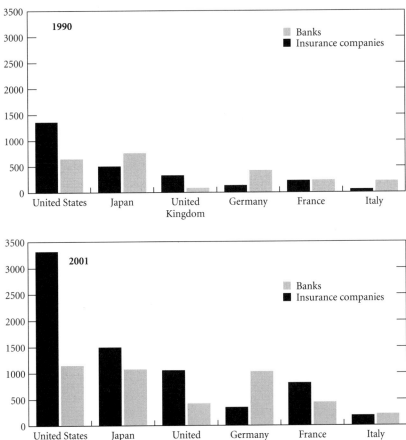

Sources: OECD, *Institutional Investors Yearbook*, various years; and OECD, *Bank Profitability: Financial Statements of Banks*, various years.

- *The prevailing level of premiums.* During the 1990s and early 2000s, premiums tended to grow at an inflation-adjusted rate of about 5 percent (higher for life, lower for nonlife before 2000)—well below average rates attained during the 1980s (see Figure 11.8 and Table 11.1).
- *The performance of financial markets.* Since the early 1980s, insurance companies in the major countries have been increasingly successful in reaping investment returns that compare favorably with the yield on domestic government bonds (see Figure 11.8).

Figure 11.4. Holdings of Securities Relative to Domestic Market Size
(Percent)

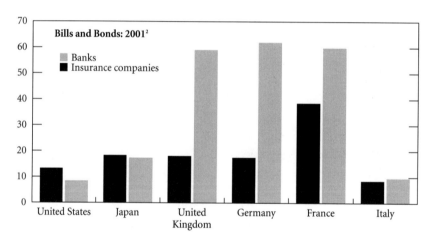

Sources: OECD, *Institutional Investors Yearbook*, various years; and OECD, *Bank Profitability: Financial Statements of Banks*, various years.

Note: Bank holdings include resident and nonresident holdings.

[1]For Germany, France, and Italy data refer to resident and nonresident holdings.

[2]For Germany and France data refer to resident and nonresident holdings.

Since the mid-1990s, insurance loss ratios (relative to premiums) ranged from 57.2 percent in Japan to 82.9 percent in France (see Table 11.2, which focuses on nonlife companies). Expense-to-premium ratios ranged from 22.4 percent in France to 35.2 percent in Japan. Adding these two ratios into the "combined ratio" gives a standard, widely used measure of the overall

Figure 11.4. Holdings of Securities Relative to Domestic Market Size (*concluded*)
(*Percent*)

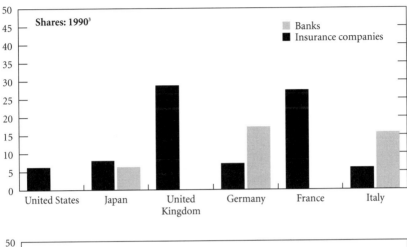

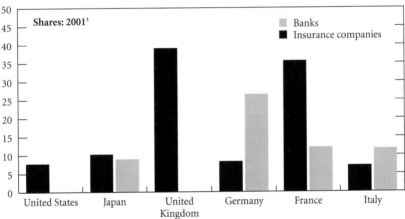

Sources: OECD, *Institutional Investors Yearbook*, various years; and OECD, *Bank Profitability: Financial Statements of Banks*, various years.
    Note: Bank holdings include resident and nonresident holdings.
    [3]Holdings of shares include resident and nonresident holdings.

profitability of an insurance company's core underwriting business (apart from the return on its market investments). As Table 11.2 and Figure 11.9 show, during 1995–2003, in most countries, nonlife insurers had combined ratios above 100 percent, implying that on a cash-flow basis and excluding investment returns, insurance underwriting was loss-making. Except in Japan, losses plus expenses exceeded premiums by 0.1 percent to 7.6 percent

Figure 11.5. United States: Corporate and Foreign Bonds
(As a percentage of total amounts outstanding; end of period)

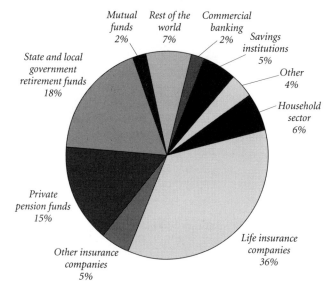

1980
Total amount outstanding: US$507.6 billion

Mutual funds 2%
Rest of the world 7%
Commercial banking 2%
Savings institutions 5%
Other 4%
Household sector 6%
State and local government retirement funds 18%
Life insurance companies 36%
Other insurance companies 5%
Private pension funds 15%

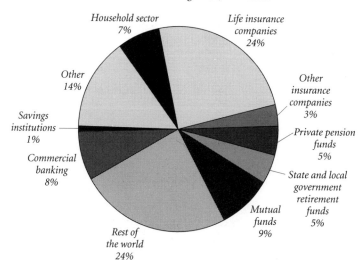

2004
Total amount outstanding: US$7,227.2 billion

Household sector 7%
Life insurance companies 24%
Other 14%
Other insurance companies 3%
Savings institutions 1%
Private pension funds 5%
Commercial banking 8%
State and local government retirement funds 5%
Mutual funds 9%
Rest of the world 24%

Source: U.S. Board of Governors of the Federal Reserve System, *Flow of Funds*.

Figure 11.6. Balance Sheet Assets of Insurance Companies: United States and Japan

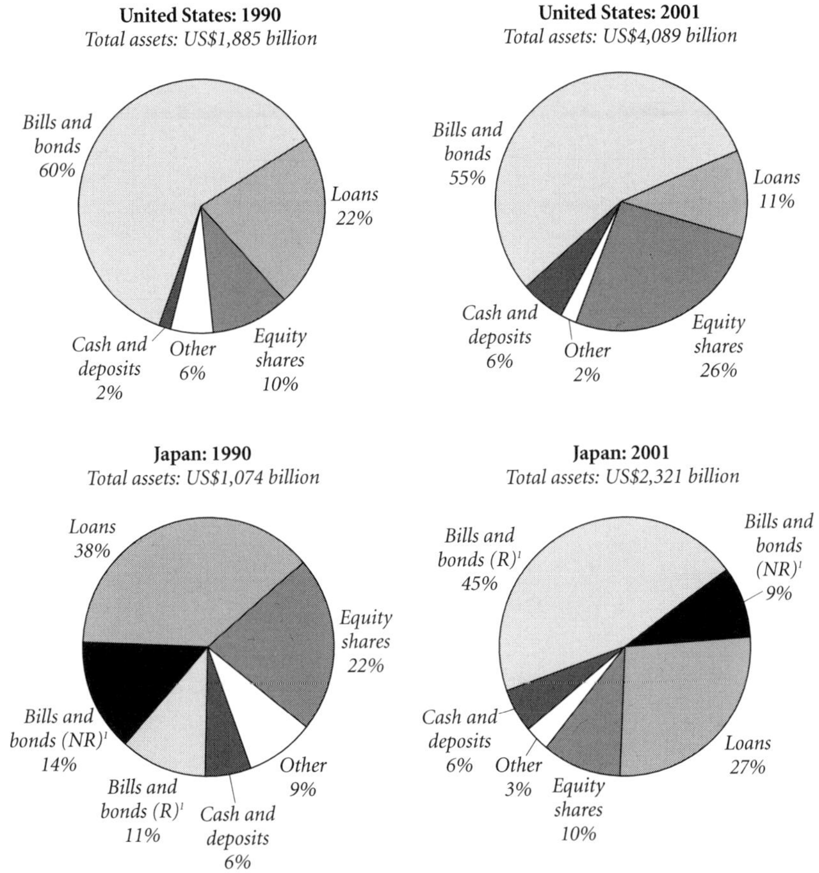

United States: 1990
Total assets: US$1,885 billion

Bills and bonds 60%
Loans 22%
Cash and deposits 2%
Other 6%
Equity shares 10%

United States: 2001
Total assets: US$4,089 billion

Bills and bonds 55%
Loans 11%
Cash and deposits 6%
Other 2%
Equity shares 26%

Japan: 1990
Total assets: US$1,074 billion

Loans 38%
Equity shares 22%
Bills and bonds (NR)[1] 14%
Bills and bonds (R)[1] 11%
Cash and deposits 6%
Other 9%

Japan: 2001
Total assets: US$2,321 billion

Bills and bonds (R)[1] 45%
Bills and bonds (NR)[1] 9%
Cash and deposits 6%
Other 3%
Equity shares 10%
Loans 27%

Source: OECD, *Institutional Investors Statistical Yearbook*, various issues.
[1]Bills and bonds issued by residents (R) and nonresidents (NR).

("Underwriting result" line in Table 11.2). In Japan, returns on underwriting were 2.2 percent.[128]

Nonlife insurers in the countries in Table 11.2 made up for underwriting losses, or augmented underwriting returns, through investment. Investment yields ranged from 2.5 percent in Japan (reflecting low government

---

[128]In the late 1990s, the positive results in Germany and Japan partly reflect accounting conventions that exclude some expenses or include investment income in the combined ratio. See Swiss Re (2001).

Figure 11.7. Balance Sheet Assets of Insurance Companies: Selected Euro Area Countries and United Kingdom

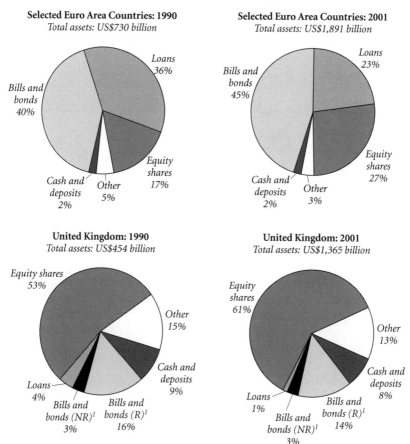

Selected Euro Area Countries: 1990
Total assets: US$730 billion

Loans 36%
Bills and bonds 40%
Equity shares 17%
Cash and deposits 2%
Other 5%

Selected Euro Area Countries: 2001
Total assets: US$1,891 billion

Loans 23%
Bills and bonds 45%
Equity shares 27%
Cash and deposits 2%
Other 3%

United Kingdom: 1990
Total assets: US$454 billion

Equity shares 53%
Other 15%
Cash and deposits 9%
Loans 4%
Bills and bonds (NR)[1] 3%
Bills and bonds (R)[1] 16%

United Kingdom: 2001
Total assets: US$1,365 billion

Equity shares 61%
Other 13%
Cash and deposits 8%
Loans 1%
Bills and bonds (NR)[1] 3%
Bills and bonds (R)[1] 14%

Source: OECD, *Institutional Investors Statistical Yearbook*, various issues.
Note: Selected euro area countries are France, Germany, and Italy.
[1]Bills and bonds issued by residents (R) and nonresidents (NR).

bond yields and declining stock prices) to 8.4 percent in the United Kingdom, and translated into net investment results (expressed as a percent of premiums) ranging from 9.3 percent to 18.8 percent. Net of taxes and other expenses, underwriting and investment results translated into profit margins from 1.2 percent (Japan) to 11.1 percent (United Kingdom), and returns on equity from 3.2 percent (France) to 14.3 percent (United Kingdom).

Figure 11.8. Global Insurance Industry Results

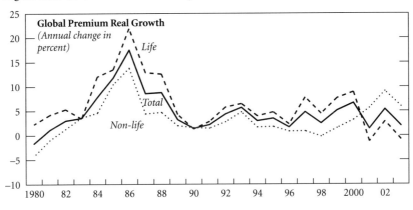

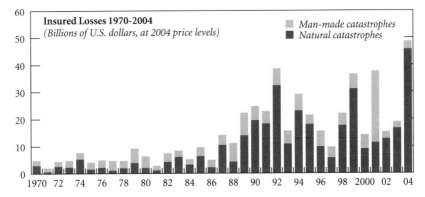

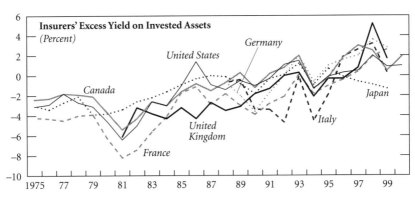

Source: Swiss Re Economic Research & Consulting.

Table 11.1. Life Insurance: Premium Growth Rates

	Single Premiums as a Percent of Total Life Business			Average Annual Growth Rates 1995–2003 (percent)		Average Annual Growth Rates 2000–2003 (percent)	
	1995	2000	2003	Single Premiums	Annual Premiums	Single Premiums	Annual Premiums
United States[1]	12.7	15.6	18.2	6.6	0.5	6.7	0.4
Japan	9.8	6.8	16.7	4.7	–2.1	35.1	0.1
United Kingdom	47.4	76.9	71.4	14.8	1.7	–10.5	–1.0
France	69.2	71.7	...	...	...	...	...
Germany	9.3	11.6	13.0	7.1	2.1	5.1	1.0
Italy[2]	36.9	60.1	70.6	31.0	8.7	22.7	–4.5
Netherlands	38.7	46.3	47.1	10.2	6.7	2.0	1.6
Switzerland	48.8	55.4	50.8	3.4	2.4	–2.8	3.3

Source: Swiss Re Economic Research & Consulting.
[1]Only personal life business.
[2]Figures for 2003 are estimates.

In the life insurance industry, reaping strong investment returns has been especially important for companies that have high guaranteed rates of nominal return on existing policies. In the 1980s and early 1990s, insurance companies offered high guaranteed returns on insurance policies, reflecting the ability to earn very strong market returns on asset portfolios, high premium incomes, and in some countries, high minimum rates mandated by regulators. As nominal bond yields sank during the 1990s amid declining inflation and the euro area convergence process, meeting these guarantees became more challenging. In Japan and Switzerland, government bond yields slid below guaranteed rates on existing policies.

During the 1990s, insurers responded to an environment of lower real premium growth by managing asset portfolios more actively and shifting the asset mix. Between 1990 and 2001, insurers' investments in corporate equities rose from 17 percent to 27 percent in the euro area, from 53 percent to 61 percent in the United Kingdom, and from 10 percent to 26 percent in the United States (see Figures 11.6 and 11.7).[129] In addition, the development of emerging markets and corporate bond markets, including the market for lower-rated credit instruments, offered insurance companies opportunities to raise investment returns. Active asset management together with realized capital gains from rising bond and share prices enabled insur-ance companies in most countries to earn an investment yield above that of the long-term government bond yield in their home country (see Figure 11.8).

Shift into Newer Financial Market Activities

In the 1990s, periods of soft premiums and low bond yields also spurred innovations that fostered convergence between insurance and capital markets. Insurers divested less profitable insurance risks in the form of catastrophic risk ("Cat") bonds—bonds with payoffs linked to a catastrophic event. Reinsurers also diversified their insurance business by developing the profitable "alternative risk transfer" (ART) market for customized reinsurance products that bridge the gap between traditional insurance and banking products.[130] Examples include contingent capital, which gives an

---

[129]Some of the shift in equity allocations may reflect stock price changes. In Japan, for example, the share of insurers' assets allocated to equity shares shrank from 22 percent to 10 percent.

[130]Major reinsurers estimate return on equity in the ART business to be in the range of 20 percent to 25 percent, well above typical rates for traditional reinsurance business. (Reinsurance is insurance for insurance companies. Reinsurance products [and companies] provide insurance against some of the risks incurred by insurance companies in their insurance contracts.)

Table 11.2. Profitability Decomposition of Major Nonlife Insurance Markets
(*Percent of net premiums*)

	United States 1995–2003	Canada 1996–2003	United Kingdom 1996–2003	Germany 1995–2003	France 1995–2003	Italy 1995–2003	Japan 1995–2003
Loss ratio	79.1	74.5	69.4	71.1	82.9	81.0	57.2
Expense ratio	26.6	30.4	31.8	26.0	22.4	24.2	35.2
Underwriting result[1]	–7.6	–5.7	–7.1	–0.1	–6.8	–6.1	2.2
Investment yield[2]	6.6	7.1	8.4	6.9	5.9	4.2	2.5
Asset leverage	262.5	205.2	220.3	221.0	223.5	198.4	446.1[3]
Net investment result	16.8	15.1	18.8	14.8	13.0	9.3	9.9
Other expenses to earnings	–1.2	0.3	0.8	–1.9	–1.5	1.6	–9.2
Profit margin (pre-tax)	9.2	9.7	12.5	12.8	4.7	4.8	2.9
Tax rate	18.4	35.7	10.5	41.3	28.9	38.5	58.8[4]
Profit margin (after-tax)	7.2	6.5	11.0	7.4	3.0	3.1	1.2
Solvency	98.6	87.0	78.4	128.8[5]	98.2	…	…
ROE[2]	7.3	7.4	14.3	5.7[5]	3.2	…	…

Source: Swiss Re Economic Research & Consulting.
Note: Loss, expense, policyholder dividend and combined ratios for the United States, Canada, and the United Kingdom are net of reinsurance, whereas for Germany, France, Italy, and Japan they are for direct business (prior to cessions to reinsurers).

[1]Includes policyholder dividend.
[2]Investment result in percent of assets of previous year.
[3]Includes reserves for maturity-refund policies, which are about 45 percent of assets and 30 percent of premiums.
[4]Excludes 1999 because in 1999 taxes were paid despite pre-tax losses, resulting in a calculated negative 631 percent tax rate for 1999.
[5]1997–2003

Figure 11.9. Nonlife Insurance: Combined Ratios in the Industrialised Countries
(In percent)

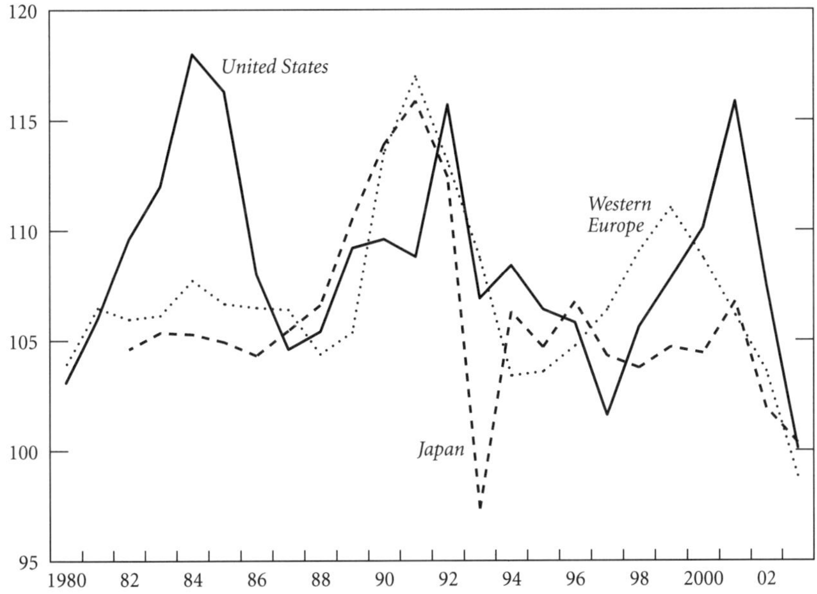

Source: Swiss Re Economic Research & Consulting.

insurance company the option to replenish its capital if it is adversely affected by a natural catastrophe; captive insurance, which permits large conglomerates to insure themselves by pooling risks in a separate entity; and finite reinsurance, which is a form of self-insurance that permits a policyholder to spread an insurance loss over a predetermined period of time.

Insurance companies also sought to diversify their large investment portfolios and funding sources. For example, they became more important participants in credit derivatives markets, helping banks to hedge and diversify their credit exposures.[131] Market participants indicate that insurance companies are more active buyers of collateralized debt obligations (CDOs), private equity, funds of hedge funds, and reverse convertible securities. On the funding side, U.S. life insurance companies have issued

---

[131]See IMF (2002b), Chapter III. It has frequently been suggested that differences in the regulatory treatment of financial risks between banks and insurers may have created opportunities for regulatory arbitrage, but the Joint Forum cautions that "comparisons of individual elements of the different capital frameworks are potentially inappropriate and misleading" (Joint Forum, 2001b, p. 5).

funding arrangements (FAs) and guaranteed investment contracts (GICs), issuance of which grew rapidly to about $40 billion to $50 billion in 2001 (JP Morgan, 2001). According to market participants, funds so generated were generally invested in higher-yielding securities with similar maturities to the FA/GIC, generating a positive spread.

In 2001, the deterioration in credit and equity markets and huge claims associated with September 11 adversely affected insurers' profits and caused the failure of a few weaker, lower-tier institutions. Subsequently, an improved appreciation of the risks in newer activities, and a firming of insurance premiums amid an increase in demand for insurance, led a number of insurance companies to reevaluate their capital markets activities. In addition, market participants suggest that a number of less-active firms withdrew from activities such as ART and credit derivatives. As a consequence, these newer activities are concentrated among a few large players. Over time, higher premiums may heighten competition in the insurance business, putting downward pressure on premiums and leading to a renewed interest in newer, more profitable activities.

Financial Efficiency and Stability Questions Raised by Insurers' Financial Activities

As noted, relatively little is known about the environment in which insurance and reinsurance companies conduct their financial market activities, and about how the existing regulatory framework should address resulting issues. The remainder of this chapter examines five forward-looking financial stability issues to broaden the understanding of the challenges that lie ahead for the insurance and reinsurance industries and more generally for the international financial community:

- the balance between official oversight and market discipline;
- information about financial markets activities;
- the legal frameworks for insurance and financial markets;
- leverage in individual firms and the overall industry;
- systemic implications, if any, of insurance and reinsurance company instability.

Official Oversight and Market Discipline

As with commercial and investment banking, the soundness of insurance and reinsurance companies and the financial stability of these industries rely on both official oversight and private market discipline. The regulatory and supervisory framework for the insurance industry is primarily oriented toward policyholder protection; thus, it ensures that reserves and capital are adequate and that investments are relatively safe and liquid, so that insurers can pay claims and other cash flows to policyholders on a timely basis. Insurers usually face restrictions on the concentration of balance-sheet investments in asset classes such as fixed income, equity, and real estate.[132] Regulation of off-balance-sheet instruments ranges from broad guidelines to outright prohibition of derivatives transactions that do not directly hedge risks associated with insurance business.[133]

Reflecting its policyholder-protection orientation and the fact that insurers are not deposit-taking institutions, official oversight of the insurance industry in many jurisdictions is less focused on financial market risks when compared with the official oversight of commercial banks. For example, European Union capital requirements reflect the volume of insurance business exclusively. In Australia, Canada, Japan, and the United States the regimes include capital charges for risks on the asset side of the balance sheet, but questions nonetheless remain about whether capital fully reflects the underlying risks.[134] The major Australian insurer HIH filed for liquidation in March 2001, but its administrator reported that it was insolvent as early as June 2000 and possibly earlier. In Japan, questions arise about the quality of capital, which may include deferred tax credits and one year's future income, and the adequacy of risk weights for equity and other exposures.

Reinsurance regulation is less uniform across countries than insurance regulation. In some countries—the United Kingdom and the United States, as well as Denmark, Finland, and Portugal—reinsurers face regulations similar to those applied to primary insurers; in others they are unsupervised. Many reinsurers are located in offshore centers where they face particularly light regulation and supervision, reflecting a view that the wholesale participants in the reinsurance market are more sophisticated and well informed than the retail participants in the primary insurance market, and therefore are better able to assess the risks of their counterparties. Nevertheless, the

---

[132]See EU Directives 92/49/EEC and 92/96/EEC, Articles 21–22, in European Commission (2002a; 2002b).

[133]For example, relevant EU directives provide that derivatives may be used to hedge risks or "facilitate efficient portfolio management," whereas the German regulatory authority publishes a list of permitted derivatives instruments and restricts how they may be used.

[134]In 2001, the U.K. Financial Services Authority proposed the introduction of more flexible prudential standards for insurance companies, along the conceptual lines of the Basel Capital Accord's three-pillar approach (Davies, 2001).

limited regulation of reinsurers in some jurisdictions has raised concerns that reinsurance regulation may need strengthening, and that reinsurance arrangements may reduce the transparency of insurance company accounts and transfer less risk than is apparent.[135]

Supervisory frameworks for insurers and reinsurers have been under active discussion in the official community. The Joint Forum of banking, securities, and insurance supervisors has underscored key differences in risk management practices and regulatory capital requirements across the three sectors (Joint Forum, 2001a and 2001b). The Forum more recently clarified the difficult challenges in enhancing disclosure and transparency in the insurance industry, and in the financial industry more generally (Joint Forum, 2004) and in 2005 published the findings of its study of the credit risk transfer market, including the involvement of insurance companies (Joint Forum, 2005). The International Association of Insurance Supervisors (IAIS) "Principles on Capital Adequacy and Solvency" recommends that capital adequacy and solvency regimes should be sensitive to risks in investments and off-balance-sheet exposures. The IAIS also developed principles for the supervision of reinsurance companies (IAIS, 2002a) and published a set of core principles for supervisory insurers (IAIS, 2003). In the European Union, the 2002 EU "Solvency I" Directives improved solvency requirements, increased supervisors' powers for early intervention, and allowed member states to put in place more stringent solvency requirements. An ongoing "Solvency II" project—scheduled to replace Solvency I in 2007—is considering issues including asset-liability matching, treatment of reinsurance cover, accounting and actuarial policies, and "double gearing" within financial conglomerates (a situation in which two companies structure a transaction in which they each have a claim on the same capital).[136] In addition, observance of insurance core principles in IMF member countries are assessed under the IMF/World Bank Financial Sector Assessment Program (FSAP) (see IMF and World Bank, 2001). Because official oversight is oriented more toward policyholder protection than managing financial market risks, the soundness of insurers and reinsurers relies heavily on market discipline. For example, credit rating agencies inform policyholders and creditors about insurers' financial strength and

---

[135]IAIS (2000, p. 4); and European Commission (2002a). IAIS (2002b) discusses supervisory standards for evaluation of reinsurance cover. The chairman of the U.K. Financial Services Authority recently remarked that two collapsed U.K. insurance companies had "financial reinsurance treaties, of doubtful value, with unregulated reinsurers" (Davies, 2002).

[136]Information on Solvency II can be found on the European Commission's Web site at http://europa.eu.int/comm/internal_market/insurance/solvency_en.htm#solvency2. A useful summary is provided in Annex 3 of BIS, 2003.

insurers strive for high ratings to maintain investors' and policyholders' confidence. In addition, risk managers at some banks partly rely on credit ratings in evaluating their counterparty risk exposures to insurers and the risks in financial products sold by insurers. Finally, counterparties increasingly use Standard and Poor's assessments of risk-based capital that are based on its proprietary capital adequacy model.

Reflecting these considerations, market participants—and some officials—regard the credit rating agencies as the de facto regulators for insurers and reinsurers.[137] Ratings agencies are uncomfortable with this perception and role. Seasoned analysts consider insurance companies to be opaque and complex, and find it difficult to fully evaluate insurers' financial market activities and assess whether the risks are well managed. Similarly, some counterparty institutions of insurers and reinsurers question whether ratings fully reflect the potential counterparty risks. These institutions have further developed their internal credit analysis of their exposures to insurers and reinsurers and tightened counterparty risk management, sometimes by taking more collateral.

Disclosure and Transparency

Less information seems to be available—to officials and private financial stakeholders—on the market activities of insurance companies than on the activities of commercial and investment banks, particularly in four areas.

First, official data to assess whether capital adequately supports insurers' financial risks is limited. Regulatory reports typically contain sparse information on risks in the asset side of the balance sheet and on off-balance-sheet activities in the derivatives markets. In addition, features of accounting standards in the insurance industry, such as limited application of mark-to-market or fair-value accounting to liabilities, and the opacity of actuarial assumptions underlying valuations, may reduce the usefulness of reported data.

Second, relatively little is known about whether insurance companies' management of market and credit risks has kept pace with their growing involvement in the markets. Although some major insurers have sophisticated financial modeling systems, market participants, credit rating agencies, and officials have raised questions about the effectiveness of some insurers'

---

[137]For example, IAIS (2000, p. 51) refers to rating agencies as "private market supervisors." IAIS (2002b, p. 3) notes that "reinsurers in some jurisdictions are directly supervised; other jurisdictions rely on rating agencies in assessing the security of a reinsurer." European Commission (2002b, Chapter 9) discusses the rating agencies' role in the market disciplining mechanism for insurance companies.

and reinsurers' internal risk management and controls for managing their asset-market activities as well as the market risks (mostly interest-rate risk) embedded in their liabilities.[138] For example, life insurers have relied on careful analysis of mortality probabilities, based on detailed and lengthy panel data, in pricing insurance premiums. Because mortality risk is relatively stable over time, profit and loss flows on portfolios of life insurance contracts have been fairly predictable. Market participants suggest that some insurers have tried to adapt the actuarial approach to managing the risks in their financial activities. This strategy has drawbacks, particularly for credit investments where data are lacking and where default probabilities can change sharply and unpredictably with economic and financial developments. These insurers have reportedly since bolstered their credit risk analysis to bring it closer to the standards attained by banks, but the actual extent of progress is unknown.[139]

Third, regulatory and shareholder reports do not consistently disclose the size of, or amount at risk in, off-balance-sheet positions, or the extent to which derivatives are used for hedging rather than yield enhancement. The only aggregate information on insurers' involvement in over-the-counter (OTC) derivatives appears to be the survey figures compiled by the British Bankers' Association on the credit derivatives market (British Bankers' Association, 2004).

Fourth, the migration of financial risks between insurance companies and other financial institutions makes it more challenging to track the distribution of risks in financial systems,[140] raising questions about the extent to which insurance companies are participating in segments such as CDOs and asset-backed commercial paper. There are also questions about the extent to which financial institutions have used financial insurance contracts, particularly in place of derivatives contracts, to hedge financial risks.

Legal Risks in Financial Insurance Contracts

Financial insurance contracts between insurance companies and the internationally active commercial and investment banks have given rise to

---

[138]The IAIS recently noted that "it is questionable whether insurance undertakings—and the insurance supervisors—still have adequate insight into the professionalism and appropriateness of the reinsurance companies, and in the risk exposure policy of globally active reinsurance companies" (IAIS, 2000, p. 4).

[139]See Financial Services Authority (2002, p. 31). European Commission (2002b, p. 53) suggests that "asset risk . . . is often more significant in the risk profile than many insurers believe."

[140]International Monetary Fund (2002c), Chapter III, suggested that the activities of nontraditional investors in credit risk transfer markets might distort prices in credit markets.

some high-profile legal disputes. For example, in the "Hollywood Funding" transactions of 2001, structured notes issued to finance a number of films to be made by Flashpoint Ltd. included credit enhancements in the form of insurance policies written by Lexington Insurance, a subsidiary of American International Group. Bondholders evidently understood the credit enhancements to be in the form of credit guarantees, which require the insurer to pay the bondholders upon default. Lexington argued that the contracts allowed it to refuse to pay if a specified number of films were not produced, and also allowed it to dispute or investigate claims prior to paying. Flashpoint never made any films, and Lexington asserted a right to investigate the claim and delay payment.

In another high-profile case, JP Morgan and Enron were counterparties in forward contracts involving physical delivery of natural gas and oil to JP Morgan. JP Morgan obtained surety bonds from insurance companies to mitigate the risk that Enron would fail to deliver.[141] When Enron filed for bankruptcy protection, JP Morgan sought payment of $965 million on these bonds from the insurers. The insurers refused to pay on the grounds that the counterparties never intended to settle the forward contracts with physical delivery, and claimed that the contracts were a front to obtain the surety bonds as collateral against what JP Morgan and Enron intended as loans from JP Morgan to Enron. JP Morgan allegedly used the surety bonds instead of credit derivatives because the bonds cost much less—perhaps 90 percent less—than credit default swaps (Kochan, 2002). The case was settled out of court just before it was due to go to jury trial in January 2003: JP Morgan received about $600 million from the insurers and took a pre-tax charge of about $400 million to recognize the net loss from the transaction.

These two disputes illustrate the key differences in the legal and operational frameworks underlying insurance and financial contracts. For example, under U.K. law, insurers can delay payment by invoking a "material disclosure" provision to claim that their financial insurance counterparty withheld material information about the underlying risk. By contrast, no such provision applies to OTC derivatives documented under International Swaps and Derivatives Association (ISDA) contracts. In addition, ISDA contracts require immediate payment, whereas insurance contracts may pay off over a period of years, particularly if insurers exercise their right to dispute the claim.

---

[141]A surety bond is a contract issued by the surety guaranteeing that the surety will perform certain acts promised by another or pay a stipulated sum, up to a limit, in lieu of performance should the principal fail to perform. See IMF (2002b).

Reflecting these disputes, some of the major global banks no longer use insurance instruments to manage financial risks and instead use ISDA derivatives contracts, particularly when dealing with insurers. Others have become highly selective in choosing insurance transactions and in choosing counterparties that have a track record of timely payment. In addition, some London market participants now craft contracts to limit the use of "material disclosure" provisions. One major rating agency now examines "willingness to pay" when rating insurance policies used to provide credit enhancements or financial guarantees. Notwithstanding this progress, the understanding and management of these risks still need to evolve.

Leverage

At first glance, balance sheet information suggests that insurance companies are typically overcapitalized to a much larger extent than commercial banks. Major insurers' capital ratios often exceed the regulatory minimum by two to four times, compared with approximately one to two times for banks (Joint Forum, 2001b, p. 53). A closer look suggests that insurers hold excess capital in part to cover financial risks not covered in their regulatory requirements. As noted earlier, capital requirements in some countries primarily reflect insurance risks—the liability side of the balance sheet—rather than investment risks on the asset side. Rating agencies and counterparties therefore look for capital ratios that are well above minimum standards. In their view, insurers are becoming more sensitive to risk-based capital allocation and are moving to upgrade their internal capital management systems.

Despite this progress, questions have been raised about whether some Japanese and European insurance companies are adequately capitalized on a risk-adjusted basis relative to their financial and insurance risks.[142] For example, insurance companies' capital may not fully reflect the substantial implicit options embedded in their balance sheets. On the asset side, some insurance companies hold securities such as convertible bonds that have embedded options. On the liability side, many life insurers have issued guaranteed return policies that amount to call options on interest rates sold to policyholders. Falling interest rates increase both the value of these options to policyholders and the implicit corresponding liability for insurers. For a variety of insurance companies, market returns on safe instruments have fallen below promised rates on existing policies originated earlier. In Japan,

---

[142]See Fukao and JCER (2002); Procter, Nordhaus, and Hocking (2002).

guaranteed returns average 4 percent, compared with investment returns of less than 2 percent; in Switzerland, insurers are mandated to offer guaranteed returns of 4 percent on compulsory private "second-pillar" pensions, compared with 10-year bond yields of about 3.6 percent.

There are also broader questions about whether capital in the global insurance and reinsurance industry is sufficient to support prudently the total amount of insurance risk in the global financial system, both presently and in the immediate future as demand for insurance products grows. The global insurance industry experienced significant shocks in the period 2001–2004 (see middle panel of Figure 11.8). In 2001, total insured losses to the nonlife industry from natural disasters were estimated to have amounted to $11.5 billion, up from $7.5 billion in 2000. Equity market declines were estimated to have erased some $20 billion from insurers' balance sheets. Enron's collapse was estimated to result in $4 billion to $5 billion in losses on securities and insurance policies. The terrorist attacks in the United States on September 11, 2001, were estimated to have cost insurers $50 billion to $60 billion worldwide. Finally, a string of natural disasters in the period 2002–2004, culminating in the Asian tsunami, are estimated to have cost insurers some $70 billion. Overall, these estimated losses total some $160 billion, only about $20 billion to $30 billion of which has been replaced by fresh inflows of capital (total capital in the insurance industry is estimated to have been around $480 billion in 2002).[143]

Possible Systemic Financial Problems of Insurance Company Failure

Extensive discussions with both market participants and officials suggest the international financial community believes that insurance company insolvencies would be unlikely to have systemic effects on financial stability, for several reasons. First, in most cases the existing combination of market discipline and official oversight seems to have detected and addressed insurers' financial fragility before it posed significant risks to financial market stability, notwithstanding the fact that some problems have been privately and socially costly. For example, the March 2001 failure of Australian insurer HIH does not seem to have caused significant or persistent volatility in either Australian or global capital markets, despite its international presence,

---

[143]There are questions about whether the nonlife industry was overcapitalized during the 1990s, but the large estimated losses relative to new inflows may have motivated the U.K. Financial Services Authority chairman's remark that "we believe it important for the long-term health of the [nonlife insurance] industry, and its clients, that there is some strengthening of the industry's capital base" (Davies, 2002).

including operations in Europe, Asia, North America, and Latin America; an estimated $2.8 billion in losses for the firm; and the risk to some 2 million policyholders and a number of creditors, including globally active banks in Europe and the United States.

Second, liquidity and solvency problems involving insurance companies are generally unlikely to cause a rapid liquidation of investment portfolios—including derivatives positions—and market turbulence. In a typical insolvency proceeding, life insurers stop taking on new policies, and their remaining long-term policies—some with maturities of decades—are sold off to other insurers and are allowed to run off over a period of years. Similarly, property and casualty insurers tend to pay off claims slowly, reducing the potential immediate pressure on liquidity. On occasions when a sharp increase in insurance claims potentially puts pressure on liquidity, litigation or investigation of claims may delay payment. Financial counterparts rely increasingly on collateral arrangements to manage counterparty and credit risk exposures.

Third, the newer financial market and insurance activities, although evidently rapidly growing, are relatively small in relation to both insurers' balance sheets and to overall capital markets. Although precise estimates of market size are not available, only about $13 billion in ART is estimated to have been issued since 1996, and total capital devoted to ART amounted to only about $20 billion in 2002. In addition, the share of CDOs held by insurers is unknown, but even if they held all of the $500 billion current total, it would constitute a small fraction of the $10 trillion in financial assets held by insurers in the major countries at the end of 2001. This suggests that a disruption in these newer activities or deterioration in these assets would be unlikely to affect the viability of a major insurer.

Conclusion

As this chapter suggests, despite limited information, many observers involved with the industry in meaningful ways are comfortable with the judgment that the international systemic risks associated with the financial market activities of insurance companies are relatively limited compared to those of the major internationally active banks and commercial banks. Nevertheless, uncertainties remain about whether insurers hold adequate capital against financial risks; whether their management of market risk has kept pace with their expanding involvement in the market, and the size and extent of their off-balance-sheet activities; and the potential migration of financial risks from banking to insurance sectors. In this light, it might be worthwhile asking whether some combination of limited information, limited regulation, and high leverage could make insurers and reinsurers more vulnerable to rapid and turbulent collapses.

An insurance or reinsurance company collapse could affect financial stability through at least two channels. First, it could affect the financial conditions of counterparty commercial banks, investment banks, and other financial institutions through direct credit exposures such as loans and credit lines. Financial stress at a large global insurance or reinsurance company could thereby adversely affect a major financial institution that plays a key role in the major payment and securities settlement systems. It could also adversely affect bank balance sheets if the affected firm were part of a bancassurance conglomerate (IMF and World Bank, 2001, p. 5). Banks that belong to bancassurance conglomerates may be more vulnerable to market risks than solo banks because of the more stringent regulatory restrictions that apply to banks' market exposures, and may also be exposed to reputational risk if their insurance arm experiences financial distress. However, few conglomerates include both a large insurance company and a large complex banking operation. Second, the failure of a large reinsurer could adversely affect OTC derivatives counterparties and bank counterparties in credit-risk transfer transactions such as credit derivatives.

Other questions can be raised about the financial-stability implications of reinsurers' financial problems. Major insurance companies actively hedge insurance risks with reinsurance companies and thereby have extensive counterparty relationships with reinsurers. In effect, the reinsurance companies are part of the risk management framework and an important line of defense against insurance company illiquidity and insolvency, because they help to pool the insurance risk. Over the years, counterparty exposures may have become more concentrated amid consolidation in the global reinsurance industry. This relationship poses risks: could a systemic insurance event—possibly the confluence of several major catastrophes to which a critical mass of reinsurers are exposed—create the strong potential for financial distress involving a number of reinsurers simultaneously?

If several major reinsurers simultaneously experienced financial stress, a large number of major primary insurers could be at risk that their reinsurance hedges could fail to perform as expected, and leave many primary insurers with unhedged financial and insurance exposures. It is difficult to know how insurers would rebalance their activities and exposures to manage the sudden change in their risk profiles but adjustments could include cutbacks in the provision of insurance, withdrawals from capital markets, and attempts to unwind OTC derivatives hedges and liquidate part of their portfolios to return their financial and insurance risk profiles to more desirable positions.

To assess these risks and have a more credible understanding of these potential scenarios, the international community needs better information about the financial activities of insurers and reinsurers, especially the size, extent, and nature of reinsurance cover, and the potential for a critical mass of major reinsurers to simultaneously experience financial difficulties. In addition, it may be desirable to assess further whether the limited regulation of insurers' and reinsurers' financial activities creates an unlevel playing field in relation to banks (Joint Forum, 2001b).

12

Ongoing National and Global Challenges

The changes in the financial market landscape since the early 1970s, and the rapid acceleration of those changes in the 1990s and beyond, have resulted in unprecedented growth and unprecedented challenges, including the growing importance of safeguarding financial stability.

Part I of this study examined finance as a mechanism that facilitates economic processes such as resource allocation, risk pricing and distribution, and economic growth and social prosperity. It also established a conceptual foundation for understanding financial stability as a public good and why both private-collective and public policy involvement might be beneficial and even necessary for achieving and maintaining financial stability.

Building on this conceptual foundation, Part II proposed a practical definition of financial stability and a broad generic framework for safeguarding it. It further identified and examined the important analytical and measurement challenges in both applying a framework and improving it. It also discussed the natural interest and role of a central bank in ensuring financial stability.

Part III examined how developments during the past several decades have dramatically altered the nature of national and international finance. The forces of globalization, as detailed in Chapter 8, have combined with the development of ever-more sophisticated financial instruments and markets (illustrated in Chapters 9 through 11), to produce an international financial system open to more participants, but cloaked in a level of complexity that masks the nature, ownership, and systemic importance of the system's underlying financial risks. The national authorities and international bodies responsible for ensuring and maintaining the stability of this financial system are coming to grips with their need for a framework that allows them to monitor and regulate the system without reining in the benefits it provides, thereby safeguarding financial stability while maintaining efficiency.

Challenges in Review

The globalization of finance is a result of the same technical advances in communications and information technology that have made the world's economies more interconnected on a business, personal, and political level. Financial markets are linked to one another, physically through computerized connections, and financially through the use of one market's assets to diversify the risks created in another market. As reviewed more thoroughly in Chapter 8, globalization has led to tighter integration of national financial markets; the greater importance for markets of nonbank financial institutions, such as hedge funds, insurance companies, and pension funds; the greater engagement of nonfinancial institutions in financial activities; as well as the emergence of hybrid entities that added financial endeavors to their core businesses—auto manufacturers and industrial giants, for example. In addition, the once-staid backbone of finance, the banking sector, has diversified into new lines of business that allow it to compete more aggressively with new entrants into the business of finance. Thus, banks are providing more "finance" and doing less lending, as measured in relative terms.

The resulting advances make international financial markets more liquid, contribute to the worldwide mobility of capital, and allow financial flows and asset prices to adjust more quickly. On the whole, markets and market participants benefit tremendously from greater efficiency.

Along with such valuable benefits, of course, come new and unmeasured risks. Market interdependencies, and the complexity of those interdependencies, contribute to the potential for volatility, turbulence, and crises to spread far beyond the entity, or even the country, of origin. The speed with which globalization has occurred has left two clear gaps in the usual system of checks and balances. First, although the efficiency of private finance has been enhanced by globalization, the appropriateness and effectiveness of regulatory and supervisory approaches has lagged behind. Second, emerging market countries accessing international capital markets—in some cases for the first time—often are faced with riding a financial roller coaster as they experience good times and bad. Finance is now easier to obtain in world markets, and many emerging markets have benefited in good times from their newfound access to international finance. But because emerging-market countries often have not made concomitant reforms in their macroeconomic, microeconomic, and financial structures, they lack smoothing mechanisms and the resilience required to brake the adverse consequences of the roller coaster's descent when faced with unexpected financial turmoil.

Chapter 8 suggests the crises and turbulence of the 1990s and early 2000s should result in three lessons: First, greater supervisory attention needs to be paid to internal risk management and control systems, to management's understanding of risk issues, and to corporate governance mechanisms. Second, market discipline is an effective and crucial tool. Errant companies should be allowed to fail and be liquidated, and this can happen without causing instability if financial supervisors have insight into risk levels and interconnectivity through regulatory disclosure. Third, international financial stability is a global public good requiring more regular and effective—and perhaps even binding—international coordination mechanisms.

Delving one layer below the surface of globalization, Chapter 9 examines the development of over-the-counter (OTC) derivatives and markets, which in many ways make up the core of liquidity and finance in the international financial system. OTC derivatives allow financial risks to be tailored to preferences and tolerances, contributing to more complete financial markets. The trade-off is that OTC derivatives can also contribute to vulnerabilities because they are unregulated to a large extent, disclosure is poor, and transparency is an issue. OTC derivatives also can introduce layers of complexity that make risks harder to manage: not only must the risk of default and loss given default be assessed and managed, but the potential changes in the value of credit extended must be assessed, and the ultimate link between the derivative and the underlying asset market must be understood.

Roughly two-thirds of OTC derivatives instruments are simple forwards and swaps, generating little additional risk and thus not deserving of undue regulatory scrutiny. Nonetheless, OTC derivatives are emblematic of the widening gap between regulated and regulator. Regulation has had its greatest impact on OTC derivatives in the effort put into avoiding regulation—through choice of jurisdiction, legal structure, and the structure of trading, clearing, and settlement. The financial institutions that trade heavily in OTC derivatives—the top 20 or so global financial institutions—are safeguarded by virtue of being well capitalized, supervised (so far), and partially insured (with safety nets); but spillovers and contagion can affect the stability of markets and countries only indirectly linked, as demonstrated by the effects of the Long-Term Capital Management (LTCM) crisis in 1998.

The policy issues raised in Chapter 9 challenge those entities operating in areas that could be sources of instability to take responsibility for enhancing stability. Private financial institutions must improve risk management and control systems, but the fact that little has been done in this regard since the near collapse of LTCM suggests that it is a complex problem, perhaps somewhat ignored because of the existence of financial safety nets. The public and private sectors should work together to identify and overcome inconsistent incentives and signals. The official sector in league with national legislatures should work to reduce legal and regulatory uncertainties, especially with regard to clearinghouse arrangements, closeout procedures during bank-ruptcy, and netting. Supervisory bodies must also work with financial insti-tutions to strike a balance on information disclosure. In principle, creditors would demand information sufficient to allow them to gauge risks and risk concentrations adequately; reality indicates otherwise, due to competitive pressures and the perception that confidentiality may be at stake. Therefore, the official sector must define its role such that counterparties receive ade-quate information, but not at the expense of reducing the private informa-tion advantage and efficiency. Finally, both private entities and the public sector must work to reduce systemic risk. Foremost among these efforts must be the drive within private institutions to be well managed and sufficiently capitalized. Authorities can provide additional incentives in this direction, including through capital requirements for off-balance-sheet credit risks.

Credit risk transfer vehicles, such as credit default swaps and collateral-ized debt obligations, allow credit origin to be separated from credit risk bearing, thus contributing to the efficiency and completeness of financial markets (Chapter 10). By allowing entities other than banks to take on credit risk, the overall concentration of risk becomes more dispersed and credit exposures can be managed more flexibly. Compared to OTC deriva-tives, the notional value of credit risk transfer vehicles is small; the associated risk, however, is huge, because credit exposure can rise to up to 100 percent of the notional amount.

Credit risk transfer vehicles subject financial market stability to the same challenges as OTC derivatives—complexity, regulatory arbitrage, new market participants—then add the additional uncertainties of poorly defined credit default events. The complexity of these vehicles combined with return-seeking but inexperienced market participants leads to a potential magnifica-tion of the risks, further exacerbated by the reduction in transparency of the institutional distribution of credit risk. Because exposures have been shifted outside the banking system—to hedge funds, pension funds, insurance companies—traditional regulatory and supervisory functions that would uncover potential volatile concentrations of risk do not come into play.

The Railtrack, Enron, and JP Morgan episodes examined in Chapter 10 illustrate that experiencing an outcome that credit risk transfer vehicles are designed to cover is not sufficient to trigger payment. The way in which that outcome occurs is also significant. Thus, better documentation is needed to help refine the definition of a credit event and what constitutes a default.

Retail investor involvement in credit risk transfer vehicles raises investor protection issues. In addition to high net worth individuals investing directly in such vehicles, other retail investors are becoming exposed through mutual funds and hedge funds that invest in credit risk transfers. Insufficient disclosure and transparency, combined with the inexperience of the investor could lead to investment mistakes, rapid unwinding of positions once the mistakes are discovered, and a tendency toward increased volatility in credit prices and spreads.

The insurance and reinsurance industry has become a significant player in the international financial market (Chapter 11). Several forces compelled the industry to step beyond its traditional role and pursue more finance-related activities. In addition to needing to offset underwriting losses and to pay for high guaranteed returns offered to policyholders in the 1980s and 1990s, insurance companies are fulfilling the demand from the remainder of the financial sector for insurance against capital risk. In doing so, insurance companies have brought an innovative approach to capital markets, developing new instruments that bridge the gap between insurance and banking. These instruments include "Cat" bonds, with payoffs triggered by catastrophic events, and customized reinsurance products available in the "alternative risk transfer" market.

Although observers foresee little possibility of a systemic impact from the possible failure of an insurance company due to its financial activities, issues similar to those that apply throughout the rest of the financial system arise. Among them are the balance between official oversight and market discipline, the need for disclosure and transparency, the understanding of legal obligations, and capital adequacy. Despite regulatory differences among countries, the overriding focus is on policyholder protection, with little concentration on the asset side of the balance sheet or on off-balance-sheet activities. Thus, little information is available regarding internal risk management and controls. Insurance companies also have different legal obligations than financial companies. Finally, although capital is typically more than adequate, it is not clear that some European and Japanese companies are properly capitalized on a risk-adjusted basis.

Conclusion

The challenges to financial stability identified in Part III, separately and collectively, lead to the strong conclusion that further and continuous reforms are desirable and should be aimed at striking a better balance between relying on market discipline and relying on official or private-collective action. In some countries—most of them advanced countries with mature markets—a rebalancing toward greater reliance on market discipline is desirable. In other countries—many with poorly developed markets—strong efforts need to be made to improve the financial infrastructure through private-collective and government expenditures and commitments, and to target the role of government to enhance the effectiveness and efficiency of market mechanisms for finance.

As the discussion in Part III suggests, the following areas are most in need of general reform:

- Private market incentives need to be realigned, including within firms, to improve internal governance at the board-of-directors level, to improve management and risk controls, and to improve the alignment of incentives at the board, management, and staff levels.
- Regulatory incentives need to be reevaluated, as does their consistency with private market incentives, to reduce moral hazard.
- Disclosure by a wide range of financial and nonfinancial entities needs to be enhanced, to improve the potential for effective market discipline and to improve private-collective and official monitoring and supervision.
- Market transparency needs to be improved, to reduce asymmetries in markets and the tendency toward adverse selection.
- Legal certainty needs to be clarified where it is still ambiguous, such as with closeout procedures for credit derivatives and other complex structured financial instruments.
- Comprehensive and appropriately targeted frameworks need to be developed and implemented for monitoring, assessing, and ensuring financial stability and to restore it when this fails.
- International cooperation and coordination in financial-system regulation, surveillance, and supervision needs to be increased, to eliminate international gaps of information and analysis and to reduce opportunities for regulatory arbitrage.

The complexity of the challenges and the rapidity and creativity with which new financial instruments are developed and disseminated require the systemic approach to safeguarding financial stability examined in Part II of this study, and in particular in Chapter 6. The financial system, working within the context of the broader economic, social, and political systems, affects the performance of the economy and well-being of society. In turn, those systems must operate hand in hand to safeguard the stability of the financial system, and the constellation of tools they provide must be used to ensure economic stability.

Ultimately, the goal is to maintain financial stability so that the financial system is capable of performing its three key functions: the intertemporal allocation of resources from savers to investors and the allocation of economic resources generally; the assessment, pricing, and allocation of forward-looking financial risks; and the absorption of financial and real economic shocks and surprises.

Glossary

Barrier options: Also known as knock-out, knock-in, or trigger options. Path-dependent options that are either activated (knocked in) or terminated (knocked out) if a specified spot rate reaches a specified trigger level or levels between inception and expiry. Before termination, knock-out options behave identically to standard European-style options, but carry lower initial premiums because they may be extinguished before reaching maturity. By contrast, knock-in options behave identically to European-style options only if they are activated and so also command a lower premium.

Book value: The value of an asset that appears on a balance sheet based on historic cost or the original purchase price.

Broker: An intermediary between buyers and sellers who acts in a transaction as an agent, rather than a principal; charges a commission or fee; and—unlike a dealer—does not buy or sell for his or her own account or make markets. In some jurisdictions, the term "broker" also refers to the specific legal or regulatory status of institutions performing this function.

Cherry picking: A practice in some bankruptcy proceedings of enforcing contracts favorable to the bankrupt and abrogating related obligations to the unsecured creditors.

Clearing and settlement: The process of matching parties in a transaction according to the terms of a contract and the fulfillment of obligations (for example, through the exchange of securities or funds).

Clearinghouse: An entity, typically affiliated with a futures or options exchange, that clears trades through delivery of the commodity or purchase of offsetting futures positions and serves as a central counterparty. It may

---

Note: Many of the items in this glossary were adapted from G. L. Gastineau, 1992, *Swiss Bank Corporation Dictionary of Financial Risk Management;* JP Morgan/Risk Management, 2001, *Guide to Risk Management;* Schinasi and others (2000); selected issues of IMF, *International Capital Markets: Recent Developments, Prospects, and Key Issues;* and selected issues of IMF, *Global Financial Stability Report.*

also hold performance bonds posted by dealers to assure fulfillment of futures and options obligations.

Closeout netting (see *Netting arrangement*): A written contract to combine offsetting credit exposures between two or more parties when a contract is terminated.

Closeout procedures: Steps taken by a nondefaulting party to terminate a contract prior to its maturity when the other party fails to perform according to the contract's terms.

Collateral: Assets pledged as security to ensure payment or performance of an obligation.

Collateralized debt obligation (CDO): Securitized interests in pools of assets, usually comprising loans or debt instruments. A CDO may be called a collateralized loan obligation or collateralized bond obligation or a collateralized mortgage obligation if it holds only loans or bonds or mortgages, respectively. Investors bear the credit risk of the collateral. Multiple tranches of securities are issued by the CDO, offering investors various maturity and credit risk characteristics, categorized as senior, mezzanine, and subordinated/equity, according to their degree of credit risk. If there are defaults or the CDO's collateral otherwise underperforms, scheduled payments to senior tranches take precedence over those of mezzanine tranches, and scheduled payments to mezzanine tranches take precedence over those to subordinated/equity tranches.

Credit derivative: A privately negotiated agreement that explicitly shifts credit risk from one party to the other. A bilateral financial contract that isolates credit risk from an underlying instrument and transfers that credit risk from one party to the contract (protection buyer) to the other (protection seller). There are two main categories of credit derivatives: instruments such as credit default swaps in which contingent payments occur as a result of a credit event; and instruments including credit spread options, which seek to isolate the credit spread component of an instrument's market yield.

Credit exposure: The present value of the amount receivable or payable on a contract, consisting of the sum of current exposure and potential future exposure.

Creditor stay exemption: The exclusion of certain creditors from the automatic stay provision of the bankruptcy code, which generally limits creditors' capacity to directly collect debts owed by a bankrupt party, including through netting of outstanding contracts. An example is the U.S. Bankruptcy Code statutory exceptions for repurchase agreements, securities contracts, commodity contracts, swap agreements, and forward contracts, where counterparties can close out exempt OTC derivatives positions outside of bankruptcy procedures.

Credit risk: The risk associated with the possibility that a borrower will be unwilling or unable to fulfill its contractual obligations, thereby causing the holder of the claim to suffer a loss.

Cross-currency swap (or *Currency coupon swap*): A variant of the standard interest-rate swap in which the interest rate in one currency is fixed, and the interest rate in the other is floating.

Currency carry trade: A strategy in which an investor borrows in a foreign country with lower interest rates than the home country and invests the funds in the domestic market, usually in fixed-income securities.

Currency derivatives: Derivatives contracts involving the exchange of two or more currencies at a specified price and date. For example, see currency option.

Currency option: The right, but not the obligation, to buy (call) or sell (put) a currency with another currency at a specified exchange rate (strike price) during a specified period ending on the expiration date.

Dealer: An intermediary who acts as a principal in a transaction, buys (or sells) on his or her own account, and thus takes positions and risks. The dealer earns profit from bid-ask spreads. A dealer can be distinguished from a broker, who acts only as an agent for customers and charges commission. In some jurisdictions, the term "dealer" also refers to the specific legal or regulatory status of institutions performing this function.

Derivatives (exchange-traded and over-the-counter): Financial contracts whose value derives from underlying securities prices, interest rates, foreign exchange rates, market indexes, or commodity prices. Exchange-traded derivatives are standardized products traded on the floor of an organized exchange and usually require a good faith deposit, or margin, when buying or selling a contract. Over-the-counter derivatives, such as currency swaps and interest rate swaps, are privately negotiated bilateral agreements transacted off organized exchanges.

Dollar (or other currency) put option: A contract that gives the holder the right to sell dollars (or other currency) at a predetermined price.

Down-and-out call (put) option: A call (put) option that expires if the market price of the underlying asset drops below (rises above) a predetermined expiration price.

Equity swap: A swap in which the total or price return on an equity is exchanged for a stream of cash flows based on a short-term interest rate index.

Foreign-exchange forward: A contractual obligation between two parties to exchange a particular currency at a set price on a future date. The buyer of the forward agrees to pay the price and take delivery of the currency and is said to be "long the forward," while the seller of the forward agrees to deliver the currency at the agreed price on the agreed date. Collateral may be deposited, but cash is not exchanged until the delivery date.

Forward contract: A contractual obligation between two parties to exchange a particular good or instrument at a set price on a future date. The buyer of the forward agrees to pay the price and take delivery of the good or instrument and is said to be "long the forward," while the seller of the forward agrees to deliver the good or instrument at the agreed price on the agreed date. Collateral may be deposited, but cash is not exchanged until the delivery date. Forward contracts, unlike futures, are not traded on organized exchanges.

Forward rate agreement (FRA): A contract determining an interest rate to be paid or received on a specified obligation beginning at a start date in the future. A notional principal contract such as an FRA need not be with the party on the other side of the obligation that the FRA contract is linked to. Any given gain or loss on the FRA is similar to a gain or loss on an option or futures contract with regard to its impact on the return of an underlying position.

Futures: Negotiable contracts to make or take delivery of a standardized amount of a commodity or security at a specific date for an agreed price, under terms and conditions established by a regulated futures exchange where trading takes place. Futures are essentially standardized forward contracts that are traded on an organized exchange and subject to the requirements defined by the exchange.

Haircut: The difference between the amount advanced by a lender and the market value of collateral securing the loan. For example, if a lender makes a loan equal to 90 percent of the value of marketable securities that are provided as collateral, the difference (10 percent) is the haircut.

Hedging: The process of offsetting an existing risk exposure by taking an opposite position in the same or a similar risk, for example, through purchasing derivatives.

Intermediation: The process of transferring funds from an ultimate source to the ultimate user. A financial institution, such as a bank, intermediates credit when it obtains money from a depositor and relends it to a borrowing customer.

Knock-in options: See Barrier options.

Knock-out options: See Barrier options.

Legal risk: Risks that arise when a counterparty might not have the legal or regulatory authority to engage in a transaction or when the law may not perform as expected. Legal risks also include compliance and regulatory risks, which concern activities that might breach government regulations, such as market manipulation, insider trading, and suitability restrictions.

Leverage: The magnification of the rate of return (positive and negative) on a position or investment beyond the rate obtained by direct investment of own funds in the cash market. It is often measured as the ratio of on- and off-balance-sheet exposures to capital. Leverage can be built up by borrowing (on-balance-sheet leverage, commonly measured by debt-to-equity ratios) or through the use of off-balance-sheet transactions.

LIBOR (London Inter-Bank Offered Rates): The primary fixed income index reference rates used in the Euromarkets. Most international floating rates are quoted as LIBOR plus or minus a spread. In addition to the traditional Eurodollar and sterling LIBOR rates, yen LIBOR, Swiss franc LIBOR, and so forth, are also available and widely used.

Liquidity: The ability to raise cash easily and with minimal delay. Market liquidity is the ability to transact business in necessary volumes without unduly moving market prices. Funding liquidity is the ability of an entity to fund its positions and meet, when due, the cash and collateral demands of counterparties, credit providers, and investors.

Loss given default: Usually refers to the loss on the principal of a loan once the borrower defaults.

Margin: The amount of cash or eligible collateral an investor must deposit with a counterparty or intermediary when conducting a transaction. For example, when buying or selling a futures contract, it is the amount that must be deposited with a broker or clearinghouse. If the futures price moves adversely, the investor might receive a margin call—that is, a demand for additional funds or collateral (variation margin) to offset position losses in the margin account.

Market maker: An intermediary that holds an inventory of financial instruments (or risk positions) and stands ready to execute buy and sell orders on behalf of customers at posted prices or on its own account. The market maker assumes risk by taking possession of the asset or position. In organized exchanges, market makers are licensed by a regulating body or by the exchange itself.

Market risk: The risk that arises from possible changes in the prices of financial assets and liabilities; it is typically measured by price volatility.

Mark-to-market: The valuation of a position or portfolio by reference to the most recent price at which a financial instrument can be bought or sold in normal volumes. The mark-to-market value might equal the current market value—as opposed to historic accounting or book value—or the present value of expected future cash flows.

Master agreement: Comprehensive documentation of standard contractual terms and conditions that covers a range of OTC derivatives transactions between two counterparties.

Moral hazard: Actions of economic agents that are to their own benefit but to the detriment of others and arise when incomplete information or incomplete contracts prevent the full assignment of damages (or benefits) to the agent responsible. For example, under asymmetric information, borrowers may have incentives to engage in riskier activities that may be to their advantage, but which harm the lender by increasing the risk of default.

Netting arrangement: A written contract to combine offsetting obligations between two or more parties to reduce them to a single net payment or receipt for each party. For example, two banks owing each other $10 million and $12 million, respectively, might agree to value their mutual obligation at $2 million (the net difference between $10 million and $12 million) for accounting purposes. Netting can be done bilaterally—when two parties settle contracts at net value—as is standard practice under a master agreement, or multilaterally through a clearinghouse. Closeout netting combines offsetting credit exposures between two parties when a contract is terminated.

Notional amount or principal: The reference value (which is typically not exchanged) on which the cash flows of a derivatives contract are based. For example, the notional principal underlying a swap transaction is used to compute swap payments in an interest rate swap or currency swap.

Off-balance-sheet items: Financial commitments that do not involve booking assets or liabilities, and thus do not appear on the balance sheet.

Off-the-run (U.S. Treasury bonds): All Treasury bonds and notes issued before the most recently issued bond or note of a particular maturity. Once a new Treasury security of any maturity is issued, the previously issued security with the same maturity becomes the off-the-run bond or note. Because off-the-run securities are less frequently traded, they typically are less expensive and therefore carry a slightly greater yield.

On-the-run (U.S. Treasury bonds): The most recently issued U.S. Treasury bond or note of a particular maturity. The on-the-run bond or note is the most frequently traded Treasury security of its maturity. Because on-the-run issues are the most liquid, they typically are slightly more expensive and, therefore, yield less than their off-the-run counterparts.

Operational risk: Risk of losses resulting from management failure, faulty internal controls, fraud, or human error. It includes execution risk, which encompasses situations where trades fail to be executed, or more generally, any problem in back-office operations.

Option: A contract granting the right, and not the obligation, to purchase or sell an asset during a specified period at an agreed price (the exercise price or strike price). A call option is a contract that gives the holder the right to buy from the option seller an asset at a specified price; a put option is a contract that gives the holder the right to sell an asset at a predetermined price. Options are traded both on exchanges and over the counter.

Over-the-counter (OTC) market: A market for securities where trading is not conducted in an organized exchange but through bilateral negotiations. Often these markets are intermediated by brokers or dealers. Examples of OTC derivatives transactions include foreign exchange forward contracts, currency swaps, and interest rate swaps.

Performance bonds: Bonds that provide specific monetary payments if a counterparty fails to fulfill a contract, thereby providing protection against loss in the event the terms of a contract are violated.

Potential future exposure: The amount potentially at risk over the term of a derivatives contract if a counterparty defaults. It varies over time in response to the perceived risk of asset price movements that can affect the value of the exposure.

Replacement value or replacement cost: The current exposure adjusted to reflect the cost of replacing a defaulted contract.

Repurchase agreement: To buy (sell) a security while at the same time agreeing to sell (buy) the same security at a predetermined future date. The price at which the reverse transaction takes place sets the interest rate (or repo rate) over the period of the contract.

Swap: A derivatives contract that involves a series of exchanges of payments. Examples are agreements to exchange interest payments in a fixed-rate obligation for interest payments in a floating-rate obligation (an interest rate swap), or one currency for another (a foreign exchange swap) and reverse the exchange at a later date. A cross-currency interest rate swap is the exchange of a fixed-rate obligation in one currency for a floating-rate obligation in another currency.

Tesobono swap: A popular instrument used by Mexican banks in the period prior to the Mexican crisis of 1994–95. Tesobono swaps allowed Mexican banks to leverage their holdings of exchange-rate linked Mexican treasury bills (Tesobonos). A bank received the tesobono yield and paid U.S. dollar LIBOR plus a premium (in basis points) to an offshore counterparty, which in turn hedged its swap position by purchasing tesobonos in the spot market.

Total return swap: A form of credit derivative. A bilateral financial contract in which one party (the total return payer) makes floating payments to the other party (the total return receiver) equal to the total return on a specified asset or index (including interest or dividend payments and net price appreciation) in exchange for amounts that generally equal the total return payer's cost of holding the specified asset on its balance sheet. Unlike with a credit default swap, the floating payments are based on the total economic performance of a specified asset and are not contingent upon the occurrence of a credit event.

Value at Risk (VaR): A statistical estimate of the potential mark-to-market loss to a trading position or portfolio from an adverse market move over a given time horizon. VaR reflects a selected confidence level, so actual losses during a period are not expected to exceed the estimate more than a pre-specified number of times. VaR is the maximum potential loss that can be incurred on a given financial position over a determined time period, and at a certain level of probability.

Bibliography

Acemoglu, D., and F. Zilibotti, 1997, "Was Prometheus Unbound by Chance? Risk, Diversification and Growth," *Journal of Political Economy,* Vol. 105 (Issue 4), pp. 709–51.

Acharya, Viral, 2001, "A Theory of Systemic Risk and Design of Prudential Bank Regulation" (Working Paper, London Business School—Institute of Finance and Accounting). Available via the Internet: http://ssrn.com/abstract=236401

Akerlof, George A., 1970, "The Market for 'Lemons': Quality Uncertainty and the Market Mechanism," *Quarterly Journal of Economics,* Vol. 84 (August), pp. 488–500.

Akyuz, Yilmaz, ed., 2002, *Reforming the Global Financial Architecture* (New York: United Nations).

Allais, Maurice, 1947, *Economie et interet,* 2 Volumes (Paris: Imprimerie Nationale).

Allen, F., 2005, "Modelling Financial Instability," *National Institute Economic Review,* No. 192 (April), pp. 57–67.

———, and D. Gale, 2004, "Financial Intermediaries and Markets," *Econometrica,* Vol. 72 (July), pp. 1023–61.

Allen, M., C. Rosenberg, C. Keller, B. Setser, and N. Roubini, 2002, "A Balance Sheet Approach to Financial Crisis," IMF Working Paper No. WP/02/210 (Washington: International Monetary Fund).

Andrews, David M., C. Randall Henning, and Louis W. Pauly, eds., 2002, *Governing the World's Money* (Ithaca, New York: Cornell University Press).

Arthur, W. B., John H. Holland, Blake LeBaron, Richard Palmer, and Paul Taylor, 1997, "Asset Pricing Under Endogenous Expectations in an Artificial Stock Market," in *The Economy as an Evolving Complex System II,* Conference proceedings of the "Global Economy Workshop," August 1995, Studies in the Sciences of Complexity, Vol. XXVII, ed. by W. Brian Arthur, Steven N. Durlauf, and David A. Lane (Reading, Massachusetts: Addison-Wesley), pp. 15–44.

Bagehot, Walter, 1873, *Lombard Street* (London: Paul Kegan, 14th ed.).

Bank for International Settlements, 1998, "Implications of Structural Change on the Nature of Systemic Risk" (unpublished; Basel).

———, 2000, "Report on Lender of Last Resort," Committee on Global Financial Systems (Basel).

———, 2001a, "Consolidation in the Financial Sector," report by the Group of Ten Working Party on Financial Sector Consolidation (Basel).

————, 2001b, "Cycles and the Financial System," *71st Annual Report,* Chapter VII (Basel), pp. 123–41.

————, 2003, "Trends in Risk Integration and Aggregation," The Joint Forum, Basel Committee on Banking Supervision (Basel).

Bank of England, 1997, "Memorandum of Understanding Between H.M. Treasury, the Bank of England and the Financial Services Authority." Available via the Internet: www.bankofengland.co.uk.

————, 1999, *Financial Stability Review,* No. 7 (London).

————, 2000, *Financial Stability Review,* No. 8 (London).

————, 2001, *Financial Stability Review,* No. 9 (London).

Barkin, J. Samuel, 2003, *Social Construction and the Logic of Money* (Albany, New York: State University of New York Press).

Barnett, William A., John Geweke, and Karl Shell, eds., 1989, *Economic Complexity: Chaos, Sunspots, Bubbles, and Nonlinearity* (Cambridge: Cambridge University Press).

Barr, N., 1998, *The Economics of the Welfare State* (Oxford: Oxford University Press, 3rd ed.).

Barrell, R., E. P. Davis, and O. Pomerantz, 2005, "Costs of Financial Instability, Household-Sector Balance Sheets and Consumption," NIESR Discussion Paper No. 243 (London: National Institute of Economic and Social Research).

Basel Committee on Banking Supervision, 1995, *Basel Capital Accord: Treatment of Potential Exposure for Off-Balance-Sheet Items* (Basel: Bank for International Settlements).

————, 2000a, *Banks' Interactions with Highly Leveraged Institutions: Implementation of the Basel Committee's Sound Practices Paper* (Basel: Bank for International Settlements).

————, 2000b, *Sound Practices for Managing Liquidity in Banking Organisations* (Basel: Bank for International Settlements).

————, 2004, *International Convergence of Capital Measurement and Capital Standards: A Revised Framework* (Basel: Bank for International Settlements).

Beales, Richard, and Jennifer Hughes, 2005, "New York Fed Calls Meeting on Derivatives," *Financial Times* (New York: August 25), p. 16.

Beck, T., A. Demirgüç-Kunt, and R. Levine, 2003, "Bank Concentration and Crises," NBER Working Paper No. 9921 (Cambridge, Massachusetts: National Bureau for Economic Research).

Bernardo, A. E., and I. Welch, 2004, "Liquidity and Financial Market Runs," *The Quarterly Journal of Economics,* Vol. CXIX (February), pp. 135–58.

Bisignano, Joseph, 1998, "Towards an Understanding of the Changing Structure of Financial Intermediation: An Evolutionary Theory of Institutional Survival," Societe Universitaire Europeenne de Recherches Financieres (SUERF) Studies #4 (Amsterdam).

Blaschke, W., M. Jones, G. Majnoni, and S. Peria, 2001, "Stress Testing of Financial Systems: A Review of the Issues, Methodologies, and FSAP Experiences," IMF Working Paper No. WP/01/88 (Washington: International Monetary Fund).

Borch, Karl H., 1990, *Economics of Insurance* (Amsterdam: North-Holland).

Bordo, M., 2000, "Sound Money and Sound Financial Policy," paper prepared for the conference "Anna Schwartz–The Policy Influence," American Enterprise Institute, Washington, April 14.

Bordo, Michael, Barry Eichengreen, Daniela Klingebiel, and Maria Martinez-Peria, 2001, "Is the Crisis Problem Growing More Severe?" *Economic Policy,* Vol. 16 (April), pp. 51–82.

Borio, Claudio, 2003, "Towards a Macroprudential Framework for Financial Supervision and Regulation?" BIS Working Paper No. 128 (Basel: Bank for International Settlements).

Borio, Claudio, and Philip Lowe, 2002, "Asset Prices, Financial and Monetary Stability: Exploring the Nexus," BIS Working Paper No. 114 (Basel: Bank for International Settlements).

Braudel, Fernand, 1977, *Afterthoughts on Material Life and Capitalism* (Baltimore, Maryland: Johns Hopkins University Press).

Brenner, Reuven, 2001, *The Force of Finance: Triumph of the Capital Markets* (New York: Texere Publishing Limited).

British Bankers' Association, 2004, *BBA Credit Derivatives Report 2003/2004,* BBA Enterprises Ltd. (London).

Brock, William A., 1986, "Distinguishing Random and Deterministic Systems: Abridged Version," *Journal of Economic Theory,* Vol. 40 (October), pp. 168–95.

———, 1997, "Asset Price Behavior in Complex Environments," in *The Economy as an Evolving Complex System II,* Conference proceedings Volume XXVII in Studies in the Sciences of Complexity, ed. by W. Brian Arthur, Steven N. Durlauf, and David A. Lane (Reading, Massachusetts: Addison-Wesley), pp. 385–423.

Bryant, John, 1980, "A Model of Reserves, Bank Runs, and Deposit Insurance," *Journal of Banking and Finance,* Vol. 4 (December), pp. 335–44.

Campbell, J., and R. Shiller, 2001, "Valuation Ratios and the Long-Run Stock Market Outlook: An Update," NBER Working Paper No. 8221 (Cambridge, Massachusetts: National Bureau of Economic Research).

Capie, Forrest, 2000, "The Evolution of the Lender of Last Resort: The Bank of England" (unpublished; City University, London, Business School).

Caprio, Gerard Jr., and Daniela Klingebiel, 1997, "Bank Insolvency: Bad Luck, Bad Policy, or Bad Banking," *World Bank Economic Review* (January).

———, 1999, "Episodes of Systematic and Borderline Financial Distress," (unpublished; Washington, The World Bank).

Caprio, Gerard Jr., Daniela Klingebiel, Luc Laeven, and Guillermo Noguera, 2003, "An Update of the Caprio-Klingebiel Database," (unpublished; Washington, The World Bank). Available via the Internet: http://www1.worldbank.org/finance/html/database_sfd.html

Cass, David, and Menahem E. Yaari, 1966, "A Re-Examination of the Pure Consumption Loans Model," *Journal of Political Economy,* Vol. 74 (June), pp. 353–67.

Chant, John, 2003, "Financial Stability as a Policy Goal," in *Essays on Financial Stability,* Bank of Canada Technical Report No. 95 (Ottawa: Bank of Canada).

Coase, Ronald, 1960, "The Problem of Social Cost," *The Journal of Law and Economics,* Vol. 3 (October), pp. 1–44.

Committee on the Global Financial System (CGFS), 2005, "Stress Testing at Major Financial Institutions: Survey Results and Practice." CGFS Publication No. 24. Available via the Internet: http://www.bis.org/publ/cgfs24.htm

Cornes, Richard, and Todd Sandler, 1996, *The Theory of Externalities, Public Goods, and Club Goods* (Cambridge, England: Cambridge University Press).

Corrigan, Gerald E., 1999, Testimony on Behalf of Counterparty Risk Management Policy Group before the Subcommittee on Capital Markets, Securities and Government Sponsored Enterprises, Committee on Banking Financial Services, U.S. House of Representatives (Washington DC: March 3). Available via the Internet: http://financialservices.house.gov/banking/3399coth.htm

————, 2005, "Transmittal Letter," *Toward Greater Financial Stability: A Private Sector Perspective* (New York). Available via the Internet: http://www.crmpolicy group.org.

Counterparty Risk Management Policy Group, 1999, "Improving Counterparty Risk Management Practices" (New York).

Counterparty Risk Management Policy Group II, 2005, *Toward Greater Financial Stability: A Private Sector Perspective* (New York). Available via the Internet: http://www.crmpolicygroup.org.

Covitz, Daniel M., Diana Hancock, and Myron L. Kwast, 2000, "Mandatory Subordinated Debt: Would Banks Face More Market Discipline?" (working paper; Washington: Board of Governors of the Federal Reserve System).

Crockett, A., 1996, "The Theory and Practice of Financial Stability," *De Economist,* Vol. 144 (No. 4), pp. 531–8.

————, 1997, "The Theory and Practice of Financial Stability," *GEI Newsletter,* Issue No. 6 (United Kingdom: Gonville and Caius College Cambridge).

————, 2000a, "Marrying the Micro- and Macroprudential Dimensions of Financial Stability," remarks before the Eleventh International Conference of Banking Supervisors, Basel, September 20–21. Available via the Internet: http://www.bis.org/speeches/sp000921.htm

————, 2000b, "In Search of Anchors for Financial and Monetary Stability," speech at the SUERF Colloquium, Vienna, April 27–29. Available via the Internet: http://www.bis.org/speeches/sp000427.htm

————, 2001a, "Market Discipline and Financial Stability," speech at the Banks and Systemic Risk Conference, London, May 23–25. Reprinted in Bank of England's *Financial Stability Review,* Issue 10 (June), pp. 166–73. Available via the Internet: http://www.bis.org/speeches/sp010523.htm

————, 2001b, "Monetary Policy and Financial Stability," speech at the HKMA Distinguished Lecture, Hong Kong, February 13. Available via the Internet: http://www.bis.org/speeches/sp010213.htm

Cunningham, D. P., and J. D. Cohn, 2005, "U.S. Netting Legislation: The Financial Contract Provisions Title IX of the Bankruptcy Reform Act of 2005 (S.256)," memorandum for the International Swaps and Derivatives Association (Allen and Overy LLP, March).

Das, Udaibir S., Mark Quintyn, and Ken Chenard, 2003, "Does Regulatory Governance Matter for Financial System Stability: An Empirical Analysis," paper prepared for Bank of Canada Conference, "The Evolving Financial System and Public Policy," Ottawa, December.

Davies, Howard, 2001, Remarks at the Insurance Institute of London Annual Luncheon, London, March 9.

————, 2002, "Rational Expectations—What Should the Market, and Policyholders, Expect from Insurance Regulation?" The Association of Insurance and Risk Management (AIRMIC) Annual Lecture, London, January 29. Available via the Internet: http://www.fsa.gov.uk/Pages/Library/Communication/Speeches/2002/sp87.shtml

Davis, Phillip, 2002, "A Typology of Financial Instability," *Financial Stability Report,* No. 2, (Vienna: Oesterreichische Nationalbank).

De Bandt, Oliver, and Philipp Hartmann, 1998, "What is Systemic Risk Today?" in *Risk Measurement and Systemic Risk, Proceedings of the Second Joint Central Bank Research Conference* (Tokyo: Bank of Japan), pp. 37–84.

————, 2000, "Systemic Risk: A Survey," ECB Working Paper No. 35 (Frankfurt: European Central Bank).

Demirgüç-Kunt, Asli, and Ross Levine, eds., 2001, *Financial Structure and Economic Growth: A Cross-Country Comparison of Banks, Markets, and Development* (Cambridge, Massachusetts: MIT Press).

DNB (De Nederlandsche Bank), 2000, "Guardian of Financial Stability," *DNB Quarterly Bulletin,* No. 4 (December), pp. 5–10.

Deutsche Bank, 2002, *Credit Derivatives Outlook,* Deutsche Bank (January).

Deutsche Bundesbank, 2003, "Report on the Stability of the German Financial System," *Monthly Report* (December).

Dewatripont, Mathias, and Jean Tirole, 1993, *The Prudential Regulation of Banks* (Cambridge, Massachusetts: MIT Press).

Diamond, Douglas W., 1984, "Financial Intermediation and Delegated Monitoring," *Review of Economic Studies,* Vol. 51 (July), pp. 393–414.

Diamond, Douglas W., and P. Dybvig, 1983, "Bank Runs, Deposit Insurance and Liquidity," *Journal of Political Economy,* Vol. 91 (June), pp. 401–19.

Diamond, Douglas W., and Raghuram G. Rajan, 2001, "Liquidity Risk, Liquidity Creation and Financial Fragility: A Theory of Banking," *Journal of Political Economy,* Vol. 109 (April), pp. 287–327.

————, 2002, "Banks, Short Term Debt and Financial Crises: Theory, Policy Implications and Applications," CRSP Working Paper No. 518 (Center for Research in Security Prices, Graduate School of Business, University of Chicago).

Diamond, Peter A., 1965, "National Debt in a Neoclassical Growth Model," *The American Economic Review,* Vol. 55 (December), pp. 1126–50.

Dodd, Randall, 2001, "The Role of Derivatives in the East Asian Financial Crisis," Financial Policy Forum, The Derivatives Study Center. Available via the Internet: http://www.financialpolicy.org/DSCSPR1.PDF

Duisenberg, Wim F., 2001, "The Contribution of the Euro to Financial Stability," in *Globalization of Financial Markets and Financial Stability—Challenges for Europe* (Baden-Baden, Germany: Nomos Verlagsgesellschaft).

Eatwell, John, and Lance Taylor, 2000, *Global Finance at Risk: The Case for International Regulation* (New York: The New Press).

———, eds., 2002, *International Capital Markets: Systems in Transition* (Oxford: Oxford University Press).

European Central Bank, 1999, "Possible Effects of EMU on the EU Banking Systems in the Medium to Long Term," (Frankfurt: European Central Bank).

European Commission, 2002a, "Study into the Methodologies for Prudential Supervision of Reinsurance with a View to the Possible Establishment of an EU Framework," (Brussels).

———, 2002b, "Study into the Methodologies to Assess the Overall Financial Position of an Insurance Undertaking from the Perspective of Prudential Supervision," study performed by KPMG, (Brussels).

European Union Economic and Financial Committee, 2000, "Report on Financial Stability," Brouwer Report (Brussels).

Evans, Owen, A. M. Leone, Martin Gill, and Paul Hilbers, 2000, "Macroeconomic Indicators of Financial System Soundness," IMF Occasional Paper No. 192 (Washington: International Monetary Fund).

FDIC, 1997, *An Examination of the Banking Crises of the 1980s and Early 1990s,* Vol. 1, (Washington: Federal Deposit Insurance Corporation).

———, 1998, *Managing the Crisis: The FDIC and RTC Experience 1980–1994* (Washington: Federal Deposit Insurance Corporation).

Fell, J., 2004, "Organising Financial Stability Analysis," in *De Nederlandsche Bank Proceedings of the Symposium on Financial Stability: Policy Challenges in the Asian Era,* Amsterdam, October.

Fell, J., and G. Schinasi, 2005, "Assessing Financial Stability: Exploring the Boundaries of Analysis," *National Institute Economic Review,* No. 192 (April), pp. 102–117.

———, 2005, "Assessing Financial Stability: Conceptual Boundaries and Challenges," in *Financial Stability Review* (Frankfurt: European Central Bank). Available via the Internet: http://www.ecb.int/pub/pdf/other/financialstabilityreview200506en.pdf

Ferguson, Roger, 2002, "Should Financial Stability Be An Explicit Central Bank Objective?" (Washington: Federal Reserve Board).

Ferran, E., and C. Goodhart, eds., 2001, *Regulating Financial Services and Markets in the 21st Century* (Oxford: Hart).

Financial Services Authority, 2002, *Cross-Sector Risk Transfer,* discussion paper, (London).

Fitch Ratings, 2001, "Use of Insurance Policies as Credit Enhancements in Structured Finance," *Structured Finance Special Report,* June 18.

Flood, Merrill M., 1952, "Some Experimental Games," Research Memorandum RM-789 (Santa Monica, California: Rand Corporation).

Folkerts-Landau, David, and Carl-Johan Lindgren, 1998, *Toward a Framework for Financial Stability,* World Economic and Financial Surveys (Washington: International Monetary Fund).

Folkerts-Landau, David, and Alfred Steinherr, 1994, "The Wild Beast of Derivatives: To Be Chained Up, Fenced In or Tamed?" in *The AMEX Bank Review Prize Essays: Finance and the International Economy,* Vol. 8 (New York: Oxford University Press for American Express Bank).

Foot, Michael, 2003, "What is 'Financial Stability' and How Do We Get It?" The Roy Bridge Memorial Lecture, Financial Services Authority, United Kingdom, April 3.

Fosler, Gail, 2004a, "Thinking About Risk," *Straight Talk,* Vol. 15, No. 8 (New York: The Conference Board, September).

———, 2004b, "Financial Stability and Systemic Risk," *Straight Talk,* Vol. 15, No. 9 (New York: The Conference Board, October).

Freixas, Xavier, and Jean-Charles Rochet, 1997, *Microeconomics of Banking* (Cambridge, Massachusetts: MIT Press).

Freixas, Xavier, Bruno Parigi, and Jean-Charles Rochet, 1999, "Systemic Risk, Interbank Relations and Liquidity Provision by the Central Bank," CEPR Working Paper No. 2325 (London: Centre for Economic Policy Research).

Freixas, Xavier, Curzio Giannini, Glenn Hoggarth, and Farouk Soussa, 1999, "Lender of Last Resort: A Review of the Literature," *Financial Stability Review,* Issue 7 (November), pp.151–67.

———, 2000, "Lender of Last Resort: What Have We Learnt Since Bagehot?" *Journal of Financial Services Research,* Vol. 18 (October), pp. 63–87.

Fukao, Mitsuhiro, and Japan Center for Economic Research (JCER), eds., 2002, "The Life Insurance Crisis Will Continue," (*Seiho Kiki wa Owaranai,* in Japanese), (Tokyo: Tokyo Keizai Shimposha).

Garber, P., 1998, "Derivatives in International Capital Flows," NBER Working Paper No. 6623 (Cambridge, Massachusetts: National Bureau of Economic Research).

García-Herrero, Alicia, and P. del Rio, 2003, "Financial Stability and the Design of Monetary Policy," Documento de Trabajo No. 0315, Banco de España, Madrid.

Gastineau, G. L., 1992, *Swiss Bank Corporation Dictionary of Financial Risk Management* (Chicago: Probus Publishing Company).

Geanakoplos, John, 1997, "Promises Promises," in *The Economy as an Evolving Complex System II,* Conference proceedings Volume XXVII in Studies in the Sciences of Complexity, eds. W. Brian Arthur, Steven N. Durlauf, and David A. Lane (Reading, Massachusetts: Addison-Wesley).

Geithner, Timothy, 2004a, "Changes in the Structure of the U.S. Financial System and Implications for Systemic Risk," remarks before the Conference on Systemic Financial Crises, Federal Reserve Bank of Chicago (October 1, 2004). Available via the Internet: http://www.ny.frb.org/newsevents/speeches/2004/gei041001.html

———, 2004b, "Hedge Funds and Their Implications for the Financial System," keynote address at the National Conference on the Securities Industry, New York (November 17). Available via the Internet: http://www.ny.frb.org/newsevents/speeches/2004/gei041117.html

Goodhart, Charles, 1989, *Money, Information and Uncertainty* (Cambridge, Massachusetts: MIT Press, 2nd ed.).

———, 1995, "Price Stability and Financial Fragility," in *Financial Stability in a Changing Environment,* ed. by K. Kawamoto, Z. Nakajima, and H. Taguchi (London: Macmillan).

Greenspan, Alan, 1998, "Risk Management in the Global Financial System," remarks before the Annual Financial Markets Conference of the Federal Reserve Bank of Atlanta, Miami Beach, Florida, February 27.

———, 1999, "Do Efficient Markets Mitigate Financial Crises?" speech before the 1999 Financial Markets Conference of the Federal Reserve Bank of Atlanta, Sea Island, Georgia, October 19.

———, 2000, "Over-the-Counter Derivatives," testimony before the Committee on Agriculture, Nutrition and Forestry, United States Senate, February 10.

———, 2002, Testimony before the U.S. House of Representatives Committee on Financial Services, February 27, 2002. Available via the Internet: http://www.federalreserve.gov/boarddocs/hh/2002/february/testimony.htm

———, 2005, "Risk Transfer and Financial Stability," remarks to the Federal Reserve Bank of Chicago's 41st Annual Conference on Bank Structure, Chicago, Illinois, May 5.

Greenwood, Jeremy, and Boyan Jovanovic, 1990, "Financial Development, Growth and the Distribution of Income," *Journal of Political Economy,* Vol. 98 (October), pp. 1076–107.

Group of Ten, 2001, *Consolidation in the Financial Sector* (Basel: Bank for International Settlements).

Haldane, Andrew, 2001, "The Financial Stability Forum (FSF): Just Another Acronym?" in *Regulating Financial Services and Markets in the 21st Century,* ed. by E. Ferran and C. Goodhart (Oxford: Hart).

———, 2004, "Defining Monetary and Financial Stability" (unpublished; London: Bank of England).

Handbook of Credit Derivatives, 1999, ed. by J. C. Francis, J. S. Frost, and G. Whittaker (New York: McGraw-Hill).

Hicks, Sir John, 1935, "A Suggestion for Simplifying the Theory of Money," *Economica,* Vol. 2 (February), pp. 1–19.

———, 1967, *Critical Essays on Monetary Theory* (Oxford: Clarendon Press).

Hill, Andrew, and Gary Silverman, 2002, "JP Morgan and Insurers Go To Court Over Enron: Dispute About Surety Bonds Raises Doubts About How Banks Transfer Their Credit Risks," *Financial Times* (London), January 15, p. 19.

Hill, Andrew, J. Labate, C. Pretzlik, G. Silverman, and P. T. Larsen, 2002, "SEC Investigates Credit Risk of US Bank 'Loans': Exposure of JP Morgan and Citigroup to Enron Raises Fears Shareholders Were Misled," *Financial Times* (London), January 16, p. 19.

Hills, Bob, and David Rule, 1999, "Counterparty Credit Risk in Wholesale Payment and Settlement Systems," *Bank of England Financial Stability Review,* Issue 7 (November), pp. 98–114.

Hills, Bob, David Rule, Sarah Parkinson, and Chris Young, 1999, "Central Counterparty Clearing Houses and Financial Stability," *Bank of England Financial Stability Review,* Issue 6 (June), pp. 122–34.

Hoelscher, David, and Marc Quintyn, 2003, *Managing Systemic Banking Crises* (Washington: International Monetary Fund).

Hoggarth, Glenn, and Victoria Saporta, 2001, "Costs of Banking System Instability: Some Empirical Evidence," *Bank of England Financial Stability Review,* Issue 10 (June), pp. 148–65.

Hoggarth, G., and J. Whitley, 2003, "Assessing the Strength of UK Banks through Macroeconomic Stress Tests," *Bank of England Financial Stability Review,* Issue 14 (June), pp. 91–103.

Houben, Aerdt, Jan Kakes, and Garry Schinasi, 2004, "Towards a Framework for Safeguarding Financial Stability," IMF Working Paper WP/04/101 (Washington: International Monetary Fund) and DNB Occasional Paper Vol. 2 (No. 1).

Hutchison, Michael, and Ilan Noy, 2002, "How Bad Are Twins? Output Costs of Currency and Banking Crises," Pacific Basin Working Paper Series No. PB02-02, (San Francisco: Federal Reserve Bank of San Francisco).

Ineichen, A. M., 2001, "The Search For Alpha Continues: Do Fund of Hedge Funds Managers Add Value?" UBS Warburg research note (London).

Institutional Investor, 2004, January.

International Association of Insurance Supervisors (IAIS), 2000, *Reinsurance and Reinsurers: Relevant Issues for Establishing General Supervisory Principles, Standards and Practices* (Working Group on Reinsurance, Basel).

———, 2002a, *Principles on Minimum Requirements for Supervision of Reinsurers* (Basel).

———, 2002b, *Supervisory Standard on the Evaluation of the Reinsurance Cover of Primary Insurers and the Security of their Reinsurers* (Basel).

———, 2003, *Insurance Core Principles and Methodology* (Basel).

International Monetary Fund, 1995, *International Capital Markets: Developments, Prospects, and Key Policy Issues,* World Economic and Financial Surveys (Washington).

———, 1996, *International Capital Markets: Developments, Prospects, and Key Policy Issues,* World Economic and Financial Surveys (Washington).

————, 1998a, *International Capital Markets: Developments, Prospects, and Key Policy Issues,* World Economic and Financial Surveys, Chapter V (Washington).

————, 1998b, *World Economic Outlook and International Capital Markets: Interim Assessment,* World Economic and Financial Surveys (Washington).

————, 1999, *International Capital Markets: Developments, Prospects, and Key Policy Issues* (Washington).

————, 2000, *International Capital Markets: Developments, Prospects, and Key Policy Issues* (Washington).

————, 2002a, "Selected Topic: The Role of Financial Derivatives in Emerging Markets" *Global Financial Stability Report,* (December), 54–70.

————, 2002b, "Stability Implications of Global Financial Market Conditions," *Global Financial Stability Report* (March), 23–47.

————, 2002c, "The Financial Market Activities of Insurance and Reinsurance Companies," *Global Financial Stability Report* (June), 30–47.

————, 2004a, *Compilation Guide on Financial Soundness Indicators,* Washington.

————, 2004b, "Global Financial Market Developments," *Global Financial Stability Report* (September), 8–80.

————, and World Bank, 2001, "Experience with the Insurance Core Principles Assessments Under the Financial Sector Assessment Program," prepared by the staffs of the IMF and the World Bank (Washington).

————, 2003, *Analytical Tools of the Financial Sector Assessment Program* (Washington).

Jevons, W. S., 1871, *The Theory of Political Economy* (London: Penguin, Reprint 1970).

Joint Forum, 2001a, *Core Principles: Cross-Sectoral Comparison* (Basel: Bank for International Settlements).

————, 2001b, *Risk Management Practices and Regulatory Capital, Cross-Sectoral Comparison* (Basel: Bank for International Settlements).

————, 2004, "Financial Disclosure in the Banking, Insurance and Securities Sectors: Issues and Analysis" (Basel: Bank for International Settlements).

————, 2005, "Credit Risk Transfers" (Basel: Bank for International Settlements).

JP Morgan, 2001, *The Insurance Industry and FA/GIC Bonds* (New York).

JP Morgan/Risk Management, 2001, *Guide to Risk Management* (London: Risk Waters Group).

Kawamoto, K., Z. Nakajima, and H. Taguchi, eds., 1995, *Financial Stability in a Changing Environment* (London: Macmillan).

Keynes, John Maynard, 1930a, *A Treatise on Money,* Vol. I (London: Macmillan, Reprint 1958).

————, 1930b, *A Treatise on Money,* Vol. II (London: Macmillan, Reprint 1960).

————, 1936, *The General Theory of Employment, Interest and Money* (London: Macmillan, Reprint 1957).

Kindleberger, Charles, 1993, *A Financial History of Western Europe* (Oxford: Oxford University Press, 2nd ed.).

————, 1996, *Manias, Panics and Crashes* (Cambridge: Cambridge University Press, 3rd ed.).

Kirman, Alan P., 1997, "The Economy as an Interactive System," in *The Economy as an Evolving Complex System II,* Conference proceedings Volume XXVII in Studies in the Sciences of Complexity, eds. W. Brian Arthur, Steven N. Durlauf, and David A. Lane (Reading, Massachusetts: Addison-Wesley), pp. 491–532.

Kiyotaki, Nobuhiro, and Randall Wright, 1993, "A Contribution to the Pure Theory of Money," *Journal of Economic Theory,* Vol. 53 (April), pp. 215–35.

Knight, Frank H., 1921, *Risk, Uncertainty, and Profit* (Cambridge: The Riverside Press).

Kochan, Nick, 2002, "Enron Fallout: Why Insurers Fail Banks," *The Banker* (March), London, pp. 16–19.

Kocherlakota, Narayana, 1998, "Money is Memory," *Journal of Economic Theory,* Vol. 81 (August), pp. 232–51.

Kregel, J. A., 1998, "Derivatives and Global Capital Flows: Applications to Asia," *Cambridge Journal of Economics,* Vol. 22 (November), pp. 677–92.

Kroszner, Randall S., 1999, "Can the Financial Markets Privately Regulate Risk? The Development of Derivatives Clearinghouses and Recent Over-the-Counter Innovations," *Journal of Money, Credit and Banking,* Vol. 31 (August, part 2), pp. 596–623.

Large, Sir Andrew, 2003, "Financial Stability: Maintaining Confidence in a Complex World," *Bank of England Financial Stability Review,* Issue 15 (December), pp. 170–4.

Leahy, Michael., S. Schich, G. Wehinger, F. Pelgrin, and T. Thorgeirsson, 2001, "Contributions of Financial Systems to Growth in OECD Countries," OECD Working Paper No. 280 (Paris: Organisation for Economic Co-operation and Development).

Leijonhufvud, Axel, 1997, "Macroeconomics and Complexity: Inflation Theory," in *The Economy as an Evolving Complex System II,* Conference proceedings Volume XXVII in Studies in the Sciences of Complexity, ed. by W. Brian Arthur, Steven N. Durlauf, and David A. Lane (Reading, Massachusetts: Addison-Wesley), pp. 321–336.

Levine, Ross, 1999, "Law, Finance and Economic Growth," *Journal of Financial Intermediation,* Vol. 8 (Issue 1–2), pp. 8–35.

————, 2003, "More on Finance and Growth: More Finance, More Growth?" The Federal Reserve Bank of St. Louis, *Review,* Vol. 85 (July/August), pp. 31–46.

Lindgren, Carl-Johan, Gillian Garcia, and Matthew Saal, 1996, *Bank Soundness and Macroeconomic Policy* (Washington: International Monetary Fund).

Llewellyn, David T., 2001, "A Regulatory Regime for Financial Stability," Working Paper No. 48 (Vienna: Oesterreichische Nationalbank).

Maier-Rigaud, Frank P., and Jose Apesteguia, 2004, "The Role of Rivalry: Public Goods versus Common-Pool Resources," MPI Collective Goods Preprint 2004/2 (Bloomington, Indiana: Max Planck Institute for Research on Collective Goods, Indiana University).

Malz, Allan M., 1995, "Currency Option Markets and Exchange Rates: A Case Study of the U.S. Dollar in March 1995," *Current Issues in Economics and Finance,* Vol. 1 (July), pp. 1–6.

Mandelbrot, Benoit B., 1997, *Fractals and Scaling in Finance: Discontinuity, Concentration, Risk,* Selecta Volume E (New York: Springer Verlag).

Mathieson, Donald J., Jorge E. Roldos, Ramana Ramaswamy, and Anna Ilyina, 2004, *Emerging Local Securities and Derivatives Markets,* World Economic and Financial Surveys (Washington: International Monetary Fund), pp. 69–90.

Minsky, H. M., 1977, "The Financial Stability Hypothesis: An Interpretation of Keynes and an Alternative to 'Standard' Theory," *Nebraska Journal of Economics and Business,* Vol. 16 (Winter), pp. 5–16.

———, 1982, *Inflation, Recession and Economic Policy* (Sussex: MIT Press Wheatsheaf).

Mishkin, Frederick, 1999, "Global Financial Instability: Framework, Events, Issues," *Journal of Economic Perspectives,* Vol. 13 (Fall), pp. 3–20.

National Bank of Belgium, 2002, *Financial Stability Review,* No. 1, Brussels.

Neely, C. J., 2004, "The Federal Reserve Responds to Crises: September 11th Was Not the First," *Federal Reserve Bank of St. Louis Review,* Vol. 86 (March/April), pp. 27–42.

Norwegian Central Bank, 2003, *Financial Stability Review,* Vol. 1, Oslo. Available via the Internet: http://www.norges-bank.no/english/financial_stability/

Nystedt, Jens, 2004, "Derivative Market Competition: OTC Markets versus Organized Derivative Exchanges," IMF Working Paper WP/04/61 (Washington: International Monetary Fund).

———, 2003, *Institutional Investors Statistical Yearbook, 1992–2001* (Paris).

———, various years, *Bank Profitability, Financial Statements of Banks* (Paris).

Olson, Mancur, 1965, *The Logic of Collective Action* (Cambridge, Massachusetts: Harvard University Press).

Oosterloo, Sander, and Jakob de Haan, 2003, *A Survey of Institutional Frameworks for Financial Stability,* De Nederlandsche Bank Occasional Studies, Volume 1, Number 4 (Amsterdam: De Nederlandsche Bank), pp. 10–16.

Organisation for Economic Co-operation and Development (OECD), 2002, "Risk Transfer Mechanisms," Committee on Financial Markets, DAFFE/CMF(2002)5 (Paris).

Padoa-Schioppa, Tommaso, 1999, "EMU and Banking Supervision," lecture given to the London School of Economics, February 24.

———, 2003, "Central Banks and Financial Stability: Exploring the Land in Between," in *The Transformation of the European Financial System,* ed. by Vitor Gaspar, P. Hartmann, and O. Sleijpen (Frankfurt: European Central Bank).

———, 2004, *Regulating Finance: Balancing Freedom and Risk* (Oxford: Oxford University Press).

Paulos, John Allen, 2003, *A Mathematician Plays the Stock Market* (New York: Basic Books).

Persson, M., and M. Blåvarg, 2003, "The Use of Market Indicators in Financial Stability Analysis," *Economic Review,* Sveriges Riksbank, pp. 5–28.

Poundstone, William, 1992, *Prisoner's Dilemma* (New York: Doubleday).

Prati, Alessandro, and Garry J. Schinasi, 1997, "European Economic and Monetary Union and International Capital Markets: Structural Implications and Risks," IMF Working Paper 97/62 (Washington: International Monetary Fund).

————, 1999a, "Financial Stability in European Economic and Monetary Union," Princeton Studies in International Economics No. 86 (Princeton, New Jersey: Princeton University).

————, 1999b, "Will the European Central Bank Be the Lender of Last Resort in EMU?" paper prepared for 21st Colloquium of the Societe Universitaire Europeenne de Recherches Financieres (SUERF), "The Euro: A Challenge and Opportunity for Financial Markets," Frankfurt, Germany, October 15–17.

Procter, Rob, Espen Nordhaus, and Jon Hocking, 2002, "Downgrading on Embedded Concerns," *Morgan Stanley Equity Research: European Insurance* (New York).

Rajan, Raghuram G., 1997, "The Past and Future of Commercial Banking Viewed through an Incomplete Contract Lens," *Journal of Money, Credit and Banking*, Vol. 30 (August), pp. 524–50.

Rajan, Raghuram G., and Luigi Zingales, 2003, *Saving Capitalism from the Capitalists* (New York: Crown Business).

Ranciere, R., 2002, "Credit Derivatives in Emerging Markets," (unpublished, New York: New York University, Stern School of Business).

Sahajwala, R., and P. van den Berg, 2000, "Supervisory Risk Assessment and Early Warning Systems," Basel Committee on Banking Supervision Working Paper No. 4 (Basel: Bank for International Settlements).

Samuelson, Paul A., 1958, "An Exact Consumption-Loan Model of Interest With or Without the Social Contrivance of Money," *Journal of Political Economy*, Vol. 6 (December), pp. 467–82.

Sandler, Todd, 1992, *Collective Action: Theory and Applications* (Ann Arbor: The University of Michigan Press).

Santa Fe Institute, 1988, *The Economy as an Evolving Complex System,* Conference Proceedings Volume V in Studies in the Sciences of Complexity, ed. by Philip W. Anderson, Kenneth J. Arrow, and David Pines (Santa Fe, New Mexico: Addison-Wesley).

————, 1994, *Complexity: Metaphors, Models, and Reality,* Conference Proceedings Volume in the Studies in the Sciences of Complexity, ed. by George Cowan, David Pines, and David Meltzer (Cambridge, Massachusetts: Perseus Books).

————, 1997, *The Economy as an Evolving Complex System II,* Conference Proceedings Volume XXVII in Studies in the Sciences of Complexity, ed. by W. Brian Arthur, Steven N. Durlauf, and David A. Lane (Reading, Massachusetts: Addison-Wesley).

Schinasi, Garry J., 1992, "Balance Sheet Constraints and the Sluggishness of the Current Recovery," Annex I, *World Economic Outlook,* World Economic and Financial Surveys (Washington: International Monetary Fund).

————, 1994, "Asset Price Inflation, Monetary Policy, and the Business Cycle," IMF Paper on Policy Analysis and Assessment 94/6 (Washington: International Monetary Fund).

————, 1995, "Asset Prices, Monetary Policy, and the Business Cycle," *Finance and Development,* Vol. 32 (June).

————, 2003, "Responsibility of Central Banks for Stability in Financial Markets," IMF Working Paper 03/121 (Washington: International Monetary Fund, June); also published as Chapter 17 in *Current Developments in Monetary and Financial Law—Volume 2,* 2003 (Washington: International Monetary Fund).

————, 2004a, "Defining Financial Stability," IMF Working Paper WP/04/187 (Washington: International Monetary Fund).

————, 2004b, "Private Finance and Public Policy," IMF Working Paper WP/04/120 (Washington: International Monetary Fund).

———— and Monica Hargraves, 1992, "Asset Price Deflation, Balance Sheet Adjustment, and Financial Fragility," Annex I, *World Economic Outlook,* World Economic and Financial Surveys (Washington: International Monetary Fund).

————, 1993a, " 'Boom and Bust' in Asset Markets in the 1980s," *Staff Studies for the World Economic Outlook,* World Economic and Financial Surveys (Washington: International Monetary Fund).

————, 1993b, "Monetary Policy, Financial Liberalization, and Asset Price Inflation," Annex I, *World Economic Outlook,* World Economic and Financial Surveys (Washington: International Monetary Fund).

Schinasi, Garry J., and R. Todd Smith, 2000, "Portfolio Diversification, Leverage, and Financial Contagion," *IMF Staff Papers,* Vol. 47 (December), pp. 159–176; also IMF Working Paper 99/136 (Washington: International Monetary Fund).

Schinasi, Garry J., Burkhard Drees, and William Lee, 1999, "Managing Global Finance and Risk," *Finance & Development,* Vol. 36 (December), pp. 38–41.

Schinasi, Garry J., Monica Hargraves, and Steven Weisbrod, 1993, "Asset Price Inflation in the 1980s: A Flow of Funds Perspective," IMF Working Paper 93/77 (Washington: International Monetary Fund).

Schinasi, Garry J., Sean Craig, Burkhard Drees, and Charles Kramer, 2000, "Modern Banking and OTC Derivatives Markets: The Transformation of Global Finance and its Implications for Systemic Risk," IMF Occasional Paper No. 203 (Washington: International Monetary Fund).

Schumpeter, J., 1934, *The Theory of Economic Development* (Cambridge: Harvard University Press).

Schwartz, Anna J., 1986, "Real and Pseudo-Financial Crises," in *Financial Crises and the World Banking System,* ed. by Forrest Capie and Geoffrey E. Woods (New York: St Martin's).

Shubik, Martin, 1997, "Time and Money," in *The Economy as an Evolving Complex System II,* Conference proceedings Volume XXVII in Studies in the Sciences of Complexity, ed. by W. Brian Arthur, Steven N. Durlauf, and David A. Lane (Reading, Massachusetts: Addison-Wesley), pp. 263–84.

————, 1999, *Theory of Money and Financial Institutions* (Cambridge, Massachusetts: MIT Press).

————, 2001, "On Understanding Money," *World Economics,* Vol. 2 (January–March), pp. 95–120.

Smith, R. Todd, and H. van Egteren, 2005, "Interest Rate Smoothing and Financial Stability," *Review of Financial Economics*, Vol. 14, pp. 147–171.

Sornette, Didier, 2003, *Why Stock Markets Crash: Critical Events in Complex Financial Systems* (Oxford and Princeton: Princeton University Press).

Steinherr, Alfred, 1998, *Derivatives:The Wild Beast of Finance* (New York: Wiley & Sons).

Stiglitz, Joseph E., 2000, *Economics of the Public Sector* (New York: W. W. Norton and Company).

Stock, James H., and Mark W. Watson, 2003, "Has the Business Cycle Changed? Evidence and Explanations," paper presented at the Federal Reserve Bank of Kansas City symposium, "Monetary Policy and Uncertainty," Jackson Hole, Wyoming, August 28–30.

Summer, Martin, 2003, "Banking Regulation and Systemic Risk," *Open Economies Review*, Vol. 14 (January), pp. 43–70.

Sveriges Riksbank, 2003, *Financial Stability Report*, No. 2, Stockholm.

———, 2004, *Financial Stability Report*, No. 1, Stockholm.

Swiss Re, 2001, "Profitability of the Non-Life Insurance Industry: It's Back-to-Basics Time," *sigma* No. 5/2001 (Zurich: Swiss Reinsurance Company).

Thaler, Richard H., 1992, *The Winner's Curse: Paradoxes and Anomalies of Economic Life* (New York: Maxwell Macmillan International).

Thom, Rene, 1972, *Structural Stability and Morphogenesis: An Outline of a General Theory of Models*, trans. by D. H. Fowler (Reading, Massachusetts: W. A. Benjamin, Inc.).

Thornton, Henry, 1802, *An Enquiry into the Nature and Effects of Paper Credit of Great Britain* (New York: Augustus Kelley, Reprint 1978).

Tietmeyer, Hans, 1999, remarks at the conference of the Center for Financial Studies "Systemic Risk and Lender of Last Resort," Frankfurt, June.

Tobin, James, 1980, "Discussion by James Tobin," in *Models of Monetary Economics*, ed. by J. Kareken and Neil Wallace (Minneapolis: Federal Reserve Bank of Minneapolis).

———, 1992, "Money as a Social Institution and Public Good," in *The New Palgrave Dictionary of Money and Finance*, ed. by J. Eatwell, M. Milgate, and P. Newman (London: Macmillan).

Truman, Edwin, 2003, *Inflation Targeting in the World Economy* (Washington: Institute for International Economics).

Tucker, Paul M. W., 2005, "Where Are the Risks," remarks at the Euromoney Global Borrowers and Investors Forum (London, June 23). Available on the Internet at: http://www.bankofengland.co.uk/publications/speeches/2005/speech251.pdf

———, 2004a, "Managing the Central Bank's Balance Sheet: Where Monetary Policy Meets Financial Stability," Lecture to mark the fifteenth anniversary of Lombard Street Research (London: Bank of England, July 2004). Available on the Internet at: http://www.bankofengland.co.uk/publications/speeches/2004/speech225.pdf

———, 2004b, Keynote Speech at the National Association of Pension Funds Annual Investment Conference in Edinburgh (London: Bank of England, March 19).

Available on the Internet at: http://www.bankofengland.co.uk/publications/speeches/2004/speech216.pdf

United States, Board of Governors of the Federal Reserve System, 1999, "Using Subordinated Debt as an Instrument of Market Discipline," Staff Studies No. 172 (Washington).

————, 2000, "Improving Public Disclosure in Banking," Staff Study 173 (Washington: Federal Reserve System).

United States, Commodity Futures Trading Commision, 1999, *Regulation of Over-the-Counter Derivatives Transactions* (Washington).

United States, Comptroller of the Currency, 2005, "OCC Bank Derivatives Report–Fourth Quarter 2004," Available via the Internet: www.occ.gov.

United States Joint Senate Committees on Agriculture, Nutrition, and Forestry and Banking, Housing, and Urban Affairs, 2000, Testimony by Federal Reserve Chairman Greenspan, SEC Chairman Levitt, and Treasury Secretary Summers, June 21. Available via the Internet: http://agriculture.sennate.gov/Hearings/Hearings_2000/June_21__2000/june_21__2000.htm

United States, President's Working Group on Financial Markets, 1999a, "Hedge Funds, Leverage, and the Lessons of Long-Term Capital Management," Report of the President's Working Group on Financial Markets (Department of the Treasury, Board of Governors of the Federal Reserve System, Securities and Exchange Commission, Commodity Futures Trading Commission) (Washington).

United States, President's Working Group on Financial Markets, 1999b, "Over-the-Counter Derivatives Markets and the Commodity Exchange Act," Report of the President's Working Group on Financial Markets (Department of the Treasury, Board of Governors of the Federal Reserve System, Securities and Exchange Commission, Commodity Futures Trading Commission) (Washington).

Van der Zwet, 2003, "The Blurring of Distinctions between Financial Sectors: Fact or Fiction?" Occasional Studies No. 2 (Amsterdam: De Nederlandsche Bank).

Van Hedge Fund Advisors LLC, 2005, "Size of the Hedge Fund Universe." Available via the Internet: http://www.hedgefund.com/abouthfs/universe/universe.htm

Volcker, Paul A., 1984, "The Federal Reserve Position on Restructuring of Financial Regulation Responsibilities," *Federal Reserve Bulletin*, Vol. 70 (July), pp. 547–57.

————, 1998, "Emerging Economies in a Sea of Global Finance," The Charles Rostov Lecture at the Paul H. Nitze School of Advanced International Studies, Johns Hopkins University (Washington DC: April 9). Available via the Internet: http://www.house.gov/jec/hearings/imf2/volker.htm

————, 1999, "The Implications of Globalism is Globalism," The Joseph I. Lubin Memorial Lecture, Stern School of Business (New York: April 20). Available via the Internet: http://www.trilateral.org/membship/membtxts/pv/990420.htm

————, 2002, "Accounting, Accountants, and Accountability in an Integrated World Economy," Remarks to the World Congress of Accountants (Hong Kong: November 19). Available via Internet: http://www.iasb.org/uploaded_files/documents/8–128–021119-pav.pdf

Wellink, Nout, 2002, "Central Banks as Guardians of Financial Stability," speech at the seminar "Current Issues in Central Banking," Oranjestad, Aruba, November 14.

White, William, 2003, "Are Changes in Financial Structures Extending Safety Nets?" in *Macroeconomics, Monetary Policy and Financial Stability: A Festschrift for Charles Freedman*, BIS Working Papers No. 145 (Basel: Bank for International Settlements).

World Bank, 1999, "Processing the Economy's Financial Information," in *World Development Report 1998–99* (Washington: World Bank).

Worrell, DeLisle, 2004, "Quantitative Assessment of the Financial Sector: An Integrated Approach," IMF Working Paper WP/04/153 (Washington: International Monetary Fund).

———, and Leon Hyginus, 2001, "Price Volatility and Financial Instability," IMF Working Paper WP/01/60 (Washington: International Monetary Fund).

Index

trust, human, 18–19, 31, 79;
   fragility, 80

uncertainty, 16; finance, 65
underwriting losses, investments and, 248–57
United Kingdom Financial
   Services Authority,
   134, 144; financial stability definition, 95
United States: Federal
   Reserve System, 95,
   136–37, 145, 148; finan-

cial stability definition,
   95; financial system,
   101–102; repurchase
   market, 148
unit-of-account service, 61
universal acceptability, 56

value at risk (VaR), 284
value of services, relative, 34
variables, distribution, 113
volatility, 72; OTC derivatives, 190–91, 208–13
Volcker, Paul, 136–37

vulnerabilities, 182; judging
   scope and impact,
   110–13. *See also* risks

wealth accumulation, 36–37
Wellink, Nout, financial stability definition, 97
willingness to pay, 266
worker-owner promise, 34

yen, OTC currency options,
   196–97

About the Author

Garry J. Schinasi is an Advisor in the Finance Department of the International Monetary Fund (IMF). He received his Ph.D. in economics from Columbia University in 1979, and, before joining the IMF, he was on the staff of the Board of Governors of the U.S. Federal Reserve System from 1979 to 1989. From 1992 to 2001, Mr. Schinasi held various positions in the IMF's Research Department. He contributed to the IMF's semiannual *World Economic Outlook* (1992–94), was a comanager of the IMF's capital market surveillance exercise (1994–2003), and was coauthor and coeditor of *International Capital Markets: Developments, Prospects, and Key Policy Issues* (1994–2001) and the *Global Financial Stability Report* (2002–03). Mr. Schinasi has published articles in *The Review of Economic Studies, Journal of Economic Theory, Journal of International Money and Finance,* and other academic and policy journals.